THE
WORLD GUIDE
to
HOUSE
PLANTS

edited by
Anthony Huxley

THE
WORLD GUIDE
to
HOUSE PLANTS

edited by
Anthony Huxley

CHARLES SCRIBNER'S SONS
New York

This book offers a unique understanding of the plants we grow indoors. They are arranged in ten geographical regions so that you can discover where your plants come from and how, in many cases, this influences the way you should look after them.

Within each region the plants are arranged alphabetically. Simply turn to the *World Map* on page 16, or to *The Illustrated Plant Index* on page 206, in order to find where your plants are discussed in detail.

First published in Great Britain by Macmillan London Limited
First published in the United States by Charles Scribner's Sons

Library of Congress Cataloging in Publication Data
Main entry under title:

The World guide to house plants.

Includes indexes.
1. House plants – Origin. 2. House plants – Ecology.
3. Indoor gardening. 4. Botany – Ecology. I. Huxley,
Anthony Julian, 1920–   .
SB419.W838 1984   635.9'65   83-27147
ISBN 0-684-18164-9

Conceived, designed and produced by Pilot Productions Limited, London

Special thanks to
Rob Shone for the line illustrations, and
James Culver for his design and cartographic assistance

Typesetting by Fleetlines Typesetters, Southend-on-Sea, Essex
Colour origination by Fer Crom 2, Barcelona, Spain
Made and printed by Henri Proost et Cie, Turnhout, Belgium

Contents

Introduction

Today homes, offices, shops, restaurants, airports – in fact almost anywhere where people get together – are decorated with foliage plants in pots. It is something of a shock to realize that this widespread use of plants for display dates only from the end of the second world war. Now they are a way of life, grown for sale in millions.

It is of course true that our Victorian forefathers grew a great variety of plants in pots indoors, but the introduction of gas lighting with incandescent mantles put paid to most: plants are very susceptible to fumes. Of those that survived, the indestructible aspidistra became a symbol of the Victorian era – quite unjustly in terms of plant taste – and the palm the inescapable accompaniment of hotel lounges and ballrooms. In the thirties the cactus and other succulents became popular in keeping with the trend to pure, simple forms in architecture, interior decoration and household objects. The foliage house plant disappeared in a reaction against Victorian and Edwardian exuberance and clutter.

After the war the house plant started its renaissance in Britain, largely under the influence of the Danes and the Dutch. In the United States the fashion had not completely died, but it gained fresh momentum after the war. My own career in horticulture began at the same time, and my interest – already attuned to succulents – immediately extended to the whole world of house plants.

Certainly these plants opened up a whole world of quite unknown families, and I suspect that my addiction to them had more than a touch of collector's mania in it. But for a long time I remained ignorant of their natural lives, just as I had the haziest idea of their countries of origins and the conditions in which they grow in the wild.

One learned slowly about these plants being in botanical groups, and even more slowly about their habitats and the resulting cultural implications. To grow them one followed

Having followed in the footsteps of some of the botanical explorers, I have first-hand knowledge of the kinds of terrain where our house plants grow, and hope to pass on the excitement and astonishment that their natural habitats can provide.

advice from the past or from those who were growing them commercially. It was 25 years before I actually set foot in a tropical jungle and saw – and felt – for myself what these growing conditions actually meant. That exciting journey was a revelation indeed, and when I saw a plant I had grown at home I felt as though I was discovering it anew.

It's fun to travel, at least in spirit, through exotic lands in search of your favourite plants: sometimes you can even discover who it was that first collected them. But there is much more to this than the satisfaction of armchair travel. By looking at the conditions in which our plants grow in nature, we can begin to understand how to treat them at home. We can

discover the reasons why each plant prefers this or that level of light, heat and humidity. It isn't enough to say that if a plant comes from the tropics (as many do) it must prefer bright light, for if for example it lives on the floor of a tropical rain forest (where shade is normal) it most certainly will not.

Without this sort of knowledge the house plant is defenceless against whim. It will be put in a place where it looks well, however unsatisfactory the conditions may be. By learning about their origins we can realize that they cannot but have definite likes and dislikes – *tolerances* imposed by evolution in a specific habitat. Then these climatic "niches" can be correlated with those in our own homes. It is probably a surprise for many to think of rooms as having climates, but in terms of plants they certainly do, varying from room to room and also within each room.

The main factors of room climate which we need to consider are those of temperature and light. The essential air humidity (which can never be divorced from temperature schedules) is rarely present in adequate amounts but can usually be provided. Then we have full responsibility for providing water and food, since all our house plants have their roots in the totally artificial environment of a pot – the aspect of culture which differs most from their natural life. We can see why it is that confining their roots in pots obliges us to provide each plant with carefully monitored food and water schedules that make up for the inadequacies of their new, artificial growing conditions.

What we are learning is to treat house plants as *living* entities, rather than as objects of furnishing or fashion bought off a shelf. No plant will survive if its natural temperature and light ranges are exceeded. There is, however, no simple equation between wild and domestic growing conditions.

Some plants live in a variety of habitats. Thus coleus is basically a jungle plant but is also found in clearings.

Some plants in nature may live in very poor light, and sprawl around, putting down roots as they go. If given better light in cultivation they are likely to grow less thin and spindly, and stay attractively compact. Examples are tradescantia, plectranthus, and hypoestes which gets very thin in poor light.

Again, in nature, plants often live in low light because that provides a niche where they can exist with minimum competition. It does not always mean that these conditions are essential for growth; they have developed tolerance to low light in exchange for free growing conditions.

Also, seeds don't choose where they fall! One sometimes sees bromeliads which normally live high up in the sunny, hot canopy growing quite happily on the jungle floor, though their growth habit may be looser and thinner. This can mean that plants in cultivation look different to the same species in the wild.

Another point to bear in mind when comparing natural habitats with desirable cultural conditions is that plants in commercial cultivation may be the results of much hybridization and are thus quite far removed from the wild species under whose name they may still be known. The coleus is an example: the commercial plant was described from Javanese garden forms and probably derived from three wild species a very long time ago. Genera affected in this way include:

Achimenes
Many begonias especially rex,
    semperflorens, and corallina
    varieties
Caladium
Codiaeum
Columnea, named varieties
Cordyline, named varieties
Dieffenbachia, named varieties
Dracaena, named varieties
Epiphyllum (derived from at
    least 4 genera)
Episcia hybrids
Fatshedera (2 genera)
Fuchsia
Impatiens
Philodendron, named varieties
Saintpaulias
Streptocarpus hybrids.

The hybrids or varieties so involved have been placed on the regional maps according to their *parents'* natural habitats.

Finally, temporary florist plants have almost all been derived from many species, i.e. Calceolaria, Capsicum, Chrysanthemum, Cineraria, Erica, Narcissus, Primula, Solanum, Tulipa.

Plants also have specific ways of growth which it is best to co-operate with; they will look better to start with. This brings us to the other vital

aspect of house plants – they are there to enhance our rooms, to give a feel of life to our surroundings. These plants bring us into contact with nature, a contact which is particularly important to those who live in flats or apartments without access to a garden.

Needless, I hope, to say this book also contains absolutely down-to-earth cultural advice, always linked with the theme of understanding the plants' natural home and growth habits. No home can truly reflect our house plants' natural climates – nor would we want it to! But we can make the best of what there is and improve it locally.

Working on this book has opened my own eyes to a considerable degree. Plant after familiar plant has been placed in a new light, failures have been explained, ideas formed for improving the lot of plants I grow. I hope it does the same for all who use it, and also restores to our house plants the sense of romance, adventure, even awe which I find always accompanies sighting a plant in the wild.

The book's contributors
I would like to thank the experts who have made very distinct contributions to this book:

Richard Gilbert (author and chairman of the *Saintpaulia and House Plant Society*) for material about the cultivation of each plant.

Jeff Grimes (phyto-geographer, late of the Royal Gardens at Kew) and his botanist wife, Hannah, for their material about plant origins, and climatic and vegetational information.

Richard Gorer (author and Fellow of the Royal Horticultural Society) for his material about plant hunting and the history of growing plants indoors.

Anthony Huxley

From the wild to the home

What is a house plant?

The definition of a satisfactory house plant must be: any plant which will live year in, year out in an average room in a temperate climate, and look attractive at all seasons. To do this it must rely mostly on its foliage effect, since few flowers last long on any plant. And it must be evergreen, retaining its leaves all the time; deciduous plants which drop their leaves for a period of rest are not permanently decorative.

Customarily we also bring indoors many temporary or "gift" plants for their attractive flowers or fruits. These are usually bought in bud or flower; many are short-lived and must be discarded after their short spell of beauty. You cannot expect to bring those to maturity in room conditions. These are not true house plants but they are included here because most people crave for flowers and we need to know how best to treat them to give them as long a life as possible.

The true house plant – evergreen and living from year to year (perennial), comes in all shapes and sizes, with leaves varying enormously in colour, pattern, form and texture. A few add flowers to their other charms, and with these the main criterion is that they can repeat this performance even in room conditions.

But it is important to realize that house plants fall into all the normal categories we are familiar with when thinking of ordinary garden plants. They can be trees, shrubs, perennials, creepers and climbers. Because they are to be grown indoors they are, in gardeners' terms, *tender* – they will not stand frost. The plants we grow in gardens are, to varying degrees, *hardy*, which simply means that they will survive most winters in the locality in which we garden.

Although "hardy" and "tender" are sometimes used of house plants it is misleading to do so. It is much better to think of them in a range from tough – tolerant of variable conditions in a house – to delicate – needing special cosseting indoors.

House plants fall into the same categories as garden plants.

Trees and shrubs

Trees and shrubs in the home may sound out of place, but the maximum size of such plants in pots – as house plants inevitably are – is usually a fraction of their potential in the open ground. Trees and shrubs are woody, which means that some of the cells in their stems lignify and, when thick enough, turn to wood. But woody house plants take on very different forms to garden trees, with trunk and branches arising from them, or shrubs with no central stem: they include plants as varied as ficus, grevillea, cordyline, dracaena, yucca, palms and pandanus.

In fact, whether or not a plant is woody is of little importance to the house plant grower. It does not necessarily mean that it is erect or self-supporting.

Non-woody house plants

Non-woody or herbaceous perennials are equally varied in form. They can form bushes like shrubs, clumps with leaves springing from the roots at soil level, or have their leaves in rosettes arising from a central point, in which leaves are spirally arranged. (The rosette also occurs in many woody plants).

In some cases, forms of growth are consistent within specific families. The bromeliads are the most important house plants of this type: almost all have rosettes, varying from flat to upright, of stiff hard foliage – mostly they are tough and tolerant indoors.

But however the leaves are carried, the arrangements all fulfil a purpose – the essential energy-producing task of photosynthesis.

Flower or leaf?

The majority of true house plants do not flower indoors readily and even if they did their flowers are often insignificant. There are some exceptions. Bromeliads are often bought with well-developed flower spikes or associated leaf colouring; flowering continues for many weeks but eventually the flowering rosette dies.

One important genus which under proper conditions flowers well is the African violet (saintpaulia), and the same can be said of the busy Lizzies or impatiens, though these need periodic renewal from cuttings. A number of other perennial house plants produce decorative flowers, but the house plant grower relies chiefly on leaf colour, pattern and texture for permanent display, adding plants grown specifically for flowers from time to time.

Cacti and some of the other succulents will flower, though they may be considered a specialized type of house plant both as to taste and cultivation, needing in particular a carefully controlled resting season as described later.

Temporary "gift" plants

Most of the flowering pot plants must be regarded as temporary in room conditions, even if they are naturally perennial, and unless greenhouse or similar facilities are available they are best treated like a bunch of flowers, to be discarded when over. These temporaries fall into categories.

Annuals

Some are annuals whose life from seed to flower takes place within one 12-month period, examples being cineraria, calceolaria and exacum. In the wild these plants may behave like short-lived perennials but in cultivation are discarded after flowering.

Another group are true perennials: some of them shrubs like azalea, cytisus, hydrangea that come from temperate climates, some herbaceous like the big pelargonium group usually called "geraniums". Although the latter *can* be kept going and flowering in cool, sunny rooms, they and the shrubs are usually difficult to keep alive indoors and must have greenhouse treatment if they are to flower again.

Bulbs and the rest

The other major group of flowering plants are fleshy-rooted and often all referred to as "bulbs", though technically they are divided into bulbs, corms, rhizomes and tubers, which are different types of fleshy storage organs which allow these plants to rest quite dry. Examples are hyacinths, tulips, hippeastrum and amaryllis (bulbs), crocuses (corms), smithianthas (rhizomes), and cyclamen and gloxinia (tubers).

Most of these plants lose their foliage and roots entirely for many months and exist as dry organs. Although they come from a variety of habitats, they all have in common a long dry season during which they survive in this way.

A few do retain foliage all year, for instance *Haemanthus albiflos*, but are not often decorative when out of flower and hence best committed to a greenhouse. The clivia, though often referred to as such, is not a true bulb;

it has very fleshy roots to retain water and a "crown" of thick leaf-bases rather like a leek.

What all plants need to survive

At the most basic level every plant needs light, moisture and certain foods, although in vastly varying amounts which depend, plant by plant, very closely on their original habitats.

Even to understand the essential processes by which a plant lives is a great help in getting it to grow well. The essential difference between plants and animals is that animals have to eat and digest food for energy while plants produce it from light by the unique process of *photosynthesis*. This is carried out through chlorophyll, a substance found in all plants whether they are microscopic algae or forest trees. It is usually sited in leaves, and sometimes in other parts. Chlorophyll gives leaves their basic green colour, though it may be overlaid with other pigments which produce the patterns and colourings that make many foliage house plants look attractive.

What is photosynthesis?

Photosynthesis is a scientific term which, quite simply, means "putting together by light", and it makes plants independent of the need of animals to absorb carbohydrates. The chlorophyll absorbs energy from light (not necessarily direct sunlight, as we shall see) and uses this energy to combine water and carbon dioxide into glucose, a simple sugar.

Carbon dioxide is obtained from the air surrounding the plant, passing into the leaves through tiny pores called stomata which are usually located on leaf undersides. In most plants water is absorbed from the soil and through roots, and passed up to the leaves through conduits formed of cells, called xylem; but a number of house plants (especially the epiphytes) have roots largely for attachment. These absorb moisture directly through the leaves.

In the photosynthetic process, oxygen is discharged by leaves as a waste

product. However, the plant needs oxygen to transform the basic glucose into energy for immediate growth, into proteins and oils used in other ways, and into starch for food reserves. In what may appear to be a totally contradictory process called *respiration*, oxygen is taken into the plant, where it acts on the sugar and transforms it as required, releasing carbon dioxide in the process. Respiration takes place mainly at night while photosynthesis can of course only take place when there is light.

In order to extract the very small amounts of carbon dioxide from the air, the leaf pores have to be open during photosynthesis. This is the weak spot of the plant's life process, for it means that a great deal of water is lost through the leaf pores by *transpiration*.

Stomata automatically close when air is dry and open when it is moist, but some water is still lost through them, and by direct evaporation from the leaf surfaces, in very hot, dry conditions. Leaves therefore have to be insulated against excessive evaporation, and many are coated with wax or tiny hairs for this purpose. If the amount of water lost through leaves is greater than the water the roots can absorb and pump up the plant stem, the plant will start to wilt and in time will collapse.

The processes of growth, including the production of a plant's flowers or reproductive organs, and the resulting seeds or fruits by which plants increase, require certain minerals. The typical plant obtains these from the soil; they are present in water taken in via the roots. But epiphytes also absorb them through their leaves and stems from decaying debris around the plant.

Glucose made in the leaves, and the complex food materials resulting from respiration and the presence of these minerals are passed to other parts of the plant by a distinct set of cellular conduits called phloem. These continue right into the roots because these need nourishment.

9

What do house plants need to survive?

Outside their native environments, house plants need all the care and understanding we can give them. It is not enough to be able to recognize the common symptoms of ill-health and treat them. Once your favourite plant's leaves turn brown or yellow, it is already too late. We must look at and minimize the *causes* of ill-health, and we can do this in part by understanding how nature has conditioned plants to tolerate certain growing conditions and not others.

Each house plant is a product of its environment, the most important feature of which is climate. It is, of course, neither necessary nor desirable to reproduce their natural environments in the home. Plants develop an ability to survive a *range* of climatic conditions. But by investigating their environments we can discover the limits beyond which they cannot be expected to survive. These limits are first and foremost set by the range of weather they are designed to grow happily in in nature.

In what climates do our house plants grow?

The majority of (but not all) house plants grow within the tropics. The tropics are demarcated by imaginary lines of latitude called the Tropic of Cancer (which lies 23° 27′ north of the Equator) and the Tropic of Capricorn (latitude 23° 27′ south).

There is a widely accepted definition of "tropical" as an area where the average monthly temperature never falls below 64°F (18°C) and where there is never a cold season. It is, however, most certainly not true that there is a uniform climate within the tropics. There are hot, steamy jungles, high mountainous forests (as wet but relatively cool), regions of savanna and monsoon climates, and hot, arid areas too.

Many house plants also grow naturally in temperate zones, where there are variable weather patterns. It is in areas where plants have to withstand a great diversity of climate that we find some of our most

Very often, by investigating what conditions our plants prefer in nature, we can deduce how best to look after them in our homes. Above: a free-draining, rocky rooting medium; below: *a stream provides high humidity on an eastern Andean slope in Ecuador.*

tolerant house plants.

What growing conditions in nature influence plant needs in the home?

Details of temperature and rainfall are given, region by region, in the main plant lists. But regional climate alone is an inadequate guide to the requirements of plants in cultivation.

How altitude affects climate

Altitude modifies temperature and rainfall. The higher the terrain, the colder the air. An increase in altitude of about 200m (650ft) tends to lower the temperature by 1–2°F (1°C).

There is also likely to be a greater variation between daytime and night-time temperatures, night-time temperature tending to fall dramatically. Light intensity can be high, and the presence of clouds can increase humidity. Altogether it is not surprising that different types of plant (with different needs) occur at different

The tree line, an abrupt halt to vegetation at high altitude

altitudes.

Aspect
Just as altitude affects the growing conditions of a plant, so the position of a slope is significant too. North facing slopes in the northern hemisphere and south facing slopes in the southern hemisphere receive less energy from the sun and are therefore cooler than flat land or slopes that face the equator.

How oceans affect temperature
Large bodies of water heat up and cool down much slower than areas of land. Consequently, they moderate the temperature of the air that is blown across them. As this air reaches land, it will, in turn, moderate the temperature of the air there.

The hotter areas of the earth are the sub-tropical deserts with *continental* climatic influences. These regions have clear skies and the sun's energy is used, virtually exclusively, to heat

the air and the land, there being little rainfall to evaporate. The absence of cloud explains the dramatic fall in temperature during the night.

How soil influences growing conditions
Superficially, soil appears to be a simple substance in which all plants grow, but invariably it is very complex in structure. Its importance is in its degrees of efficiency with which it stores the nutrients and water that all plants need. In the *Key to Vegetational Zones*, the different soils which in nature support house plant growth are described. Later, on page 182, we see how potting mixtures should be composed to suit plant needs in the home.

All soil types are formed by the breakdown of rock, so the type of soil found in a locality is ultimately deter mined by the type of parent rock.

Rock is broken into smaller and

smaller fragments by a process called weathering.

This weathering process eventually results in the production of relatively fine particles which are the basis of soil. Depending on the type of parent rock, more or less of these weathered particles are dissolved in rain and ground water to provide some of the essential nutrients for plants and to help determine how acid or alkaline the soil is. (The latter being a vital home cultivational consideration.)

Besides the weathering process, the withering and breakdown of old roots and the aerial parts of plants – rapid at first, then slower – affects the soil. It does so in two distinct ways:

Firstly, it alters the physical structure of soil by creating *humus*. This is the jelly-like substance which coats minute particles of soil, helps them retain nutrients more effectively, creates a good "crumb structure" (which aids the retention of moisture yet ensures the drainage of excess water), encourages root growth, aids natural propagation by providing a good bed for seeds to grow, and darkens light soils to aid heat retention.

Secondly, the breakdown of organic matter releases chemicals which, in conjunction with those released from the weathered parent rock particles, can lower the pH level and make the soil more acidic. Different plants prefer different pH levels.

The final aspect of soil to bear in mind is its fauna. Earthworms, beetles and other insects, and many more live animals, live in the soil itself and affect its structure by burrowing, moving it around, and secreting different materials and chemicals.

All plants tend to be ideally suited to a particular soil type, and in the wild a plant will *only* grow and thrive in its ideal substrate. In cultivation we have to create an artificial medium (p.182) which makes up for the fact that then there is no soil fauna activity, no natural addition of water, humus or nutrients.

How neighbouring vegetation influences growing conditions

In the tropics where the sun is always almost directly overhead, a considerable amount of solar energy reaches the surface of the earth. This is due to the fact that the rays of the sun have less far to travel to the earth than at any other point, and less of their energy (intensity) is absorbed by the atmosphere. At greater latitudes the rays take an oblique and thus longer path through the atmosphere, and much more solar energy is absorbed *en route*.

We would be wrong to expect all house plants from the tropics to require bright light, however.

In the forest, light levels vary considerably. At ground level, light intensity is less than 1% and often as low as 0.1% of full daylight. But thanks to their adaptation no individual leaf will be blocked from the light by others, whether on a trunk, in a clump or rosette formation.

Most trees grow to reach a middle tree-canopy level, are less exposed to the sun than those "emergent" trees (that can reach 45m (150ft)), and form the most dense layer of larger thick leaves. Some light does filter through this canopy layer of course, and nature helps it on its way by reflecting it downwards off the trees' large and shiny leaves.

Far below, the creeping plant spreads its leaves from stems laying flat on the forest floor to catch what light it can; while the climbing plant holds its leaves outwards from stems clambering upward, through, or on, other vegetation. Thanks to their adaptation to this environment, no individual leaf will be blocked completely from the light by others. Some climbers simply scramble up to the light (like *Cissus antarctica*, though its relation *C. rhombifolia* has tendrils to help it on its way). The most prominent climbers among house plants – the ivies from more temperate climes and the philodendron from sub-tropical and tropical rain forests – have aerial roots which adhere to moist bark. Mainly for

Adaptations to dry heat
The succulent stems of a ferocactus (below right) are its water-storage organs. In the lithops (right) succulent leaves have evolved into a single conical body to survive an erratic water supply. Below: *a bulbous haemanthus from South Africa has evolved to store moisture while resting.*

attachment, these roots can also absorb moisture. In philodendrons, and the related monstera (Swiss cheese plant, as it is commonly known), the aerial roots can extend from the upper parts of the plant right down to the ground (sometimes 30m (100ft) or more) and carry water to the top in parallel with the stem.

What can plants themselves tell us of their cultivational needs?

In order to resist excessive water loss caused by the extreme heat, or compensate for the virtual absence of water in arid regions, plants develop various adaptations in their leaves and root systems. If we recognize these we can adjust our cultural schedules to suit them.

Epiphytes, in the main, grow high in the canopy, where the light is intense, and rely upon trees for their support. Their main survival problem is water, as they can only obtain it when it rains. Many have masses of aerial roots to absorb as much rain as possible, whereas others (like the

bird's nest fern, *Asplenium nidus*) produce their own moisture-retaining soil by collecting organic matter in their funnel-like sets of leaves. The epiphytic bromeliads, on the other hand (a very important group of house plants including aechmea, billbergia, nidularium, vriesea, etc), develop thick waxy or mealy leaves to protect themselves from excessive evaporation in the face of the strong equatorial sun. They also present their leaves in "vase" or "cup" shapes in order to collect rainwater when it comes. The water is then absorbed directly into the plants by special cells near the leaf bases.

Epiphytes that grow at lower levels in the forest are protected from the intense drying effect of the sun by higher vegetation, and consequently display little or no water-retaining adaptations. Here, where light levels are relatively low, we also find the papery-leaved caladiums that would soon wilt and die if exposed to fierce sunlight. Their leaves contrast strongly with those of *Ficus elastica* (the popularly durable rubber plant). In nature it can grow 30m (100ft) high and has developed its thickly cuticled leaves to withstand the heat and avoid excessive moisture loss.

Clearly it would be wrong to expect plants that are not naturally adapted to withstand such growing conditions to thrive upon strong light in the home. And this logical connection (one of many) between natural growing conditions and home care schedules is developed in specific terms when we consider the plants themselves.

Plant adaptations in arid regions
Contrary to popular belief, a not inconsiderable amount of rain falls each year in sub-tropical and semi-deserts. And because the plants which inhabit these regions grow relatively far apart (and have large root systems), they enjoy almost as much water as the plants tightly packed together in a humid forest. The drier the region, the further apart the plants grow, their root systems spreading out in search of moisture.

In pots at home, cacti and other

Jungle adaptations
Epiphytes growing high in the tree canopy have to withstand intense light; see below the "rigging" of their aerial roots. Right: Vriesea splendens, an epiphytic bromeliad adapted to resist excessive evaporation. Below right: *the papery-leaved caladium adapted to the low light of a jungle floor.*

succulents have their root systems artificially restricted, and when they are watered they require drenching and then must be left to dry out thoroughly, allowing their special moisture-retaining systems to look after their needs. These systems have developed in nature to survive periods of drought when their water-absorbing roots die. In aloe and crassula, the water-storage organs are their succulent leaves; in cacti and species of *Euphorbia* and *Stapelia*, succulent stems perform the same function. In some species of *Asparagus*, succulent roots serve as underground water-storage organs.

Apart from the true succulents, all other types of plant require some water to be available even during the dry period. In semi-arid regions there are plants that have soft leaves that wilt under dry conditions and may drop during lengthy dry periods; only the youngest leaves, protected within hair-covered buds, survive. Other plants have small, hard leaves that can reduce water loss to a minimum when water is scarce. Yet others shut all their stomata and undergo a period of starvation; the leaves of

these will eventually dry out, turn yellow and drop, the plants surviving dry periods but appearing pitifully crippled.

Once we learn to recognize what plants can tell us by their leaf and root characteristics, we can use the information together with what we know about a plant's local climate and make sense of specific care schedules.

Plant tolerances
From the climate of a particular locality (known as a plant's micro-climate and definable in terms of regional climate modified by such variables as altitude, aspect, and the degree of shelter offered by neighbouring vegetation) and from what we can learn about a plant's morphology (the organic adaptations a plant makes in response to its micro-climate), we can attribute temperature and light tolerances to a plant growing in a home environment.

Clearly those plants which experience a variety of conditions in the wild make most successful house plants, but *no plant will survive if its natural temperature or light ranges are exceeded at either end of the scale.* And because most plants popularly cultivated indoors originate in the tropics (and are used to higher temperatures than we can comfortably provide them), it is safe to say that it is the lower level of a plant's temperature range that is more likely to be exceeded.

But it is absolutely vital to understand that temperature schedules cannot be divorced from advice about humidity.

A rain forest plant may tolerate a temperature of 100°F (88°C) but *only* if it can rely upon daily rain keeping the humidity (moisture level in the atmosphere) high. Whereas succulents (including cacti) coming from arid regions do not require water or even water vapour at similar temperatures. Dry heat is no problem for long periods thanks to their water-storing fleshy tissues.

13

Tropical (evergreen) rain forest

Characteristics

Predominantly trees, mainly slender with thin bark, small crowns (due to crowding of canopy) and shallow roots (many develop stilt roots or plank buttresses). The warmer and wetter the climate, the larger their leaves tend to be (though those that are exposed to direct sun are usually smaller). There may be 3 distinct layers of tree: the "emergent" trees reaching 45m (150ft), the "canopy" an almost continuous leafy layer of trees where crowns may top 37m (120ft), and the "middle" layer of smaller trees, often indistinguishable from the "canopy" layer. Below this is the dark forest floor.

Due to lack of clear-cut seasons one tree may be in full bloom while neighbours of the same species may only be in leaf; sometimes branches of the same tree may be at different stages.

Apart from trees, there are shrubs, herbs, lianas and epiphytes, which use trees for support in their search for light.

Light levels

Low. At ground level less than $1\frac{1}{4}$% of full daylight, so vegetation on forest floor is sparse. Some light is reflected downwards by shiny foliage.

Soils

Usually brown loams, often waterlogged and swampy. Surprisingly poor and acid; vegetation decays rapidly but nutrients are as rapidly absorbed by roots. Little goodness is lost from the soil due to leaching, despite high rainfall. Once vegetation is removed, however, and the rapid cycle stopped, the soil is unable to support any rich regrowth.

Water

Wet; usually at least 100mm (4in) rain per month, though some months drier than others. Humidity is always high, and encourages the luxuriant plant growth. Many plants (e.g. *Ficus elastica* – the rubber plant), have leathery leaves with thick cuticles to stop excess water loss when in direct, intense sunlight. Plants at lower levels in forest are protected by the tree canopy acting as an insulating layer. Epiphytes either store their water in fleshy tissues or absorb it from the moist air through hanging roots.

Tropical moist and dry deciduous forest, savanna and grassland

Found in tropical areas not covered by rain forest. Forest is often cleared to create savanna and grassland.

Type of vegetation is determined by (a) the amount and frequency of rainfall, and (b) the duration of the dry season. As (b) increases, the uppermost tree layer becomes deciduous, lower layers remaining evergreen as in the rain forest (such areas are known as tropical semi-evergreen forests). As (a) decreases and (b) increases still further, all trees become deciduous to prevent further water loss through their leaves, creating either moist or dry deciduous tropical forest.

Deforested areas in wetter areas will turn to savanna. There is a gradual transition from wooded areas with grassy undergrowth to predominantly grassy areas in which woody plants are more or less evenly distributed (i.e. savanna), and then to grassland without woody plants.

Characteristics

The leaf loss of woody plants is a response to the dry season. Deciduous trees shed leaves when the lack of water is acute; the plants are not actually dormant – many flower at this time, probably stimulated by the temperature rise. Water loss through petals is minimal, so there is no threat to plant survival. Plants in these areas have fewer stomata (leaf pores), a fact which diminishes transpiration.

Aerial grass shoots die down during the dry season and form a dense layer protecting their growing points; growth recommences immediately the rains arrive.

Light levels

Low at ground level in dense forest, but increasing when leaves are shed.

As the trees become sparser, so light at ground level increases and undergrowth becomes more grassy.

Soils

Soils vary from deep loam to freer draining, fine sand; they become significant in cleared areas as rainfall decreases. In deep, loamy soils that are capable of retaining water, savanna prevails; in stony soils (where water may be unevenly distributed) trees and thorny bushes with wide-spreading roots prevail. In the fine, sandy soils that are capable of holding adequate water, grass is successful as its finely divided roots can permeate a small area of soil to extract maximum moisture efficiently.

Water

The factor that controls the type of vegetation. There is always a dry period which, as we have seen, plants are adapted to survive. If rainful is so low that only surface layers of soil are moistened, the grass survives but the trees die. With higher rainfall, trees thrive, enlarge their crowns and shade out the grasses.

Sub-tropical deserts and semi-deserts

Characteristics

Plants have evolved various methods of beating the effects of low and often erratic rainfall:

1. Horizontally spreading root systems expand to encompass an area capable of yielding as much water as would suffice for a plant in a tropical forest. The drier the region the further apart are the plants.

2. Ephemerals grow and flower in brief wet periods and survive drought by dormancy or as seeds in the ground.

3. Succulents with water storage

systems in their fleshy tissue can survive up to 12 months without taking up water.

4. Plants (more characteristic of semi-arid regions) have soft leaves which wilt in prolonged periods of drought, but produce new, young leaves that are protected by hair-covered buds.

5. Some plants have small, hard leaves specially designed to reduce water loss.

Light levels
Always very high, except beneath dense scrub. Plants have to be able to withstand intense sunlight.

Soils
Soil texture is important as it determines how much water can be retained in the soil after the precious rain has fallen. In humid and wet areas of the world, sandy soils are dry as they can retain only small amounts of water, whereas clay soils are wet and generally more suitable for growth. In arid areas, water still deeply penetrates sandy soils, but the drying action of the sun only acts on surface layers leaving deeper soil relatively wet and exploitable by roots. Conversely, in dry areas of clay soils only the surface is moistened by rain, this either runs off or is rapidly evaporated by the sun, leaving no water for plant growth.

Fertile areas are often found where run-off rainwater settles: e.g. gullies and valleys, and on sand dunes which, if deep enough, can store sufficient water for roots of suitable plants to reach.

Water
Rainfall tends to be very low and often irregular. In some areas a regular early morning dew helps alleviate the problem.

Sclerophyllous vegetation with winter rains

Often, as in the Mediterranean, this type has replaced natural evergreen forest destroyed by Man.

Characteristics
Most plants flower in spring, some again after the autumnal rains, but there is a period of relative dormancy in the dry summer period. The characteristic method of conserving water is by thick leathery sclerophyllous leaves that defy the evaporating effects of the dry period.

Light levels
In woodland, light at ground levels tends to be low, though in scrubby areas there is more.

Soils
When cleared of trees the soil is exposed to sun and wind and the lack of decaying vegetable matter diminishes soil fertility. The original, spongy, brown forest soils lose their structure, the rain washes away the fertile soil particles, and expose bare rock. The remaining pockets of soil are deficient in humus and prone to drought. Soil is often red in colour due to the mineral decomposition of the parent rock, rich in iron.

Water
Winter is wet and warm (frosts are very rare) and summer is hot and dry. Many plants complete their life-cycles before summer. Where soil moisture is adequate, many species can survive – some woody species have roots penetrating rocks to a depth of 10m (over 30ft).

Warm temperate wet evergreen forests

Tropical rain forest gives way to subtropical forest as latitude increases, and these in turn give way to warm temperate forest.

Characteristics
A luxuriant forest very similar to the tropical rain forest but as the average temperature falls so the size of leaf decreases. Tropical species become rarer, and those tree-ferns that flourish in cooler damp climates, abound.

Light levels
This is a dense forest and little light permeates through the canopy to reach the lower levels of vegetation.

Soils
Similar to tropical rain forest, though the Kauri forests of New Zealand grow on heavy clay soils.

Water
The climate is wet and very humid throughout the year; there is no shortage of water so the plants show no water-retaining characteristics.

Temperate deciduous forests

Characteristics
A leaf colour change and leaf shedding in autumn is characteristic. It is probably due to decreasing day length, and is certainly an adaptation to survive the cold season.

The length of growing season determines the type of local vegetation – deciduous plants need at least 4 months growing to build up reserves for flowering, fruiting and leaf formation during the following season; evergreen plants need only about 1 month. Thus prevailing conditions determine whether local vegetation is evergreen or deciduous.

Light levels
Beneath the tree cover the light is low (often as little as 0.6% of full daylight), temperatures are cool and humidity high.

All herbaceous species on the forest floor are shade tolerant and moisture loving (annuals are rare). Many take advantage of the more accessible sunlight in spring before the trees come into leaf, plant leaves yellow and die when the trees leaves expand; if exposed to more light this happens even earlier in the growing season (i.e. this is not a response to reduced light as might be expected). They then lay dormant, covered by a protective layer of autumn leaves and snow.

Soils
A wide variety of soil types support different types of forest.

Water
Rain falls throughout the year and there is no period of drought.

15

The map shows, by colour coding, the ten regions of the world that are the ten sections of the *World Guide to Plant Origins and Home Cultivation*. The genera with which the book deals are listed here and have been keyed into the regions where they grow naturally and the sections of the *World Guide* in which their cultivation is described in detail. Hybrids are dealt with in the regions where their parents originated.

Additionally, any particular species can be traced through *The Illustrated Plant Index* on page 206.

Achimenes ☐
Acorus ■☐
Adiantum ☐☐☐
Aechmea ☐
Aeonium ■
Aeschynanthus ☐
Aglaonema ☐
Aloe ☐
Ananas ■
Anthurium ☐☐
Aphelandra ☐
Araucaria ■
Asparagus ☐☐
Aspidistra ■
Asplenium ▨
Astrophytum ☐
Begonia ■
Beloperone ☐
Billbergia ☐
Blechnum ☐☐
Brassaia ☐
Browallia ☐
Brunfelsia ☐
Bryophyllum ☐
Caladium ☐
Calathea ☐
Calceolaria ☐
Callisia ☐
Campanula ■
Capsicum ☐☐
Carex ■
Caryota ☐☐
Catharanthus ☐☐
Cephalocereus ☐
Cereus ☐
Ceropegia ☐
Chamaecereus ☐
Chamaedorea ☐
Chlorophytum ☐
Chrysanthemum ■
Cineraria ■
Cissus ☐☐

☐	**North and Central America, and West Indies**	
☐	**South America**	
☐	**Europe and North Africa**	
☐	**Tropical Africa**	
☐	**South Africa**	
☐	**Madagascar**	
☐	**India**	
■	**Central and East Asia**	
☐	**South East Asia**	
☐	**Australia, New Zealand and the Pacific Islands**	

Citrus ☐■
Cleistocactus ☐
Clivia ☐
Cocos ▨
Codiaeum ☐
Coleus ☐
Columnea ☐
Cordyline ☐☐☐
Cotyledon ☐
Crassula ☐
Crocus ■
Crossandra ☐
Cryptanthus ☐
Ctenanthe ☐
Cyclamen ■
Cyperus ☐☐☐
Cyrtomium ☐☐☐
Cytisus ■
Davallia ☐☐☐
Dieffenbachia ☐☐
Dizygotheca ☐

Dolicothele ☐
Dracaena ☐☐☐☐
Echeveria ☐
Echinocactus ■
Echinocereus ■
Echinopsis ☐
Epiphyllum ☐
Episcia ☐☐
Erica ☐
Euphorbia ☐☐
Exacum ☐
Fatshedera ■
Fatsia ■
Faucaria ☐
Ferocactus ☐
Ficus ☐☐■☐☐
Fittonia ☐
Fuchsia ☐
Gasteria ☐
Graptopetalum ☐
Grevillea ☐

Guzmania ☐☐
Gymnocalcium ☐
Gynura ☐
Haemanthus ☐
Hamatocactus ■
Haworthia ☐
Hedera ■
Hemigraphis ☐
Heptapleurum ☐
Hibiscus ☐
Hippeastrum ☐
Howea ■
Hoya ☐☐■
Hyacinthus ☐
Hydrangea ■
Hypoestes ☐
Impatiens ☐☐
Jasminum ■■
Kalanchoe ☐☐
Kleinia ☐
Lantana ■

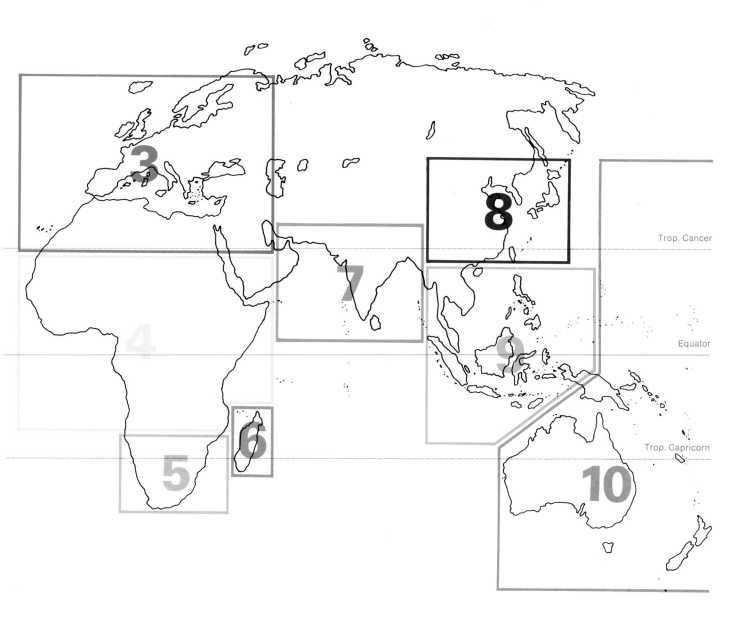

Lithops ▫	Pelargonium ▫	Rhapis ■	Spathiphyllum ▫
Lobivia ▪	Pellaea ▫▫	Rhipsalidopsis ▫	Stapelia ▫
Mammillaria ■	Pellionia ▫	Rhododendron ■	Stenotaphrum ■
Maranta ▫	Peperomia ▪▫	Rhoeo ▪	Strelitzia ▫
Microcoelum ▪	Philodendron ▪▫	Rochea ▫	Streptocarpus ▫
Mimosa ▪	Phoenix ▪▫	Rohdea ■	Strobilanthes ▫
Monstera ▪	Phyllitis ▪	Rosa ■	Stromanthe ▪
Narcissus ▪	Pilea ▪▪▫	Ruellia ▫	Syngonium ▪
Neoregelia ▫	Pisonia ▪	Saintpaulia ▫	Tetrastigma ▫
Nephrolepis ▪	Pittosporum ■	Sansevieria ▫	Thunbergia ▫
Nerium ▪	Platycerium ▪▫	Saxifraga ■	Tillandsia ▪▫
Nidularium ▫	Plectranthus ▫▫▪	Schlumbergera ▫	Tolmiea ▪
Notocactus ▫	Pleomele ▪	Scindapsus ▫▫	Trachycarpus ■
Oplismenus ▪	Plumbago ▫	Sedum ▪■	Tradescantia ▪▫
Opuntia ▪▫	Podocarpus ■	Selaginella ▫▫▫	Trichocereus ▪
Pachyphytum ▫	Polypodium ▪	Senecio ▪	Tulipa ▪
Pachystachys ▫	Polystichum ■	Setcreasea ▪	Vallota ▫
Pandanus ▪	Primula ▫■	Sinningia ▫	Veltheimia ▫
Parodia ▪	Pseuderanthemum ▪	Smithiantha ▪	Vriesea ▪
Passiflora ▫	Pteris ▪▫▫	Solanum ▪	Yucca ▪
Pedilanthus ▪	Rebutia ▪	Sparmannia ▫	Zebrina ■

17

North and Central America, & West Indies

Here house plants grow in tropical rain, montane and sub-tropical forests, high open areas, grassland, and desert. Each requires the care appropriate to its habitat; special measures (noted in the text) are required to match humidity with temperature for those which enjoy the hot, moist conditions of the rain forest. Examples are the Swiss cheese plant, maidenhair, hare's foot and nephrolepis ferns, the flamingo flower, columnea, dieffenbachia, epiphyllum, episcia, guzmania, peperomia, syngonium and tillandsia.

North and Central America
North and Central America cover an area of about 8.2 million sq.miles. Central America, which reaches as far north as Texas and as far south as the northern border of Colombia, is made up of land that has a high, central plateau with lowland coastal plains on either side. These high plateau areas are separated by many small valleys with pleasant climates and fertile soil.

Climate
In the United States, the climate varies greatly between both north and south, and coast and interior. Summers are generally hot, and in the coastal areas, quite humid. Winters are mild on the west coast, but colder east of the Rockies. In the east the annual rainfall is about 1,000mm (40in) and it falls throughout the year, whereas the central plains receive about 500mm (20in), mainly in the summer. Winters are wettest on the west coast, with 1,800mm (70in) in the north but only 200mm (8in) in the desert areas to the south. The southernmost areas of the country are tropical.

Vegetation
Tundra
This is found in the northernmost part of the continent and runs southwards into Central America along the mountains. There are no trees, so the vegetation is dominated by herbs and low shrubs. The growing season is short, temperatures are low and winds are usually strong.

Coniferous forest
Coniferous forests are common in the northern hemisphere. Here they cover the rest of Canada, the area to the south of the tundra; they also grow along the mountain chains and down the western coast as far as central California.

Deciduous forest
This covers a large area of the eastern United States from the Great Lakes in the north as far as eastern Texas and Florida (though some evergreens will be found too)

Grassland
Grasslands cover the massive central area of North America from Indiana west to the Rockies and from southern-central Canada to parts of northern Mexico, as well as a few smaller areas further to the west.

Symbols

Plants from tropical and sub-tropical forests:

 Ground level plant

 Canopy level plant

 Shrub level plant

 Canopy level climber

 Low level climber

 Canopy level epiphyte

 Low level epiphyte

Other categories of forest and woodland:

WT Warm temperate wet evergreen

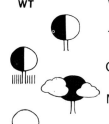 Temperate deciduous

Open areas of forest

Montane/cloud forest

Savanna

Plants from other areas:

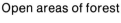 Water margins

 High open areas

 Arid areas

Grassland and steppe

 Sclerophyllous/maquis/dry bush

Temperature/light home-care symbols:

Sunlovers (direct sun)

Bright light (75–60% full sun)

Good light (50–25% full sun)

Light shade (10% full sun)

Shade (5–3% full sun)
(*See pages 178–179*)

Cool (45–55°F (7–13°C))

Medium (55–65°F (13–18°C))

Warm (65–75°F (18–24°C))
(*See pages 172–173*)

These are the prairies.

Bordering the grassland is coniferous forest, deciduous forest, desert, shrubland and woodland.

Rainfall is not very high, a maximum of 1,000mm (40in) in the south-east reducing to only 250mm (10in) at the base of the Rocky Mountains. Much of the rain falls during the growing season, mainly in May and June.

Temperatures can be extreme, as low as −31°F (−35°C) and as high as 113°F (45°C). The cold winters and the late summer drought limit the growing season to 120 days in the north and 200 days in the south.

Many of the grassland plants have most of their mass below ground in corms, bulbs, tubers etc; this helps them to survive the drought period as well as the burning. Many of the plants show water-conserving characters.

Desert grassland is found in the south-western United States and northern Mexico. Growing with the grasses are shrubs including the creosote bush, acacias, yuccas and prickly-pear cacti.

Deserts

There are two areas of hot deserts. One from north-western United States through Nevada and Utah to western Mexico, and the other covers southern New Mexico and Texas and northern-central Mexico. These two desert areas are separated by desert grassland. All of these areas have low rainfall that can fall at any time; most of the rain, in fact, falls during heavy cloudbursts, and much of the water runs off and is of no use for plant growth. Temperatures are usually high during the day and low at night, sometimes below freezing. The wind is often strong and sand and dust storms are common.

The vegetation is usually in two low open shrub layers, but in some places are found plants with tree-like growth above them. There is a sparse and patchy herb layer. On the whole the shrubs are widely spaced due to the

root competition for soil moisture; creosote bush, sagebush, yuccas and acacias are very common. Most of the herbs are ephemerals, which grow and flower after the rains.

Temperate shrubland, woodland and savanna

Shrubland or thicket vegetation is dominated by dense shrubs or small shrubby trees; woodland is dominated by trees, but the crowns do not touch; and savanna is even more open with trees covering only about 30% of the surface and with a well-developed herb layer. Woodland and shrubland are found in the Rocky Mountains; woodland, shrubland and forest grow along much of the Californian coast; and temperate savanna is found in central United States.

The Californian woodland is sclerophyllous and often called Chaparral; it is found from southern Oregon to northern Baja California. This area has cool and wet winters and hot, dry summers typical of a Mediterranean climate; rainfall is 350–750mm (14–29½in). In the winter the temperature can average as low as freezing point, whereas summer temperatures reach a maximum of 95°F (35°C).

Tropical vegetation

This occurs from South America northwards through Central America and the Caribbean Islands to northern Mexico and also includes the southern tip of Florida. The climate is generally warmer and wetter than that found in the temperate zones and most of the vegetation is tropical rain forest, though throughout much of Central America, there are areas of true savanna.

The lowland tropical rain forest experiences only slight variations of temperature; the average temperature throughout the year is about 77°F (25°C). Rainfall is high, but with local variations. Despite slight seasonal fluctuation, there is no completely dry period and active growth continues throughout the year. Humidity is always high and a heavy

dew usually forms overnight.

There is a great wealth of plant species. Most of the trees are evergreen, with the leaves having a life of about 14 months; they are shed in constant succession. Lianas are common, often growing so densely that they hold up dead trees that would otherwise have crashed to the forest floor. Epiphytes are also very common; the shade-loving ferns tending to grow low in the forest, and the light-loving flowering plants high in the canopy. Most of the herbs that grow on the forest floor tend to be ferns; many of them can reach heights of several metres.

The lower montane forests above tropical rain forest, at altitudes of over 250m (820ft). Humidity is very high due to the stationary clouds around the mountains. Rainfall is very high, but due to the fact that most of the land is sloping, there is some run off, and very little water-logged ground.

The montane rain forest (or cloud forest) grows at somewhat higher altitudes. Humidity, fog and cloud are at an absolute maximum, but due to the increased height, temperatures are 22–36°F (12–20°C) lower than those found in the lowland tropical rain forest.

The montane thicket (a high mountain forest) grows at altitudes of over 4,000m (over 13,000ft).

The elfin woodland is the highest tree zone, where temperatures average 59°–68°F (15–20°C) with great daily fluctuations; there is always a lot of cloud cover.

Tropical savanna exists in areas scattered throughout Central America and the Caribbean Islands.

West Indies
Climate
As in most tropical areas where reaonably elevated land is found (over 15,000 sq.miles are above 500m (1,650ft) altitude), the climate varies and at the higher levels quite low temperatures are experienced. All

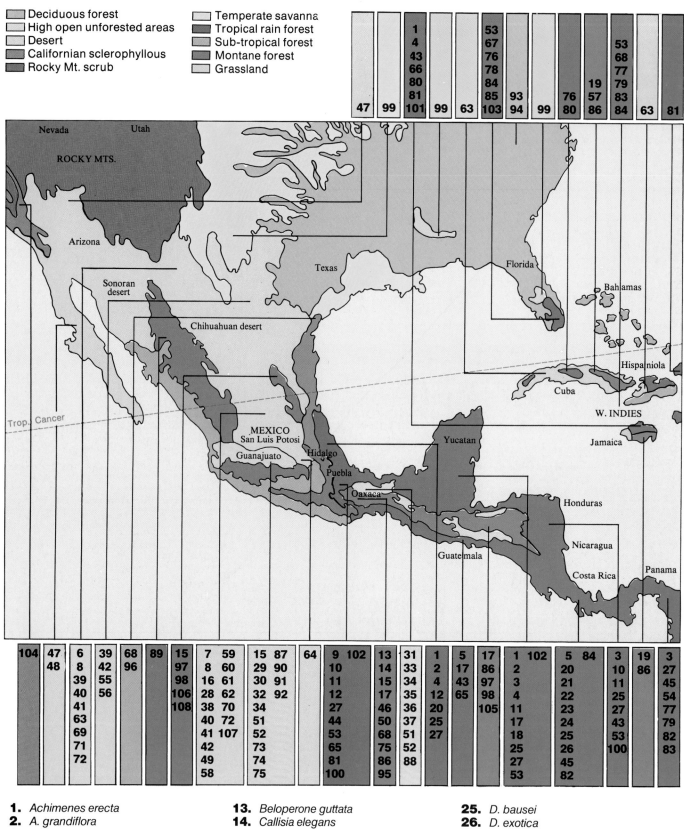

Deciduous forest
High open unforested areas
Desert
Californian sclerophyllous
Rocky Mt. scrub

Temperate savanna
Tropical rain forest
Sub-tropical forest
Montane forest
Grassland

1. Achimenes erecta
2. A. grandiflora
3. A. longiflora
4. Adiantum tenerum
5. Anthurium scherzerianum
6. Astrophytum asterias
7. A. myriostigma
8. A. ornatum
9. Begonia boweri
10. B. erythryophylla
11. B. gracilis
12. B. Maphil

13. Beloperone guttata
14. Callisia elegans
15. Capsicum annuum
16. Cephalocereus senilis
17. Chamaedorea elegans
18. C. seifrizii
19. Cissus rhombifolia
20. Columnea banksii
21. C. gloriosa
22. C. linearis
23. C. microphylla
24. Dieffenbachia amoena

25. D. bausei
26. D. exotica
27. D. maculata
28. Dolicothele longimamma
29. Echeveria affinis
30. E. agavoides
31. E. derenbergii
32. E. elegans
33. E. gibbiflora
34. E. harmsii
35. E. leucotricha
36. E. setosa

20

Cloud forest with orchids and bromeliads in the Costa Rica Mountains

slightly higher altitude. Forests are widespread, and some immense locust trees are estimated to be over 4,000 years old.

The structure of the vegetation is a broad spectrum of different types, often of very limited distribution: from mangroves on Haiti and Santo Domingo, to tropical rain forest, to coniferous forest, to shrubby thickets, to areas with a dense covering of palms, to many open and cultivated areas. On the whole, the tropical rain forests of Central America, closely resemble the vegetation of the West Indies.

Steep country in the Jamaica rain forest defies botanizing.

of the islands are in the north-easterly trade wind belts, and except for part of the Bahamas, the average annual temperature at sea level is about 77°F (25°C). The climate is maritime with the intense heat moderated by the trade winds and the cool nights.

The shorter of its two wet seasons usually starts in April and lasts for only a few weeks. After this is a dry season that lasts until September when the main rainy season begins. In this wet season, lasting until December, hurricanes are frequent and often damaging. From December the dry season once again begins, but there are fresh winds and the occasional showers. Annual rainfall is about 1,500mm (59in).

Vegetation
The vegetation is very varied and rich and many wild and cultivated species have been introduced from elsewhere in the world. Plants cultivated in temperate areas usually grow well and often quite close to others that require tropical conditions; though the temperate crop is grown at a

Plant hunting in the area

Rear-admiral Bligh in the West Indies

We have all heard of the mutiny on the *Bounty*, but it seems less well-known that Bligh, by then Rear-admiral, made a second journey in the ship, *H.M.S. Providence*, which successfully delivered the breadfruit plants to the West Indies. On his return he had a magnificent collection of plants for Kew, the famous English botanical garden, including the first really outstanding maidenhair ferns.

Messrs Smith and Perrin, who had been tending the breadfruit, obtained the large-leaved *Adiantum macrophyllum*; a doctor known as Thomas Dancer provided *A. trapeziforme* and yet another medical man, Arthur Broughton, supplied Bligh with *A. tenerum*, probably the most widely grown of all the maidenhairs. *Providence* brought them back in 1793. Though brought from Jamaica, all the genus have a wide distribution over tropical America and may well have been cultivated plants. *Providence* also carried a number of peperomias including *P. magnoliaefolium*, while *P. obtusifolium* was being grown by Philip Miller in 1739. Philip Miller was curator of the Chelsea Physic Garden in London, the second oldest botanical garden in the country, the oldest being in Oxford.

Theodor Hartweg and Central American cacti

Before the Veitch collectors, whom we shall consider later, Britain had two collectors in Central America. In 1837 Theodor Hartweg, collecting for the London Horticultural Society (it was not yet Royal) arrived in Mexico, where he collected for some years, making journies also to Colombia and to Guatemala. He sent back very large collections made up of numerous species. Among these were a number of cacti, of which *Cephalocereus senilis* is perhaps the best known, but he also sent 40 different species of Mammillaria, of which 22 were still unnamed, when he published his report in 1846. His next sending included *Fuchsia fulgens*, the main parent, with *F. magellanica*, of the hybrid fuchsias, which have been so popular for so long. During his trip Hartweg went to Guatemala, but this had been well explored by an attractive figure, George Ure Skinner.

George Ure Skinner and Achimenes grandiflora

At the age of 27 he went to Guatemala and set up a business with a Herr Klee, which was very successful. His partner was *chargé d'affaires* of Hanover and Prussia. Skinner had always been a keen amateur naturalist and on arriving in Guatemala sent specimens of birds and of insects to the Manchester Natural History Museum. Then James Bateman, one of the first of the true enthusiasts for orchids, wrote to Skinner and asked him to collect orchids for him. Skinner eventually became an enthusiastic collector of plants of all kinds, but the house plant grower's greatest debt to him is the introduction of *Achimenes grandiflora*.

20th Century expeditions

Few new house plants have been received from Central America or South America during this century, although a number of cryptanthus hybrids have been bred in the U.S.A. However a new sedum, *S. morganianum*, with hanging branches is one recent introduction and a very strange one it is. A plant was purchased in a Mexican market and all the plants in cultivation would seem to derive from this original purchase. That is odd enough in itself, but even more remarkable is that the plant has never been found in the wild, nor were any other cultivated specimens found at the time of the original purchase. In 1936 another Mexican plant came into cultivation, although it had been known before. This was the shrimp plant, best known as *Beloperone guttata*, but which should probably really be called *Justicia brandegeana*. This is, of course, one of the most popular of all house plants and there must now be more plants in cultivation than survive in the wild.

ACHIMENES
(GESNERIACEAE)

Achimenes from the warm and humid parts of Mexico, Honduras, Panama and Jamaica are more suited to growing in a sunny porch or conservatory than the windowsill, where they are usually shy to flower. They grow from a scaly rhizome up to 25mm (1in) long, and growth will only start if temperature is right–around 60°F (15°C). In temperate climates they have a period of dormancy from late September to early April when they should be kept

completely dry at the roots, still in their pots.

Leaves may be thin and pointed or heart-shaped, and are usually slightly hairy. Flowers are a narrow tube shape but flare out into five rounded lobes. Colour is usually strong, blue or purple, pink or red shades, but some are white or streaked with deeper coloured veining.

For best effect several rhizomes should be planted in one pot, on their sides just below the surface of the mixture. Most need some form of thin cane support

A. erecta (syn. *A. coccinea*) – bright red.
A. grandiflora – deep reddish purple.
A. longiflora – blue with white throat.

Many hybrids are available from specialist growers, including:
Ambroise Verschaffelt – white with purple veining.
Little Beauty – deep pink, yellow eye.
Paul Arnold – large, violet purple.

Watering: Water sparingly at first after potting up and until a good root system has been built up. Thereafter water generously and then allow the mixture to begin drying out before giving more. As flowers become fewer in the early autumn, start to reduce watering ·

Potting mixture: Use a mixture of equal-parts peat, leaf mould and vermiculite or perlite with a little dolomite lime added .

Propagation: Each rhizome makes several new ones each year and a stock of plants can be built up quite quickly.

Special points: Feed established plants every two weeks with a high potash liquid fertilizer from the time that growth is say 10cm (4in) high until early September. If intended to grow plants upright, provide support early.

ADIANTUM TENERUM
(POLYPODIACEAE)

A. tenerum, a maidenhair fern from Florida, the West Indies, and Mexico is recommended (but see also South America and Australasia).
Its fan-shaped pinnae are fringed or crested at the edges (particularly the types Farleyense and Gloriosa). It may grow to 60cm (2ft) tall.

Watering: Keep moderately moist at the roots but never sodden. Fronds will shrivel if the mixture dries out completely; dunk periodically in a bowl or bucket of water for 15 minutes in warmer months.

Potting mixture: Use $\frac{1}{4}$ peat, $\frac{1}{4}$ leaf mould, $\frac{1}{4}$ sharp sand or perlite and $\frac{1}{4}$ soil-based potting mixture.

Propagation: Divide up overcrowded clumps in spring.

Special points: Stand pots on trays of moist pebbles. When older fronds start to brown at the edges, cut them down right to the base; new ones will take their place. Avoid draughts. Very little feeding is necessary; do so only every two or three months during the growing season with a half-strength fertilizer.

ANTHURIUM SCHERZERIANUM
(ARACEAE)

A. scherzerianum (flamingo flower) dwells in the humid rain forests of Guatemala and Costa Rica. It makes virtually no stem and lance-shaped leaves 20–20.5cm (8–10in) long held on long leafstalks.

Spathes are oval, shiny, brilliant scarlet and pierced by a twisting, orange spadix. Some kinds have darker red spathes spotted white.

Watering: Water plentifully during the active growth period, allowing a little drying out between applications. Be more sparing during winter.

Potting mixture: Ideally equal parts mixture of coarse leaf mould and peat, otherwise a peat-based mix.

Propagation: Divide overcrowded clumps in spring, ensuring that each detached piece has some roots attached and a growing point. Use a propagator if available.

Special points: The recommended potting mixture has little plant food built into it and it is essential that regular liquid feeding is given. Use a half-strength liquid fertilizer, every two weeks while growth is apparent. A very humid atmosphere is essential;

BEGONIA
(BEGONIACEAE)

See South America for general discussion of genus and species cultivation.

B. boweri Said to have been found originally 4,000 feet up in a shady ravine by a stream in Mexico, *B. boweri* also grows in green savanna in Costa Rica. It is the parent of a group of low-growing offspring (a little easier to grow than the parent) called boweri hybrids having passed on one typical characteristic, black, stitch-like markings and eyelash-like bristles on leaf edges, prompting the name eyelash begonia. Basic leaf colour is a fresh green and the small flowers may be white or shell-pink.

B. erythrophylla is a hybrid with two Mexican parents and is often sold as *B. feastii* or beefsteak begonia. Leaves are round, shiny, 8–10cm (3–4in) across, deep olive green above with a "beefsteak" red on the underside. Flowers are small and pink. There is a form *B. e*. Helix, where one lobe of the leaf curls over another part, like the turn of a corkscrew.

B. gracilis (Mexico) is one of two "hollyhock begonias" with a fleshy, erect stem to 60cm (2ft), pale green, almost round, scallop-edged leaves, and rosy pink flowers tucked (like those of a hollyhock) into the leaf axils, near the tops of the stems. It produces small bulbils in the leaf axils in autumn.

B. Maphil , a boweri seedling, has star-shaped leaves with bristly white hairs on the edges, long red-spotted stalks (also bristly) and pale pink flowers in early spring.

Leaf colour is a mixture of light but bright green, gold and chocolate-brown. **23**

Cacti

Begonia boweri, *found 4,000ft up in a shady ravine by a Mexican stream*

Begonia gracilis, *the hollyhock begonia.*

BELOPERONE GUTTATA
(ACANTHACEAE)

Drejerella guttata and *Justicia brandegeana* are two synonyms, the common name – shrimp plant – at least remains the same. Native of Mexico, it makes a small shrub 30–36cm (12–14in) tall with rather dull, slightly hairy leaves, a bushy habit if growing points are pinched out periodically, and shrimp-like flowerspikes. These are terminal, in small clusters, 8–10cm (3–4in) long and made up of overlapping reddish brown and pink bracts through which peep thin, white tubular flowers. Flowerspikes are produced from spring through to late autumn.

Watering: Water sparingly, allowing the mixture to dry out a little before repeating.

Potting mixture: Use a mixture of three parts soil-based mix with one part coarse peat or if available leaf mould.

Propagation: Take tip cuttings 8–10cm (3–4in) long (removing any young flowerspikes) in spring. See below.

Special points: Most plants need cutting back hard in the spring and the tips can be used for making new plants. See that several rooted cuttings are potted together to make a bushy effect. Feed actively growing plants every two weeks. Pinch out growing tips if growth becomes straggly.

Desert cacti from Central America

Jungle cacti are discussed in their appropriate alphabetical positions in the general plant listing, but since other cacti share the same cultural needs they are discussed here together.

Watering: Water plentifully during the growing period, allowing the potting mixture to dry out partly before watering again. In the rest period water only enough to keep the mixture from drying out entirely.

Potting mixture: Use $\frac{3}{4}$ soil-based mixture and $\frac{1}{4}$ coarse sand or grit well mixed, and pot preferably in clay pots.

Special points: Feed once a month in the growing period, April to September. Ensure a winter rest in cool conditions and good light. Repot in spring only if old pot is filled with roots.

ASTROPHYTUM
Astrophytums are low-growing, round or cylindrical cacti from the high deserts of north and central Mexico, found at between 3,000 and 6,000 feet where they experience a cool, dry winter. The body (stem) is divided into segments by ribs, some are spineless, others fiercely armed; most have yellow, daisy-like flowers around an inch across.

A. asterias (sea-urchin cactus) is like a slightly flattened ball up to 10cm (4in) across and 40mm (1½in) wide with eight raised ribs.

Cephalocereus senilis, *from Mexico, is known as old man cactus*

A. myriostigma (bishop's mitre or monk's hood) starts round but gradually elongates to cylindrical. Maximum size in pots is 10cm (4in) across and 20cm (8in) high. It has 5–8 very pronounced ribs and is spotted with fine white hairs, that look like scales.

A. ornatum (ornamental monk's hood) can grow to 30.5cm (1ft) tall and 15cm (6in) through. Stout yellow-brown spines densely cover the edges of the ribs usually 8 in number. Flowers can be 9cm (3–4in) across.

CEPHALOCEREUS SENILIS
A columnar cactus from central Mexico, known as

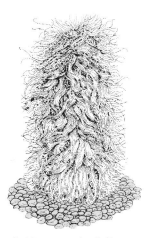

"old man cactus". Its many shallow ribs are virtually hidden by silvery hairs that shield its body from intense sun and dry desert winds. Grown from seed. Beware mealy bugs.

DOLICHOTHELE LONGIMAMMA

Closely related to *Mammillaria*, this single species from central Mexico is basically globular and covered with conical tubercles, each tipped with a star-shaped cluster of 12mm ($\frac{1}{2}$in) pale yellow spines. 5cm (2in) across, its yellow, bell-shaped flowers appear during the summer. Raised from seed; alternatively offsets.

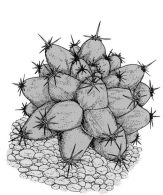

ECHINOCACTUS

The barrel cactus, as its name suggests, is globular and ribbed and experiences very hot days and cold nights in its native Mexico and Texas.

E. grusonii (golden barrel cactus) has large fierce golden-yellow spines. Unlikely to flower in pot.

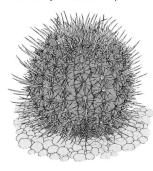

E. horizonthalonius has small, slow-growing, curved yellow spines, and a white "bloom" on its body. Pink bell-shaped flowers appear in summer on plants that have reached 15cm (6in) in diameter. Both are raised from seed.

ECHINOCEREUS

The hedgehog cactus has clump-forming cylindrical stems, and is either upright or sprawling. From Mexico and southern Texas.

Opuntia basilaris, *growing in southern California*

Mammillaria elegans, *from central Mexico*

E. knippelianus is from 7.5–10cm (3–4in) high, with dark, blue-green, broad ribs and white, bristly spines. Pink, summer flowers.

E. pectinatus can grow to 25cm (10in), but more usually from 10–12cm (4–5in). It has broad, medium green ribs, the many short white spines in

an unusual and attractive comb formation giving the plant a white appearance. Its flowers are pink and up to 7cm (3in) across.

E. pentalophus (syn. *E. procumbens*) is sprawling, to 15cm (6in) long, with deep indentations between its warty ribs. Large, violet-pink summer flowers. Most species are raised from seed; branching kinds provide side-shoots which can be used as cuttings.

FEROCACTUS

Also known as hedgehog cactus, it is squat, ribbed and globular. From Baja California and Mexico, it is noted for its stout, often hooked spines.

F. acanthodes has long, bristle-like red spines. *F. fordii* is densely covered with long, needle-like spines. *F. latispinus* is globular at first but over the years elongates to cylindrical. It grows to 30cm (12in) tall and 20cm (8in) across. None make offsets; can be grown only from seed.

HAMATOCACTUS

These are globular or cylindrical, ribbed cacti from Mexico and southern Texas. They are summer or autumn flowering, and subsequently sometimes produce attractive red berries.

25

H. hamatacanthus (Turk's head) has shiny, yellow flowers with a red centre. *H. setispinus* (strawberry cactus) is free-flowering with yellow petals, red at their base. Raised from seed.

MAMMILLARIA

This large family comes mainly from central Mexico, but some originate in the West Indies. Either globular or cylindrical, they are clump-forming and covered with tubercles (no ribs). Some are covered with white hair, others with spines. Flowers appear in rings on the previous year's growth in between the tubercles. White, yellow, pink or red, they arrive bell-shaped from spring to early summer and may be followed by red berries. *M. hahniana*

Recommended kinds include *M. bocasana, M. celsiana, M. elegans, M. erthyrosperma, M. gracilis, M. hahniana M. prolifera, M. zeilmanniana*, but most of the numerous species are worth growing.

Ensure that when plants have made their clusters, water does not lodge between the tightly packed plant bodies. Rot may ensue. Divide over-crowded clumps in spring.

OPUNTIA

Opuntias are distributed over much of the American continent, from Canada in the north to Patagonia in the south. A typical habitat could be the arid plateau of Mexico or the thorn savanna of northern Argentina where grasses do not thrive. Most have flattened, round or pear-shaped segments joined together by only a narrow strip. Some are cylindrical. Segments may carry spines, but usually have barbed bristles (called glochids) scattered over the "pads". Only the smaller kinds flower as house plants.

Recommended are *O. basilaris* 20–30cm (8–12in), *O. cylindrica* 60cm (2ft), *O. imbricata* 20–30cm (8–12in),

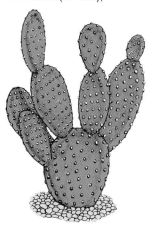

O. microdasys (bunny's ears) 30cm (12in), *O. rufida* 20–25cm (8–10in), *O. salmiana* 30cm (12in). *O. subulata* (can grow to a metre), *O. vestita* 45cm (18in).

Pads root easily in spring or early summer. Also grown from seed.

CALLISIA ELEGANS
(COMMELINACEAE)

This distinctive relative of the very popular tradescantias is a native of

the moister parts of Mexico where it creeps over rocky ground to form large patches of ground cover. It is still widely sold under its now obsolete name, *Setcreasea striata.*

Leaves are olive green, striped lengthwise with white. The leaf underside is a soft purple. Stems are upright at first but later start to trail. When grown in hanging baskets the colourful underside of the leaves is seen to advantage. Small creamy-white flowers are occasionally produced and last but one day.

Good light is essential keep tight, characteristic growth.

Looks unhappy in winter; cut off long, untidy growths then, and maybe rest it out of sight.

Watering: Water generously but then allow the mixture to dry out considerably before giving more. Feed with a standard liquid fertilizer every month from spring to early autumn.

Potting mixture: Use a soil-based mixture, lightened by adding up to a quarter-part coarse peat.

Propagation: Young bushy plants are much the best; start fresh cuttings each spring, planting at least 4 tip cuttings in the one pot.

Special points: Tolerant of a wide range of temperatures with a minimum level of 50°F (10°C), it is best to rest at 50–60°F (10–15°C) in winter.

CAPSICUM ANNUUM
(SOLANACEAE)

Capsicums are peppers, those grown as house plants are ornamental peppers prized for their colourful, long-lasting, pod-like fruits. Today's hybrids are derived from wild forms native of Mexico, Colombia and the southern United States and are usually called Christmas or winter peppers as they appear on the market in late autumn and early winter. Fruit shape can be round, cone-like or slender-pointed and fruit colour from ivory white, bluey-purple, green, red or orange. Many change fruit colour as they age. The best are the small bushy kinds.

Culture: Raised from seed. Tolerant of quite bright light, Keep cool; water generously – always enough to make the mixture thoroughly moist – stand on trays of moist pebbles for extra humidity. Throw away when fruits start to shrivel.

CHAMAEDOREA
(PALMAE)
(syn. *Collinia elegans,
Neanthe bella*)

C. elegans from the moister parts of Mexico and Guatemala is the only chamaedorea widely grown as a house plant. These dwarf palms (rarely above 1.2m (4ft) tall) grow in the filtered light below taller trees and so prefer bright but filtered light indoors (an east or west-facing window is ideal). Fronds are feathery, up to 60cm (24in) long and broken down into several 15cm (6in) long leaflets on either side of the midrib. A short green trunk may develop in time, mature plants producing sprays of tiny, yellow, bead-like flowers – but no fruit or seeds indoors.

C. seifrizii from Yucatan (Mexico) makes slender stems topped with narrower bluish-green leaflets. Rarely seen.

Watering: Water generously during the growing season, sparingly during the winter.

Potting mixture: Use an equal parts mixture of soil-based mix and coarse peat.

Propagation: Not practicable in the home.

Special points: Tolerate dry air but do better when stood on pebble trays. Look out for red spider mites. Feed every two weeks from spring to early autumn. Take care when repotting.

CISSUS RHOMBIFOLIA
(VITACEAE)

C. rhombifolia (grape ivy) still popularly known as *Rhoicissus rhomboidea* from Colombia, Brazil and the West Indies, has leaves made up of three leaflets, each on its own very short stalk. Colour is dark green with a hint of brown but new leaves carry a soft silvery down for a short while. *C.r.* Ellen Danica, a Danish form, has leaflets that are larger and strongly serrated leaf margins.

Watering: Water moderately during the growing period and sparingly during the winter.

Potting mixture: Use a soil based mixture.

Propagation: Take tip cuttings in spring and keep warm and humid, either in a propagator or within a plastic bag.

Special points: Feed every two weeks during the growing season with the standard liquid fertilizer. Tendrils attach themselves to supports, but plants should be trained into place. Nip out growing tips periodically to encourage bushy growth. All are capable of making 1.8–2.4m (6–8ft) tall plants, but pruning will keep plants within bound. Cut out any spindly growth after winter. Watch out for red spider

mites, particularly if the air is dry.

COLUMNEA
(GESNERIACEAE)

Columneas are epiphytic plants from Costa Rica that use small pockets of decaying leaves etc. as footholds in the crotches of tree branches, their arching or fully trailing stems festooning the branches. Stems may be 90cm (3ft) or more in length. Rain is normally a daily occurrence and humidity very high. Leaves, on very short stalks, are arranged on the stems in opposite pairs, the large tubular flowers appearing on new growth, mostly at the stem tips.

As house plants they like filtered light, an east or west-facing window being ideal or a southern one (in N. hemisphere) with direct sun broken by a translucent curtain. They need a good level of humidity to thrive. Excellent for hanging baskets.

C. banksii is a hybrid between *C. oerstediana* (Costa Rica) and *C. schiediana* (Mexico). Leaves are dark-green and slightly shiny, flowers scarlet and up to 7.5cm (3in) long. Blooms most of the year, stem length indoors 90cm (3ft).

C. gloriosa, a species with slender, trailing stems, dark-green leaves covered with purple hairs on the upper side and reddish hairs on the underside. Flowers scarlet with yellow patch at the throat and up to 7.5cm (3in) long – most of the year.

C. linearis spreads rather than trails (growing upright at first) and branches regularly. Leaves are shiny, dark green, and at 7.5cm (3in), are longer than most other popular columneas. Flowers are deep pink, covered with fine hairs and up to 4cm (1½in) long – usually in summer.

C. microphylla, another Costa Rican, but with thin trailing stems up to 1.2m (4ft) long indoors. Leaves are round, set close to each other, up to 12.5mm (½in) across and dark green. Stems and leaves are densely covered with reddish-brown hairs. Flowers appear mainly in spring and are bright orange-scarlet with a yellow throat.

Modern hybrids (banksii goes back as far as 1918) derived from very mixed parentage and prized for their compact habit of growth and free-flowering habit include:–

C. Alpha is the best of the yellow-flowered hybrids. Growth short and much-branched. Flowers at an early stage. Blooms 6.5–7.75cm (2½–3in) long.

C. Chanticleer, vigorous and tolerant, with a compact habit. Flowers

27

Columnea linearis, *an epiphyte from Costa Rica*

light orange and to 4cm (1½in) long.

C. Mary Ann has deep-pink flowers 4cm (1½in) long, and narrow dark green leaves.

A number known as the Cornell hybrids (raised at Cornell University, U.S.A.) are exceptional and have started to appear on the market.

Capsicum annuum *in Dominica, West Indies*

Watering: Water very moderately, giving only enough to just moisten the growing mixture. Use water at room temperature.

Potting mixture: Use a mixture of equal-parts coarse peat or leaf mould, and perlite.

Propagation: Take tip cuttings (ideally without flowers) 7–10cm (3–4in)

long in spring or summer. A propagating case is a big help.

Special points: High humidity is an absolute essential, so stand on trays of moist pebbles or plunge pots into peat moss and avoid close contact with heating appliances. Feed every two weeks with a high potash liquid fertilizer during the growing season.

Repot every two years. Do not pinch out growing tips as this may delay blooming.

**DIEFFENBACHIA
(ARACEAE)**

Dieffenbachias have the common name "dumb cane" – dumb, because the leaves and stems contain a poison, calcium oxalate, which if it gets in the mouth causes severe inflammation and temporary loss of speech, and cane from the notched (often scarred)

stem. Growth is upright, stem stout and unbranched. Leaves are large, 30-60cm (1–2ft) long and 20–30cm (8–12in) wide on arching stalks. Most are marked with yellow or white, but this may be very pronounced or just light flecking. The greater the leaf variegation the brighter the light these plants need, but never direct sunlight: most prefer to be in filtered light. In the wild they grow in hot and humid areas usually among trees, but are adaptable for the home.

A selection of kinds could include:
D. amoena (Costa Rica).
D. bausei, a hybrid (*maculata* x *weirii*).
D. exotica (Costa Rica) with mainly cream leaves.
D. maculata (syn. *D. picta*) from a wide area of Central America.

Many hybrids are available.

Watering: Water moderately throughout the year if the room is warm, more sparingly in winter if the temperature falls below 60°F (15°C).

Potting mixture: Use a soil-based potting mixture to which has been added up to one-third extra peat or leaf mould.

Propagation: Tip cuttings (beware of the sap) will root in spring in a propagator and sections of stem 7.5–10cm (3–4in) long, will also root and send out new shoots if planted on their sides in warmth.

Special points: Feed every 2 weeks during active growth. Ensure high humidity by using pebble-filled trays or plunge pot into moist peat. Growth can be quite rapid in good conditions and plants may need moving on into larger pots each spring.

ECHEVERIA
(CRASSULACEAE)

Echeverias are mostly Mexican succulent plants that are spread over a wedge of land (mainly away from the coastal strips) running from the north almost down to Guatemala. Having spent much of their heavy rain over the eastern seaboard, the trade winds reach the higher altitudes and provide moderate rainfall and lower temperatures. Echeverias can be found on precipitous cliff faces, on rocky hillsides, among scrubby bushes and deciduous and pine forests.

Some are small ground-hugging plants, others make small bushy shrubs. All make leaf rosettes but these can be tight with closely overlapping leaves or may be much looser. Most are smooth-leaved, covered with a waxy "bloom", but some have hairy leaves.

E. affinis was introduced only about 20 years ago,

having been found in scrubland and under sparse-leaved trees. It forms a squat rosette around 10cm (4in) across with deep brownish-black leaves that have earned it the name Black Echeveria. Deep colour develops only if the plant is grown in bright sun and if it is dryish at the root. Flowers bright red.

E. agavoides is low-growing, up to 15cm (6in) across, with fleshy, pale-green pointed leaves tipped with brown. Flowerspike tall, blooms yellow, but tipped red. Rarely produces offsets.

E. derenbergii makes a dumpy cushion of many rosettes, each about 50mm (2in) across. Leaves are blue-green, rounded, and thickly coated with silvery bloom – each reddish-brown tipped. Crook-shaped flowerstalks carry reddish-orange flowers.

E. elegans makes tight rosettes up to 10cm (4in) across of light blue-green leaves thickly coated with white bloom. Summer, pink and yellow flowers are carried on long, pink stalks.

E. gibbiflora grows to 60cm (2ft) tall. Its varieties are more attractive than the species and include: var. carunculata with cameo-like or warty growths on the fleshy grey-green leaves; var. crispata with wavy leaf margins; var. metallica with more

rounded leaves and a bronzy, metallic hue.

E. harmsii (syn. *Oliveranthus elegans*) forms a small, much-branched sub-shrub with leaves clustered together at the tips. The mid-green, lance-shaped leaves are softly hairy and brown tipped. Flowers are large (up to 25mm (1in) long), scarlet with tips turned back to show the yellow lining. Gets straggly; re-root annually.

E. leucotricha makes a small, branching sub-shrub with light-green leaves densely covered with short, bristly, white hairs. Leaf tips can, in bright sun and when dry at the root, have a reddish hue. Flowers red.

E. setosa is very low-growing with dark-green leaves thickly covered with short, white hairs. Red and yellow flowers appear in spring.

E. shaviana comes from pine forest regions of Mexico, hugs the ground very close and makes a wavy-edged rosette of greyish-blue leaves shot with pink shades. Pink flowers are carried on foot long stalks in spring and summer.

Watering: Water moderately throughout the growing period and very sparingly during the winter rest period. Avoid wetting the leaves.

Potting mixture: Use a soil-based potting mixture to which has been added up to $\frac{1}{4}$-part coarse sand or perlite.

Propagation: The quickest method is to use offsets,

which root easily. A number can produce new plants from single leaves; choose plump leaves and dibble the stem end into moist, sandy mixture.

Special points: Beware of mealy bugs that can settle between the closely-packed leaves. Feed actively growing plants every two weeks with a half-strength fertilizer. Avoid touching the leaves of those plants with a mealy bloom as they are easily spoiled.

EPIPHYLLUM HYBRIDS
(CACTACEAE)

The epiphyllums grown as house plants are practically all hybrids with their origins in wild plants found as epiphytes in the tropical rain forests of large parts of central and South America and the West Indies. Their leafless flattened stems may grow to 60cm (2ft) long and 50mm (2in) wide. They are notched at the edges and often segmented, supporting large trumpet-shaped flowers, mainly in spring. Flowers may be white, cream, yellow and orange shades, all shades of pink and red, bi-coloured, very large (up to 15cm (6in) across) or small

29

and produced in considerable quantities. The really large flowered kinds must have their rather gawky stems supported, but smaller flowered forms can be grown in hanging baskets – their stems trailing down. Many named forms are available from specialist growers.

Watering: Water generously during spring and summer and moderately at all other times. Avoid really hard water.

Potting mixture: Use a rooting medium of equal parts soil – and peat-based mixtures, adding some coarse sand or perlite to guarantee openness.

Propagation: Detach sections of stem 10–15cm (4–6in) long in spring and early summer, allow to dry for a day or two before planting in a growing mixture.

Special points: Feed every two weeks with a high-potash liquid fertilizer from early spring until flower buds are well developed; stop feeding then for 3 or 4 weeks; restart and then continue until early autumn. Stand on pebble filled trays or plunge pot into moist peat, and in warm rooms, mist-spray the stems. Place out of doors in a sheltered place for the late summer and early autumn. Move small plants on into larger pots each spring – 12–15cm (5–6in) is usually the maximum size needed – thereafter replace with fresh mixture. These plants flower best if pot-bound (see index). Tie in stems to supports as necessary and cut out (or back) old stems when they become long.

EPISCIA
(GESNERIACEAE)

The genus ranges from southern Mexico down to Brazil and Peru, occupying the warm and often very humid rain forests. Some are grown principally for the beauty of their foliage, others for their bright flowers.

E. dianthiflora from Mexico produces velvety green leaves with scalloped edges and white flowers frilled at the petal edges. Best for a warm sunny porch or conservatory – will not do well in dry air.

E. lilacina (Panama, Costa Rica) is a bit sprawling and untidy but has beautiful bronzy-green leaves with a bright-green rib area and large lilac flowers. Also needs better growing conditions than the average room.

Watering: Water generously during the active growing period but more sparingly during the winter rest period. See potting mixture (in this case the two are closely inter-connected).

Potting mixture: A fast-draining mixture is absolutely essential. An ideal mixture would be equal-parts sphagnum moss, peat and perlite or vermiculite, but if the sphagnum moss is not available it can be dispensed with. A surface layer of sphagnum is a refinement.

Propagation: The plants that develop at the ends of stolons root very easily if potted separately; keep warm and humid. Single leaves, with a short stalk attached (like those of the African violet) will root and develop small plantlets.

Special points: A really high level of humidity is essential if plants are to develop to their full potential. Stand on trays of moist pebbles or plunge pots into moist peat, or keep in a terrarium. Feed actively growing plants with a general purpose liquid fertilizer every two weeks. Plants are shallow-rooting and do best in wide-topped pans and hanging baskets where their offsets can send down roots. Episcias will not tolerate cool conditions.

Cygnet – a hybrid of *E. dianthiflora* and *E. punctata*, light-green velvety leaves, flowers white with purple spots.

EUPHORBIA PULCHERRIMA
(EUPHORBIACEAE)

The two most popular house plant euphorbias are totally different in appearance and culture. See also Madagascar for *E. milii*. The only obvious link is that they are both shrubs, with an acrid, milky sap and tiny flowers wedged between very much more striking floral bracts.

E. pulcherrima, the poinsettia, originates in central America (particularly the drier parts of Mexico), but is grown in the tropics world-wide. It has spineless stems, large, soft, emerald-green leaves and very large, red, pink or

cream bracts. There are many named varieties available, some able to flower out of season and on relatively short stems.

Special treatment is required to encourage a second-season flowering, namely short day-lengths at crucial bract-development stage. It is almost as if they need to withdraw completely from the unsettling growing environment of the home if they are to come out for more than one flowering period. Better, perhaps to treat them as temporaries.

Culture: Give good light; keep cool; water moderately; avoid draughty position.

FUCHSIA
(ONAGRACEAE)

F. fulgens is native to Mexico. Most of today's varieties have a very mixed parentage, though are mainly derived from *F. fulgens* and *F. magellanica*, which grows in Chile and Argentina. See South America for a full discussion of today's fuchsias.

GRAPTOPETALUM
(CRASSULACEAE)

Graptopetalums are low-growing Mexican succulents closely related to echeverias. Their fleshy leaves are arranged in tight rosette shapes, stems are short, but branch regularly resulting in a clustering effect.

G. pachyphyllum rarely exceeds 10cm (4in) high with bluish-green leaves. Rosettes to 25mm (1in) across, flowers red.

G. paraguayense makes rosettes of whitish grey leaves to 15cm (6in) across on thick stems. Flowers white.

Watering: Water moderately during the growing period and more sparingly in winter.

Potting mixture: Use a mixture of ¼-part coarse sand and ¾-parts soil-based mixture.

Propagation: Rosettes of leaves root very easily in spring and early summer, and individual leaves lightly pushed into a porous mixture will also root.

Special points: Watch out for mealy bugs that are prone to settle in between the tightly packed leaves. Handle the plants carefully; leaves drop at a touch.

GUZMANIA
(BROMELIACEAE)

Guzmanias are epiphytic bromeliads, mainly from the Andean rain forests of Colombia, Panama and Ecuador, but also widely spread through much of Tropical America. (See also South America.)

G. monostachia (syn. *G. tricolor*) has spiky-looking bright-green leaves and a tube-shaped flowerhead made up of many greenish-white bracts, tipped with orange or red and striped with purple. Found in the West Indies, Florida, Central and South America to the south of Brazil.

G. zahnii enjoys light shade and very high humidity in the forests of Panama and Costa Rica. Leaves have a transparent look and are finely meshed with thin red lines, running lengthwise on both upper and underside. The whole plant has a rosy, wine-coloured hue. The 30cm (12in) long

flowerstalk carries red bracts and white and yellow flowers.

Watering: Water moderately, allowing the mixture to dry out a little before giving more. Ideally use rain water.

Potting mixture: Use equal parts soil-based mixture, coarse leaf mould and peat. Other mixtures may be used but they *must* be open and quick-draining.

Propagation: Take away offsets that form around the base of the parent plant, but not before they are about 7.5cm (3in) long. Root in heated propagator.

Special points: Feed young plants every two weeks with a half strength liquid fertilizer from early spring to early autumn. To increase the level of humidity stand pots on trays of moist pebbles or plunge pot in moist peat. Small pots are adequate for these plants as they make relatively compact roots.

LANTANA CAMARA
(VERBENACEAE)

Lantanas are vigorous-growing shrubs from tropical America that have naturalized in sub-tropical areas of Florida, Texas, Trinidad and Tobago, and have become a pest in

Hawaii. As house plants they are best suited to the large cool porch or conservatory. Usually bought in bud in early spring, they have coarse-textured elliptic leaves and many small flower buds packed tightly together in clumps. Flowers (yellow, orange, red) open in succession (many change colour after a day or so) over a long period.

Watering: Plentifully during the growth period, sparingly during the rest period.

Potting mixture: Use a soil-based mixture.

Propagation: Use 7cm (3in) (non-flowering) shoots in summer.

Special points: Feed every two weeks during the active growth period. Increase humidity by standing on moist pebble trays. Keep cool for the winter rest period (45–50°F (7–10°C)). Pot on into larger pots as required (perhaps twice during the summer). Prune drastically, just as new growth starts, and nip growing tips regularly to encourage bushy growth. Young plants are better than old, replace frequently. Watch out for aphids.

MONSTERA DELICIOSA
(ARACEAE)

The Swiss cheese plant, *M. deliciosa*, is a tall growing climbing plant from the moister rain forests of Mexico and other parts of tropical America. There it clings to the bark of trees by means of pencil-thick aerial roots and is often found in the cooler mountain slopes **31**

Monstera deliciosa, *the Swiss cheese plant, from the moist rain forests of tropical America*

NEPHROLEPIS
(POLYPODIACEAE)

Nephrolepis ferns are deservedly popular house plants. Two species are usually seen but there are many forms of each kind. They are very widely distributed: *N. cordifolia* hies from Jamaican tropical rain forests as well as the sclerophyllous woodlands of Chile; *N. exaltata* and its many forms are found from Florida to Brazil, in parts of Africa, Southern Asia and even Australia. Most grow on the forest floor (but rarely in dense forests), though some take sustenance in niches of decaying leaf mould, as epiphytes. Fronds are up to 60cm (2ft) long, generally arching, with many decorative pinnae arranged in two ranks, one on each side of a central rib. The base is an underground rhizome, from which slender, furry runners or stolons grow, rooting down at intervals and making small new plants. The stolons must have a moist rootrun to develop on their own, a medium found in the wild as thick pads of moss in crevices in the bark of fallen trees or in congenial pockets of earth. As house plants they make excellent hanging basket plants.

N. cordifolia (erect sword-fern) produces fronds up to 10cm (4in) wide at the base, gradually narrowing along their length to a point. Some fronds are upright, but in time they arch over.

N. exaltata – the species is rarely seen, the many selected forms are popularly grown. Most of these

Nephrolepis cordifolia *from Jamaican tropical rain forests*

forms are known collectively as Boston ferns.

Fronds are more arching than of *N. cordifolia* and the pinnae may be divided and sub-divided several times or frilled or crested at the edges.

Watering: Water moderately. Nephrolepis must never be allowed to dry out completely at the root at any time, although those grown at lower temperatures during the winter need very careful watering. Dunk hanging baskets in a bowl or bucket of water periodically during the warmer months.

Potting mixture: Use a peat-based potting mixture or an equal-parts mixture of peat with a soil-based mix.

Propagation: Propagate by

at between 3,000 and 4,000 feet, where temperatures may fall to 50°F (10°C). Young leaves are heart-shaped and entire but as plants get older so leaves become incised at irregular intervals from the edge almost to the midrib; additionally, holes may appear on each side of the midrib. The incisions enable leaves better to withstand strong winds and provide an explanation for another common name, hurricane plant. Maximum growth indoors around 2.4m (8ft).

Watering: Water moderately at all times.

Potting mixture: Use a mixture of ⅔ soil-based mix and ⅓ coarse peat or leaf mould.

Propagation: This is difficult because of the size of cuttings (ideally a maximum of two leaves) but is possible in spring with a heated propagator or in a warm room when planted and enclosed in a large plastic bag.

Special points: Feed every 2 weeks during the growing season with a standard liquid fertilizer for best cut leaves. Stand on large trays filled with moist pebbles.

Thick heavy stems develop and need training to stout stakes, tying in securely.

Aerial roots become untidy and are best directed into the pot early on. Pot on into larger pots each spring, topdress once maximum pot size is reached.

splitting up overcrowded clumps in spring.

Special points: Feed well-established plants with a nitrogenous feed every two weeks during the active growth period. Provide extra humidity by standing plants grown in pots on trays covered with moist pebbles and handspray hanging basket plants. Ideal for moist bathrooms or kitchens.

OPLISMENUS HIRTELLUS
(GRAMINEAE)

Only Variegatus, the variegated form of this relation of the grass plant, is popular. It comes from the West Indies and from Texas to Argentina. Resembling a narrow, thin-leaved tradescantia with green, white and pink stripes, it makes a good basket or trailing plant.

Watering: Water plentifully during the active growing season and sparingly in winter.

Potting mixture: Use a soil-based mixture.

Propagation: Tip cuttings 5–7cm (2–3in) long, root very easily in spring and early summer.

Special points: Plant 8–10 rooted cuttings in a hanging basket for best effect. Feed once a month with standard fertilizer whilst growth is active. Renew frequently, young plants are better than old.

PACHYPHYTUM
(CRASSULACEAE)

Pachyphytums are low-growing succulent plants from Mexico closely related to *Graptopetalum* and *Echeveria*, which they resemble. Prized mainly for their decorative leaves, they also carry bell-shaped flowers in spring and summer. Most have a waxy bloom on their leaves which is easily spoiled by handling.

P. amethystinum (syn. *Graptopetalum amethystinum*) grows about 10cm (4in) high with blue-grey leaves that take on an amethyst hue as they age. Pink flowers.

P. oviferum (Moonstones) grows to 15cm (6in) tall and carries thick and fleshy grey leaves thickly coated with a white mealy bloom; they look like sugared almonds. Bright red flowers.

P. pachyphytoides is a hybrid, growing to 38cm (15in) tall with 7.5–10cm (3–4in) long greenish-white

leaves tinged purple. Pink flowers on a long stalk.

Watering: Water moderately in period of active growth and sparingly during a winter rest period – which should be encouraged.

Potting mixture: Use ⅔ soil-based mix and ⅓ coarse sand or perlite.

Propagation: Use branches 7–10cm (3–4in) long in spring.

Special points: Do not give liquid fertilizer, this encourages soft, untypical growth. Pot on into the next size pot each spring.

PEDILANTHUS TITHYMALOIDES
(EUPHORBIACEAE)

Polypodium aureum, *growing epiphytically*

This pedilanthus is a leafy succulent belonging to the spurge family – with its typical milky, noxious, sap – and distributed over a large area, from Florida, through Central America to Colombia.
Stems are woody at the base, green and succulent. The species has straight stems but the sub-species most commonly grown, *S.t. smallii*, has zig-zag stems with fleshy, oval leaves pointing at every angle. In time it forms a bushy shrub to 60cm (2ft) tall. A variegated leaved form, *P.t.s.* Variegatus, has creamy leaf margins which may take on a reddish hue in really bright light and when the plant is hard-pressed for water. The red-bracted flowers are rarely produced in cultivation.

Watering: Water sparingly during the period of active growth and hardly at all in the winter rest period. Too much water causes rot.

Potting mixture: Use a mixture of ⅔ soil-based mix and ⅓ coarse sand or perlite.

Propagation: Tip cuttings 50mm–12cm (2–5in) long will root in spring. Allow each cutting to dry out, unplanted, for 24 hours to stop the flow of sap and

33

thereafter water very sparingly until new growth indicates that stems have rooted.

Special points: Cuttings and broken stems "bleed", staunch by dipping the cut end in water. Feed every month with half strength liquid fertilizer from spring to end of summer.

PEPEROMIA
(PIPERACEAE)

All peperomias are native of the moister parts of the West Indies and the tropical rain forests of South America. Many grow as epiphytes, occupying the middle structure of the giant forest trees. They all enjoy the dappled half light (made up of short shafts of direct sun and periods of filtered light). Their thick, fleshy leaves enable them to store water to withstand short periods of drought. Air is normally very humid. Roots are fibrous and forage deep into the moss and moist debris of the tree limbs over which they creep. Flowers are held in tightly-packed white or cream-coloured spikes on a reddish base, and are said to resemble a rat's tail. Most make neat, low-growing plants rarely above 23–30cm (9–12in) tall. (See also South America.)

P. magnoliifolia (syn. *P. tithymaloides*) is from the West Indies, Panama as well as the northern areas of South America, and is the strongest growing peperomia commonly used indoors. Its glossy, oval, fleshy leaves may reach 15cm (6in) long and are a deep green often "shot"

with reddish purple. The variegated form, Variegata, with red speckled stems and leaves liberally streaked with pale-yellowy-green, is more commonly grown.

P. obtusifolia is an erect sub-shrubby plant from the Everglades of Southern Florida, Mexico, and Venezuela. Leaves are fleshy, shiny and almost oval, a deep green with red edging. There are several variegated-leaved forms; Alba, Albo-marginata, Greengold and Variegata.

P. orba Astrid (or Princess Astrid) is a light-green leaved hybrid kind with red-streaked stems and a low habit of growth. Origin unclear as it has never been seen growing wild.

P. scandens (syn. *P. serpens*) is a trailer from Peru, the West Indies, Panama and Brazil. Only the variegated form is grown as a house plant. Leaves are heart-shaped, about 50mm (2in) long, green with yellow border. Leafstalks are red, and stems may grow to 60cm (2ft) in length.

P. verticillata from the West Indies can grow up to 30.5cm (1ft) tall. Its deep-green, pointed leaves are arranged in whorls of 3–6 at intervals up its reddish stem.

Watering: More than anything else, over-watering kills peperomias. Water sparingly at all times and avoid wetting leaves and stems – rot can set in if water collects where several stems join.

Potting mixture: Peat-based potting mixtures suit

them best.

Propagation: All kinds can be propagated by using 50mm–7cm (2–3in) long tip cuttings. The rooting mixture needs to be just moist and one made up of equal-parts coarse sand and peat is best.

Special points: These plants will not tolerate temperatures below 50°F (10°C), and only then if they are fairly dry at the root. They do however have high humidity in their native habitat and in a warm room need to stand on trays filled with moist pebbles. Small pots are normally adequate as they make little root. If stems tend to elongate without branching, nip out the growing points to encourage breaks.

PHILODENDRON
(ARACEAE)

See South America for full description of genus, and cultural guide.

P. scandens is the most widely spread of all philodendrons, native of most of tropical America, but with a subspecies found in South Mexico. It is also the most popular kind in cultivation and the easiest to grow. Leaves are 10cm (4in) long, on short leafstalks, have a bronze tinge when first they unfurl but later become leathery and dark green. Very adaptable to being grown indoors.

P. wendlandii forms a

rosette of waxy, deep-green, lance-shaped leaves – arranged like a shuttlecock. The central leaf rib is particularly pronounced at the base. Leaf spread can be 90cm–1.2m (3–4ft), but height is less than 60cm (2ft). It grows in the wild from Nicaragua to Panama, usually perched high in the tree tops in dappled sunlight.

PILEA INVOLUCRATA
(URTICACEAE)

The friendship plant is often sold under its old name of *P. pubescens*. Leaves are almost circular, deeply quilted, (a dark green with a bronze hue), almost stalkless, and arranged tightly together in pairs. Stems divide regularly to produce clustering hummocks. A form sold as *P. mollis* (also *P.* Moon Valley) has a looser appearance, leaves that are a yellowy green with thin bronze veining, and relatively large pink flower clusters.

Watering: Water moderately during active growth, more sparingly in the winter rest period.

Potting mixture: Use a peat-based mixture, or an equal-parts mixture of peat and soil-based mixture.

Propagation: Tip cuttings and side shoots root very easily from late spring, through the summer. Start new plants each year.

Special points: Stand on moist pebble trays. Feed fortnightly from late spring to end summer.

POLYPODIUM AUREUM
(POLYPODIACEAE)

The hare's foot fern, *P. aureum*, can be found in sub-tropical forests from Florida to Argentina. The base is rhizomatous, crawling over the surface of a potting mixture and around the edge of its container. Rhizomes are covered with furry brown hair and silver scales.

Fronds have long stalks and are made up of up to 12 pairs of 15–20cm (6–8in) long pinnae or leaflets. *P.a.* Glauca has blue-green fronds and *P.a.* Mandaianum rippled and curled pinnae.

Watering: Water plentifully during active growth but more sparingly if temperature falls below 55°F (12°C).

Potting mixture: Use an equal parts mixture of soil-based mix and leaf mould or coarse peat.

Propagation: Cut off a 7cm (3in) long section of rhizome in spring and peg it down into contact with moist growing mixture and keep warm and humid.

Special points: Use half-pots or shallow pans to allow the rhizomes extra room to spread. Move on into larger containers, in spring, when the rhizomes have covered the surface of the mix. Use half-strength liquid fertilizer every 2 weeks when growth is active. Make air more humid by standing pots on trays of moist pebbles, or plunge pots into moist peat.

PTERIS CRETICA
(POLYPODIACEAE)

P. cretica (Florida, Ethiopia, Himalayas, India, Italy, Japan, Middle East) is the most popular of the genus. Fronds reach 30cm (12in) in length and are made up of several pointed pinnae or segments fanning out from a common point. *P.c.* Albo-lineata has creamy white central lines on the pinnae, and *P.c.* Wimsettii, crested pinnae.

Watering: Keep well watered during the warmer months when growth is active, more sparingly if temperatures or light levels are low.

Potting mixture: Use a peat-based mixture.

Propagation: Divide overcrowded clumps in spring, seeing that some rhizome is attached to each piece.

Special points: Use half-strength general fertilizer every 2 or 3 weeks while growing is active. Make the air more humid by standing pots on moist pebble trays or plunging in moist peat.

RHOEO SPATHACEA
(syn. *Rhoeo discolor*)
(COMMELINACEAE)

R. spathacea is a tradescantia relative from Mexico, Guatemala and the West Indies, where it can be regarded as a persistent weed. The species has dark-green lance-shaped leaves, 20–25cm (8–10in) long, purple below and held in an upright, rosette shape. More favoured is *R.s.* Variegata or *R.s.* Vittata with leaves finely striped with yellow, sometimes tinged pink. Small white flowers peep through purple-green, cup-like bracts wedged in the leaf axils, from which it gets such popular names as Boat Lily and Moses-in-the-Cradle.

Watering: Water plentifully during the growth period and very sparingly in the winter rest.

Potting mixture: Use a soil-based potting mixture lightened by ⅓ extra peat.

Propagation: Use offsets produced around the base; can also be grown from seed.

Special points: Feed with the standard liquid fertilizer every two weeks during the growth period. Ensure air is made more humid by standing on trays of moist pebbles. Pot on into larger pots each spring. Good in hanging baskets.

SEDUM
(CRASSULACEAE)

The kinds grown as house plants are mainly Mexican, succulent, mostly with fleshy, stalkless leaves, but they can be tiny-leaved creepers or small shrubs. Some produce flowers (usually white and small) at an early stage, others take a year or two. (See also C. & E. Asia.)

S. adolphi (golden sedum) grows to 15cm (6in) high and across with bronze-yellow leaves.

S. allantoides forms a bushy plant with trailing stems and grey-green, club-shaped leaves.

S. bellum grows 15cm (6in) tall and 25–30cm (10–12in) across – a hummock of tightly-packed rosettes, the leaves being thickly covered with white meal. The flowerspike takes at least a year to develop fully and open up into a mass of white flowers in late winter.

S. morganianum (donkey's tail or jade plant) has never been found in the wild: the first plants were found in a Mexican market. It trails to 60cm (2ft), making stems that are totally hidden by overlapping pale green leaves with a thin dusting of white bloom. Good in a hanging basket. Beware when handling as leaves fall off at the slightest touch.

S. pachyphyllum grows upright with cylindrical, red-tipped, fleshy leaves.

35

Anthuriums and rhoeos are both natives of Guatemala.

S. rubrotinctum (Christmas cheer) has upright stems at first (later sprawling) that carry fleshy, egg-shaped leaves in rosettes near the tips. If kept well-watered and in some shade they are green, if kept dryish at the root and in full sun they are a rich red.

Watering: Water moderately in active growth period and sparingly at other times.

Potting mixture: Use ⅔ soil-based mix and ⅓ coarse sand or perlite.

Propagation: By tip cuttings, or in many cases, single leaves pushed into potting mix.

Special points: No feeding is needed. Use shallow pans, half-pots or hanging baskets. Pot on, if necessary, into larger pots in spring.

SELAGINELLA
(SELAGINELLACEAE)
Selaginellas form tight seeds. All thrive on high humidity and are best suited to the bottle garden or Wardian case. The genus is very large and covers large tracts of the world's surface.

S. apoda (east North America) commonly called moss-like hummocks or loose fern-like fronds. Although not ferns they often resemble them and do produce spores rather than creeping moss, forms dense clumps of pale green stems.

S. emmeliana (syn. *S. pallescens*) – North America – has upright, branching stems to one foot tall. Pale green, white edged fronds, fan out giving an open appearance.

S. martensii (Mexico) grows erect at first (to 15–20cm (6 or 8in) without branching) and then fans out into many fine segments. Stilt-like roots reach down for water and food. The cultivar Watsoniana has silvery white and pale green fronds.

Watering: Water plentifully throughout the year – never allowing the mixture to dry out.

Potting mixture: Use a mixture of ⅔ peat and ⅓ coarse sand or perlite.

Propagation: Take short tip cuttings 25–50mm (1–2in) long in spring, keep warm and humid until rooted.

Special points: Do not feed at other than ¼-strength standard liquid fertilizer every two weeks during the growing period. "Normal" feeding will result in coarse, untypical growth. Use shallow pans or half-pots. Move on into larger pans as plants grow over the edge of the older ones. Make the air more humid by standing on trays filled with moist pebbles, or grow in a terrarium.

SETCREASEA PURPUREA
(COMMELINACEAE)
(syn. *S. pallida*)

This close relative of the tradescantia is a native of N.E. Mexico, where it spreads over rocky and stone-strewn areas, rooting down at convenient spots into pockets of earth. The stony surface gives some shade to the roots and small scrubby bushes give some overhead protection from the fierce sun. It quickly forms large patches of ground cover. Leaves are lance-shaped, 10–15cm (4–6in) long and up to 25mm (1in) wide, a rich violet purple shade, lightly covered with a mealy cuticle and sparse hairs (particularly where the stalkless leaves grasp the stems). Small 3-petalled flowers of strong magenta-pink appear from late spring through summer; each lasts just one day.

Watering: Give a thorough drenching and then allow the mixture to dry out almost completely before applying more. Too much water gives sappy, weak, poorly coloured and untypical growth.

Potting mixture: Use a soil-based potting mixture.

Propagation: Cuttings, 7–10cm (3–4in) long, root extremely easily if they are cut immediately below a node and planted in a peat-and-sand mixture.

Special points: Setcreaseas are tolerant of a very wide temperature range, they grow well in warm rooms and can tolerate temperatures down to 45°F (8°C), if dry at the root at the time. Feed every two weeks through spring and summer with a standard liquid fertilizer. In good conditions setcreaseas are fast-growing and may need moving on into larger pots 2 or even 3 times during the growing season. Since old, pot-bound plants lose their colour and vigour, it is wise to root new potfuls at least once a year. Shoots that have produced a clump of flowers are best cut out to allow new growing points to develop. Really bright light produces the best leaf colour.

SMITHIANTHA
(GESNERIACEAE)

Smithianthas (temple bells) are a small genus from the tropical mountain forests of Mexico and Guatemala with scaly, rhizomatous rootstocks. Both leaves and flowers are attractive: the former are heart-shaped, beautifully felted with fine hairs in contrast to the general leaf coloration, and arranged in opposite pairs or whorls. The flowers are shaped in a spire, composed of a number of showy, 50cm (2in) tubular

blooms, resembling those of a foxglove. Flowers open in succession from the bottom of the spire to the top, over a period of 6–8 weeks. There is a considerable period of dormancy.

S. cinnabarina (Mexico and Guatemala) grows to 60cm (2ft) tall and 45cm (18in) through. Its leaves are dark green, flushed red. Flowers are red with spots of orange yellow at the mouth. It is one of the longer-flowering kinds with the main and side spires offering colour from early summer to early winter.

S. zebrina (Mexico: Vera Cruz) may grow taller, and has dark-green, soft, silky-haired leaves heavily streaked through the vein areas with reddish-brown and purple. The outside of the flower is red, the inside pale yellow spotted red. Flowering period early summer to autumn.

Watering: Water moderately, allowing the mixture to dry out a little before giving more. Gradually dry off when flowering stops.

Potting mixture: Use a mixture of equal parts leaf mould, coarse peat and perlite or vermiculite, adding a little dolomite lime

to cut down acidity.

Propagation: Plants can be increased by breaking up the large rhizomes into 12–25mm ($\frac{1}{2}$–1in) long pieces when potting up in spring; they make smaller plants the first year but in the second year attain normal size.

Special points: Warmth (minimum 65°F (18°C)) and high humidity is essential; stand on wide trays of moist pebbles to increase atmospheric humidity. Pot the large rhizomes singly in spring in half-pots and move on into larger pots as necessary. Provide thin cane supports for the flowerspikes.

STENOTAPHRUM
SECUNDATUM
VARIEGATUM
(GRAMINEAE)

The rather coarse-textured buffalo grass, *S. secundatum*, is grown as a house plant only in its variegated-leaved form, the plain form hailing from south Carolina, Florida and Texas. It makes a good hanging basket plant, particularly when viewed against a light. Stems are flattened and creep, rooting whenever they can. Clusters of cream-coloured

Tillandsia usneoides, *the rootless Spanish moss, festoons trees in great swags and looks like mattress stuffing.*

leaves, finely lined with green, blunt-ended but otherwise grass-like soon form a dense, but light-coloured mass. Propagate frequently.

Watering: Apply plentifully in the growth period and sparingly in winter.

Potting mixture: Use a soil-based mixture.

Propagation: Use tufts of leaves with a short length of stems attached.

Special points: Pot 3 or 4 rooted clumps up together in one shallow basket or half-pot (they are surface-rooting). Feed no more often than once a month with standard liquid fertilizer, or growth will become soft and untypical.

SYNGONIUM (ARACEAE)

Syngoniums are tropical climbing plants from the forests of Central America and the West Indies. Related to the philodendrons they climb up the trees, fixing their aerial roots into the rough surface of tree bark. Indoors they can be trained up stakes and moss poles or used as trailers in hanging baskets.

S. angustatum Albolineatum (Mexico, Nicaragua): Deeply lobed leaf segments, with white and silvery markings in vein areas.

S. auritum (Jamaica, Hispaniola): Leaves have 5 segments, the central one long; leaf spread on a mature plant is 30cm (12in) square.

S. podophyllum: Arrow-shaped central lobe and two small back-swept lobes. Emerald Gem is a compact form.

Watering: Water moderately while plants are active and sparingly through a short winter rest period.

Potting mixture: Use equal parts soil-based mix and leaf mould or peat.

Propagation: Use tip cuttings 7–10cm (3–4in) long in late spring or early summer.

Special points: A good deal of humidity is required or leaves may shrivel. Stand on moist pebble trays or plunge in moist peat. Feed actively growing plants every 2 weeks. Provide supports for climbing plants and tie in stems. Encourage short aerial roots to grow into moss poles by keeping moss moist.

TILLANDSIA USNEOIDES (BROMELIACEAE)

T. usneoides, the "Spanish moss" of the Everglades and the moister parts of the

stretch from Texas to Argentina, is the real oddity of the genus – see also South America. Rootless, this plant festoons trees in great swags, comprising many, tangled, silvery-grey stems or leaves, looking like mattress-stuffing – which is just what it is used for in South America. Flowers are pale green, interesting but insignificant. It is usually acquired dangling on threadlike stems from a piece of cork or cork-bark.

Watering: Spray daily; most of its needs are provided from moisture in the air.

Potting mixture: None.

Propagation: Staple sections onto blocks of cork.

Special points: Local humidity must be high: stand above (but not in) bowls of water in a warm room. Mist-spray daily.

TOLMIEA MENZIESII (SAXIFRAGACEAE)

Tolmieas are from the west coast of North America where the winters are relatively mild, making them suitable for cool rooms or unheated porches etc. Leaves are medium green, roughly heart-shaped with toothed edges, held on long

stalks. Leaves and stalks are covered with fine, bristly hair. A striking feature is the way some mature leaves carry a miniature plant on the upper side, weighing down the leaf and creating a trailing effect, good in hanging baskets. Easy to grow and propagate.

Watering: Water moderately throughout the year.

Potting mixture: Use soil-based mixture.

Propagation: Take off leaves with well-developed plantlets already formed with 25mm (1in) of stalk still attached. Dibble the stalk into rooting mixture with the leaf blade just touching the mixture. Or layer into a nearby pot.

Special points: Feed every two weeks during the growing season. Pot on in spring as necessary. Use 4 to 6 rooted cuttings in one hanging basket for best effect. Renew frequently.

TRADESCANTIA (COMMELINACEAE)

The simple, yet striking plants we call wandering Jews are in nature occupants of the floor of the tropical rain forests of Mexico and South America. There they enjoy the constant warmth (around 80°F (27°C)), high and steady humidity, filtered light and the protection from extremes of climate given by the high and middle range of forest canopy. Rainfall can equal 2m (80in), falling at regular intervals throughout the year. Tradescantias creep

over the forest floor sending down shallow clumps of roots into the thin layer of fertile soil from virtually every node. They thrive best when they reach a spot where perhaps a tall tree has fallen to give them a glimpse of the sky. Gaps between the nodes are wide when the quality of the light is poor; growth is more compact when light conditions are better.

Leaves are fleshy, arranged alternately along the stems; the 3-petalled flowers may be white, pink or blue, and each lasts just one day.

T. albiflora Albovittata (C. America) is a fast-growing, robust kind with 5–7cm (2–3in) peppermint-green leaves, liberally striped lengthwise with white.

T. sillamontana comes from North East Mexico and has thick white felt-like hair covering the mid-green leaves. Flowers are a strong pink.

Watering: Give thorough soakings but then allow the mixture to begin to dry out before applying more.

Potting mixture: Use a soil-based potting mixture.

Propagation: Cuttings of all tradescentias root very easily, throughout most of the year. They will even produce roots if 5–7.5cm (2–3in) long cuttings are stood in a glass of water. Plant 4–6 cuttings in one pot for a quick, bushy effect and propagate at least once a year as young plants are much more attractive than older ones.

Special points: Feed plants every two weeks with a standard liquid fertilizer

once roots have filled the pots. Nip out the growing tips periodically to induce bushy, much-branched growths. Should any non-variegated shoots appear on plants with variegated foliage, cut them out right to the base or they will develop at the expense of the more colourful ones. Ideal for hanging baskets in an east or west-facing window.

YUCCA ELEPHANTIPES (AGAVACEAE)
(syn. *Y. guatemalensis*)

A native of Mexico but widely cultivated in Guatemala, *Y. elephantipes* grows to 14m (45ft) tall in often very harsh terrain, but usually where its fleshy roots can search widely for water – i.e. in deep soil and under rocks. As a house plant it has recently rocketed to popularity, partly due to a fashion for tall, bare-because chunky lengths of stems (trunks) to 1.8m (6ft) in length have been imported from Central America, induced to root and produce tufts of soft

stemmed plants and partly and pliant, lance-shaped, dark-green leaves. Yuccas will tolerate a wide range of temperatures and a certain amount of dry air. Some of the best ones seen are growing in south-facing (and sometimes unheated) porches.

Watering: Water thoroughly during the growing season (spring to autumn) but then allow to dry out considerably before applying more. Water sparingly during the winter rest period, particularly if grown cool. Water stored in the bulky stems can carry the plant through short periods of drought.

Potting mixture: Use a soil-based potting mixture and, because of the weight of the stout stems, wide-bottomed clay pots. These help to keep the rather top-heavy plants from falling or being knocked over.

Propagation: Use small offsets that develop around the base of the plants, in spring.

Special points: Feed every 2 weeks during the growing season only.

ZEBRINA PENDULA (COMMELINACEAE)

Zebrinas grow wild in the moister parts of Mexico and neighbouring Guatemala. They are very closely related to the tradescantias and with them share the common name, wandering Jew. Their pointed-oval leaves are medium green but marked with two silvery green stripes, the underside being a rich purple. Stems

may trail to 60cm (2ft) in length – to make good basket plants – or they may be trained up light supports. A form, *Z.p.* Purpusii, is a rich reddish purple on both leaf sides, particularly when grown in some sun. These plants behave quite diffe-rently when exposed to really bright light: leaves are less lush and fleshy, often curled round a little at the edges, but they do take on a much richer coloration than when grown in poorer light.

Watering: Water moderately during the active growth period and sparingly during the winter. By being kept relatively dry at the root, leaf colour is improved. Tolerant of a wide temperature range.

Potting mixture: Use a soil-based mixture.

Propagation: Replace older plants with young rooted tip cuttings at least once a year, as young plants are far better than older ones. Pot several cuttings in one pot in spring for the best bushy effect.

Special points: Pinch out growing points to encourage branching. Feed well established plants every two weeks with the standard liquid fertilizer from spring to early autumn.

South America

South America is both a botanist's paradise and the richest source of indoor plants. George Gardner, describing one part of his Brazilian travels in 1846, noted: "The whole country through which we had passed for nearly two days was one vast flower garden, where 'like a child at a feast', I knew not which object to grasp first; everything was not only new to me, but each more beautiful and more curious than the other." Epiphytic ferns and bromeliads, desert and mountain cacti, shrubs, climbers and trailing plants, nearly all kinds of house plant are here.

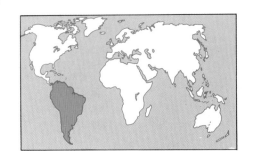

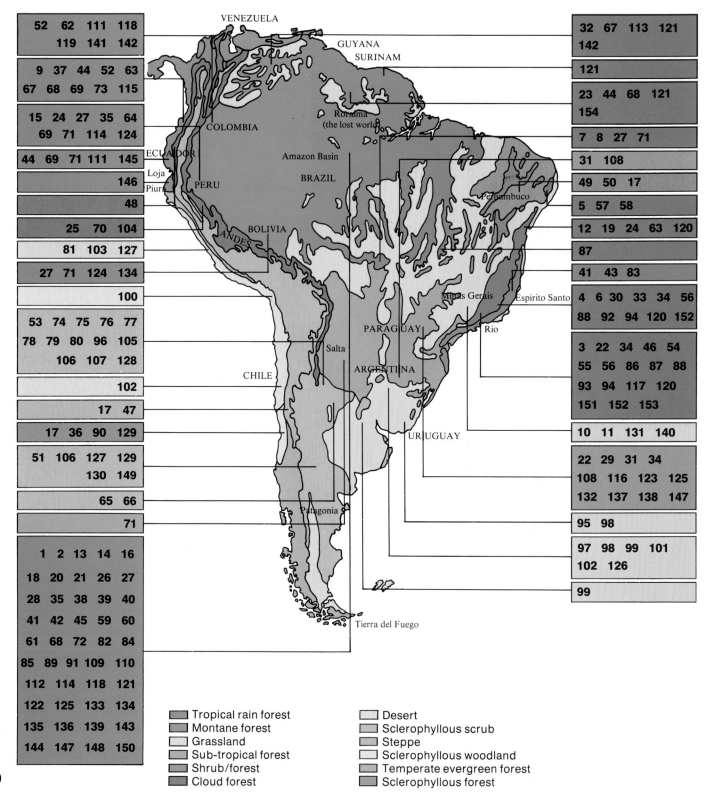

Left boxes	Right boxes
52 62 111 118 119 141 142	32 67 113 121 142
9 37 44 52 63 67 68 69 73 115	121
15 24 27 35 64 69 71 114 124	23 44 68 121 154
44 69 71 111 145 146	7 8 27 71
48	31 108
25 70 104	49 50 17
81 103 127	5 57 58
27 71 124 134	12 19 24 63 120
100	87
53 74 75 76 77 78 79 80 96 105 106 107 128	41 43 83
102	4 6 30 33 34 56 88 92 94 120 152
17 47	3 22 34 46 54 55 56 86 87 88 93 94 117 120 151 152 153
17 36 90 129	10 11 131 140
51 106 127 129 130 149	22 29 31 34 108 116 123 125 132 137 138 147
65 66	95 98
71	97 98 99 101 102 126
1 2 13 14 16 18 20 21 26 27 28 35 38 39 40 41 42 45 59 60 61 68 72 82 84 85 89 91 109 110 112 114 118 121 122 125 133 134 135 136 139 143 144 147 148 150	99

Place names on map: VENEZUELA, GUYANA, SURINAM, COLOMBIA, Roraima (the lost world), ECUADOR, Loja, Piura, PERU, Amazon Basin, BRAZIL, Pernambuco, BOLIVIA, ANDES, Minas Gerais, Espirito Santo, PARAGUAY, Rio, Salta, ARGENTINA, CHILE, URUGUAY, Patagonia, Tierra del Fuego

Legend:
- Tropical rain forest
- Montane forest
- Grassland
- Sub-tropical forest
- Shrub/forest
- Cloud forest
- Desert
- Sclerophyllous scrub
- Steppe
- Sclerophyllous woodland
- Temperate evergreen forest
- Sclerophyllous forest

1. *Adiantum capillus-veneris*
2. *A. raddianum*
3. *Aechmea fasciata*
4. *A.* Fosters Favourite
5. *A. fulgens*
6. *A.* Royal Wine
7. *Ananas bracteatus*
8. *A. comosus*
9. *Anthurium andraeanum*
10. *Aphelandra chamissoniana*
11. *A. squarrosa*
12. *Begonia alleryi*
13. *B. compta*
14. *B.* Corallina de Lucerna
15. *B. hiemalis*
16. *B. limmingheiana*
17. *B. luxurians*
18. *B. maculata*
19. *B. metallica*
20. *B. scharfii*
21. *B. schmidtiana*
22. *B. semperflorens-cultorum*
23. *B. serratipetala*
24. *B. thurstonii*
25. *B. tuberhybrida*
26. *Billbergia amoena rubra*
27. *B. decora*
28. *B.* Fantasia
29. *B. horrida*
30. *B. iridifolia*
31. *B. nutans*
32. *B. venezuelana*
33. *B. vittata*
34. *B. zebrina*
35. *Blechnum brasiliense*
36. *B. occidentale*
37. *Browallia speciosa*
38. *Brunfelsia pauciflora calycina*
39. *Caladium hortulanum*
40. *Calathea bachemiana*
41. *C. lancifolia*
42. *C. lindeniana*
43. *C. makoyana*
44. *C. ornata*
45. *C. picturata*
46. *C. zebrina*
47. *Calceolaria herbeohybrida*
48. *Capsicum annuum*
49. *Cereus jamacaru*
50. *C. peruvianus*
51. *Chamaecereus sylvestrii*
52. *Cissus rhombifolia*
53. *Cleistocactus straussii*
54. *Cryptanthus acaulis*
55. *C. bivittatus*
56. *C. bromelioides tricolor*
57. *C. fosteranus*
58. *C. zonatus*
59. *Ctenanthe lubbersiana*
60. *C. oppenheimiana*
61. *C. setosa*
62. *Dieffenbachia amoena*
63. *D. bowmannii*
64. *D. imperialis*
65. *Echinopsis eyriesii*
66. *E. multiplex*
67. *Episcia cupreata*
68. *E. reptans*
69. *Fittonia verschaffeltii*
70. *Fuchsia* hybs.
71. *Guzmania lingulata*
72. *G. monostachia*

73. *G. musaica*
74. *Gymnocalcium baldianum*
75. *G. bruchii*
76. *G. denudatum*
77. *G. mihanovichii*
78. *G. platense*
79. *G. quehlianum*
80. *G. saglione*
81. *Lobivia hertrichiana*
82. *Maranta leuconeura*
83. *Microcoelum weddellianum*
84. *Mimosa pudica*
85. *Neoregelia carolinae*
86. *N. concentrica*
87. *N. marmorata*
88. *N. sarmentosa*
89. *N. spectabilis*
90. *Nephrolepsis cordifolia*
91. *N. exaltata*
92. *Nidularium fulgens*
93. *N. innocentii*
94. *N. purpureum*
95. *Notocactus apricus*
96. *N. concinnus*
97. *N. leninghausii*
98. *N. ottonis*
99. *N. scopa*
100. *Opuntia cylindrica*
101. *O. salmiana*
102. *O. subulata*
103. *O. vestita*
104. *Pachystachys lutea*
105. *Parodia aureispina*
106. *P. chrysacanthion*
107. *P. sanguiniflora*
108. *Passiflora caerulea*
109. *Peperomia argyreia*
110. *P. caperata*
111. *P. fraseri*
112. *P. griseoargentea*
113. *P. obtusifolia*

114. *P. scandens*
115. *Philodendron angustisectum*
116. *P. bipennifolium*
117. *P. bipennatifidum*
118. *P.* Burgundy
119. *P. erubescens*
120. *P. imbe*
121. *P. pedatum*
122. *P. scandens*
123. *P. selloum*
124. *Pilea spruceana*
125. *Polypodium aureum*
126. *Rebutia calliantha*
127. *R. kupperana*
128. *R. miniscula*
129. *R. senilis*
130. *R. xanthocarpa*
131. *Rhipsalidopsis gaertneri*
132. *R. rosea*
133. *Ruellia makoyana*
134. *Schlumbergera bridgesii*
135. *S. truncata*
136. *Sinningia cardinalis*
137. *S. leucotricha*
138. *S. pusilla*
139. *S. speciosa*
140. *Solanum capsicastrum*
141. *Spathiphyllum* Mauna Loa
142. *S. wallisii*
143. *Stromanthe amabilis*
144. *S. sanguinea*
145. *Tillandsia cyanea*
146. *T. lindenii*
147. *Tradescantia blossfeldiana*
148. *T. fluminensis*
149. *Trichocereus spachianus*
150. *Vriesea fenestralis*
151. *V. hieroglyphica*
152. *V. psittacina*
153. *V. saundersii*
154. *V. splendens*

Climate

This is the only continent to extend far into the southern temperate latitudes, but as it tapers towards the South Pole it does not suffer the extremes of temperature of the northern continents and their continental climates. In South America the winters are warmer and the summers cooler than in North America or Asia, and at no time are there freezing temperatures at sea level. South America has the largest area of truly tropical climate to be found in any continent, but due to the high altitude of the Andes it also has temperate and sub-arctic climates.

Except in the south, the winds blow parallel to the Andes on the west coast and bring heavy rain to Ecuador and Colombia. South of this to 30°S, the western side of the Andes is very dry due to the effect of the Humboldt current, and what little rain does fall comes, in fact, during the coolest months. South of 35°S there is much rain mainly falling during autumn and winter. On the whole, the Andes are a barrier to circulation, but south of 40°S they are low and the westerly winds can cross them bringing heavy rain on the Chilean side (but only sparse rainfall in Patagonia). Further north around Colombia, Venezuela and Guyana, where the trade winds blow, the bulk of the rain falls during July. The equatorial zone tends to be very wet with two periods of exceptional wetness. The Plate estuary northwards to the Tropic of Capricorn receives warm rainy winds throughout the year.

The tropical areas tend to be cooler than expected, even when taking into account the increased altitude; this is due to its greater cloudiness, heavier rainfall and denser forests.

41

Amazon domain

This covers most of the area to the south of Central America that is found in the tropics. It is an area where the climate is hot and humid and it is densely covered with vegetation.

The Amazon province covers a massive area and includes most of northern Brazil, much of Guyana and Venezuela, and the east of Colombia, Ecuador, Peru and Bolivia. It is a hot and humid area with temperatures averaging 80°F (26°C) with little variation. There is no dry period, thus no seasons. Rainfall: 2,000–2,600mm (80–100in).

The characteristic vegetation of this province is rain forest

The Pacific province lies in the north of the continent on the western side of the Andes. This is one of the most humid regions in the world and has a rainfall of over 10,000mm (390in) a year. Temperatures are always high and vary very little.

The vegetation is tropical rain forest, very much like that found in the Amazon province.

The Yungas province, between the vast Amazon basin and the Andes is a long narrow strip of vegetation running parallel to the mountains and confined to the tropics. It is cooler than the Amazon and Pacific provinces, but it is still very humid. It is between 500 and 3,000m high (1,600–10,000ft), and with such an increase in altitude, temperature and rainfall levels drop rapidly.

The vegetation is mainly cloud forest.

The Venezolana province lies to the north of the Yungas. It has a vegetation intermediate between tropical rain forest and the woodland of the Yungas. Rainfall is about 1,500mm (60in) and the temperature fairly hot at about 57–80°F (14–28°C). The communities of trees vary from wet rain forest, to drier woodland types with areas of savanna with thickets and shrubs.

The Cerrado, or "secret" province, covers about 25% of Brazil in the south-east of the country as well as the north-east of Paraguay. This is a plateau area between 500 and 1,000m (1,600 and 3,200ft) high and it has a yearly rainfall of 1,200–2,000mm (47–80in). The temperature is only fairly warm, 70–77°F (21–25°C), due to the increased altitude.

The Parana province includes the southernmost part of Brazil, the very north of Argentina and the east of Paraguay. The rainfall, which is about 1,500–2,000mm (60–80in), falls mainly during the summer giving a dry winter period. The climate is warm, averaging from 61°F (16°C) to 72°F (22°C). The area is mountainous with low ridges that rise in the east; most of the area is only about 1,000m (3,300ft) high, but rises to 3,000m (10,000ft) at the coastal mountains.

The vegetation is predominantly subtropical with *Araucaria* woods and elevated savanna, the latter due to Man's clearance of wooded areas.

The true Savanna province is found in the north of the area from the Venezuelan plain stretching eastwards to Columbia. Its principal climatic characteristic is a very wet period followed by a very dry one. The hot dry period determines the type of vegetation; grassland either without trees or with clumps of small trees scattered here and there.

The Atlantic province occupies the coastal strip (no wider than 75 miles) from the east-most point of Brazil southwards to the north of Uruguay. The climate is hot and humid with temperatures averaging 68–77°F (20–25°C). Rainfall is at least 2,000mm (80in) and in some places 4,000mm (158in); it falls throughout the year, though there is slightly less during the southern hemisphere winter.

The climax vegetation is rain forest.

The Paramo province occupies the high mountain areas of Venezuela, Colombia, and Ecuador, between altitudes of about 3,800 and 4,500m (12,500 and 14,750ft). It is a region with few trees, often mist covered and it receives much rain and snow. At night the temperatures are low, reaching below freezing point. The dominant plants are grasses, with woody shrubs growing about 3m (10ft) tall.

Guyanan domain

The Guyanan domain comprises a small area in the north of South America and consists of the plateau area of Guyana, Venezuela and Brazil; it is entirely surrounded by the Amazon province and its tropical rain forest vegetation. This domain consists of elevated areas over 2,000m (6,500ft) high of which Roraima – the "Lost world" – is probably the best known. In general these areas are steep sided and very difficult to enter. The upper levels are undulating and usually covered by rich savanna vegetation.

There are estimated to be over 8,000 different plant types in the area.

Chaqueno domain

Apart from eastern Brazil, this occupies the area as far south as 40°S, and to the west as far as the Andes. The climate is variable, but on the whole continental, with little to adequate rain, mild winters and hot summers. The vegetation, not sur-

prisingly adapted to conserve water, is varied: deciduous forests, thickets or herbaceous steppes. Many of the plants are legumes, especially acacias and caesalpinias; there are also masses of cacti and bromeliads.

The Caatinga province is the eastern part of Brazil and within the tropics.

It is an arid area (much of it cleared by Man years ago) with a rainfall of only 400–750mm (16–30in) a year and a high average temperature of 79–81°F (26–27°C). The rainfall is unreliable, some years being much drier than others.

The Chaquena province extends from the south of Bolivia to the west of Paraguay and to the north of Argentina. It has a continental climate and is only slightly raised above sea level. Rainfall of 1,200mm (47in) is at its maximum in the east reducing to only 500mm (20in) in the west. It is warm with temperatures averaging 68–73°F (20–23°C). In the west the rain falls mainly during the summer months, whereas in the east it falls throughout the year and there is no distinct dry period.

The Espinal province is further to the south in the northern part of Argentina. The vegetation is either trees adapted to conserve moisture, or steppe. The climate is fairly hot and humid in the north becoming cooler and drier in the south. In the south, the rainfall is only about 350mm (12in); in the north it reaches 1,000mm (39in).

The Prepunena province is situated further to the west and at higher altitudes, from 1,000 to 3,400m (up to 11,000ft) in the Andes. Here, the mountains dramatically affect the climate and make the area very hot and dry, with rain falling only in the summer.

The Mountain province lies to the south of the small Prepunena province and occupies the arid areas of Argentina from 27°S to 44°S. The area is varied with gravelly hills, plateaux and ranges of mountains.

Rainfall is never more than 250mm (10in), but the temperature varies quite appreciably throughout the year.

The Pampas province is well known for its grassy steppe vegetation. It covers a large area in the north-east of Argentina, Uruguay and southern Brazil. It is a gently undulating area with small mountains up to 1,200m (4,000ft) high and has a warm temperate climate where rain falls throughout the year. The rainfall reduces from north to south and from east to west, the maximum being 1,200mm (47in) and the minimum 600mm (24in). Temperatures vary by up to 63°F (17°C) during the year.

Andes-Patagonian domain

The High Andes province includes the areas of the Andes over 4,200m (13,800ft) in the tropics, over 3,000m (10,000ft) at 34°S, over 2,000m (6,500ft) at 40°S and over 500m (1,600ft) in Tierra del Fuego. It is always cold and most of the precipitation is as snow and hail.

The vegetation is mainly short, tough grasses and small bushes with only a few herbs. It is an unpleasant area in which to live, but there is a great variety of tussock, rosette or cushion-form plant species.

The Punena province is the large, raised "altiplano" area of Peru and Bolivia between 3,200 and 4,400m (10,500 and 14,400ft) high. The climate is cold and dry and has large fluctuations of temperature. Rainfall diminishes from east to west and north to south with the maximum being 700mm (28in), and the minimum a mere 50mm (2in).

The vegetation is steppe with plants 40–150mm (1.5–6in) tall.

The Desert province runs along the west coast by the side of the Pacific from 5°S to 30°S. Rainfall is very low, 100mm (4in) or less; only on the slopes of the Andes is there any reasonable rainfall during the summer.

The Chilean province, the central Chilean area, has a sclerophyllous vegetation. Winter rains are prevalent and the area is warm.

Sub-antarctic domain

To the south of the Chilean sclerophyllous zone is *the sub-antarctic zone*. With an increase in rainfall, *Nothofagus* forest grows, and these deciduous trees lose their leaves during the cool winter months. Even

further south, where the rainfall is 2,000–3,000mm (6,500–10,000ft), *Nothofagus* forest is replaced by temperate, evergreen rain forest.

43

Elfin forest near the summit plateau of Mont Roraima (the "Lost World" mountain)

Plant hunting in South America

By far the largest number of house plants are South American in origin and these countries were closed to foreign botanists until they left the Spanish and Portuguese rule.

However a quite surprising number of South American plants did get into cultivation during the 18th century. For example among the aroids, the popular *Caladium bicolor* had, presumably, been brought from Brazil by some Portuguese amateur who established it in his garden on Madeira. Thence it was sent by their correspondent to Kennedy and Lee, who introduced it to cultivation in 1773. In 1759 Philip Miller in the Chelsea Physic Garden was growing a Monstera with perforated leaves, some 15cm (6in) long, at least one and possibly two dieffenbachias.

The journals of Allan Cunningham

In 1814 Sir Joseph Banks obtained permission from the Portuguese for two Kew collectors to visit Brazil; these were Allan Cunningham, later to do so much valuable work in Australia, and James Bowie, who did rather less valuable work in South Africa. The expedition journal was written by Allan Cunningham. One of its most valuable aspects is that he noted the temperatures two or three times a day: e.g. on July 11th at Sao Paulo,

Cunningham noted: "Morning frosty. Strong hoar frost on plants; the Bananas and Coffee trees suffered much from it." Low temperatures seem to have been very frequent during July. There was another frost on the 25th. This information should have been invaluable for the Kew gardeners and the fact that Brazilian plants are often exposed to low temperatures should encourage the house plant grower.

Cunningham sent back more than 700 packets of seeds and the number of plants that are actually ascribed to this expedition is somewhat small for so large a collection. It certainly sounds as though much of the material was lost before it could flower. We do know, however, that at least two plants that are still grown as house plants came out of this expedition and here is their account:

"August 31st. Thursday 8 a.m. 69°. 5 p.m. 73°. Morning fair but cloudy. This morning we left the Ranxo and travell'd about 5 leagues, arrived at a large Ranxo called Formosa, a short distance from Capt. Mor. Our mules were completely tired out this day on account of the steepness of the road in many places; the ascents and descents being exceedingly fatiguing.

"This day we collected legumens of a

climber, supposed to be a scarlet-flower'd diadelphous shrub before noticed on our way to St Paulo, No 345. On the sides of the road on the mountain we collected seeds of a sp. of Ruellia, very much allied to *R. formosa*, but smooth, No. 413 – gathered the fruit of a gardenia without spines from a tree about 30 feet high (on the margin of a wood) with large leaves, No 347 – seeds of a beautiful species of begonia, leaves very large and acuminated, No 342 . . . another species, a climber, with undulated subreniform leaves, No 343, seeds of a sp. of Asclepias, follicle large and woolly, No 384, seeds of a climbing shrub, flowers octandrous, capsule ventricose (Cardiospermum?) 373, specimens of Myrtus sp. leaves ferrugineous and peduncles hairy & specimens of Paullinia sp. red flowers.

"This day we travell'd a very high, steep and mountainous road. Day cool, evening fine. Turned and shifted specimens which were very damp."

Plant collectors invariably number their gatherings. Cunningham had two sets of numbers; one for seeds and one for pressed specimens, but other collectors may make only one list in which seeds and specimens are numbered consecutively.

"November 24th. Friday. 8 a.m. 75°. 12 n. 82°. 4 p.m. 74°. Morning very fine. Attending to specimens and writing forward journal. Day close and hot. In the afternoon upon the mountains. Collected seeds and specimens of *Turnera spp.* (allied to *T. sidoides*, persoon, but shrubby) No 625, specimens of *Piper spp.* with large leaves in shaded situations and margins of woods. In damp leafy woods collected specimens of a curious plant, flowers blue, hexandrous *(Tradescantia spp.)*, specimens of a shrub, flowers pentandrous, white in spikes, petioles long, gibbous, specimens of *Celtis spp.* . . . beneath a large timber tree gather'd from the ground a small yellow fruit of a disagreeable bitter taste and said to act as an emetic (3-seeded). From the ground collected some fruit, 1-seeded red, No 691, and plants of

Kaempferia, leaves very large, velvety, purple beneath".

The velvety leaves belonged, in point of fact, to *Calathea zebrina*. In the earlier entry it is the beautiful begonia which interests us. It is not very often that Cunningham describes a plant as beautiful, and it would be obvious to the Kew growers that this merited special care. Indeed it did, since it turned out to be *Begonia corallina*.

The adventures of George Gardner

George Gardner published his *Travels in the Interior of Brazil* in 1846: he was able to travel into northern parts of the country and move far more freely than had been possible twenty years earlier. As a botanist he seems to have been somewhat austere, but elsewhere he displays an unexpected sense of humour. He mentions, for example, that a rich landowner refused to teach his daughters to read and write for fear that the one would read novels, while the other might write love letters. Again, his description of the steps taken to cope with a possible rebellion, although too long to quote here, is hilarious.

Alas, his Wardian cases were so poorly constructed that his list of introductions is not as large as might have been expected. He is credited with the first achimenes to get into cultivation.

William Lobb, the Veitch collector

Shortly before leaving, Gardner went again to the Organ Mountains, long regarded as the richest part of Brazil, in order to collect plants and to ascend to the highest point. He found, however, that it had been climbed about six weeks previously by "Mr Lobb, an English gardener, who had been sent out by a nursery-man to collect seeds and living plants". This was William Lobb, the first and one of the most successful of the Veitch collectors. The bulk of his collecting was done in Chile, but he also sent plants from Brazil of which *Begonia coccinea* is sometimes seen as a house plant. On his way back from his second expedition, which lasted from 1845-8, he seems to have

The Amazon rain forest, stretching far into the distance, is interrupted only by the huge, meandering curves of a river.

managed to visit Venezuela and Colombia and from this area he collected *Calathea ornata*.

Schomburghk in Guyana

By far the most vivid account of botanising in the tropics come from Richard Schomburghk in 1876. The actual exploration of Guyana lasted from 1840-4, although Richard's brother, Robert, had made a previous exploration in 1835-9. Robert was working for the British government, Richard for the Prussian. Rain forests must have been frequent for these South American explorers, but few describe them. Here, however, is Schomburghk: "No idea can be formed of a Mora forest; it is so thick that the sight of heaven is denied to those who enter it. Everything is drowned in a mass of shadows; the eye can only behold a labyrinth of gigantic proportions which astonish and overawe him, garnished with a dome of foliage that darkens the atmosphere and renders it intolerably dark and gloomy. Lianes of immense thickness entwine with giant arms these trunks, and ramp to the highest branches, where they crown these giants; then again grow down from this giddy height on to the smaller trees, the branches of which they entwine and so fetter one tree to another with a network, and hold in their strong arms those giants

standing close on the banks of the rivers, whose secure position is often undermined by the rapid streams, thus preventing their sudden fall; but should such a giant succumb, by his fall he will carry all the trees entwined by the same lianes, to destruction with him."

Linden and the Belgian explorers

From about 1843 the exploration of most of eastern South America was organised by Belgians, principally by Linden and his collectors, but in 1843 Kew, now under the excellent direction of Sir William Hooker, sent William Purdie to Jamaica and the following year to Colombia. Among his sendings were *Episcia cupreata*, *Begonia fuchsioides* and *Ruellia macrantha*, all of which have been used as house plants.

In 1841 Jean Jules Linden arrived with Louis Schlim in Venezuela. He had previously visited Cuba and Mexico on a government mission, but his 1841 trip seems to have been a private mission or perhaps one financed by a syndicate. According to one report he was also Belgian vice-consul at Caracas, the capital of Venezuela. Linden and Schlim botanised chiefly in Venezuela, but they got into Colombia and also visited Cuba. The expedition ended in 1845. Apart from *Aphelandra* 45

A. B. Graf, botanist explorer and author/publisher of Exotica *(the most comprehensive cyclopaedia of exotic plants), with a* Vriesea hieroglyphica *collected in the rain forest on the Serra do Mar in southern Brazil.*

aurantiaca, none of Linden's actual sendings show much in the house plant line, yet this expedition was to have far-reaching consequences. Schlim continued exploring Colombia later, accompanied by a Herr Funck. Schlim and Funck sound rather like the comic relief in Viennese operetta, but they did manage to send back *Calathea villosa* var. *pardina* and *C. metallica.* On his return Linden had set up a nursery in Luxembourg, specifically for the introduction of new plants. This nursery was moved to Brussels in 1853, when Linden was appointed director of the botanic garden there. Linden sent out collectors to all parts of South America and his example was followed by other Belgian nurserymen. Louis van Houtte of Ghent seems to have had several collectors, although only the name of Ghiesbreght can be assigned with certainty to van Houtte. A Brussels nurseryman, de Jonghe, had a M. Libon collecting for him in Brazil in 1846. Another nurseryman, Mackoy, had the splendid peacock plant,

Calathea makoyana, named in his honour, and usually when nurserymen were honoured in this fashion it means that it was their collector who discovered or introduced it. There are innumerable tropical plants with epithets such as *lindeniana, veitchiana, sanderiana,* etc, so it may well be an unknown Mackoy collector who brought back this splendid plant. Unfortunately we can put few names to these collectors. We know that in the 1870s Edouard André, who became a revered French botanist, was collecting for Linden and among his sendings were *Philodendron andreanum* and its juvenile form, long known as *P. melanochryson* and a popular, but difficult house plant, the popular painter's palette, *Anthurium andreanum.* It is reasonably certain that other philodendrons came from this expedition.

Another collector was a remarkable man, Gustave Wallis, who was later to collect for Veitch. He is commemorated in the now very popular *Spathiphyllum wallisii,* as well as in other plants less well-known. His life shows a triumphant overcoming of what most would think unsurmountable obstacles in becoming a plant collector. He was born in 1830 a deaf mute, but by the age of six he was taught to articulate, although his speech remained defective. He also, in his teens, became proficient in several foreign languages. He was, after some initial hesitation, trained as a gardener. Nothing more seems to be known about him until we find him in 1856 opening a nursery financed by a German house, in Southern Brazil. The German firm failed and Wallis was left stranded and impoverished in Brazil. He offered his services to Linden who accepted them, and Wallis, apparently, journeyed the whole length of the Amazon from its mouth to its source. In 1870 he entered the Veitch service, his first expedition being rather oddly to the Philippines, and unsuccessful. In 1872 he went to Colombia and it was from this expedition that the spathiphyllum came, as well as an enormous-leaved anthurium and a choice form of

Dieffenbachia seguine now known as var. *liturata.* He died in Panama at the early age of 48.

Towards the end of the 19th century the various continental nurseries combined to form Horticolteur Internationale which financed the sending out of expeditions, mainly to South and Central America.

The famous Veitch Nursery expeditions

Veitch having done so well with William Lobb in Chile (see above) followed up in 1859 by sending Richard Pearce to Chile, but he also visited Peru and Bolivia in 1862 to search for plants with fine foliage. During this trip he collected all the parent species which make up the present race of tuberous begonias and his name is well commemorated in *Begonia pearcei* with its velvety leaves and fine yellow flowers. In Bolivia he collected *Calathea veitchii.* He made a second expedition in 1863 from which came *Dieffenbachia pearcei* and *Sanchezia nobilis.* He also sent back *Hippeastrum leopoldii,* which, with its huge scarlet trumpet, has been the principal ingredient in the modern race of amaryllis. In 1867 Pearce left for S. America, this time to collect for another nurseryman William Bull. He was taken ill when he arrived in Panama and died at a young age. He is also said to have discovered several peperomias, but we have no details as to which they were.

Veitch also had a collector, David Bowman, in Brazil in 1866 and it was from him that they received *Dieffenbachia bowmannii.* He was yet another collector who succumbed to tropical diseases, dying from dysentery at Bogata in his thirtieth year. Bowman was also probably responsible for the introduction of the Rugby Football plant, *Peperomia argyreia.* This was originally known as *P. sandersii,* and since Bowman was also collecting for Mr Wilson Saunders, as well as Veitch and the Royal Horticultural Society, and since the plant arrived from Brazil in 1866, he seems the most likely sender.

Preparing plant specimens in Mato Grosso, Brazil

ADIANTUM
(POLYPODIACEAE)

Maidenhair ferns are among the most popular of all indoor ferns. The genus has a worldwide distribution but the most popular house plants are those from tropical America. Their delicate, roughly triangular fronds are divided into many small fan-shaped pinnae (or leaflets), held on thin, usually black, hair-like stalks. Fronds rise from creeping rhizomes. In nature they may grow on moss-covered rocks or fallen trees on the floor of humid forests, but some are epiphytes. None will thrive unless the rooting mixture is moist yet free draining. The name adiantum means "able to shed water".

A. capillus-veneris (Venus-hair) is found worldwide from tropical to temperate climes. Fronds are erect, 30cm (12in) long, light green but with a glaucous bloom. It is understandably the most tolerant of cooler conditions.

A. raddianum (syn. **A. cuneatum**) is Brazilian and called the Delta maidenhair after the D-shaped pinnae. It is more delicate than most others but is by no means difficult. Fronds are 30–46cm (12–18in) long and much divided. There are a number of named forms including Decorum, Fragrantissimum and, perhaps the easiest indoors, Fritz-Luthii with dense overlapping pinnae.

Watering: Keep moderately moist at the roots but never sodden.

Potting mixture: Use $\frac{1}{4}$ peat, $\frac{1}{4}$ leaf mould, $\frac{1}{4}$ sharp sand or perlite and $\frac{1}{4}$ soil-based potting mixture.

Propagation: Divide up overcrowded clumps in spring.

Special points: Stand pots on trays of moist pebbles. When older fronds start to brown at the edges, cut them down right to the base; new ones will take their place. Avoid draughts. Very little feeding is necessary; do so only every two or three months during the growing season with a half-strength fertilizer.

AECHMEA
(BROMELIACEAE)

Aechmeas are mainly epiphytic bromeliads from the mountainous regions of a wide area stretching from Mexico through to Argentina. They can be found in trees only just above sea-level and also high up in cloud forests. Their usually sparse roots hold them fast to the rough surface of tree bark or rocks. Leaves are arranged in a rosette shape, clasped tightly together at the base to form a watertight central cup in which rain and dew collect. A common name is urn plant, after the general shape. Water and plant food can be absorbed by the special cells at the base of the leaves.

A. fasciata is found in full sun in the upper layers of the forest canopy of south Brazil (Rio de Janeiro) at elevations from 450 to 1,200m (1,500 to 4,000ft). Leaves are grey-green, armed with spines at the edges and crossbanded with mealy-white scurf (actually scales). The pink flowerhead, shaped like a drumstick, remains attractive for several months and carries small, very short-lived, pale-blue flowers.

A. fulgens var. **discolor** has much softer leaves and grows on trees but is more likely to be found on the lower limbs, where there is more shade – or even on the ground. It also thrives at lower altitudes. Its chief habitat is south Brazil (Pernambuco). Leaves are a dullish olive-green above and shiny purple beneath. Purple flowers held about 30cm (1ft) above the foliage, are followed by red berries.

A. Foster's Favorite is a small-growing hybrid between two Brazilian species and is prized for its polished, dark-red leaves. Blue flowers are followed by dark-red berries. Growth is unlikely to be more than 30cm (1ft) high and through.

Another hybrid, Royal Wine, has leaves with a shiny olive-green upperside and a wine-red underside, with blue flowers followed by orange berries.

Watering: Water moderately allowing the mixture to dry out partly between applications. The central cup can be kept filled with fresh water (empty the old water out periodically or it will start to smell) but leave empty from the time the flowerstalk starts to develop. Give half-strength liquid fertilizer every two weeks during the growing season.

Adiantum raddianum, *one of the more delicate maidenhair ferns*

Potting mixtures: Use equal parts leaf mould, peat and sharp sand. Other similar combinations are possible but all must be open and quick-draining.

Propagation: Remove offsets when they are well developed (not before) and root in the normal growing mixture, preferably with bottom heat.

Special points: Roots are sparse and plants do best when grown in relatively small pots. Rosettes that have flowered can be cut down with a sharp knife and the offsets grown on still attached to the old rootstock. This results in a plant with two or more rosettes. A spell in the garden during the summer months often induces flowering.

ANANAS
(BROMELIACEAE)

Ananas are terrestrial bromeliads and include the pineapple. Their exact area of origin is unknown but *A. bracteatus* is almost certainly a native of southern Brazil. The edible pineapple, *A. comosus*, has been cultivated in tropical America since the 16th century, and by native Indians possibly before that time. Pineapples are grown from sea-level to 1,800m (6,000ft) and are a commercial crop plant throughout the warmer parts of the world. The variegated-leaved forms are the most popular as house plants. Fruit is unlikely to be produced indoors, though fruiting plants of *A. bracteatus* can sometimes be obtained.

A. bracteatus Striatus (red pineapple) from southern Brazil is also used in the home only when young. Its leaves are similarly coloured, but are wider – to 6–7cm (2½in).

Ananas comosus Variegatus (Bahia, Mato Grosso) has long, sword-shaped, spiny-edged leaves with broad cream borders. In strong sunlight the cream parts are suffused with pink. This can make a very large plant in time; young plants are normally used indoors.

Watering: Water moderately throughout the year, allowing the mixture to dry out a little before applying more.

Potting mixture: Use an equal parts mixture of soil-based compost and coarse leaf mould or peat.

Propagation: Use good-sized offsets that appear around the base of older plants. A propagator is needed to induce these to root. Pineapple tops in good condition can sometimes be rooted in warmth, but not reliably. These will not, of course, be variegated.

Special points: See that humidity is high by standing on trays of moist pebbles or plunging in moist peat. Feed every two weeks during the growing season.

ANTHURIUM ANDRAEANUM
(ARACEAE)

Anthuriums come from the humid rain forests of tropical America. There they are epiphytic or terrestrial, using living trees, rotting fallen trees or the forest floor for anchorage. From S.W. Colombia comes *A. andraeanum* (painter's palette). Deep green, heart-shaped leaves, 15–20cm (6–in) long, provide a perfect foil for the waxy, shield-shaped spathes which may be white, pink, salmon or red.

Watering: Water plentifully during the active growth period, allowing a little drying out between applications. Be more sparing during winter.

Potting mixture: Use an equal parts mixture of coarse leaf mould and peat.

Propagation: Divide overcrowded clumps in spring, ensuring that each detached piece has some roots attached and a growing point. Use a propagator if available.

Special points: The recommended potting mixture has little plant food built into it and it is essential that regular liquid feeding is given. Use a half-strength liquid fertilizer, every two weeks while growth is apparent. A very humid atmosphere is essential, stand on moist pebbles.

APHELANDRA
(ACANTHACEAE)

These Brazilian plants thrive on the high humidity and regular downpours in the rain forests. They adapt satisfactorily to indoor conditions but will not do well unless humidity is high and temperatures above 55°F (13°C). Lower leaves tend to fall at lower temperatures. Stems of the two widely cultivated sorts are stout and fleshy, leaves are broadly elliptic, dark green but heavily striped in the vein areas with white. Flowers are yellow and peep through a four-sided, cone-shaped spike of bracts that is yellow tinged red.

A. chamissoniana has a narrow, yellow spike, and leaves 10–15cm (4–6in) long.

A. squarrosa (saffron spike or zebra plant) has several forms: Louisae – leaves 20–25cm (8–10in) long, orange-yellow bracts; Brockfeld – compact, darker green areas; Dania – silvery leaf markings.

Watering: Water plentifully during the active growth period as they are thirsty plants. Reduce watering during the winter but never allow the mixture to become less than moist.

Potting mixture: Use a soil-based mixture.

Propagation: Use tip cuttings and side shoots in spring, rooting them in a propagator or inside a plastic bag in a warm room.

Special points: Plants that have flowered should be cut down to a pair of lower leaves in spring (the top and sideshoots being used in propagation), otherwise they will become too tall. Shake off most of the compost from the old plant and give fresh; pot on as necessary. Stand pots on moist pebbles or plunged in moist peat. Watch out for aphids which tend to collect on the new leaves.

BEGONIA
(BEGONIACEAE)

More than a thousand begonia species exist (and there are perhaps ten times as many hybrids) distributed over several large areas of the world.

Tuberous begonias have corky, underground tubers up to 7.5cm (3in) across and send up usually very juicy stems, fleshy leaves and large or small flowers. Some sprawl and make excellent hanging basket plants. Tuberous begonias have a period of dormancy when top growth dies down and plants need virtually no water. *Semi-tuberous*

Tuberous begonias are the result of intensive cross-hybridization. Rhizomatous kinds scramble about putting down roots wherever they make contact with a suitable growing medium. Here are two finding sustenance on ruined buildings.

kinds have persistent stems and retain their top growth during the winter – even though they usually stop growing then. The Christmas-flowering kinds produce little basal growth but have a dormant period during late spring through summer.

Rhizomatous kinds have a thick, fleshy rhizome (sometimes gnarled and wood-looking) which may creep over the surface of the potting mixture but may also (less often) be semi-upright. Leaves can be of practically any shape, but flowers are usually small, white or in pink shades, and carried in large trusses in early spring. These plants store a certain amount of water and plant food in the rhizome and can endure reasonable periods of neglect.

Fibrous rooted begonias can be hirsute – leaves, stems and even flowers are covered or sprinkled with hairs. Alternatively they can be cane-stemmed, when stems are smooth, knotted at intervals like bamboo, or just bushy. The wax begonias, *B. semper-florens* hybrids are of this kind.

49

TUBEROUS BEGONIAS

B. hiemalis hybrids are a mixture of various Andean species of begonia but include the "blood" of *B. socotrana* from Socotra Island in the Indian Ocean. Stems are usually a very deep red and up to 45cm (18in) tall; leaves are fleshy, coloured deep green to almost chocolate; flowers are single, about 7cm (2½–3in) big, and usually strong red with a yellow centre. Plants sold have names like Fireglow, Schwabenland and Elatior.

B. tuberhybrida is the name given to a host of large-flowered hybrids with parents from the Andes. Stems are very fleshy, rarely above 38cm (15in) indoors, leaves sappy and male blooms huge, comprising many layers of petals. White, pink, red, orange and yellow forms exist, some with frilly petal edges, some with edges piped in another colour or shade. They are far from easy to grow well in the home, needing high humidity, very careful watering and the right level of light.

Other recommended tuberous begonias originate elsewhere and are described fully in the following sections:

South African species
B. cheimantha hybrids (Gloire de Lorraine type)
B. dregei
B. sutherlandii
B. weltoniensis

Central American species
B. gracilis

Central and East Asian species
B. grandis (syn. *B. evansiana*)

Watering: As plants come out of dormancy, water sparingly at first until roots become established; thereafter be moderate, allowing some drying out before watering again. Stop watering those that lose their top growth when leaves yellow in the autumn and give just a little water through the winter to those that retain stems and leaves.

Potting mixtures: Use an equal parts mixture of soil-based and peat-based mixture.

Propagation: Use the bulbils that form in the leaf axils of those that make them. Take these off in the autumn and store dry at around 50°F (10°C) in a small container (matchbox or tin), planting them in spring in a seed tray and potting individually when 25–50mm (1–2in) high.

Stem cuttings of the semi-tuberous-rooted can be taken in spring and larger tubers of *B. tuberhybrida* can be cut with a knife in two or more pieces (each with a growing point) once new growth is obvious in the spring.

Special points: Moist pebble trays are a considerable advantage while plants are in growth.

Do not pull away dying growth in the autumn; leave on the plant until it is easily freed. Take tubers of the large-flowered kinds out of their pots and store in *just* moist peat until spring. Start these off into growth in trays filled with moist peat, potting up when necessary.

Feed actively growing plants every two weeks with a high-potash liquid fertilizer.

RHIZOMATOUS BEGONIAS

B. limmingheiana (syn. *B. glaucophylla*) is a trailing plant from Brazil where it scrambles over the ground and puts down roots from the nodes whenever it comes into contact with a suitable growing mixture, or up moss-covered tree trunks. Indoors it is usually grown as a hanging basket plant. Leaves are pointed ovals, shiny and medium green; brick-red flowers appear in winter.

Rhizomatous begonias originating outside of South America include:

Central American species
B. boweri
B. erythrophylla
B. Maphil (a boweri seedling)

South East Asian species
B. masoniana (syn. *B.* iron Cross)

Indian sub-continent
B. rex-cultorum

Watering: Water plants in growth moderately but allow considerable drying out before applying more.

The usually thick rhizome can store a certain amount of moisture and endure short periods of drought.

Give only enough during the winter to prevent shrivelling. Some leaves may fall in winter but they will be replaced quickly in spring.

Potting mixture: Use either an equal-parts mixture of coarse leaf mould and soil-based mix, or a peat-based mixture. Good drainage is essential.

Propagation: Rhizomes can be cut into 5–7.5cm (2–3in) pieces (they usually have some roots attached to them), and placed *on* the surface of a peat and sand rooting mixture, in a propagator or potted within a plastic bag. Most will also make new plants from single leaves (rooted in the same way as saintpaulia leaves) with 25–50mm (1–2in) of leafstalk attached.

Special points: Maintain high humidity around the plants. Move on into larger containers only when the rhizomes have crept across the potting mixture. Half pots or pans are usually most suitable as the roots are shallow.

FIBROUS-ROOTED BEGONIAS

B. alleryi – a hybrid between *B. gigantea* (Sikkim) and *B. metallica* (Brazil) – is one of the hirsute begonias, growing 90–122cm (3–4ft) tall.

Tooth-edged, hairy leaves are browny-green with reddish veins on the underside. Flowers are pale pink and covered with fine, silky, silver hair.

B. compta is a tall-growing plant from Brazil, having bamboo-like stems notched at intervals, with grey-green silky leaves boldly striped around the vein areas with silvery-grey. Flowers are a dull white.

B. Corallina de Lucerna (a hybrid between a species from Brazil and one from Malaysia) is similar to many other forms with names like

Lucerna and President Carnot. All grow to 1.5m (5ft) tall, with white-spotted, deep olive-green leaves, shot with bronze in bright light, a red underside, and very large trusses of coral-red flowers. It is difficult to tell the difference between them.

B. luxurians (Brazil) makes tall red stems and unlikely, palm-like leaves, divided into many finger-shaped leaflets, drooping slightly from a red-spotted central point. Flowers, small and dull, bloom in spring.

B. maculata. The name means "spotted begonia" and was given to this species because it was the first found with spotted leaves. From Brazil, this species makes smooth (bamboo-like) stems, deep green leaves spotted silver above and deep red beneath, and pink flowers.

There is a more heavily marked form, *B.m.* Wightii, with white blooms.

B. metallica (Brazil) grows to 90cm (3ft) tall, has shiny surfaced, metallic, deep-olive-green leaves marked particularly strongly around the vein areas with reddish purple, and with a red underside. Flowers appear in tight ball-like clusters of pink with red beards.

B. scharffi (syn. *B. haageana*) from Brazil is a popular, tall-growing hirsute plant with deep olive-green leaves, burgundy red underneath. All parts are covered with soft, short hair and the white flowers in dense clusters are speckled with red hairs.

B. schmidtiana is a small, much-branched creeping plant from Brazil. Leaves and stems are hairy, flushed red, particularly in the indented vein areas. It makes a non-stop display of small pink flowers and is good in baskets.

B. semperflorens-cultorum (wax or bedding begonia). Semperflorens means everblooming and aptly describes these most rewarding plants. Today's hybrids are of complex parentage (mainly species from Brazil and north Argentina) and may have glistening green, bronzy-green or chocolate coloured leaves. Flowers can be white, pink, red or bicoloured, usually single but also semi-double and fully double. They flower when very young and continue to produce flowers through most of the year.

B. serratipetala is a full-branching, fibrous-rooted begonia from New Guinea. Its leaves are sharply pointed, with edges crinkled and deeply cut, bronze-green with pink, raised spots. Flowers are red, some with serrated edges. Often wrongly called *serratifolia*, due to the serrated leaf edges.

B. thurstonii (a hybrid between two Brazilian species, *B. metallica* and *B. sanguinea*) has shiny, metallic bronze and green leaves (scarlet below) and pink flowers with red beards. Stems are red and up to 60cm (2ft) long. It is best seen against the light in an east or west-facing window.

Watering: Water moderately, allowing the mixture to dry out a little between waterings. Water sparingly in winter, particularly if the temperature falls below 5°F (10°C).

Potting mixture: Use an equal-parts mixture of soil-based and leaf mould or coarse peat.

Propagation: Take short tip cuttings of most kinds in spring. Use basal shoots of *B. semperflorens* as these branch freely; tip cuttings of this kind are inclined to continue to grow unbranched. Make quite sure that cuttings of the hairy stemmed kinds are not more than *just* moist while rooting; they are particularly prone to rot rather than root if too moist.

Seed of several kinds is available, though this is very fine and should not be covered; just sow on the moistened surface.

Special points: With the cane-stemmed sorts keep a special watch for powdery mildew, which may start with small spots on leaves or stems and gradually spread. A steady state of moderate moisture at the roots is the best safeguard. Pot on into larger pots each spring, and stake and tie in as necessary. Few of these plants insist on high humidity but it is a great help in warm rooms.

Feed all plants every two weeks during the growing season. All begonias prefer good light without hot, direct sun but thrive in an east or west-facing window for most of the year.

BILLBERGIA (BROMELIACEAE)

Most billbergias are native of eastern Brazil but some also come from Uruguay, Argentina and Venezuela. They grow over a wide range of altitudes, from just above sea-level to 1,500m (5,000ft). The majority are epiphytes, forming clumps on tree limbs, fallen trees low down in the forest, or clinging to moist rocks. exposures. Flowers are tubular, usually nodding, blue and green and backed with large, highly decorative pink or red bracts. Flowers of all billbergias are short-lived.

B. amoena Rubra grows to 60cm (24in) tall and has a tubular shape, with leaves of a rosy hue spotted with white or yellow.

B. decora, from Brazil , Bolivia and Peru, reaches 45cm (18in) high. Leaves are strongly cross-banded with meal.

B. Fantasia, a hybrid between two Brazilian species (*B. saundersii* and *B. pyramidalis*), grows 30cm (12in) high. Its coppery-red leaves are very heavily spotted with white and pink. Best colour is achieved in sun. Bracts are bright-red and the upright blue flowers have red petals.

B. horrida is a squat plant with leaves armed at the edges with dark spines and an erect flowerspike.

B. iridifolia grows no more than 30cm (12in) tall. Shape is tubular with leaf tips recurving.

B. nutans, the most widely distributed (Brazil, Argentina and Uruguay) is the most popular and the simplest of all bromeliads to grow. This species and *B. windii* (an offspring) tend to form dense clumps of growths.

B. venezuelana is limited to a small, hot and dry area of Venezuela where it is often seen clinging to cliffs. It may grow to 90cm (3ft) tall. Leaves mottled with wine-red and silver, flower spike spectacular.

B. vittata is tubular shaped, to 75cm (2½ft) tall, olive-green with a dull purplish hue and banded with silvery scales.

B. zebrina grows naturally in both moist rain forest and dry areas. It forms a cup-like base with the upper parts of the purplish bronze, silver-banded leaves flaring out.

Watering: Keep the potting mixture moist at all times, never sodden. Rain water is best as it leaves no white lime deposit.

Potting mixture: Use equal proportions of soil-based mixture and leaf mould; any open mixture can be used.

Propagation: Take off well-developed side shoots from the base of the plants in late spring. They will often have some roots already attached and normally can

Blechnum occidentale, *the hammock fern, grows from the West Indies to Chile.*

be planted directly into a recommended growing mixture. Use small pots at first.

Special points: A few months in a shady position in the garden during the summer months greatly improves the leaf colouration and usually encourages flowering. Feed plants that have filled their pots with roots, every two weeks from spring to early autumn.

BLECHNUM (POLYPODIACEAE)
Blechnums are ferns from tropical America and the tropical islands of the south-west Pacific. Their fronds are usually arranged in a loose rosette shape but they may grow from an underground creeping rhizome or in the case of

some mature plants sprout from the top of a scaly trunk. Fronds are divided into two ranks of often wavy-edged pinnae, not uniform in size or shape.

B. brasiliense (Brazil and Peru) makes a stout, dark brown trunk after several years of growth, when young it sends out lance-shaped fronds that are tinged copper and up to 60cm (2ft) long from a rough-textured brown core.

B. occidentale (tropical America – from the West Indies to Chile) is called the hammock fern and sends up arching fronds with

slightly drooping pinnae of a rich green from creeping rhizomes. Fronds are usually around 38cm (15in) long and 12.5cm (5in) wide.

Watering: Water generously during the growth period and moderately in winter.

Potting mixture: Use equal parts soil-based mixture and leaf mould or coarse peat. Provide good drainage.

Propagation: The tree-fern-type blechnums occasionally send up small offsets at the base. Use these for propagation. *B. occidentale* can be broken up into many sections, each with a 7.5–10cm (3–4in) piece of rhizome. Spring and early summer are best periods.

Special points: Increase humidity with pebble-covered trays and plunge pots into moist peat. Mist fronds in dry, hot conditions. Move on into the next size pot only when pots are filled with roots.

BROWALLIA SPECIOSA
(SOLANACEAE)

B. speciosa from Colombia is a rather sprawling sub-shrub, 45–60cm (18–24in) tall, that produces bell-

shaped, violet-blue flowers, up to 50mm (2in) across in autumn and, if the light is good enough, into early winter. Named forms are available which may be more compact, with white flowers or in other shades of blue. Good in hanging baskets.

Culture: Raised from seed sown early in the year. Give bright light, moderate watering, fortnightly feeding with a high-potash fertilizer, and discard when past their best.

BRUNFELSIA PAUCIFLORA CALYCINA
(SOLANACEAE)

Brunfelsias are small evergreen shrubs from

Brazil, with leathery, lance-shaped leaves 7.5–12.5cm (3–5in) long and clusters of flat-faced, violet-purple blooms made up of five lobes and a tiny white eye. An interesting feature is that the flowers gradually lose much of their colour as they age and prompt a common name: yesterday-today-and-tomorrow. The form normally grown is Eximia, with rather larger flowers than the species; Floribunda is dwarf and floriferous, while Macrantha has especially large blooms. The species is often erroneously called *Brunfelsia calycina*, which is in fact a separate variety differing in botanical detail.

Watering: Water moderately during the growing period and sparingly in winter.

Potting mixture: Use a soil-based mixture.

Propagation: Take tip cuttings in spring – use a propagator.

Special points: Feed actively growing plants with a high-potash liquid fertilizer during the growth period only. Increase humidity by standing on a moist pebble tray or plunging in moist peat. Repot only when it is clearly

necessary; these plants flower best when roots are restricted. Prune plants drastically, cutting out at least half the old growth, just as new growth starts in spring (detached pieces may be used in propagation).

CALADIUM HORTULANUM HYBRIDS
(ARACEAE)

Caladiums are tuberous rooted plants from the humid rain forests of the tropics (mainly Brazil), where they often grow in clearings. They are prized

for their highly decorative, brightly coloured or variegated leaves. These

are heart- or arrow-shaped, papery thin, easily damaged and difficult to keep in good condition unless a very high level of humidity is maintained. Often, therefore, they are treated as temporary plants, to be enjoyed and then discarded. The hybrids are a little easier to grow than the wild species. All have a long (dormant) rest period.

Watering: Water moderately during the growing season, allowing the mixture to start to dry out before applying more. Dry off as leaves yellow.

Potting mixture: Use a peat-based mixture.

Propagation: Small tubers develop around the parent tuber and are used in propagation.

Special points: Avoid draughts. Stand on trays of moist pebbles and mist spray the leaves at least daily. If plants are retained for another year, leave the tubers in their pots-keep at around 55°F, (10°C) and give a little water once a month. Repot and start again in spring, ideally in a heated propagator.

Caladiums, with their papery thin leaves require high humidity indoors.

Cacti

Cacti from deserts and mountains

Jungle cacti are discussed in their appropriate alphabetical positions in the general plant listing, but since other cacti share the same cultural needs they are discussed here together.

Watering: Water plentifully during the growing period, allowing the potting mixture to dry out before watering again. In the rest period water only enough to keep the mixture from drying out entirely. Plants which have had insufficient water may start to shrivel.

Potting mixture: Use ¾ soil-based mixture and ¼ coarse sand or grit well mixed, and pot preferably in clay pots.

Special points: Feed once a month in the growing period, April to September. Ensure a winter rest in cool conditions and good light. Repot in spring only if old pot is filled with roots.

CEREUS

C. jamacaru (Brazil) usually makes a single column in cultivation and may grow to 90cm (3ft). Blue-green; six or more ribs; yellowish spines.

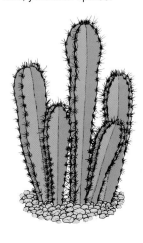

C. peruvianus from central Brazil is another bluish columnar plant, branching when old. Its variety, *C.p.* Monstrosus, is a bizarre mutation with thickened, distorted, branching stems and twisted uneven ribs.

The species are grown from seed, though side shoots can be used as cuttings if produced (as is the case with *C. p.* Monstrosus).

CHAMAECEREUS SYLVESTRI

The peanut cactus, a particularly popular succulent, is small, much-clustering, and free-flowering, and hies

from western and northern Argentina. Its spirally ribbed stems (about the size of a finger) are covered with short, white spines. Large bright scarlet flowers, 25mm (1in) across, appear in early summer; each lasts one day but they arrive in succession over a period of two to three weeks. There are a number of hybrids. If kept too dry at the root and in *very* bright sun, this cactus can take on a reddish or brown hue. Opposite extremes can cause soft, sappy growth. Can be grown from seed, or the stem joints used as cuttings.

CLEISTOCACTUS STRAUSSII

A slender, columnar cactus, known as silver torch, from Argentina and Bolivia. Can reach 1.2m (4ft) tall and may branch at its base. Its many fine ribs are covered with short,

silvery-grey spines. Propagate from seed and cuttings from side growths if produced.

ECHINOPSIS

The globular, sea urchin cactus grows in the pampas of south Brazil and Uruguay, and the thorn savanna of northern Argentina. Summer rains make the pampas green but as autumn sets in, it becomes drier and winter is virtually rainless; temperatures fall to 40–45°F (5–7°C). Flowers are trumpet shaped on a long tube, sweetly scented and inclined to open in the evening.

E. eyriesii has fragrant, white flowers, 20–25cm (8–10in) long and 10–12cm (4–5in) wide. *E. multiplex* has fragrant, pale pink flowers, 17–20cm (7–8in) long and 10–12cm (4–5in) wide. Both are raised from seed or by rooting offsets.

GYMNOCALYCIUM

Chin cacti are relatively small, globular and ribbed. Summertime, funnel-shaped flowers are large and may be white, yellow, red or pink. They appear on long flower tubes and in bud form completely lack hair (the Latin name for the chin cactus literally means "naked bud").

Recommended are *G. baldianum, G. bruchii* (syn. *G. lafaldense*), both from Argentina; *G. denudatum* from S. Brazil to N. Argentina; *G. mihanovicii* from Paraguay; *G. platense,*

G. quehlianum and *G. saglione* from Argentina.

Root offsets or grow from seed.

LOBIVIA HERTRICHIANA

Globular, ribbed, clustering cactus from southeast Peru and Bolivia. 5cm (2in) across, its flowers in scarlet with yellow centres appear in early summer. Propagate by rooting offsets, or easily from seed.

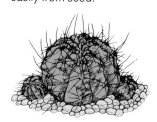

NOTOCACTUS

A genus of globular to cylindrical cacti from sub-tropical South America. All produce ribs; some make offsets at the base; all flower readily when small and some are prized for their

Cacti dominate this high-altitude, low-rainfall zone in the mountain province of Argentina.

decorative spines as much as for their striking flowers.

N. apricus (Uruguay) has large flowers, yellow with

reddish outer petals.
N. concinnus (S. Brazil and Uruguay) is free-flowering with yellow-red stigma.
N. leninghausii (Brazil), the golden ball cactus, has golden spines and can eventually grow to 60cm (2ft) tall. Rarely flowers. No offsets.
N. ottonis (S. Brazil, Uruguay & N. Argentina) is clump-forming and has bright yellow flowers.
N. scopa has bright yellow flowers. All are relatively easy to grow from seed which is freely available.

OPUNTIA
Species that originate from South America include
O. cylindrica (from Ecuador to Peru),
O. salmiana (from S. Brazil to N. Argentina),
O. subulata (Chile and Argentina), and *O. vestita* (Bolivia). *O. cylindrica* is as its name suggests a cylindrical type; others have round or pear-shaped, flattened segments joined together by a narrow strip.

PARODIA
Globular or cylindrical cacti, normally 10–12cm (4–5in) high and 10–15cm (4–6in) across with spiny tubercles. They bloom in late spring and summer, and grow naturally on the arid slopes of northern Argentina.

Parodia chrysacanthion

Three popular kinds are
P. aureispina: 20cm (8in) tall, yellow flowers 40mm (1½in) across;
P. chrysacanthion: golden yellow blooms, 50mm (2in) across; *P. sanguiniflora:* blood red blooms, 50mm (2in) across. All are shallow rooted; use half pots or pans.

REBUTIA
Rebutias are small desert cacti from the dry grasslands and thorn savannas of sub-tropical and temperate areas of Argentina and Bolivia. They are subject to very hot summers with occasional downpours of rain, and cold but dry winters. They start producing flowers when quite young (around two years from seed) and can be relied on to bloom each year. Stems are globular or cylindrical, pale or dark green and covered with spirally arranged rows of tubercles, each carrying a tuft of short white or brownish spines. Trumpet-shaped flowers, up to 5cm (2in) across, appear in late spring and early summer in rings around the base of the

plants. Blooms open in succession, each lasting two or three days.

Recommended kinds include: *R. calliantha* (blood-red flowers),

R. kupperana (deep red),
R. minuscula (light red),
R. senilis (pale red) and *R. xanthocarpa* (pale pink). There are many hybrids available.

TRICHOCEREUS SPACHIANUS
Erect columnar cactus from Argentina, up to 37.5cm (15in) tall in time. It branches from the base and rarely flowers in cultivation. Propagated by the removal of a basal branch, or cutting off and re-rooting the top of an old plant.

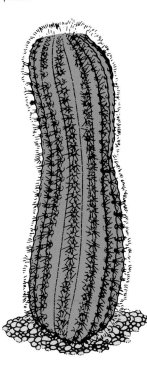

55

Calathea ornata *lives low down in humid forests*.

CALATHEA
(MARANTACEAE)

Calatheas are foliage plants from the tropical rain forests – mainly southern Brazil – that thrive on high humidity, and are closely related to maranta. Their mainly oval leaves, on long stalks, rise from a creeping rootstock.

C. bachemiana is grey-green with darker markings on the underside.

C. lancifolia (syn. **C. insignis**) has sword-shaped, wavy-edged leaves up to 45cm (18in) long but only 5cm (2in) wide. Pale green with darker markings.

C. lindeniana has large dark-green leaves with thin olive-green stripes in herring-bone fashion.

C. makoyana, commonly called peacock plant, has light olive-green upper leaf surface, feathered with very distinctive silvery markings and a similarly patterned

underside shot with a pinkish-red hue.

C. ornata, from Guyana, Colombia and Ecuador, has deep olive-green leaves with fine pink-white lines following the veining. The variety **C.o.** Sanderiana has larger and broader leaves.

C. picturata is rarely seen, but its silvered form, Argentea, is popular. Large, oval-pointed leaves are shiny, metallic green with emerald green edging.

C. zebrina is one of the most striking, with velvety emerald green leaves patterned with a paler midrib and vein areas.

Watering: Water thoroughly during the growing season, allowing just a little drying out between applications. In winter be much more sparing, but do not allow the mixture to dry out too much.

Potting mixture: Use $\frac{2}{3}$ soil-based mixture and $\frac{1}{3}$ coarse leaf mould or peat.

Propagation:
Overcrowded clumps can be divided in late spring, ensure that some roots are attached to all pieces.

Ideally use a heated propagator, if not available enclose in a plastic bag in a warm room.

Special points: Make the air more humid by standing on pebble trays. Best grown in a bottle garden or terrarium. Feed every two weeks from spring to early autumn.

CALCEOLARIA HERBEOHYBRIDA
(SCROPHULARIACEAE)

Modern-day calceolaria hybrids are derived from the Chilean species, **C. crenatiflora**. The almost circular, ballooned, pouch-shaped blooms produced in clusters at the tips of the branches give rise to such common names as slipper flower and pouch flower. Flowers can

Ctenanthes, from the warm, moist forests of Brazil, are related to marantas.

be in several shades of yellow, orange, red or autumn shades; most are spotted with a different colour or shade. Leaves are large and fleshy, usually heart-shaped and netted with fine veins.

Culture: Seed is sown in one summer to produce flowering plants in spring of the following year. Flowering period can be 6–8 weeks. Give good light but avoid direct sun; cool conditions will extend the life of the plants. Soak pots in water periodically to ensure a thorough wetting and never allow the mixture to dry out completely. Discard when blooms fade.

CAPSICUM ANNUUM
(SOLANACEAE)

Capsicums are peppers, those grown as house plants being ornamental peppers prized for their colourful, long-lasting, pod-like fruits. Today's hybrids are derived from wild forms native of Mexico, Colombia and the southern United States and are usually called Christmas or winter peppers as they appear on the market in late autumn and early winter. Fruit shape can be round, cone-like or slender-pointed and fruit colour from ivory white, bluey-purple, green, red or orange. Many change fruit colour as they age. The best are the small bushy plants.

Culture: Tolerant of a wide range of light, including some sun, keep cool, water generously – always enough to make the mixture thoroughly moist – stand on trays of moist pebbles for extra humidity. Throw away when fruits start to shrivel.

CISSUS RHOMBIFOLIA

From northern South America (Columbia and Brazil) as well as the West Indies (the section where its culture is discussed in detail). This popular climbing and trailing plant grows in montane forests where conditions enable it to survive a good range of temperature and light. Growth is fast (with short gaps between the nodes) when given bright light, slower under poorer light. Commonly called the grape ivy, its relation the kangaroo vine *(C. antarctica)* grows wild in Queensland and New South Wales, Australia and is discussed on pages 142–3.

CRYPTANTHUS
(BROMELIACEAE)

Cryptanthus are ground-hugging, star-shaped bromeliads from eastern Brazil, found growing on the forest floor, on rotting tree trunks and in gaps in rocks. Some flourish in full sun, some in dappled shade, some in the steamy tropical air of the rain forest, others just above sea-level where the air is dry. As house plants they are very adaptable provided some basic needs are provided.

Leaves are tough (often appearing thin), usually pointed and wavy-edged and covered with scales. These scales are easily spoiled by handling, but durable and serve the plants by absorbing water and nutrients from the air or tropical downpours. Flowers are small, dull white and appear in the centre of the rosette of leaves. Once having flowered, the rosette slowly dies. Roots are invariably sparse and shallow pans are sufficient for their needs. May be grown on bromeliad "trees", driftwood, tufa or other porous stone.

C. acaulis is 15cm (6in) across, medium green covered with grey scurf.

There are pink-tinged forms, Roseus and Ruber.

C. bivittatus Minor is 15cm (6in) across, wavy edged and bronze-green with two pink lengthwise stripes.

C. bromelioides Tricolor is 30cm (12in) across, with a loose rosette, medium green, ivory white, flashed with strong pink.

C. fosteranus grows to 45cm (18in) across, and is wavy-edged, subtly striped and crossbanded, and shot with bronze and purple.

C. zonatus grows to 37.5cm (15in) across, and is wavy edged, with mixed green, brown and white bands, having thick white scurf on the underside.

Watering: Water sparingly at all times.

Potting mixture: Use an equal-parts mixture of leaf mould and coarse peat.

Propagation: Cryptanthus make offsets either right at the base (when roots may already have been made) or in the lower leaf axils. Detach the latter only when they have made 2.5–5cm (1–2in) of growth; tiny ones are difficult to root.

Special points: Provide extra humidity by keeping pots on pebble trays. Feed every month from early spring to early autumn, splashing the dilute fertilizer onto the leaves and the mixture. Half- pots or pans are adequate; move on only when essential. Can be allowed to form clumps. **57**

CTENANTHE
(MARANTACEAE)

Ctenanthes are from the warm, moist forests of Brazil, but the three kinds popular as house plants have adapted well to home conditions. They are closely related to the maranta and have almost oblong leaves; usually held horizontally with the leaf stalks almost vertical. All in time grow 60–90cm (2–3ft) tall.

C. lubbersiana is fast growing with medium-green leaves subtly marked with patches of yellowy-green.

C. oppenheimiana Tricolor is a three-coloured form with more slender, lance-shaped leaves, deep olive-green boldly marked with large, irregular patches of creamy white. Leaf underside is bright red and this tinges the paler areas on the upperside.

C. setosa has hairy (sometimes purple) leaf stalks and pale green leaves marked with a deeper colour at the vein areas.

Watering: Water moderately while in active growth and sparingly when resting.

Potting mixture: Use equal parts of leaf mould and soil-based mix.

Propagation: Use basal offsets or shoot cuttings with three or four leaves attached. Use a propagator if available.

Special points: Feed every two weeks with the standard liquid fertilizer during the growing period. Stand pots on wide trays of moist pebbles. Pot on into larger pots in spring as necessary.

DIEFFENBACHIA
(ARACEAE)

D. amoena, which grows naturally in the hot humid forests of Colombia as well as Costa Rica, was one of the genus already discussed in the section on Central American house plants. Other recommended species include *D. imperialis* from Peru, and *D. bowmannii* which comes from eastern Brazil and, as its name suggests, was first discovered in its native habitat by David Bowman in 1866

Watering: Water moderately throughout the year if the room is warm, more sparingly in winter if the temperature falls below 60°F (15°C)).

Potting mixture: Use a soil-based potting mixture to which has been added up to one-third extra peat or leaf mould.

Propagation: Tip cuttings (beware of the sap) will root in spring in a propagator and sections of stem 7–10cm (3–4in) long will

also root and send out new shoots if planted on their sides in warmth.

Special points: Feed every two weeks during active growth. Ensure high humidity by using pebble-filled trays, and plunge the pot into moist peat. Growth can be quite rapid in good conditions and plants may need moving on into larger pots each spring.

EPISCIA
(GESNERIACEAE)

All species have creeping or trailing stems, sending out nodeless stolons bearing new plants at their tips. Indoors they can cover the surface of shallow pans or be grown in hanging baskets. Leaves are arranged in a rosette shape. Flowers are tubular, flaring out at the tip into lobes which may be fringed at the edges.

Most plants grown today are hybrids or variations of two species: *E. cupreata* (Columbia, Venezuela) and *E. reptans* (Colombia, Guyana, Brazil, Peru). Good leaf coloration and freedom of flowering have become commonplace in the later forms. Although plants are shielded from the fierce sun in the wild by the leafy canopy they need better light (but not

full sun) to flower well in the home. Humidity must be high, or leaves will develop brown edges and flower buds shrivel.

Hybrids
Acajou – silvery green pattern over dark tan, flowers red-orange almost everblooming;
Chocolate Soldier – dark chocolate brown leaves with a silver midrib, red blooms;
Cleopatra – (sometimes called Pink Brocade) quilted leaf surface, light green, white and pink colouring, orange-red flowers

Watering: Water generously during the active growing period but more sparingly during the winter rest period. See potting mixture (in this case the two are closely inter-connected).

Potting mixture: A fast-draining mixture is absolutely essential. An ideal mixture would be equal-parts sphagnum moss, peat and perlite or vermiculite, but if the sphagnum moss is not available it can be dispensed with. A surface layer of sphagnum is a refinement.

Propagation: The plants that develop at the ends of stolons root very easily if potted separately; keep warm and humid. Single leaves, with a short stalk attached (like those of the African violet) will root and develop small plantlets.

Special points: A really high level of humidity is essential if plants are to develop to their full potential. Stand on trays of moist pebbles or plunge pots into moist peat, or keep in a terrarium. Feed actively growing plants with a general purpose liquid fertilizer every two weeks. Plants are shallow-rooting and do best in wide-topped pans and hanging baskets where their offsets can send down roots. Episcias will not tolerate cool conditions.

FITTONIA VERSCHAFFELTII
(ACANTHACEAE)

Fittonias are ground-hugging plants from the rain forests of Colombia, Ecuador and Peru. They creep over the ground to form large patches but can also grow on fallen trees, rocks and the lower limbs of living trees. They need only enough decaying forest debris (or moss) for their roots to hold them fast, their other needs – warmth, high humidity and regular rainfall – being part of daily life in their tropical home.

Only one species is commonly grown indoors:

F. verschaffeltii, with olive-green leaves puckered slightly by the sunken carmine-red vein areas. A silver-veined form, *F. v.* Argyroneura, is freely available and a dwarf form, *F. v.* A. Nana, is becoming popular. The dwarf form rarely grows taller than 5cm (2in), the others may reach

12.5–15cm (5–6in) at maximum. Flowers are dull yellow and insignificant.

Watering: Great care is needed when watering. If given too much stems will rot; too little and leaves will curl and shrivel. Keep *just* moist.

Potting mixture: Use a peat-based mixture.

Propagation: Short tip cuttings root easily in good conditions. Creeping stems can also be layered by placing a plant in a bowl filled with moist peat when stems will root down into the peat. They can then be cut off and potted up individually.

Special points: Fittonias are by no means easy plants to grow well in the home, and do better in the humid air of a terrarium or bottle garden. Small pots are usually adequate. Fresh young plants are better than older ones as the latter tend to lose some of their lower leaves. Feed with half-strength liquid fertilizer every two weeks during the active growth perod.

FUCHSIA
(ONAGRACEAE)

Today's fuchsias are of very mixed parentage but with their origins mainly derived from *F. fulgens* (Mexico) and *F. magellanica* (Southern Chile and Argentina). They grow high in the mountainous regions of Mexico and the Andes but some come from other parts of South America and a few from many thousands of miles away in New Zealand. There are many

hundreds of named varieties from which to choose. Most have a bushy, upright habit, though a few are trailing. All produce flowers on thin stalks from the leaf axils and these may have four or more slender back-swept sepals and a thin, bell-shaped or skirted corolla, or have a thickened "skirt" of sepals made up of several rows or layers.

Watering: Water liberally during the active growing season to keep the mixture constantly moist. Give only enough to prevent the mixture from becoming dust-dry during the winter rest period.

Potting mixture: Use a soil-based mixture.

Propagation: Tip cuttings, 5–10cm (2–4in) long, root very easily, particularly if taken at the end of the summer, and planted in a peat and sand mixture. Small plants overwintered at 50°F (10°C) and kept growing through the winter will make good flowering-sized plants for blooming from mid-spring onwards. Plant several rooted cuttings of the trailing kinds in a hanging basket.

Special points: Pinch out growing points to make bushy plants if side-growths are not made naturally, but do not do this when flower

buds are imminent or blooms will be lost. Feed every two weeks from spring to end-summer with a high potash liquid fertilizer. Older plants can be rested dryish at the root and then be cut back at the end of winter when they will make strong growth from the woody framework of stems. Stand plants on trays of moistened pebbles, (or plunge in moist peat) to increase humidity, and mist-spray hanging basket plants regularly. Watch out for aphids.

GUZMANIA
(BROMELIACEAE)

Leaves are almost always soft, shiny and pliable and arranged in a loose rosette shape. The centre of the rosette makes a shallow cup with water collecting in the angles formed at the leaf bases. The flowerhead is held clear of the foliage but may be a tall, impressive spike or a tuft of colourful bracts. Actual flowers are usually white or yellow, small and short-lived, peeping through the bracts or from the colourful flowerhead. Like most bromeliads, the rosette of leaves blooms once only.

G. lingulata, found from Central America to Paraguay, Mato Grosso, Ecuador, Bolivia and growing at heights of 900–1800m (3000–6000ft) in the Colombian Andes, it has various forms which are preferred for cultivation.

G. l. Cardinalis, grows high in the mountains, has 2.5cm (1in) wide, plain green leaves and bright red bracts.

Fittonias are ground-hugging, rain forest plants requiring only debris as a rooting medium.

HIPPEASTRUM
(AMARYLLIDACEAE)

G.l. var. Minor, rarely grows taller than 30.5cm (12in) in Brazilian and Nicaraguan rain forests. It is sometimes found totally obscuring the limbs of the trees used as its base. Bracts are orange.

G. monostachia (syn. *G. tricolor*) has spiky-looking bright-green leaves and a tube-shaped flowerhead made up of many greenish-white bracts, tipped with orange or red and striped with purple. Found in the West Indies, Florida, Central and South America to the south of Brazil.

G. musaica is found in the forests and mangrove swamps of Colombia and Panama. Its bright-green leaves are striped crosswise with thin brown lines above and netted with purple lines

below. A tall flowerstalk carries many flesh-pink, egg-shaped flowers cupped within yellow bracts.

Watering: Water moderately, allowing the mixture to dry out a little before giving more. Ideally use rain water.

Potting mixture: Use equal parts soil-based mixture, coarse leaf mould and peat. Other mixtures may be used but they *must* be open and quick-draining.

Propagation: Take away offsets that form around the base of the parent plant, but not before they are about 7.5cm (3in) long. Root in heated propagator.

Special points: Feed young plants every two

weeks with a half-strength liquid fertilizer from early spring to early autumn. To increase the level of humidity stand pots on trays of moist pebbles or plunge pot in moist peat. Small pots are adequate for these plants as they make relatively compact roots.

Hippeastrums are popular tender bulbous plants, often called amaryllis (botanists continue to argue about the correct name).

Bulbs are very large, brown-jacketed and are best grown only half buried in the potting mixture. Leaves are fleshy, strap-shaped, 3–5cm (1½–2in) wide and up to

Guzmania lingulata, *a widely distributed epiphyte from the rain forests of South America.*

45cm (18in) long, and arranged in two arching ranks. The sturdy flower bud pushes up at the side of the leaf growth, the stalk reaching 15cm (18in) tall and carrying up to four large trumpet-shaped flowers. Very large bulbs may produce two flowerstalks. Blooms range from almost pure white, all pink, red and orange shades and may be a solid one colour or streaked with paler shades, white or green.

Watering: When dry bulbs are potted up water should be given very sparingly at first, but increased when the root system and top growth develop. Start to drench the mixture once the flowerstalk is half grown but allow the mixture to dry out a little before giving more. Gradually stop water from late summer on and leave totally dry until late winter, or until new growth (hopefully a flower bud) can be seen.

Potting mixture: Use a soil-based mixture.

Propagation: Increase by taking off small bulbs that develop around the base of the larger bulb. Pot up separately and grow on.

Special points: Sun is vitally important to ripen the bulb and encourage flowering during the following year. A spell in the garden often ensures this. Feed every two weeks with a high-potash fertilizer during the growing season. As leaves yellow in autumn, gradually stop watering and feeding. Cut off the embryo seedhead as blooms fade but allow the flowerstalk to die down naturally. Repot only when absolutely

essential; topdress in other years.

MARANTA LEUCONEURA
(MARANTACEAE)

Marantas are low-growing, creeping plants from Brazil, found more often in clearings where the sun enters the forest rather than in heavy shade. The sheathed stems and leaf stalks are practically vertical, but the oval oblong blades of the leaves are held horizontally. At night the leaves partly fold together, giving rise to one of its common names, the "prayer plant".

M. l. Erythroneura (often incorrectly called *M. l.* Erythrophylla) has deep olive-green leaves, lighter green around the midrib and with red veins and leaf underside. Very colourful.

M. l. Kerchoviana, also called "rabbit's foot" and "rabbit's tracks", has light green leaves, lighter vein areas and deep brown markings in a row on either side of the midrib. The underside is slate-grey.

M. l. Massangeana is less often seen; it has dark green leaves with silvery-grey veins and mid-rib area.

Watering: Water generously during active growth and more sparingly in winter.

Potting mixture: Use a peat-based mixture.

Propagation: Divide overcrowded clumps in spring or detach sections with three or four leaves and treat as cuttings.

Special points: Provide a moist atmosphere. Plants are relatively shallow rooting and half-pots or pans are normally suitable. Feed fortnightly from spring to early autumn. Good in hanging baskets (for east or west-facing windows, *not* the south).

MICROCOELUM WEDDELLIANUM
(PALMAE)

Known also as *Cocos weddelliana* and *Syagrus weddelliana*, this palm is native of the very humid tropical rain forests of Brazil where it receives daily rain, air saturated with moisture and protection on the forest floor from drying winds and draughts.

Stems are fibrous, with loose brown fibre, fronds to 60cm (2ft) long and divided

like a feather into many, very narrow, shiny segments. Give good light without direct sun. Minimum temperature 60°F (15°C).

Watering: Water thoroughly and then allow a little drying out before repeating. Never allow to become completely dry or brown tips will develop.

Potting mixture: Use an equal-parts mixture of soil-based mix and leaf mould or coarse peat.

Propagation: Not practicable indoors.

Special points: Really moist air is essential – stand on a moist pebble tray and mist-spray regularly. Feed with a half-strength liquid fertilizer from early spring to early autumn. Be very careful when repotting not to damage the roots, repot in spring only when really necessary.

MIMOSA PUDICA
(LEGUMINOSAE)

The sensitive plant, *M. pudica*, is a small shrub from the rain forests of

61

tropical America, and is one of nature's curiosities. Its finely divided leaves are highly sensitive and if touched the segments fold together in pairs and temporarily collapse. This usually triggers off the collapse of large sections or indeed the whole of the plant, but it will recover after a short while. The stems are a little thorny and small clumps of fluffy mauve-pink flowers may appear. It is best treated as an annual

Culture: Raised from seed. Grow in a warm and sunny window, use a soil-based mix, water moderately, feed fortnightly and discard in late autumn.

NEOREGELIA
(BROMELIACEAE)

Neoregelias are epiphytic bromeliads found over large areas of Brazil. Some are from the high cloud forests, others just above sea-level around Rio de Janiero. Most thrive in some light shade and tend to be on the lower limbs of trees rather than the high leafy canopy. A distinguishing feature is the way the centre of the plant becomes flushed with colouring (usually red) as flowering time approaches. The flowerhead has no stalk; it fills the central cup at water level and the tiny flowers open up from it over several weeks.

N. carolinae makes a flat rosette up to 18 inches across; improved forms are *N. c.* Marechalii (green with carmine-red centre), *N. c.* Meyendorffii with coppery leaves whose centres go deep maroon and *N. c.*

Tricolor which is striped

with white and soft pink, with a brilliant red middle.

N. concentrica is pale green speckled purple, with black spines on the edges, and silvery grey on the underside.

N. marmorata is light green, marbled red.

N. sarmentosa is stoloniferous, dark green with purple sheen. Inner leaves are brown to red or speckled in two colours. There is no colour change at flowering time.

N. spectabilis (painted fingernail plant) is olive green, the leaf tips turning red.

Watering: Water moderately but allow a certain amount of drying out between applications. Keep the central cup filled except when flowerhead appears. Change water in cup frequently.

Potting mixture: Use equal parts leaf mould, coarse peat and sand or perlite.

Propagation: Use young offsets near the base or on the ends of the stolons. Spring is the best season for this.

Special points: Pot on only when absolutely necessary – the 12.5cm (5in) size is likely to be the maximum needed. Feed active plants every two weeks; splash

general fertilizer on the leaves and into the cup.

NEPHROLEPIS
(POLYPODIACEAE)

Excellent hanging basket plants, the popular Nephrolepis ferns grow wild in many parts of the tropics. They are described in detail in the section on North and Central America.

NIDULARIUM
(BROMELIACEAE)

Nidulariums are epiphytic bromeliads from high in the leafy canopy of the cloud forests of south and eastern Brazil.

N. fulgens has spiny-edged, light green, shiny leaves spotted darker green.

N. innocentii has metallic, dark-green leaves speckled purple, wine-red underside. A form, *N. i. lineatum*, has several ivory, lengthwise stripes.

N. purpureum has deep green leaves shot with purple, maroon on underside.

Watering: Water moderately at all times.

Potting mixture: Use equal parts leaf mould, coarse peat and sand or perlite.

Propagation: Use well-developed offsets that grow on stolons from the base.

Special points: Feed actively growing plants standard fertilizer at half strength every two weeks. Stand on trays of moist pebbles. 10–12.5cm (4–5in) pots should be maximum needed. Keep water in central cup fresh by changing frequently.

PACHYSTACHYS LUTEA
(ACANTHACEAE)

Re-introduced recently, *P. lutea* from Peru makes a small upright shrub about 45cm (18in) tall. The leaves are thin and pointed and netted with darker veining. The flowerheads are cone-shaped clusters of bright, golden-yellow bracts through which the white tubular flowers poke.

Watering: Water moderately from spring to early autumn, sparingly during the winter rest period.

Potting mixture: Use soil-based mixture.

Propagation: Use tip cuttings 7.5–10cm (3–4in) long in spring.

Special points: Stand on trays of moist gravel. Prune drastically in mid-late winter, cutting back at least half of the previous year's growth. Move on into the next size pot when some new growth has been made.

PASSIFLORA CAERULEA
(PASSIFLORACEAE)

P. caerulea is hardier than most other passion flowers although it comes from the jungles of Brazil and Argentina. It is a very vigorous climber but adapts well to indoor conditions when trained around a hoop of wire or cane. The dark-green leaves are divided into five or more pointed segments arranged like a fan; corkscrew-like tendrils haul the stems close to whatever they may contact. The flowers are the most incredible mixture of parts – blue and green with a "corona" of radiating blue and white filaments. It is ideal for a large cool space.

Watering: Water plentifully when in active growth and sparingly in winter.

Potting mixture: Use a soil-based potting mixture.

Propagation: Tip cuttings 7.5–10cm (3–4in) long root

relatively easily if kept warm and moist in late spring or summer.

Special points: In a warm room they must be stood on trays of moist pebbles or flower buds will fall. Feed every two weeks with a standard liquid fertilizer from early spring to early autumn. During late winter plants should be pruned drastically, cutting away completely all weak growth, cutting back almost to the main stems all side growths, and reducing the number of stems to four or six. Repot every spring, moving on into the next size pot whenever really necessary; overpotting will result in poor flowering. Train stems around the supports provided.

PEPEROMIA
(PIPERACEAE)

Peperomias inhabit the humid tropical rain forests of both the West Indies, Central and South America. Recommended species from Brazil, Ecuador, Peru and Venezuela include:

P. argyreia (syn. *P. sandersii*) from Brazil. It is popularly called the watermelon plant, with almost round leaves that are marked with alternate silver and dark-green bands.

P. caperata, also from Brazil, has small, very deep-green, heart-shaped leaves with a deeply corrugated surface. Leaf stalks are reddish. There is a variegated leaved form, Variegata, with 2.5–4cm (1–1½in) leaves carrying broad white or cream borders.

P. fraseri (syn. *P. resediflora*) from Ecuador has shiny-green heart-shaped leaves and an untypical fluffy, creamy-white flower spike carried on tall stalks.

P. griseoargentea (syn. *P. hederifolia*) from Brazil is often called ivy or silverleaf peperomia and carries heart-shaped, greyish-green leaves with a metallic sheen. Vein areas are darker and leafstalks pinkish.

P. obtusifolia is an erect sub-shrubby plant from Venezuela. Leaves are fleshy, shiny and almost oval, a deep green with red edging. There are several variegated-leaved forms: Alba, Albo-marginata, Greengold and Variegata.

P. scandens (syn. *P. serpens*) is a trailer from Peru, the West Indies, Panama and Brazil. Only the variegated form is grown as a house plant – Variegata. Leaves are heart-shaped, about 5cm (2in) long, green with a yellow border. Leafstalks are red and stems may grow to 60cm (2ft) in length.

Watering: More than anything else, over-watering kills peperomias. Water sparingly at all times and avoid wetting leaves and stems – rot can set in if

water collects where several stems join.

Potting mixture: Peat-based potting mixtures suit them best.

Propagation: All kinds can be propagated by using 50mm–7cm (2–3in) long tip cuttings. The rooting mixture needs to be just moist and one made up of equal-parts coarse sand and peat is best.

Special points: These plants will not tolerate temperatures below 50°F (10°C), unless they are fairly dry at the root. They do however have high humidity in their native habitat and in a warm room need to stand on trays filled with moist pebbles. Small pots are normally adequate as they make little root. If stems tend to elongate without branching, nip out the growing points to encourage breaks.

PHILODENDRON
(ARACEAE)

The Greek word *philodendron* means "tree lover" and aptly describes the members of this large and varied family of South American plants. There are two distinct kinds of philodendron, those found clambering by means of aerial roots up the trunks and along the limbs of the rain forest trees, and those that do not climb but grow perched high in the middle layers of the leafy canopy. The latter germinated and developed in a shallow patch of detritus lodged in a fork or crotch of the branches. Seedlings of the climbing kinds may have started life in the thin layer of forest floor litter but quickly took to tree trunks in search of better light.

Aerial roots develop at each leaf node and may drop 30 metres or more from tree to soil level. With age, plants may become independent of their basal roots and original stem. The warm and humid atmosphere make germination and later development an easy matter.

The non-climbing forms make a short, stout stem with large leaves on usually long stalks radiating from a central point, with a spread of a couple of metres or more. The climbing kinds may grow to 30m (100ft) in length. Most adapt well to the very different conditions found in the average home. A number display quite different characteristics when young to those they develop when more mature. See also Central America.

P. bipinnatifidum is one of the non-climbing (Americans call them self-heading) philodendrons from south eastern and southern Brazil, where it makes a large and impressive specimen. Indoors in a large pot it may eventually reach 1.25–1.5m (4–5ft) tall. Its dark green, arrow-shaped leaves are deeply incised to the point where they appear divided into separate leaflets. Long leafstalks make the spread of the plant considerable.

P. pedatum (Syn, **P. laciniatum**) is a relatively slow-growing climber from Guyana, Venezuela and Brazil. Of rather sprawling habit, it sometimes hangs from tree branches,

sending out numerous side branches in search of another foothold. Leaves are shiny, mid-green, up to 25cm (10in) long and deeply lobed into at least five distinct lobes. The back two lobes are often themselves divided. Maximum growth in the home around 1.25m (4ft).

P. selloum is a large, fast-growing non-climber from south west Brazil. It likes moist conditions and has

been found clinging to river banks and gorges, near waterfalls where the humidity is as high as 90–100%. The short, thick, trunk-like stem supports much-divided, dark-green leaves up to 38cm (15in) across. The lobe at the tip of the leaf is invariably short. A magnificent plant indoors if space allows.

P. angustisectum (syn. **P. elegans**) is Colombian and a climber with 30.5–38cm (12–14in) long leaves divided up into many narrow, finger-like, dark-green segments. It needs a support, growing to 2–2.5m (4 or 5ft) tall indoors and is a good candidate for a moss pole.

P. bipennifolium also climbs and is found in quantity in the humid forests spread over a large section of Brazil. The olive-

green leaves of young plants are roughly heart-shaped but more mature plants display the typical narrow-waisted leaves – like the body of a violin. Growth is rapid, quickly reaching 1.8m (6ft), and stout supports are needed.

P. erubescens is one of the most striking of the Colombian species and has been much used in hybridization. Its 25cm (10in) arrow-shaped leaves have a deep green upper surface and a rich, coppery-red underside. When seen against the light the effect is impressive. Provide stout stakes.

P. imbe is a native of Rio de Janeiro and the other states of south east Brazil, and a strong climber. Its heart-shaped, mid-green leaves are around 25cm (10in) long and held on leafstalks of equal length, each slightly overlapping its predecessors. In bright light there is a tinge of rusty-red on the leaf underside. Can grow to 1.8m (6ft) tall.

P. scandens is native of most of tropical America, and also the most popular kind in cultivation and the easiest to grow. Leaves are 10cm (4in) long, on short leafstalks, have a bronze tinge when first they unfurl

There are two distinct kinds of philodendron: those that clamber up trunks by means of aerial roots (these are candidates for moss poles in the home) and those that grow perched in the middle layer of the forest.

but later become leathery and dark green. Very adaptable to being grown indoors as a climber, (staked or on a moss-covered pole), allowed to trail over the edge of a plant trough of from a hanging basket.

P. Burgundy is a hybrid of complex origin – mainly South American with large shield-shaped leaves, shot with burgundy red on the underside and long leaf stalks. A parent of some of the deep red-leaved varieties.

Watering: When plants are in active growth give a thorough watering and then no more until the mixture has become fairly dry. In winter give just enough to prevent the mixture from drying out. Feed every two weeks in the active growing season with a high-nitrogen liquid fertilizer.

Potting mixture: Use a mixture of equal parts loam-based mix and rough leaf mould or coarse peat.

Propagation: Propagate climbing philodendrons by means of tip cuttings taken in spring and early summer. Plant up in peat and sand and enclose in a large plastic bag and keep warm and humid. Small offsets often appear at the base of plants and these root easily. The non-climbers are normally grown from seed which is available from specialist growers.

Special points: Good light is essential to get close, typical growth; in poor light stems become elongated. An east- or west-facing window is best. Maximize humidity in dry rooms.

Move on into larger pots every other year. Support climbing kinds with stout stakes, tie in loose stems, and tuck aerial roots into the pot as they grow. If grown on moss poles the moss *must* be kept constantly moist or roots will not use it. Will not tolerate temperatures below 55°F (13°C).

PILEA SPRUCEANA
(URTICACEAE)

Like all pileas that are grown as house plants, *P. spruceana*, from Peru and Bolivia, looks best when planted in a shallow pan: it is surface-rooting. Some authorities have claimed that the plant is in fact no more than a form of *P. involucrata* (see North & Central America). However there are named forms of *P. spruceana* that are particularly recommended: *P. s.* Norfolk is unquestionably a very fine sort with almost round leaves packed close together and forming clumps of growths. Leaves are striped metallic silver on bronze, with wine-red shading on new leaves. More upright growing kinds are *P. s.* Bronze (bronze) and *P. s.* Silver tree (silver banding on pointed deep-green leaves) the whole with an open appearance.

Watering: Water moderately during active growth, more sparingly in the winter rest period.

Potting mixture: Use a peat-based mixture, or an equal-parts mixture of peat and soil-based mixture.

Propagation: Tip cuttings and side shoots root very easily from late spring, through the summer. Start new plants each year.

Special points: Stand on moist pebble trays. Feed fortnightly from late spring to end summer.

POLYPODIUM AUREUM
(POLYPODIACEAE)

Like *Davallia fejeensis*, a member of the same family (see Australasia & the Pacific Islands), *P. aureum* is commonly called the hare's foot fern. It grows wild in sub-tropical forests from Florida to Argentina. See North & Central America for full description.

RHIPSALIDOPSIS
(CACTACEAE)

Rhipsalidopsis are epiphytic jungle cacti found in the wet and warm rain forests of south-east Brazil.

Under the upper leafy canopy they receive some protection from full sun and in the home they should not be exposed to hot summer sun. Only two species are known, but numerous hybrids have been raised from them. Stems are flattened, in jointed segments; they start growing upright but later arch over. Funnel-shaped flowers appear singly or in clusters of two or three at the ends of the stems in spring – a common name is Easter cactus. Good in hanging baskets.

R. gaertneri (syn. *Schlumbergera gaertneri*) has scarlet flowers.
R. rosea has small narrow segments, rose-pink flowers.
Hybrids include: Paleface, Electra, Spring Dazzler.

Watering: In the wild they are subject to very heavy rain and then a dry period. In the home water plentifully but allow a little drying out between applications. Give a brief (4–6 weeks) rest after flowering, watering very sparingly for that time, then renew earlier pattern.

Potting mixture: Use $\frac{2}{3}$ peat-based mixture and $\frac{1}{3}$ coarse sand or perlite.

Propagation: Stems comprising two or three segments (use a sharp blade to cut through the hard stem core) root easily in late spring or early summer. Plant several together for best effect. Can also be grown from seed.

Special points: Feed with a high-potash liquid fertilizer every two weeks from around late winter/early spring when buds are forming. Alternate this feed with a standard liquid feed after the short rest period and continue until late autumn. Stand on moist pebble trays or plunge in peat and mist-spray the stems. Renew every two or three years as younger plants are much the best.

Bromeliads, philodendrons and ferns, are utilizing a tree epiphytically.

even deeply incised – a distinguishing feature.

S. bridgesii (syn. *S. buckleyi*), a hybrid, flowers around Christmas with rose-purple or magenta blooms.

S. truncata (syn. *Zygocactus truncatus*) blooms earlier and is called crab or lobster cactus. Flowers are rose-pink.

There a number of hybrids with differing flower colour, from almost white through orange shades to deep red.

RUELLIA MAKOYANA
(ACANTHACEAE)

R. makoyana is a trailing and creeping plant from the forest areas of Brazil with velvety, elliptic, deep olive-green leaves with wide silvery vein areas and a dark blue-purple underside. Stems branch frequently and in good growing conditions may reach 60cm (2ft) in length. Flowers appear in late autumn and early winter and are rose-red, trumpet-shaped and appear singly from the leaf axils. Good in a hanging basket.

Watering: Water moderately during the growing period and very sparingly in winter, particularly if the temperature goes below 60°F, 15°C.

Potting mixture: Use half soil-based and half peat-based mixture, or leaf mould.

Propagation: Take tip cuttings in early summer, enclose in a plastic bag or use a propagator; high humidity is essential.

Special points: Dry air causes brown leaf tips and lack of flowers. Stand on trays of moist pebbles or plunge in moist peat, and mist-spray hanging basket plants. Roots are shallow and half-pots or pans are adequate. Feed actively growing plants every two weeks. Move on into larger pots in spring.

SCHLUMBERGERA
(CACTACEAE)

Schlumbergeras are epiphytic jungle cacti from southern Brazil, very closely related to rhipsalidopsis. The stems are flattened and jointed leaf-like segments, upright at first but later arching, and carry flowers with backswept petals in tiers and prominent pistils. They are late autumn- and winter-flowering and commonly called the Christmas cactus. Segments are usually notched at the edges or

Watering: In the wild the growth pattern is for stems to develop from early spring to early autumn, when watering should be plentiful; there should be a period of moderate watering until after flowering and then a 4–6 week rest period with very sparse watering – just enough to prevent drying out.

Potting mixture: Use peat-based mixture to which has been added up to $\frac{1}{3}$ extra coarse sand or perlite.

Propagation: Use stem cuttings made up of two or three segments in early spring. When taking cuttings use a sharp knife to avoid damage to the midrib.

Special points: Stand on trays of moist pebbles, and spray stems in warm periods. Do not turn plants round when flower buds have partly developed,

Gloxinias are hybrids from Sinningia speciosa.

since a change of light direction can cause them to fall off (though some bud drop is inevitable). Pot on into slightly larger pots each spring, but renew plants frequently as younger ones are better than old. Feed actively growing plants every two weeks.

SINNINGIA (GESNERIACEAE)

Few sinningia species are in cultivation; the plants generally called gloxinias are actually hybrids from *S. speciosa*, a Brazilian plant. Plants that for years were called *Rechsteineria cardinalis* are now categorised as *S. cardinalis* and those sold as *R. leucotricha* are now *S. leucotricha*. These are widely spread through central America and Brazil.

Recently more and more miniature sinningias (mainly hybrids with the Brazilian *S. pusilla* as one parent) have become available.

All sinningias have a tuberous base, usually onlypartly buried in the soil; all have a dormant period, but this may be quite short.

S. cardinalis (Brazil and Central America) starts into growth in spring, reaches about 25cm (10in) tall and carries heart-shaped to oval, slightly hairy leaves and in late summer, blood-red tubular flowers. These open in succession and provide bloom over about three months.

S. leucotricha (Brazil: W. Parana) has leaves and stems thickly coated with silky white har and pink flowers. Growth is short at first, flowers are produced and then the stems grow longer and the leaves get bigger. The white hairy coating is thickest and most effective in the early stages of growth.

S. speciosa hybrids (gloxinias) (Brazil) are virtually stemless with opposite pairs of fleshy, oval and velvety leaves and from the centre come large, slightly upturned, bell-shaped flowers. These may be white, red and pink shades, blue and purple shades, or creamy coloured. Some are ruffled at the petal edges, others piped with white or another colour or shade and some are spotted or netted with red or purple. Double-flowered and dwarf-growing forms are also available.

The miniatures, mainly hybrids with *S. pusilla* (Brazil) make a flat rosette 12.5mm ($\frac{1}{2}$in) long, with hairy leaves and violet to lavender flowers 20mm ($\frac{3}{4}$in) long. Blooms have much the appearance of a tiny blue streptocarpus. Three recommended hybrids are Dollbaby, Cindy and Freckles.

Watering: Water generously during the active growing season, allowing the mixture to dry out a little between applications. Gradually reduce the amount given as leaves yellow and dormancy starts, rest completely dry. See special points.

Potting mixture: Sinningias prefer a slightly alkaline, well-aerated potting mixture. Use equal parts peat, coarse leaf mould and perlite or vermiculite, to which has been added two teaspoons of dolomite lime per 7.5cm (3in) pot of mix.

Propagation: Short stem cuttings taken in early summer can be induced to form small tubers if planted in a propagator. Seed is the usual way of increasing the miniatures.

Special points: A high level of humidity is absolutely essential for success; stand on wide trays of moist pebbles throughout the active growing period. Tubers of the hybrids of *S. speciosa* are normally taken out of their containers, shaken free of mixture and stored for the winter in dryish peat in a plastic bag.
S. Cardinalis is best left in its pot and kept dry until being repotted in spring. The miniatures have hardly any rest period – simply do not water for, say, one month. Shallow pans are normally adequate as roots spread outwards. A half-strength liquid fertilizer can be given to the larger plants, at every watering, once 7.5–10cm (3–4in) of top growth has been made. They are greedy feeders.

SOLANUM (SOLANACEAE)

Two solanums are popular autumn- and early-winter-fruiting sub-shrubs:

S. capsicastrum from Brazil and *S. pseudocapsicum* is said to have been introduced from Madeira in 1596, but its true origins remain obscure.

S. capsicastrum (false Jerusalem cherry) has slightly hairy leaves and oval, orange fruits, 12.5–20mm ($\frac{1}{2}$–$\frac{3}{4}$in) in diameter.

S. pseudocapsicum (Jerusalem cherry) makes a larger, more robust plant

67

and has larger, slightly more rounded, orange-red fruit. There are dwarf forms of the latter which are smaller in scale but fruit size is little, if at all, reduced in size.

Culture: Raised from seed. Grow in really bright light, pot on into larger pots if necessary using a soil-based mixture, stand on trays of moist pebbles, water generously and discard when fruits fall or shrivel.

SPATHIPHYLLUM (ARACEAE)

Two spathiphyllums are popular house plants, *S. wallisi* from Colombia and Venezuela, and the

hybrid Mauna Loa, derived from the Colombian *S. floribunda* and another hybrid. Spathiphyllums are rain-forest plants that enjoy warmth and very high humidity. The rootstock is a creeping rhizome, the leaves are lance-shaped, dark green and appear from sheathed stems. The flowerhead is a white, arum-like spathe enclosing a cream-coloured spadix. The hybrid grows to 45cm (18in), while the species rarely tops 30cm (12in).

Watering: Water moderately at all times.

Potting mixture: Use a peat-based mixture.

Propagation: Divide overcrowded clumps in spring, ensuring that each piece has a stout piece of rhizome at the base.

Special points: Stand on trays of moist pebbles and mist-spray foliage weekly. Feed every two weeks during the active growth period. Watch out for red spider mites in warm rooms.

STROMANTHE (MARANTACEAE)

Closely related to maranta, stromanthes are mainly plants from the forest floor (a few may grow as epiphytes) in the warmth and high humidity of Brazilian forests. Two are popular house plants, each with feathery markings running from a central midrib of the leaf.

S. amabilis is low growing with leaves held flat. Leaf coloration is a subtle mixture of grey-green and mid-green, the leaf underside greyish.

S. sanguinea holds its leaves almost vertical and these are sword shaped, up

to 45cm (18in) long and marked emerald green on pale green, with the underside deep red.

Watering: Water moderately throughout the year.

Potting mixture: Use a peat-based mixture.

Propagation: Split up clumps in spring, retaining some of the rhizomes with each piece.

Special points: Stand on trays of moist pebbles or plunge in moist peat. Repot every other year, when the rhizomes start to grow over the side of the pots. Half-pots or pans are suitable. Feed every two weeks during the growing period.

TILLANDSIA (BROMELIACEAE)

Tillandsias are a huge family of bromeliads of diverse size and shape, some with typical bromeliad form (a rosette of leathery leaves), others with tiny grass-like leaves arranged in clumps, and one looking more like a lichen. Some are from the moist rain forests of Peru; others predominently populate large areas of high Andean mountain sides in Peru and Ecuador; some can grow anywhere, provided the air is moist, even on telegraph wires. Most protect themselves from extremes of habitat (cold, a high level of ultra-violet, or drying winds) by a covering of white or grey scurfy scales.

T. cyanea grows in full sun in Ecuador, makes stiff rosettes of leaves and a

flowerhead of many overlapping pinkish bracts. Violet-blue, 5cm (2in) flowers appear in succession over several weeks.

T. lindenii (N.W. Peru) is similar to the above but has a longer stalk to the flowerhead and deeper blue flowers.

Watering: Spray daily; little watering is required as these plants satisfy most of their watering needs from taking moisture from the air.

Potting mixture: Coarse leaf mould, half-rotted pine needles or coarse peat.

Propagation: Take well-developed offsets.

Special points: Local humidity must be high; try anything to recreate the feel of a steamy jungle – mist-spray daily; stand above (but not in) bowls of water in a warm atmosphere.

TRADESCANTIA (COMMELINACEAE)

Living on the floor of the rain forests of Mexico and South America, these Wandering Jews (as they are known) enjoy constant warmth and humidity, filtered light and the protection from climatic extremes given by the forest canopy. See also North and Central America.

T. blossfeldiana is from Argentina with deep, olive-green leaves – purple on the underside – and pink flowers. There is a striking variegated-leaved form, *T. b.* Variegata, with broad bands of pink and cream in the leaves.

T. fluminensis from Brazil and Argentina is the most widely grown kind. Its thinner leaves are striped with white or yellow with a light purple underside. There are many slightly different forms, some with purple shading in the white leaf variegation. Flowers white.

Watering: Give thorough soakings but then allow the mixture to begin to dry out before applying more.

Potting mixture: Use a soil-based potting mixture.

Propagation: Cuttings of all tradescantias root very easily, throughout most of the year. They will even produce roots if 5–7.5cm (2–3in) long cuttings are stood in a glass of water. Plant 4–6 cuttings in one pot for a quick, bushy effect and propagate at least once a year as young plants are much more attractive than older ones.

Special points: Feed plants every two weeks with

a standard liquid fertilizer once roots have filled the pots. Nip out the growing tips periodically to induce bushy, much-branched growths. Should any non-variegated shoots appear on plants with variegated foliage, cut them out right to the base or they will develop at the expense of the more colourful ones. Ideal for hanging baskets in an east or west-facing window.

VRIESEA
(BROMELIACEAE)

Vrieseas are epiphytic and terrestrial bromeliads from the rain and cloud forests of South America – mainly southern Brazil. Most have soft, pliant leaves (without barbed edges) arranged in a loose rosette. A striking flowerhead is held well clear of the foliage. In the wild they grow mainly on the lower limbs of trees where they receive dappled sunlight, but also cling to rocks and cliffs. They all enjoy really humid conditions. Those grown as house plants adapt well to home conditions, some being prized for their highly decorative leaf markings, others for their flowerhead.

V. fenestralis, a foliage type, has light green leaves patterned with a fine network of darker purple markings. It makes a plant about 45cm (18in) through. It is shy in producing its tall branched flowerstalk of green, purple-spotted bracts and yellow flowers.

V. hieroglyphica, also grown for its fine foliage, has shiny bright green leaves marked with irregular

patches in a most striking way, up to 60cm (2ft) across. It only flowers at an advanced age, its upright spike having green bracts and yellow flowers.

V. psittacina has plain yellowish-green, shiny leaves, reaching 20–30cm (8–12in) across. The very colourful flowerspike of red and yellow is produced on plants around two years old.

V. saundersii is another small plant, with matt grey-green leaves densely spotted on the underside with purple, and an attractive yellow forked flowerhead.

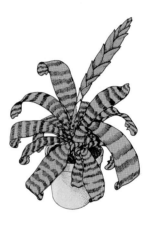

V. splendens (flaming sword), the most popular species, has dark green leaves barred with purple-black crossbanding, and a 30–38cm (12–15in) spread. The flowerspike is upright, made up of a flattened blade of bright-red bracts through which peep yellow flowers. There are a number of variants with differing bract colouring and with stronger or weaker leaf marking.

Like most bromeliads, once having flowered the rosette of leaves does not do so again, although it may remain attractive for several

months after flowering.

Watering: Water generously during the active growth period, filling up the central cup and allowing the excess to run through to the lower leaf axils and the potting mixture. Allow the mixture to dry out a little before applying more and be more sparing with water during the winter. Stop watering into the cup when the flowerspike is obvious, and place it instead around the lower leaves.

Potting mixture: Use a mixture of equal parts coarse leaf mould and rough peat.

Propagation: Few offsets are made at the very base of the plants, but these should be used for preference, for often they may have roots already attached to them. Vrieseas also make offsets in the lower leaf axils (divorced from the potting mixture). Do not detach these until they are 7.5–15cm (3–6in) long as immature offsets are difficult to root. Use a heated propagator.

Special points: Feed actively growing plants every two weeks with a half-strength liquid fertilizer, splashing it into the central cup and over the leaves (they can take up plant food). An alternative way of continuing to grow plants that have flowered is to cut down the old rosette of leaves and allow the offsets in the leaf axils to develop into a plant with multiple growing points. Stand all plants on trays of moist pebbles to increase humidity and spray plants with a handsprayer in warmer weather.

Europe & North Africa

Within the broad region of the Mediterranean, we find quite a range of plants popularly grown indoors. There are the succulent aeoniums, adapted to withstand the hot, dry summer of the Canaries and Morocco, the sclerophyllous-type dragon tree with its small, leathery leaves, evolved to survive heat, drought and the salt-laden winds off the coast of Tenerife, the bulrush or paper plant from the banks of the Nile, and, of course, bulbous plants from North Africa, Greece and Asia Minor: hyacinths, narcissi and tulips.

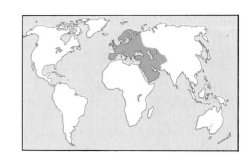

Tundra
Evergreen trees & maquis
Temperate coniferous into deciduous forest
Deciduous forest
Desert
Mountain forest
Grassland
Water margin

1. *Aeonium arboreum*
2. *A. canariense*
3. *A domesticum variegatum*
4. *A. haworthii*
5. *A. undulatum*
6. *Campanula isophylla*
7. *Cineraria*
8. *Crocus*
9. *Cyclamen persicum*
10. *Cyperus papyrus*
11. *Cytisus canariensis*
12. *Davallia canariensis*
13. *Dracaena draco*
14. *Hedera canariensis*
15. *H. helix*
16. *Hyacinthus orientalis*
17. *Narcissus*
18. *Nerium oleander*
19. *Phoenix canariensis*
20. *P. dactylifera*
21. *Phyllitis scolopendrium*
22. *Tulipa*

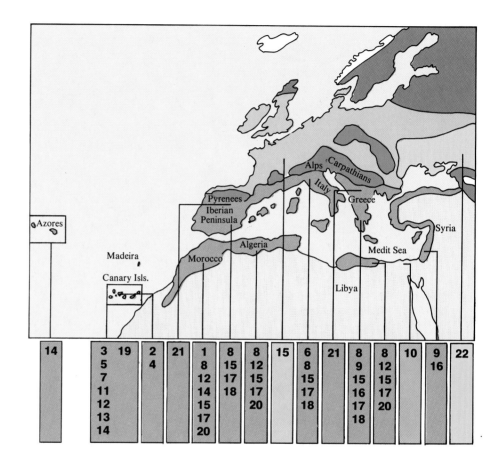

Climate

Mediterranean Europe has a warm wet winter and a hot dry summer. Much of lowland Middle East is desert, though the mountains and some of the areas affected by their mass, are wetter. Temperatures are often very high in summer, and Saudi Arabia is often the hottest place in the world with temperatures rising to 120°F (50°C).

Vegetation

In the north, part of the land is within the Arctic Circle, and the extreme climate found there only allows a tundra vegetation to grow. Further to the south, where conditions are slightly less severe, trees grow, and across the whole of northern Europe

is a vast belt of conifers, mainly spruce and pine. Apart from the trees, there is a sparse ground cover of herbaceous plants, and, in some places, a dense layer of moss. Where the climate becomes milder, south of the coniferous belt, deciduous trees grow, though throughout Europe and especially in the west, there is a wide overlap where there is a mixture of both coniferous and deciduous trees.

Much of the woodland of Europe has long ago been cut, and most of the area is now intensively farmed; in many places, however, vestiges of the original vegetation remain. More of the Middle East is cultivated than would be expected, thanks to extensive irrigation.

The other major type of vegetation is Mediterranean. This is a narrow band of vegetation around the Mediterranean Sea, it also covers the bulk of the Iberian Peninsula, coastal Morocco, Algeria, Tunisia and northern Libya. It is also found on Madeira and the Canary Islands on the lower rolling hilly land above the Mediterranean grassland in the valleys and below the oak-conifer forests of the higher land. This is a maquis area of evergreen plants among which heathers are prominent.

The trees are 15–18m (50–60ft) tall and fairly dense and often form a closed canopy; they may consist of only the evergreen oak, *Quercus ilex*.

Below the trees is a dense shrub layer 3–5m (10–16ft) tall, and made up of assorted plants like box, viburnum and phillyrea and perhaps wild roses; climbing over these and the trees may be honeysuckle, clematis and *Smilax*. The herb layer is fairly sparse due to the fairly intense shading, but includes butcher's broom, asparagus, spleenworts and sedges. Most of the shrubs begin to bloom in March, and continue until May or even June. During the dry period that follows, the vegetation is dormant until the rains again fall in autumn, at which time some trees may flower again.

In the mountains of the Mediterranean region there are two types

Evergreen forest-covered slopes of Gomera in the Canary Isles. Aeoniums grow on the cliffs.

of vegetation. On the northern margins of the area, with an increase in altitude, not only does the temperature drop but the dry season also disappears. Here the sclerophyllous forest is succeeded by deciduous oak and chestnut forest, and above this, at summer cloud height, beech and fir trees form a cloud forest. At even higher levels there may be a beech forest followed by spruce or pine.

In the remainder of the area, summer drought is still experienced up to the alpine region, and here the sclerophyllous forest is followed by various types of coniferous forest which include cedar and various junipers.

AEONIUM
(CRASSULACEAE)

Aeoniums are sub-shrubby, temperate-zone, succulent plants from North Africa, the Canary Islands and Madeira. They have been in cultivation for centuries and may now be found semi-wild along the coast of southern Europe – from Portugal to Greece – and throughout the warmer parts of most of the rest of the world. They need no more than protection from frost. All form tight rosettes of leaves, partly overlapping each other to afford protection from the drying effects of sun and wind. Some tightly hug the ground, shading the roots with their spread, others have their leaves arranged in such a way that the scarce water is directed down to their roots. Old leaves dry up and may fall off or "skirt" the stem. Stems may be scarred where old leaves were attached. Height varies from 7 or 8cm (a few inches) to 90 or 120cm (3 or 4ft). Flowerheads are

impressive and often held on stout stalks. They comprise many small, usually yellow (but may be white, pink or greenish) daisy-like flowers. A rosette blooms but once.

A. arboreum grows to 90cm (3ft) tall in Morocco, and has shiny green leaves. Stems are woody and multi-branching, constantly shedding older leaves. There is a form with deep purple leaves, *A. a.* Atropurpureum. The rosettes of both may grow to 12.5cm (5in) across.

A. canariense is low-growing, rarely more than 30cm (1ft) tall. Leaves are light green, flannely and arranged in a flat rosette which may grow to 45cm (18in) across. Older leaves are retained, clothing the

short stem. From the Canary Islands, it is commonly called giant velvet rose.

A. domesticum variegatum (syn. *Aichryson*), also from the Canaries, has small, very fleshy leaves. The wild, plain green form grows on hot dry cliffs; the recommended variegated-leaved form has cream markings, which take on a pink tinge in full sun. Rarely grows taller than 25cm (10in) and forms a dense clump of many 25mm (1in) rosettes.

A. haworthii from Tenerife is one of the commonest aeoniums in cultivation. Its hard, leathery, grey-green leaves are tinged with red at the edges. Ultimate height 45cm (18in).

A. undulatum is found in Gran Canaria at elevations of 300m (1,000ft). It forms a very thick stem, up to 90cm (3ft) tall, branches ver rarely but sends up small rosettes of leaves from the base. These small growths usually grow very little while all the energy is going into the main growth. Leaves

are shiny, dark-green and undulate at the edges. Rosette spread 25–30cm (10–12in).

Watering: Water moderately (a little more in winter if it is cold), allowing the mixture to begin drying out before more is given. Too much water leads to soft, untypical growth. Feed every two weeks with a standard liquid fertilizer from spring to early autumn.

Potting mixtures: Use a free-draining mix of 1 part sand or perlite and 2 parts loam-based compost. Move the strong growers into larger pots each spring.

Propagation: Aeoniums grow easily from seed. The rosettes of the branching kinds root easily with a 25–50mm (1–2in) length of stem attached.

CAMPANULA ISOPHYLLA
(CAMPANULACEAE)

Campanula isophylla is a trailing plant from Northern Italy. It favours south-facing rocks (sometimes limestone or chalk) where drainage is fast but where its dense

71

network of fine roots can always find moisture in the chinks between the rocks. It is almost hardy and only needs protection from frost.

Stems are up to 45cm (18in) long and carry small heart-shaped leaves with a toothed edge of a fresh lettuce green. Both stems and leafstalks are brittle and exude a white, milky sap if damaged. Pale blue, star-shaped flowers up to 4cm (1½in) across appear in quantity from late summer through to autumn.

There is a white-flowered form,Alba,and one with hairy, grey-green leaves and blue flowers, Mayi.

Watering: Water moderately throughout the long growing season, but sparingly during the winter rest period.

Potting mixture: Use a soil-based potting mixture.

Propagation: Young tip cuttings 4–5cm (1½–2in) long root easily in early spring. Plant several together in a pot for a bushy effect.

Special points: Plants branch freely and there is no need to pinch out growing points. Pot on into larger pots several times during the summer, to

flower in a 12.5cm (5in) pot. Stand on trays filled with moist pebbles during the warmer months. Can be trained as a climbing plant around miniature trellis-work. Feed every two weeks with a high-potash fertilizer once pots are filled with roots. Ideally keep at below 50°F (10°C) for the winter months.

Makes a good hanging basket plant for a sunny, or well-lit window.

CINERARIA
(COMPOSITAE)

These hybrids of very complex parentage have an ancestor from the Canary Islands. Leaves are large and fleshy and roughly heart-shaped. Flowers appear in clusters in late winter and spring and are a typical daisy shape in white, pink, orange, blue and purple shades – many with a ring of white surrounding the central disc. Technically, they are called *Senecio* hybrids.

Culture: Plants are raised from seed. Keep cool and in bright light, out of direct sun, water thoroughly (soak if necessary), watch out for aphids and discard as flowers fade.

CROCUS HYBRIDS
(IRIDACEAE)
It is the hybrids and not the

original wild species that are grown as temporary spring bulbs in the home. Their flowers are larger and more striking than the species and they also adapt better to being grown in containers. Wild plants are found around the Mediterranean shores.

Their life cycle begins with the appearance of roots while the soil is cold and climaxes into flower at the beginning of spring. Plant them up in autumn and encourage them to make an extensive root system, leaving them in the cool even until flower colour is visible. Then bring them indoors, where they have only a short life. Plant in garden when blooms fade.

CYCLAMEN PERSICUM HYBRIDS
(PRIMULACEAE)

Dracaena draco, *the dragon tree from the Canaries.*

Cyclamen are popular flowering pot plants best treated as temporary. They originate from the east Mediterranean (from Greece to Syria), have a dormant period (when the soil normally becomes too dry for growth), but enjoy a relatively long growing season. The base is tuberous, the heart-shaped leaves (which may be marbled with silvery markings), leafstalks and flowerstalks are fleshy. Flowers are five upswept petals, variously coloured white, all shades of pink, red, mauve and purple. There are some good dwarf-growing strains with smaller but sweet-scented flowers.

Culture: Raised from seed and normally bought when in bud. Grow cool, (45–55°F (7–12°C)) in bright light but without direct sun; water from below to avoid wetting the tuber. Remove any yellowing leaves and dead flowers as they fade – right to the base,or the "snag" left behind can quickly cause rot.

CYPERUS PAPYRUS
(CYPERACEAE)

C. papyrus – the bulrush of the Bible, or paper-plant from North and tropical Africa – is very tall-growing (6–8ft) – with stout bamboo-like stems topped with hundreds of threadlike, drooping bracts, and is much more a plant for the conservatory. Likes a minimum temperature of 60–65°F (15–18°C).

Watering: Keep permanently moist.

Potting mixture: Use a soil-based potting mixture.

Propagation: The easiest way is to divide overcrowded clumps in early spring. The umbrella shape of bracts at the top of the stalk can be induced to make roots by either standing it with 12mm (½in) of stem attached in water or damp sand. Pot up when some roots have formed and a little new growth appears.

Special points: Feed actively growing plants at monthly intervals with a standard liquid fertilizer. Pot on into pots two sizes larger each spring, or as required.

CYTISUS CANARIENSIS
(LEGUMINOSAE)
This is the Canary Island broom, a small shrub 30–38cm (12–15in) high and 30cm (12in) through. Leaves are made up of three small oval leaflets, flowers are bright yellow, slightly scented, pea-like, 20mm (¾in) long and borne in a terminal spike. There is a hybrid, C. racemosus, with deeper yellow, larger

flowers. Both are temporary house plants only.

Culture: Grown from seed. Give bright light but keep cool, water plentifully (soaking if necessary) and stand on moist pebble trays.

DAVALLIA CANARIENSIS
(POLYPODIACEAE)

D. canariensis (Canaries, southern Spain and North Africa) is called the deer's foot fern – pale rusty brown scales over the rhizomes. Good basket plant.

Watering: Water moderately, allowing the mixture to dry out a little

between waterings. Davallias grown in baskets should be soaked.

Potting mixture: Use an equal-parts mixture of peat-based and soil-based mixture.

Propagation: Use 5–7.5cm (2–3in) long sections of rhizome, each with two or three leaves attached. Pin down into contact with the mixture and enclose in a plastic bag or put in a propagator.

Special points: Feed actively growing plants every two weeks with a standard liquid fertilizer. Use half pots or pans as root system is shallow. Plant several small rooted sections in a hanging basket. Stand pots in trays of moist pebbles and mist fronds, rhizomes and baskets with a handsprayer (perhaps daily).

DRACAENA DRACO
(AGAVACEAE)

D. draco is the dragon tree of the Canary islands, the most tolerant dracaena of cooler conditions and the one with slightly coarse, blue-grey leaves with narrow red margins.

Watering: Water plentifully when in active growth, more sparingly in the winter.

Potting mixture: Use a soil-based potting mixture.

Propagation: Stem, tip and basal cuttings can be used in spring. Tips should be rooted in a propagator, basal shoots will normally have some roots attached and will grow if enclosed in

a plastic bag. Set 7.5–10cm (3–4in) stem cuttings upright in a peat and sand mixture. With warmth they will send down roots and develop growing points.

Special points: Give extra humidity by standing pots on trays of moist pebbles. Feed every two weeks with a standard liquid fertilizer from spring to early autumn. Repot only when really necessary. Watch out for mealy bugs that may inhabit the leaf axils. The loss of older leaves is quite normal, leaving behind the quite attractive bare stem.

HEDERA
(ARALIACEAE)
Ivies have a distribution from Japan to the Azores and from northern Europe to North Africa. Three main species exist, H. canariensis, H. colchica (hardly ever seen as a house plant), and helix. All are woody-stemmed climbing plants with short aerial roots (rarely used indoors) which fix to damp surfaces. Leaves vary enormously in shape and size, all have a leathery texture unless grown too "soft" when they are thin and untypical. In the wild they grow over the ground, over rocks and up tree trunks, particularly in wooded areas. They enjoy the typical British climate, and can tolerate a wide range of temperatures. They make easy house plants except when used in really warm rooms.

H. canariensis (from Algeria, Morocco, the Azores and the Canaries) has dark green, triangular shaped leaves, 12.5–15cm **73**

(5–6in) long and across. The variegated-leaved kinds, Gloire de Marengo and Margino-Maculata, are streaked or spotted with grey-green and creamy-yellow.

H. helix (English ivy) grows as far south as Anatolia and the Caucasus, but can also be found further north in Russia and southern Scandinavia. There are hundreds of clones, forms or varieties. The most prized kinds are those that are very free-branching, making dense growth and those with strikingly variegated leaves. Some of the best are: Adam, Boskoop, Brokamp, Glacier, Green Ripple, Harald, Hibernica, Ivalace, Luzii, Manda's Crested, Parsley Crested, and Très Coupé.

Watering: Water moderately during the growing season, allowing the mixture to dry out a little before applying more. In winter (when grown cool) water sparingly.

Potting mixture: Use a soil-based potting mixture.

Propagation: Tip cuttings of all kinds, 7.5–10cm (3–4in) long, root extremely easily if rooted in peat and sand or perlite in spring. They will also root in water.

Special points: Be sure to pot several cuttings up in one pot to get a bushy effect. Feed every two weeks with the standard liquid fertilizer from March to September inclusive. Stand on trays of moist pebbles, this is an absolute essential in warm rooms. Watch out for red spider mites if the air is dry. Pot on into slightly larger pots two or three times a year. Replenish with young plants regularly.

HYACINTHUS ORIENTALIS HYBRIDS (*LILIACEAE*)

Hyacinths are temporary bulbous plants prized for their heady, fragrant flowers in the depth of winter. The Dutch took up this plant from Asia Minor, Greece and North Africa and developed it as early as the 18th Century. Today we can choose between a large number of kinds with white, blue, pink, red and yellowy-cream flowers with small or huge columnar spikes of bell-shaped flowers. Some have double flowers. A cool, dark, rooting period extending over at least ten weeks is essential for success. Some bulbs (known as "treated" or "prepared") have been

specially treated to encourage them to bloom that little bit earlier and these may be "forced" a little by bringing them into gentle heat once flowers have emerged from the necks of the bulbs, but most prefer cool conditions until flower buds show colour.

Culture: While indoors, give bright light, keep cool, provide slim canes to support the heavy blooms and keep thoroughly moist at the root. Plant in the garden when flowers fade.

NARCISSUS (*AMARYLLIDACEAE*)

The genus narcissus includes the familiar daffodil, jonquil, paper-white narcissus etc., native of Europe, the Mediterranean and North Africa. All are temporary room plants, ideally brought into the home as their flower buds are starting to show colour, and taken to the garden when blooms fade.

Culture: Keep in bright light, cool (well below 60°F (15°C)) and well watered. Provide thin canes for support.

NERIUM OLEANDER (*APOCYNACEAE*)
Widely grown along the

Nerium oleander *in Morocco*

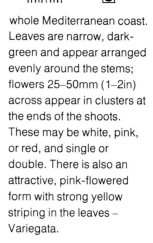

whole Mediterranean coast. Leaves are narrow, dark-green and appear arranged evenly around the stems; flowers 25–50mm (1–2in) across appear in clusters at the ends of the shoots. These may be white, pink, or red, and single or double. There is also an attractive, pink-flowered form with strong yellow striping in the leaves – Variegata.

Watering: Water moderately while new growth is being made and very sparingly during the winter rest period.

Potting mixture: Use a soil-based mix.

Propagation: Tip cuttings 7.5–10cm (3–4in) long root easily in spring (in rooting mixture or water).

Special points: Feed active plants every two weeks. Pot on into larger pots each spring, but do not over-pot as this discourages flowering. Watch out for scale insects that may collect on the leaf underside. All parts of this plant are poisonous if eaten.

PHOENIX
(PALMAE)

The date palm and its close relatives are only suitable house plants when young and trunkless. Three are popularly grown. *P. roebelinii* comes from Laos and is discussed in the section about S.E. Asia.

P. canariensis from the temperate Canaries grows to 1.2m (4ft) tall in a 30cm (12in) pot with almost a similar spread. Fronds are stiff, rather prickly and made up of many thin, pointed leaflets or segments on either side of the midrib. Tolerant of cool temperatures; useful for porches.

P. dactylifera is the date palm, anciently cultivated and probably of West Asian or North African origin. Fronds are blue-green, segments more openly spaced than the previous species and not as attractive.

Watering: Water thoroughly during the growing season and very sparingly during the winter rest period.

Potting mixture: Use a soil-based potting mixture.

Propagation: Date stones' may be planted, but a slow business. Offsets occasionally occur, detach and pot up in spring.

Special points: Feed every two weeks with standard liquid fertilizer during the growth period. Pot on into larger pots only when a mass of fine roots can be seen on the mixture surface. Topdress those that have reached maximum pot size.

PHYLLITIS SCOLOPENDRIUM
(POLYPODIACEAE)

The popular hart's tongue fern, in many forms, is found throughout Europe but also elsewhere (one variety is local in N.E. America). The strap-like fronds, soft at first but later becoming leathery, are normally undivided and rise from a branching rhizome. Frond length in a pot is around 30cm (12in). There are wavy-edged and crested kinds. Tolerant of a very wide range in temperature.

Watering: Water moderately at all times.

Potting mixture: Use a peat-based potting mixture to which has been added a little limestone (powder or chips) to counteract the acidity of the peat.

Propagation: In spring just as new fronds are unfurling divide old overcrowded clumps or take away sections of rhizomes with two or more fronds attached.

Special points: In warm rooms stand on trays filled with moist pebbles. Feed growing plants every two weeks with half strength liquid fertilizer. Repot into the next size pot each spring.

Cut away completely some of the old fronds to make room for the new ones appearing from the base.

TULIPA
(LILIACEAE)

Tulips are temporary house plants. Originally from central and west Asia, some species are popular as garden plants but those used indoors are invariably hybrids. Short-stemmed, early-flowering kinds are the most suitable.

Culture: Bring indoors only when flower buds are clear of the necks of the bulbs, Keep as cool as possible, in bright light, and water moderately (particularly if grown in bowls without a drainage hole). Take to the garden (perhaps via a garden frame) for recovery.

Phoenix dactylifera, *the date palm*

75

Tropical Africa

Tropical Africa illustrates most clearly the way an increasingly marked dry season determines gradual changes in vegetation, from lush green tropical rain forest to arid desert. *Ficus buxifolia* hies from the evergreen, hot and humid rain forests of the Congo basin, *Dracaena fragrans* from the tropical deciduous forests where some trees lose their leaves to retain moisture during the dry season, and *Kalanchoe marmorata* from the still drier savanna. Popular too (its forebears came from shady, rocky outcrops in the primeval forest of Usumbara) is the African violet.

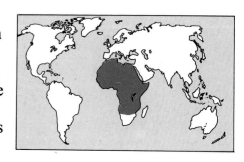

This covers the whole of Africa with the exception of the area to the south of the tropics. It is an area of just under 11 million sq miles. Most of the area is within the tropics, and most of that to the north is desert.

Forests

Mangrove forests are found along the tropical coasts; they grow especially well in the estuaries of rivers. Tropical rain forest is, surprisingly, only of very limited distribution, covering parts of the Congo Basin and the Cameroons; there are various other small and isolated pockets scattered here and there. Unusually for tropical rain forests, many areas are dominated by only a few tree species.

Cloud forest or temperate rain forest is more dense than the tropical rain forest and is the most varied and interesting of the African forests. It occurs on the high mountains of central and eastern Africa, and in places gives way to savanna and grassland. Dry forest, which varies from open park-like areas to fairly dense forest, always has a grassy ground vegetation, though shrubs and young trees are rare; the trees tend to be flat-topped and the grasses are relatively tall. This forest is most common in the southern central part of Africa from Mozambique to Tanzania across to the Congo and Angola.

Thorn forest occurs in areas of savanna where the trees are dense enough to exclude the grasses, and it is found in scattered small areas throughout all of the drier parts of Africa.

The final type of forest is the oasis which occurs throughout the desert areas and includes any trees that can survive the heat, and the strong and often sand-bearing winds.

Grassland

High grass, low tree savanna has grasses up to 4m (13ft) tall; these grass plants grow in tufts and do not form a continuous turf. This vegetation forms a distinct border zone around the tropical rain forest, and, in fact, covers a larger area than the forest.

Acacia tall grass savanna is the most widespread type of vegetation in Africa and it covers large areas. There is an even distribution of tall grasses (1–2m) (3–6ft), in which are scattered small trees up to 15m (50ft) tall; these trees are often thorny and flat topped and give the landscape the appearance of a large orchard or park.

Desert grass savanna varies from a short and even grass cover to a sparse and scattered growth of desert grasses. Small thorny trees and bushes are always scattered throughout the area, which is to be found in a strip around the desert and covers a large area of Africa.

Pure grassland without any trees (the grasses are about 1m (3ft or so) tall and form a fairly continuous ground cover) covers large areas of eastern Africa and at high levels throughout the continent.

Alpine meadowland occurs at even higher levels, and consists of low grasses and herbs; much of the area is often snow and ice covered.

Desert

Desert shrub is made up of woody and fleshy plants, and much of the Sahara is covered by this type of vegetation. In saline areas the plants are adapted to the high salt levels in the soil, and, in general, tend to be very fleshy. In the slightly wetter parts of the desert, tufts of grass grow between the shrubs which allow the area to be used for grazing.

Plant hunting in Africa

The African violet

Sightings of saintpaulia species were recorded in 1884 and 1887, but the credit for the introduction of the main species concerned, *S. ionantha*, goes to a German provincial governor whose full name was Baron Adalbert Emil Redcliffe Le Tanneur von Saint Paul-Illaire. He sent the seeds he collected to his father who in turn sent some to Herman Wendland, an eminent horticulturist and director of the Royal Botanical Gardens at Herrenhausen. The first plants to flower were duly exhibited at the International Horticultural Exhibition of 1893, at Ghent.

Wendland named these plants after their introducer — it was just as well for us that he did not go the whole way and call them Saintpaulillairea.

The seeds came from two localities between the Usumbara Mountains and the sea in northern Tanganyika, as it was then. One was at only 150 feet above the sea, the other at around 2,500 feet "in the primeval forest of Usumbara, in shady situations, on granite rocks." One of its "type localities" is the Sigi Caves which has given rise to the suggestion that the plant is a cave-dweller. In fact it grows outside the caves proper on their top ledges, among boulders, in fissures and pockets filled with humus.

Saintpaulias come from shady mountain slopes in Tanzania.

Collecting dracaenas in W. Africa

Very often plants of interest were sent back by missionaries and this may be one of these. Among house plants we are indebted to the Reverend Hugh Goldie for sending back *Dracaena goldieana* in 1872.

The firm of Sander were specialists in orchids and employed collectors for this purpose in most of the tropics. In 1892 they had a collector in the Congo and he sent back two plants that are used as house plants, the handsome silver-variegated *Dracaena sanderiana* and the rather odd plant which is usually sold as *D. godseffiana*, but which is correctly *D. surculosa* var *punctulata*. *D. surculosa* itself had earlier been collected in Sierra Leone by one of the London Horticultural Society's collectors George Don. He was given a place on H.M.S. *Iphigenia*, which was commanded by the brother of the secretary of the R.H.S., Joseph Sabine, and he visited not only places in West Africa, but also Brazil and the West Indies. All this took place in 1822. We have his journal, which is extremely difficult to decipher.

"March 29, 1822. I set off about 7 o'clock in order to visit the point a little to the west of Freetown, which was a distance of three miles from me. As soon as I entered it I found a new species of Combretum, very different from any I had ever seen

before; this makes the 13th species of this genus I have seen since I came to Sierra Leone. A little further on I met with a very curious, fine sp. of Limodorum with green flowers ... In the country the most general plant was the Butter or Tallow tree and the Cherimoya bush. ... I find I have done little good to my foot by going out" (he had stepped on some nails) "and the pain is so great I am hardly able to walk.

"March 31. About 2 o'clock this morning there was a tornado; the wind was very high and it rained, thundered and lightened without intermission for the course of an hour. In the forenoon I went down to Captain Sabine ... and understood he had been at the Sugar Loaf Mountain, about 6 miles from Freetown, where he had picked up two bulbs of *Haemanthus multiflorus*, where next morning I intend setting out to the same place to collect a few bulbs as directed by Mr Sabine, when in England.

"April 1. Went to the Sugar Loaf Mountain ... on my way I found a strange sp. of Salvia. I reached Regent's Town about 9 in the morning and went into one of the houses, where I was advised to take a man as guide to the top of the mountain. The principal trees there are a tree very nearly related to *Guiacum officinale* and another

nearly related to Sciurus(?). After half an hour on my boy and I looked very closely for the Haemanthus but only found one bulb; but in looking for this plant I met with a new sp. of gladiolus or iris, but I could not ascertain which, as it was not in leaf nor in flower ..."

The next day they went by boat to York, a distance of thirty miles. "In the afternoon I went along the beach a little way. All along the beach the land is covered with *Sansevieria guineensis* running into various varieties, which tend to confound the many species which Mr Haworth has made. *Hymenaea courbaril* is very common here.

"April 3rd ... Smith and myself went to Flint a distance of 12 miles. We kept to the sea beach all the way, which was covered in many places with *Haemanthus multiflorus*, where I gathered 200 bulbs. The bulbs are all separate; you never find them closer to each other than 1 foot and likewise you will hardly ever see them above 100 yards from the sea beach. April 9th. Packed up 4 boxes. 1 Live plants. 2 specimens. 3 seeds. 4 bulbs and a box of Lepidopterous insects. Wrote a list of the various vegetables of Sierra Leone and lists of the various boxes and sent them down to Captain Sabine in the afternoon to get them put along with the articles which he had to send home."

We shall see (C. & E. Asia) that *Dracaena fragrans* was introduced some time in the 1760's, but the variegated forms probably date from the 1870s and were raised at the Linden nursery if the cultivar name "Lindeni" is any indication. Before Bause's work the Linden nursery was especially renowned for its fine Dracaenas (which included Cordyline at that time). The other cultivar name "Massangeana" was probably given by Linden. M. de Massange was a keen amateur grower of orchids, but it would seem that he was also interested in variegated plants as he has not only the Dracaena, but also a form of *Maranta leuconeura*. On the other hand M. de Kerchove, who also has

Tropical rain forest
Savanna woodland
Grassland
Desert
Temperate rain/cloud forest
Dry forest
Scrub

1. *Begonia hiemalis*
2. *Dracaena deremensis*
3. *D. fragrans*
4. *D. goldieana*
5. *D. sanderiana*
6. *D. surculosa*
7. *Exacum affine*
8. *Ficus buxifolia*
9. *F. lyrata*
10. *Impatiens wallerana*
11. *Kalanchoe marmorata*
12. *Pellaea viridis*
13. *Plectranthus oertendahlii*
14. *Saintpaulia ionantha*
15. *Selaginella kraussiana*
16. *Thunbergia alata*

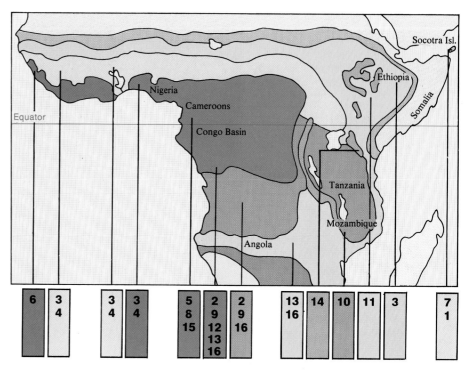

plants named in his honour, was an authority on palms.

The other African dracaena, *D. deremensis*, seems to have got into cultivation without anyone noticing, but the variegated cultivar known as "Bausei" bears tribute once again to Bause's work with this genus.

The Busy Lizzie
John Kirk, who accompanied Livingstone as physician and naturalist in the 1850s, later became consul-general at Zanzibar, whence he introduced Busy Lizzie, *Impatiens wallerana*.

African species of Ficus
There are three which are used as house plants, and here once again we are not sure by whom they were introduced. The fiddleback fig, *F. lyrata*, arrived in commerce in 1903. *Ficus vogelii* (not listed here), which seems more or less indistinguishable from *Ficus nekbudu*, was probably discovered by Dr Vogel, the botanist on the ill-fated Niger expedition, led by Captain Trotter in 1841. There would seem, however, no reason to suppose that he introduced the plant, or rather that the gardener, Ansell who accompanied him did, although it is possible that seeds were brought back. Dr Vogel died on the expedition.

The position is rather frustrating. Tropical Africa seems to have produced few house plants and those that do come from Africa seem to have arrived without our being able to name the introducer. In the case of *F. lyrata*, Sander named the plant *F. pandurata*, unaware of the earlier name: the fact that Sander named it does suggest that it was due to one of his collectors.

The levels of high evergreen forest in Tanzania, viewed through the canopy.

BEGONIA
(BEGONIACEAE)

B. hiemalis hybrids are a cross between *B. socotrana* and various Andean species. Stems are usually a very deep red, to 45cm (18in) tall, leaves fleshy, deep green to almost chocolate and with 6–7.5cm (2½–3in) single flowers, usually strong red with a yellow centre. Plants sold have names like Fireglow, Schwabenland and Elatior hybrids. See also *B. cheimantha* hybrids: S. Africa.

Most begonias come from South America; their culture is discussed in that section.

DRACAENA
(AGAVACEAE)
In the wild dracaenas range over a large part of tropical and temperate Africa and nearby. They are naturally upright-growing shrubs (rarely branching unless forced) with narrow strap-like or lance-shaped leaves, arching outwards and arranged around a woody stem. All grow relatively quickly and in 4–5 years may reach a metre and more in height. Some develop a bare stem at the base, scarred where leaves

were attached, giving the plant a palm-like appearance.

D. deremensis from the grassland and deciduous forests of tropical Africa is rarely grown, two varieties being popular: *D.d.* Bausei carries a broad white stripe down the middle of a dark green leaf, while *D.d.* Warneckii has two such stripes.

D. fragrans is one of the more tolerant of the

species, originating in Upper Guinea but sufficiently hardy to grow happily further east in the higher altitude of Ethiopia.

In cultivation it has been superseded by its variegated forms: *D.f.* Lindenii with broad, creamy-white leaf margins; *D.f.* Massangeana with a wide central yellow strip to the apple-green leaves and *D.f.* Victoria with wide yellow margins.

D. goldieana, from Upper Guinea alone, is best suited to a terrarium as it demands high and constant temperatures and high humidity. Glossy green leaves have a yellow midrib and are cross-barred with silvery grey.

D. sanderiana from the tropical rain forests of the Cameroons is a slender shrub with 25mm (1in) wide by 22mm (9in) long green and white striped leaves.

D. surculosa (syn. *D. godseffiana*) from West tropical Africa (Sierra Leone) grows only to 60cm (2ft) tall with leathery green leaves heavily spotted with cream. Two forms, Florida Beauty and Kelleri, are more colourful and a little easier to grow than the wild

Dracaenas in their dry forest habitat

type. It is commonly called gold dust.

Watering: Water plentifully when in active growth, more sparingly in the winter.

Potting mixture: Use a soil-based potting mixture.

Propagation: Stem, tip and basal cuttings can be used in spring. Tips should be rooted in a propagator, basal shoots will normally have some roots attached and will grow if enclosed in a plastic bag. Stem cuttings, 7.5–10cm (3–4in) long, set upright in a peat and sand mixture will, with warmth, send down roots and develop growing points.

Special points: Give extra humidity by standing pots on trays of moist pebbles. Feed every two weeks with a standard liquid fertilizer from spring to early autumn. Repot only when really necessary. Watch out for mealy bugs that may inhabit the leaf axils. The loss of older leaves is quite normal, leaving behind the quite attractive bare stem.

Thunbergia alata

EXACUM AFFINE
(GENTIANACEAE)

Exacum affine is a native of Socotra, off the Horn of Africa, where it is hot and dry. Small plants are on sale in late summer and make attractive, short-term house plants. Leaves are a medium green, shiny and heart-shaped; flowers are a

pale lavender blue with prominent yellow stamens and slightly fragrant. Named varieties are available from seedsmen.

Culture: Raised from seed. Give bright light (an east or west-facing window), keep cool, well watered and pot on into a slightly larger pot if necessary using a soil-based mixture. Pick off flowers as they fade to ensure continued blooming.

FICUS
(MORACEAE)

Two come from tropical Africa:

F. buxifolia from the evergreen forests of the Congo basin (Zaire) has

79

shiny, roughly triangular leaves about 25mm (1in) across, attached intermittently along arching reddish stems. 1.8m (6ft) specimens are seen, but rarely.

F. lyrata (syn. *F. pandurata*) from the grassland and deciduous forests of tropical west-Africa has large, light-green, fiddle-shaped leaves 30–38cm (12–15in) long. The leaf surface is slightly puckered – the vein areas being slightly sunken. Inclined not to branch. Maximum height indoors 2.10m (7ft).

Watering: Water moderately during the growing period and sparingly during the winter rest period. Overwatering will cause the lower leaves to fall off.

Potting mixture: Use a soil-based mixture.

Propagation: Usually air layered, but tip cuttings will root if a propagator is available.

Special points: Give standard liquid fertilizer every two weeks from spring to early autumn. Move into larger pots only when this is absolutely necessary – ficus do best when roots are a little restricted and can be grown in what may appear quite inadequate pots. Pot in spring. Top dress large specimens, in the spring. Keep the leaves clean by gently wiping with a damp

sponge, or better still, stand out in gentle rain during the warmer months.

IMPATIENS (BALSAMINACEAE)

All impatiens (Busy Lizzies) grown today as pot plants are highly developed hybrids. *I. wallerana* (Tanzania – Mozambique) has lots of large flowers in good colours, that are virtually continuously produced above relatively short stems.

Watering: Water generously while the plants are in active growth, more sparingly in winter.

Potting mixture: Use a soil-based potting mixture.

Propagation: Seed sown in early spring will quickly give flowering-sized plants. Tip cuttings will root quickly at almost any time of the year, in water or in rooting mixture – spring is best.

Special points: Plants will only make short, tight growth and flower profusely if light is bright, without hot, direct, summer sun. Feed actively growing plants with a high-potash liquid fertilizer every two weeks. Beware of aphids and red spider mites. In warm rooms make the air more humid by standing pots on trays of moist pebbles.

KALANCHOE MARMORATA (CRASSULACEAE)

Kalanchoes are small succulent plants or shrubs.

Most of the more popular kinds come from the dry bush or low sclerophyllous forest of Madagascar (see Madagascar). *K. marmorata*, however, can be found in the savanna/desert grassland bordering Ethiopia and the Somali Republic. It makes a low shrub with smooth, spoon-shaped, medium green leaves liberally spotted with brown markings and with nicked edges. White, spring flowers.

Watering: Water sparingly through the growing season and very sparingly after flowers have faded. Leaves become gross and untypical if overwatered.

Potting mixture: Use $\frac{3}{4}$ parts of soil based mixture and $\frac{1}{4}$ part coarse sand or perlite.

Propagation: Tip cuttings and offsets root very easily in spring.

Special points: Feed actively growing plants once a month with a half-strength liquid fertilizer. Watch out for mealy bugs that are apt to collect in the leaf axils.

PELLAEA VIRIDIS (POLYPODIACEAE)

P. viridis (green cliff brake) is African, grows upright with fronds 61cm (2ft) long, triangular in outline and divided and subdivided into many small pointed pinnae.

Watering: Water plentifully during active growth and moderately in winter.

Potting mixture: Use a peat-based mixture.

Propagation: Divide overcrowded clumps in spring, each piece with a section of rhizome and two or more fronds.

Special points: Feed actively growing plants every two weeks with the standard liquid fertilizer. In warm rooms stand on moist pebble tray and mist spray foliage. Move on into the next size pot when growths become cramped.

PLECTRANTHUS OERTENDAHLII (LABIATAE)

The fast-growing, creeping and trailing forms of plectranthus are those most popular as house plants.

P. oertendahlii (popularly called candle plant) is one of the most popular. Its dark-green leaves are marked with prominent white veins on the upper side and shaded deep purple on the underside.

Watering: Water plentifully during the period of fast growth from spring to early autumn, but water sparingly during the short winter rest period.

Potting mixture: Use a soil-based potting mixture.

Propagation: Tip cuttings root very easily in the spring and early summer, even in water. Young plants are best; start afresh each year.

Special points: Plant 4–6 plants in one hanging basket to get the best, bushy effect. Nip out growing points regularly to encourage side branches to develop. Feed every two weeks with the standard liquid fertilizer during the active growing season. Encourage to rest in winter.

SAINTPAULIA
(GESNERIACEAE)

The saintpaulias (African violets) grown today are far removed from the wild species that contributed to their make-up. *S. ionantha*, one species from the Usambara Mountains in the north east province of Tanzania,was an important parent, but there have been others, each contributing to the shape, size and flower colour range. Today we expect to find standard kinds, miniatures and semi-miniatures, and trailing kinds. Flowers may be single (5 petals), semi-double or fully double; white, blue, purple, pink, "red", or bicoloured: with petal edging piped with white (known as Geneva) or with flowers that start one colour and fade to another. Leaves are arranged in a rosette shape but may be plain green in various shapes and sizes, or variegated, scallop- or frilly-edged.

Hundreds of named varieties are commercially available, but those under the group name, Ballet or Rhapsodie series,have been found most viable.

These are quick to flower, their large flowers held on stout stalks, and capable of holding their blooms over a long period. A good colour range exists.

Watering: During the growth period water thoroughly but repeat only when the mixture has started to dry out. Be very sparing during the short rest period. Avoid wetting the foliage.

Potting mixture: Use a peat-based mixture.

Propagation: Divide overcrowded clumps into individual rosettes. With trailers, take small rosettes from the ends of the trailing stems. Take leaf cuttings of all kinds. The latter can be rooted in either mix or plain water. If water is used transfer into mix *very* soon after roots start.

Special points: Feed growing plants every two weeks with a high potash liquid feed. Stand on trays of moist pebbles. Move small plants on into the next size pots as required (though saintpaulias look best and flower best when grown in relatively small pots). 10cm (4in) pots (or half-pots) are normally the maximum needed, even for very large plants. In early spring repot older plants with fresh mixture into clean pots of the same size. Keep plants to one rosette of leaves (called a crown) by removing side shoots (make sure not to take out flower buds instead). The hairy leaves get dusty in time; they can be cleaned by washing with tepid water under the tap or a showerhead. Do this early in the day and only when it is warm. Keep out of direct

sun for this period – sun on beads of moisture can cause burning. African violets must have at least twelve hours of bright light daily to initiate new flower buds, although existing buds will open with less. Plants can be kept in bloom throughout the winter by providing 6–8 hours per day of supplementary artificial light.

SELAGINELLA
KRAUSSIANA
(SELAGINELLACEAE)

Selaginellas form tight moss-like hummocks or loose fern-like fronds. Although not ferns they often resemble them and do produce spores rather than seeds. All thrive on high humidity and are best suited to the bottle garden or Wardian case. The genus is very large and covers large tracts of the world's surface.

S. kraussiana (Cameroons) is fast-growing, creeps over the surface, rooting down at intervals but reaching up to one foot tall. A form, *S.k* Aurea is yellow-green.

Watering: Water plentifully throughout the year – never allowing the mixture to dry out.

Potting mixture: Use a mixture of $\frac{2}{3}$ peat and $\frac{1}{3}$ coarse sand or perlite.

Propagation: Take short tip cuttings 25–50mm (1–2in) long in spring; keep warm and humid until rooted.

Special points: Do not feed at other than $\frac{1}{8}$-strength standard liquid fertilizer

every two weeks during the growing period. "Normal" feeding will result in coarse, untypical growth. Use shallow pans or half-pots. Move on into larger pans as plants grow over the edge of the older ones. Make the air more humid by standing on trays filled with moist pebbles, or grow in a terrarium.

THUNBERGIA ALATA
(ACANTHACEAE)

T. alata, black-eyed Susan, is a fast-growing climber from tropical Africa now widely naturalized through the warmer parts of the world. Its stems twine, leaves are arrow-shaped and slightly hairy and its flowers are 5cm (2in) across, and orange with a central, chocolate-brown "eye". Yellow and cream-flowered forms are available. Best treated as an annual.

Culture: Raised from seed. Pot on, if necessary, into soil-based mixture; grow in a sunny window; water moderately and feed every two weeks with a high potash liquid fertilizer. Provide thin canes, or string around which the stems can twine.

81

South Africa

Many South African pot plants are succulents that display water-retaining characteristics to cope with the irregularity of the rainfall. Here, for example, abide the lace and partridge-breasted aloes, *Ceropegia woodii*, cotyledons, crassulas, faucarias, and the intriguing, stone-like lithops. But South Africa also gives us Cape primroses, pelargoniums (the ivy-leaved geranium was in England by 1701), heathers, begonias, and that easy-to-grow hanging basket plant, the spider plant, *Chlorophytum comosum*.

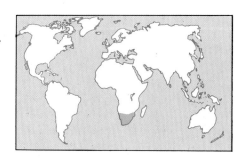

1. *Aloe aristata*
2. *A. variegata*
3. *Asparagus asparagoides*
4. *A. densiflorus* Sprengeri
5. *A. setaceus*
6. *Begonia cheimantha hybs.*
7. *B. dregei*
8. *B. sutherlandii*
9. *B. weltoniensis*
10. *Bryophyllum tubiflorum*
11. *Ceropegia woodii*
12. *Chlorophytum comosum*
13. *Clivia miniata*
14. *Cotyledon orbiculata*
15. *C. undulata*
16. *Crassula arborescens*
17. *C. argentea*
18. *C. falcata*
19. *C. lactea*
20. *C. lycopodioides*
21. *C. rupestris*
22. *Cyperus albostriatus*
23. *Cyrtomium falcatum*
24. *Dracaena hookerana*
25. *Erica gracilis*
26. *E. hyemalis*
27. *E. ventricosa*
28. *Faucaria tigrina*
29. *F. tuberculosa*
30. *Gasteria liliputana*
31. *G. maculata*
32. *G. pseudonigricans*
33. *G. verrucosa*
34. *Haemanthus albiflos*
35. *H. katherinae*
36. *H. multiflorus*
37. *Haworthia cuspidata*
38. *H. margaritifera*
39. *H. reinwardtii*
40. *H. tessellata*
41. *Kleinia articulata*
42. *K. tomentosa*
43. *Lithops fulleri*
44. *L. lesliei*
45. *Pelargonium spp.*
46. *Plumbago auriculata*
47. *Rochea coccinea*
48. *Sansevieria trifasciata*
49. *Selaginella kraussiana*
50. *Senecio macroglossus*
51. *S. mikanioides*
52. *S. rowleyanus*
53. *Sparmannia africana*
54. *Stapelia variegata*
55. *Strelitzia reginae*
56. *Vallota speciosa*
57. *Veltheimia capensis*
58. *V. viridifolia*

14	1	29	42	3	25	22	46	13	4	35	48	11
15	2	30	43	23	26		49	16	5	36		12
54	10	31	44	24	27		50	17	6			
	16	32	45	46			51	19	7			
	17	33	47	49			53	21	8			
	18	37	54	52			55	48	9			
	19	38	56	53					11			
	20	39	57						12			
	24	40	58						22			
	28	41							34			

☐ Montane forest
☐ Sclerophyllous-type bush
☐ Arid areas
☐ Sub-tropical/Warm temperate/ temperate forest
☐ Tall grass

☐ Water margin
☐ Grassland
☐ Savanna
☐ Sub-tropical bush
☐ Evergreen trees and sclerophyllous-type bush

The southernmost part of the continent of Africa from latitude 35°S, northwards to just within the tropics covers an area of about half a million square miles. The land mass appears symmetrical in both its wedge-shaped outline and its structure. The land essentially consists of a large elevated plateau with raised margins and with a fairly low lying coastal belt.

The raised plateau, by far the largest part of the area, reaches its maximum height at its edges where a sharp and distinct escarpment drops to the coastal plain. At its lowest, the plateau is about 825m (2,700ft) high; it reaches a maximum height of about 3,400m (11,000ft)

In the east (Natal) the land falls from the plateau to the sea in a series of steps, whereas in the south, where the land from the escarpment to the sea is wider, there are ranges of mountains that run parallel to the coast making the coastal strip very narrow.

Climate

There is considerable variety. Most

of the area is included in the southern warm temperate zone, though the northern part is within the tropics. Due to their elevation most of the interior areas are more temperate than might be imagined. The amount of sunlight is high and the relative humidity usually fairly low; the clear, dry atmosphere permits large, daily and seasonal temperature fluctuations.

The coastal climate especially is affected by ocean currents. A warm current flows down the eastern coast and around the south coast; a cold Antarctic current runs up the west coast with cold water coming to the surface to the north of Table Bay.

Temperatures fall into two distinct groups. In the coastal belt the range is small and frosts are rare or absent, whereas in the large elevated interior, the range is wide and frosts are common. The low temperatures are, however, never prolonged and always rise rapidly during the day.

Rainfall is also variable. Not only in amount, but also when it falls. About two thirds of the area has less than 500mm (20in) a year and much of this receives less than 250mm (10in). On mountain summits and the mountains in the southwest, rainfall is high: over 1,500mm (60in). Apart from local variations, rainfall is greatest on the east coast and decreases towards the west. Nearly all of the area has a seasonal rainfall with the largest area having a wet summer and dry winter (most of the rain falling as short, heavy thunderstorms); only a few coastal areas have rain throughout the year. Only in a small area of south-western Cape Province is the pattern different. Here, well over half of the rain falls during the winter.

Vegetation

The vegetation in this area can be divided into five main types:–

Bush

This is a sclerophyllous vegetation where the bushes, shrubs and trees have small and hard leaves; it occurs in the south-western part of Cape Province. It has a wet winter and a dry summer; the rainfall averages

The great escarpment of the Drakensburg rears vertically from surrounding grassland. Bulbs and streptocarpus grow on the steep slopes.

between 400mm (16in) and 1,200mm (47in) of which about three quarters falls in the winter months. The summer is warm, averaging about 68°F (20°C), and the winter mild, averaging about 54°F (12°C); further inland the temperature ranges are greater.

Forests

The mainly seasonal rainfall, with a distinct dry period, does not favour the development of forests. What woodland there is along the coastal plain from Natal to southern Cape Province, on the escarpment in Transvaal and on some of the northern mountains is evergreen rain forest. Although of only a limited distribution, four different types of forest can be distinguished.

Temperate forest grows up to an altitude of 1,250m (4,000ft) where water from rain or mists is available for year-round growth.

The canopy of the forest is about 15–20m (50–65ft) tall, although the odd tree may reach 45m (145ft). The

dense and dark green foliage makes the forest dark, and the ground vegetation is made up almost entirely of ferns that prefer low light conditions.

Warm temperate forest only grows at low altitudes and usually close to the sea in frost-free areas with moderate average temperatures. Rainfall is high, at least 750mm (30in) of which about three quarters falls in the summer. Although the forest appears evergreen, many trees and shrubs shed leaves to survive winter droughts.

The trees grow in two layers below which is shrub and then a herbaceous layer. Lianas are very common, herbaceous types much more so than woody ones; whereas epiphytes are few and far between and ferns survive only in the wettest parts.

In the cooler regions further to the south, the forest is drier. There is a layer of trees below which grows a denser shrub layer. Where there is sufficient light the forest floor is covered with grasses. As areas 83 become drier the forest degenerates into scrub, and in the driest areas there is an abundance of larger, water-retentive succulent plants (euphorbias and aloes are particularly common). Growing with the succulents are a variety of spiny shrubby plants, especially species of *Asparagus*.

Sub-tropical forest occurs along the eastern coastal strip where the land is low lying, the climate is fairly tropical, the rainfall is high and there is no dry season. The forest is not particularly tall, but is made up of clearly defined layers; two of trees, one of shrubs, and a stratum of herbaceous plants at ground level. The tree canopy is dense and the trees are tied together by the mass of lianas; epiphytes are present but not particularly common.

On the whole the trees are evergreen and have large compound leaves; it is interesting to note that many of these tree species are deciduous when they grow in less favourable conditions. Large palms are also common; this is sometimes called the palm belt. Near the sea only one layer of trees grows in the sand. The canopy, with its mass of lianas, is so dense that little light reaches the forest floor; consequently there is little undergrowth.

Montane forest occurs on the slopes of the mountains around northern Transvaal, as well as in some ravines.

Savanna
Towards the north of the area, where the climate is more tropical, the rainfall is seasonal with a distinct dry period. This area includes the plateau lands of central and southern-central Africa, and is covered by a savanna type of vegetation.

In the south, a temperate savanna grows up to an altitude of about 1,250m (4,000ft or so) above which there is only grassland. Rainfall varies from about 400 to 1,000mm (16 to 40in) of which three quarters falls during the summer. The vegetation is either an open bush or very small tree savanna, with acacias forming the bulk of the woody species. The grasses are rather short and dense.

Grassland
Grassland covers the central part of the plateau and forms a very extensive and uniform type of vegetation. The average annual rainfall is 500–1,500mm (20–60in), most of which falls in summer. Daily and annual temperature ranges are wide with hot days and, at least in winter, short-lived but severe frosts. In summer everything appears green and flourishing, while in winter the landscape is pale brown and dead-looking. The temperatures and rainfall that prevent the growth of trees and bushes produce here a vegetation of herbaceous plants, all of a uniform size. In some areas aloes and even asparagus bushes grow, whereas at altitude tussock-forming grasses are very common and they often grow with species of *Erica*.

Semi-desert
Where the rainfall is less than 300mm (12in) the vegetation is low, often no more than 30cm (12in) and, as expected, there are large areas of bare soil. The arid areas are found inland on part of the plateau as well as in the very south on the low-lying coastal strip.

Apart from the short woody plants, annuals are very common; in fact where flora survives it is very rich and varied. In areas where there is least chance of frost, many plants display succulent characteristics: *Euphorbia*, *Cotyledon*, *Aloe*, and *Crassula* are all very characteristic of this vegetation.

Plant hunting in South Africa
When we come to South Africa we have considerable knowledge of the collectors. One of the principal as well as the earliest collectors was Francis Masson, who also introduced from the Canary Islands the ancestor of the Cineraria, *Senecio cruentus*. South Africa is the country where the greatest number of pelargoniums grow and many of the most popular had been brought back by the Dutch from early in the 18th century and numerous other species arrived as the century advanced; Masson himself introduced 47 new species. The first to have arrived seems to have been the Ivy-leaved geranium, *Pelargonium peltatum*, which the Duchess of Beaufort was growing as early as 1701. Nine years later she had the horseshoe geranium, *P. zonale*, while in 1714 Bishop Compton was cultivating the other parent of our zonal geraniums of the present day, *P. inquinans*. It is not known by whom the first hybrid of this was made, but it seems to have turned up in Dr Fothergill's garden before his death in 1780. These were all tall shrubby plants and the dwarf bedding form was first raised about 1836, but not released commercially until 1844. Of the parents of the show pelargoniums, *P. cucullatum* was in cultivation by 1690, *P. angulosum* in 1724. *P. acerifolium* was being grown in Britain by a Mr Archibald Thompson in 1784. We have no idea who Mr Thompson was nor how he obtained this plant. Masson himself brought back *P. grandiflorum* in 1794. Another species used was *P. fulgidum*, in cultivation in 1724.

Rocky desert: enough rainfall to support "super-succulents" like lithops

The main bout of hybridization seems to have taken place in the first two decades of the 19th century and were mainly undertaken by an amateur, Sir Robert Hoare, and the Colville nursery at which Robert Sweet, the monographer of the genus, was working and who may be supposed to have been the principal planner of the hybrids. He was also responsible for the race known as "Unique" pelargoniums, which crossed *P. fulgidum* with numbers of the scented-leaved pelargoniums in the attempt to combine scented leaves with attractive flowers. Apparently the main scented-leaved species used was *P. capitatum*, which was in cultivation as early as 1690. Few plants of the Unique strain are seen nowadays, yet they are very attractive and could well be revived.

Heathers

South Africa is also noted for its great richness in heathers and until 1914 they were all cultivated in greenhouses. Few are seen nowadays as pot plants, but occasionally *Erica ventricosa* is so grown. This was brought back by Masson in 1787. The small-flowered winter heath *E. gracilis* was obtained in 1794 by Richard Williams, a nurseryman, and this still makes an appearance at Christmas. The other winter heath, *E. hyemalis*, is a mystery. It has not been found in the wild and there is no record of its introduction. It became popular around 1845.

Cape primroses

James Bowie can claim all the credit for the first of the Cape primroses, *Streptocarpus rexii*. The modern streptocarpus hybrids are of more recent date and derive from Bowie's plant and the dark red *S. dunnii* which first flowered at Kew in 1886. In recent years the inclusion of *S. johannis*, introduced as recently as 1939, has given almost continuous flowering to these hybrids. They have become, somewhat belatedly, among the most popular of modern pot plants. Two of these species were introduced fortuitously. Between 1853-5 Captain Garden sent some ferns from Natal to Kew with soil round their roots and from this soil

Tree euphorbias dominate a stretch of eastern sub-tropical bush.

appeared seedings of *S. gardenii* and *S. polyanthus*. It would seem that there has to be an element of luck even in plant introductions.

Succulents

A number of popular South African pot plants are succulents and some of the most popular came early into cultivation. The favourite partridge-breasted aloe, *Aloe variegata*, for example, was being grown by Thomas Fairchild in 1720 and the almost equally popular *Haworthia margaritifera* was being grown by Sherard in 1725. Those that did not get early into cultivation were mostly sent back by the much maligned James Bowie. We have already met him with Cunningham in Brazil and when that expedition was complete Cunningham went to Australia and Bowie to South Africa, where he collected for Kew between 1816 and

Wet sclerophyll bush country where growth is dense and luxuriant

1823. He returned to South Africa in 1827 as a freelance collector and spent a penurious life in this occupation until his death in 1869. (Some authorities kill him off in 1853, but the later date seems the more probable.) He thus probably survived to the age of 80, which casts doubts on the writers who depicted him as an habitual drunkard. John Smith, later curator of Kew, accused him of spending "his evenings in public houses, telling stories of his encounters with buffaloes etc.", while in 1889 he was accused of spending his time "among the free and easy companions of the bar parlours, recounting apocryphal stories of his Brazilian and Cape travels, largely illustrated with big snake and wildebeeste adventures."

It does not sound too terrible. In fact after Banks's death Kew was going into a bad decline, and until his resignation Bowie would have seen the plants he collected with such enthusiasm being neglected and even being lost, so one can see alcohol becoming a comfort. In any case of the more popular S. African succulents, we can credit Bowie with *Aloe aristata, Haworthia reinwardtii, H. tesselata,* and *Cotyledon undulata.*

William Burchell in S. Africa

William Burchell seems in his *Travels in Southern Africa* (1822) to have been able to indulge in details that were beyond the means and time of most explorers. His expedition lasted just on four years and he "determined on delaying my journey until I should have collected some information respecting the country and acquired some experience and knowledge of its customs and peculiarities." He insisted also in learning not only Dutch, but also the native languages. "It is not enough to have mingled with the better part of society; the Boers must be heard, the Hottentots must be heard and the slaves must be heard." He laid out some £600 in having a special waggon built, which was loaded with "six muskets and powder horns, a fowling piece and shot belt, a large rifle, two cases of pistols, a cutlass, four barrels of gunpowder, saws,

Warm wet temperate forest, humid but not as hot as tropical rain forest

hammers, hatchets, adze, sledge hammer, ropes and lines, casks and canvas bags, lanterns, an iron melting ladle, more than 50 volumes, the Atlas Celeste of Flamsteed and various surveying equipment." Few people could manage such a collection.

It was Burchell who in 1811 first discovered the extraordinary "living stones" or lithops, on a desert area south of the Orange River. He wrote about his discovery: "On picking up from the stony ground, what was supposed a curiously shaped pebble, it proved to be a plant, and an additional new species to the numerous tribe of *Mesembryanthemum* but," he went on, "in colour and in appearance bore the closest relation

to the stones, between which it was growing.... By its form and colour ... this juicy little Mesembryanthemum may generally escape the notice of cattle and wild animals."

Lithops hiding (bottom centre) among stones in their natural habitat

ALOE
(LILIACEAE)

Aloes are slow-growing succulents from the sclerophyllous bush of southern Africa; they display diverse size and habit. Those popular as house plants make low rosettes of leaves and carry pink or orange-red tubular flowers.

A. aristata (lace aloe) ranges over large areas of the habitat, from hot and arid areas to grassy mountainous slopes. It is stemless with fleshy, dark-green leaves packed together tightly to form a rosette 10–15cm (4–6in) across. Leaf margins are white and finely toothed, leaf surface is generously spotted with small white tubercles and the tip has a tapering dry point. Orange flowers appear in summer.

A. variegata (partridge-breasted aloe) comes from the south-western part of southern Africa and is

usually found growing amongst bushes in partial shade. It often does better as a house plant than in the greenhouse. Leaves are V-shaped in section and arranged semi-erect in three ranks, the ranks usually spiralling. Irregular bands of greeny-white cross the medium-green leaves giving a distinctive pattern. Coral pink flowers appear in early spring.

Both make numerous offsets around the base, forming clumps.

Watering: Water

thoroughly during the growing season, allowing the mixture to dry out a little between applications, give only enough in the winter rest period to prevent shrivelling.

Potting mixture: Use a soil-based potting mixture.

Propagation: Pot up singly the larger offsets that form around the base.

Special points: Feed every two weeks during the growing season with a standard liquid fertilizer. Shade from strong sunlight in summer. When watering avoid wetting the leaves; water lodging in the leaf axils can cause rot.

ASPARAGUS
(LILIACEAE)

These lily relatives are regularly but incorrectly called ferns on account of their finely divided foliage (actually phylloclades, or modified stems or branches). Most are from

South Africa but a few originate in Sri Lanka. See Indian sub-continent. Some are true climbers (scrambling through stronger-stemmed plants) but most make excellent hanging basket plants. They produce fleshy roots, often with pronounced tubers on them, which store water and see the plants through short periods of water shortage. Insignificant flowers are produced followed by reddish berries. In nature they live in temperate savanna and warm temperate forests.

A. asparagoides (syn. *A. medeoloides*) is a strong climber from the Cape of Good Hope, and winds its stems around thin supports. Branchlets are shiny, a fresh green and up to 50mm (2in) long.

A. densiflorus Sprengeri, from Natal but beloved of butchers' shops everywhere, makes an excellent hanging basket plant with its drooping stems clothed with needle-like branchlets – a well grown mature plant can have a spread of 60cm (2ft). *A.d.* Myers (usually called *A. myersii*), the foxtail asparagus, has needle-like branchlets arranged around the stems like plumes or a fox's brush. Some stems are held upright, the older ones arch over gracefully, stem length around 38cm (15in).

A. setaceus (more widely known as *A. plumosus*) is often called lacefern and maidenhair fern from the very fine foliage, and is used as background to buttonholes. Branches are held horizontally, displaying the flattened branchlets; stems are wiry, short at first but longer in more mature plants. There is an especially vigorous kind, Robustus, and a dwarf kind, Nanus.

Watering: Water thoroughly. allowing the mixture to dry out a little before applying more during the growing season, but more sparingly in winter. Phylloclades fall if the mixture gets too dry.

Potting mixture: Use a soil-based potting mixture.

Propagation: Increase plants by dividing overcrowded clumps in spring. A sharp knife may be needed to cut through the mass of fleshy roots but retain as many as possible.

The lace aloe, a slow-growing succulent from S. African sclerophyllous bush

Special points: Old plants lose some of their vigour due to overcrowding: break up and repot the healthy younger pieces. Feed every two weeks with a general liquid fertilizer from spring to early autumn. When potting leave the level of the potting mixture well below the pot rim level, as the fat, tuberous root sections grow they force the mixture upwards. Provide thin cane supports for climbers. .

BEGONIA
(BEGONIACEAE)

B. cheimantha hybrids (Gloire de Lorraine type) are a cross between *B. dregei* (see below) and *B. socotrana* (Socotra). They bloom during winter.

B. dregei (Natal mountains) is semi-tuberous, to 60cm (2ft) tall, red stemmed, and small maple-shaped leaved with deep purple vein areas and a red underside. Flowers white. Develops a fleshy tuber, just above ground. Rarely out of flower.

B. sutherlandii from Natal

is a small trailing plant with red stems, fresh green maple-shaped leaves and small, clear orange flowers. Bulbils appear in virtually every leaf axil in late autumn.

B. weltoniensis (summer lorraine) is a hybrid between *dregei* and *sutherlandii* and has upright, red-tinged stems, satiny, maple-shaped leaves and bright pink flowers. Top growth is retained in winter, actual growth just ceases. Easy to propagate.

Full discussion of the genus and its culture is included in the section on S. America.

BRYOPHYLLUM
(CRASSULACEAE)

Popularly called bryophyllums these plants are now officially in the genus *Kalanchoe*. Two are commonly grown, *B. tubiflorum* from South Africa and *B. daigremontianum*, both native of Madagascar. They are discussed in detail in the section on Madagascar.

CEROPEGIA WOODII
(ASCLEPIADACEAE)

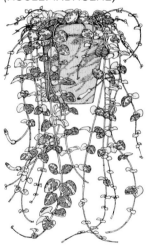

This succulent plant from temperate savanna and warm temperate forests in Zimbabwe and Natal, South Africa, has a corky, tuberous base and fine thread-like stems. The trailing stems meander through and over surrounding plants and small shrubs, rooting into suitable pockets of earth at intervals. Common names include hearts entangled and rosary vine, from the way the 20mm (¾in) heart-shaped leaves are spaced along the thin stems. Leaves are grey-green, marbled with silver on the upper side and rich purple beneath. Flowers are small, tube-shaped with a ballooned base, and reddish purple. Small tubers appear on the stems. Good in a hanging basket.

Watering: Water sparingly during the growing season and hardly at all during the winter rest period. Given too much water its leaves become thin and pale; when grown relatively dry they are fat and well coloured.

Potting mixture: Use equal-parts soil-based potting mixture and coarse sand or perlite.

Propagation: Use the small tubers that develop on the stems.

Special points: Feed once every two months during the active growth period only. Plants may be trained around small trelliswork pushed into the potting mixture. Can be grown as a small basket plant in a south-facing window.

CHLOROPHYTUM COMOSUM
(LILIACEAE)

Commonly called spider plant and St. Bernard's lily, *C. comosum* from South Africa makes an easy and very striking plant, particularly when well grown and displayed in a hanging basket with its small plantlets spilling over the edge. Leaves are soft and easily damaged, green and cream and arranged in a loose, arching rosette shape. Small, white, starry flowers are produced in summer on long yellow stems and are succeeded by groups of small plants – each tuft resembling the parent. In the wild these root down into the soil and form large carpets. *C.c.* Variegatum has green leaves edged white and *C.c.* Vittatum green leaves with a central white stripe. Though a tolerant plant, the sharpest colour leaf contrast is only possible in good light.

Watering: Water generously during the active growth period, more sparingly in winter.

Potting mixture: Use a soil-based potting mixture.

Propagation: Tufts of growth can be cut from the arching stems and treated as young plants – rooting them in a mixture of peat and sand. Alternatively they may be layered by pegging them down while still attached to the parent into nearby pots of peat and sand, detaching them when they have made some roots of their own.

Special points: Allow a few centimetres space between the surface of the potting mixture and the rim of the pot when potting, as the fleshy roots occupy space and force the mixture

upwards. In very warm rooms stand plants on trays of moist pebbles; dry air causes leaf tops to brown. When planting up baskets see that several young plants are included in one basket for maximum bushy effect.

CLIVIA MINIATA
(AMARYLLIDACEAE)

Often described as bulbous, but with the structure of a leek (a 'stem' made up of tightly overlapping leaf-bases), *C. miniata* comes from South Africa where it is found in scrubland, shielded from scorching sun by small shrubs and tall grasses. In cultivation it is tolerant of a wide range of growing conditions, including temperatures.

The leathery, dark-green, strap-shaped leaves may be up to 45cm (18in) long and are arranged in two ranks. The thick, fleshy flowerstalk pushes up from the central 'crease' of leaves around late winter and carries clusters of up to 15 trumpet-shaped, orange or orange-red flowers. Roots are thick and fleshy. There is a small-scaled type, no taller than 30cm (12in).

Watering: Water liberally during spring and summer, reduce the amount given in

the autumn and give only enough to prevent the mixture from becoming totally dry during the winter. When restarting into growth, give only a little water until new growth is clearly underway. Give liquid fertilizer every two weeks from spring to late summer.

Potting mixture: Use a soil-based potting mixture. The thick roots are inclined to push up the growing mixture allow ample space for this when potting.

Propagation: Propagate by taking off well-formed offsets in late spring

Special points: Grow in an east or west-facing window that gets some sun. See that the plant has a cool winter rest, (minimum 50°F (10°C)). Cut off embryo seedpods when flowers fall. Repot only when absolutely essential.

COTYLEDON
(CRASSULACEAE)

Cotyledons are shrubby succulents from the drier areas of sclerophyllous bush in South and southwest Africa. They display simple, stalkless leaves arranged in opposite pairs up fleshy stems. Two species are popular as house plants:

C. orbiculata makes a plant up to 50cm (20in) tall with fleshy, oval, grey leaves with reddish edges, thinly covered with white powder. Flowers orange in summer.

C. undulata, from Cape Province, is of slightly smaller size with fan-shaped fleshy leaves,

joined to the stems at the narrow base and with a wavy or scalloped tip. Dense white meal covers stem and leaves. Flowers orange-yellow in summer. Handle with great care as the white meal is easily spoiled.

Watering: Water moderately during growth period and very sparingly during the winter rest.

Potting mixture: Use a mixture of ⅔ soil-based mix and ⅓ coarse sand or perlite.

Propagation: Use tip cuttings 7.5–10cm (3–4in) long in spring.

Special points: Feed every two weeks during the growing period with a standard liquid fertilizer. Keep in a minimum winter temperature of 50°F (10°C). Move on into larger pots each spring, topdress older plants. Full sun produces the best coloured plants.

CRASSULA
(CRASSULACEAE)

Crassulas come from the drier areas of South Africa. Most are low-growing but some make small bushy shrubs. Day temperatures can be very high with a huge night-time drop causing heavy dew. Sea

mists and fogs can also move in from the coasts bringing sparse water suppliers. The flowers of most are tiny but may appear in very large numbers.

C. arborescens (syn. *C. cotyledon*) from Cape Province and Natal may grow to 75cm (2½ft) high with a thick, trunk-like stem and many branches. Leaves are almost round and fleshy, grey-green and margined with red. Rarely flowers indoors.

C. argentea (syn. *C. portulacea, C. obliqua*), also from Cape Province and Natal, grows to 1.2m (4ft) high. Its leaves are shiny green, spoonshaped, but not as the name might imply, silvery. The trunk is gnarled and gives an appearance of considerable age; the stems or branches are well proportioned and balanced, and contribute to the plant's common name of jade tree.

C. falcata is found from Cape Province to Natal and has fleshy, grey-green, sickle-shaped leaves up to 20cm (8in) long and terminal clusters of small, long-lasting, scarlet or orange-red flowers in summer.

C. lactea, from Natal and the Transvaal, is one of the easiest of crassulas, forming a rather sprawling shrub up to 60cm (2ft) tall.

Its leaves are ovate and dark-green with a line of white dots following the leaf edging. Large, multi-branched flowerheads, made up of many star-shaped, white flowers, appear in winter.

C. lycopodioides from S.W. Africa makes a small, multi-branched shrub. Its stems are competely hidden by 4 rows of tiny, scale-like dark-green leaves. Minute, yellow flowers appear in the leaf axils and could go unnoticed.

C. rupestris is distributed through the Cape Province and Namaqualand. Leaves are united in pairs on opposite sides of the stems, very fat, almost triangular, blue grey and often edged with red. Growth habit is sprawling, rarely above 30cm (12in) tall. Flowers, small, white or pale pink, are produced in winter.

Watering: Water liberally during the active growing period but always allow the mixture to dry out considerably before giving more.

Potting mixture: Use a mixture of 3 parts soil-based mixture and 1 part coarse sand or perlite.

Propagation: All the crassulas listed are extremely easy to root from tip cuttings – ideally taken in the spring or summer. Most will, in time, grow from single leaves, but the latter method is hardly ever worthwhile as stem cuttings are readily available.

Special points: Beware of mealy bugs that are partial to most succulents. *C. lycopodioides* will grow for years in a relatively small pot but the other species usually need moving on into larger pots each year. They do best on a sunny window-ledge when small and the bigger ones may need a small table to support them when reaching maturity. All benefit considerably from a summer spent in the garden, the fresh air and sun, toughening up the stems and improving leaf colour. Feed well-established plants every two weeks with the standard liquid fertilizer from spring to early autumn.

CYPERUS ALBOSTRIEATUS
(CYPERACEAE)

Cyperus are bog or riverside plants that thrive with their roots in water or very wet soil. As house plants they should be stood in deep saucers filled with water to emulate the riverside home. *C. albostriatus* (syn. *C. diffusus*) – South Africa – grows to almost 60cm (2ft) tall with tufts of basal leaves in purple-tinged sheathes

Watering: Keep permanently moist.

Potting mixture: Use a soil-based potting mixture.

Propagation: The easiest way is to divide overcrowded clumps in early spring. The umbrella shape of bracts at the top of the stalk can be induced to make roots by either standing it with 12mm (½in) of stem attached in water or damp sand. Pot up when some roots and a little new growth have formed

Special points: Feed actively growing plants at monthly intervals with a standard liquid fertilizer. Pot on into pots two sizes larger each spring, or as required.

CYRTOMIUM FALCATUM
(POLYPODIACEAE)

The holly fern, *C. falcatum*, comes from South Africa, as well as China, Japan and Polynesia. It is one of the most tolerant ferns available. Its leathery fronds to 60cm (2ft) in length are divided into 7.5–10cm (3–4in) shiny, holly-leaf-shaped pinnae of a dark green. They will spread, in time, to 60cm (2ft).

Watering: Water plentifully during the growing period, more sparingly if temperatures fall below 55°F (12°C).

Potting mixture: Use a mixture of equal parts peat- and soil-based compost.

Propagation: By division of overcrowded clumps in spring, pull apart into sections each having a piece of rhizome and 3–4 fronds.

Special points: Use half strength liquid fertilizer every two weeks during the growing period. Pot on into the next size pot only when the fronds fill the old pot. In warm rooms increase humidity by standing plants on pebble-filled trays. Periods of poor light will be tolerated but growth will be slow.

Sun-loving Crassula falcata

DRACAENA HOOKERANA
(AGAVACEAE)

In the wild, dracaenas range over a large part of tropical and temperate Africa. They are naturally upright-growing shrubs (rarely branching unless forced) with narrow strap-like or lance-shaped leaves, arching outwards and arranged around a woody stem. All grow relatively quickly and in 4–5 years may reach several feet tall.

D. hookerana comes from South Africa – Natal and the Cape of Good Hope – and has shiny green leaves with narrow white margins. There are several forms, differing little from each other.

See Africa for culture and information about other species of the genus *Dracaena*.

ERICA
(ERICACEAE)

Widely known as Cape heather, the ericas grown as house plants are from South Africa and best

treated as temporary plants. From grassland, high in cloud areas, they need cool temperatures and high humidity. Stems are woody, leaves fine and needle-like, flowers globe or bell-shaped.

E. gracilis grows to 45cm (1½ft) tall with tiny globe or bell-shaped, rose-pink flowers. There is a white variety, Alba.

E. hyemalis may reach 60cm (2ft) high with pink, white-tipped bell-shaped flowers. Flowers autumn to mid-winter.

E. ventricosa reaches 45cm (1½ft) tall and carries (from midsummer to mid-autumn) white or blush-pink flowers held erect in terminal clusters.

Culture: Give them light, but no direct sun; keep cool and humid by standing on moist pebble tray and daily mist-spraying. Keep thoroughly moist at the root; rain water is ideal.

FAUCARIA
(AIZOACEAE)

Faucarias are small succulent plants from Cape Province, South Africa, where they grow in rock crevices. Dew forms regularly, following rapid changes in temperature at night; the plants gain moisture from additional humid winds off the oceans around the Cape.

Two kinds are popular, both make low-growing rosettes of fleshy leaves and golden yellow flowers up to 5cm 2⅔in) across appear in the autumn.

F. tigrina (tiger jaw) has tooth-edged, greyish-green leaves, spotted with many tiny white dots.

F. tuberculosa makes a star shape with tooth-like warty growths on the upper surface of the dark green leaves.

Watering: Water plentifully, allowing the mixture to dry out considerably between

90

application in the growing season and give just enough to prevent shrivelling in winter.

Potting mixture: Ensure quick drainage by using 2 parts soil based mixture and 1 part coarse sand, chunky grit or perlite.

Propagation: Divide overcrowded clumps in late spring or early summer. Most pieces will have some roots attached; should there be none, allow the section to dry for 24 hours before planting in a very sandy mix.

Special points: Must be kept cool and in very bright light during the winter to ensure flowering the following year. Feed actively growing plants once a month with a half-strength liquid fertilizer.

GASTERIA
(LILIACEAE)

Gasterias are low-growing succulents and came, like faucarias, from the sclerophyllous bush of

Haworthia reinwardtii

Cape Province and south-west Africa. They have fleshy leaves usually arranged in two rows. Flowers are small and tubular and appear at the top of long flowerstalks.

G. liliputana, as the name implies, is one of the smallest. Its 38–60mm (1½–2½in), dark-green leaves, with prominent white markings, spiral into a rosette.

G. maculata has flat-topped, blunt-tipped, 15cm (6in), dark-green leaves with white bands – may also spiral.

G. pseudonigricans has leaves arranged in two ranks, those at the bottom of the layer are held flat but the higher they grow the more their leaves arch upwards at the tip. 12.5–15cm (5–6in) in length, these leaves are coloured dark green with white spots.

G. verrucosa has tapering, 10–15cm (4–6in), dark-green leaves covered with small white warty growths.

All gasterias prefer to be shaded from the midday sun.

Watering: Water moderately in the growing season and sparingly in the winter rest period.

Potting mixture: Use 3 parts soil-based mixture and 1 part coarse sand or perlite.

Propagation: Use offsets that develop around the base.

Special points: No need to feed, they are frugal plants. Use shallow pans as root growth follows that pattern. Repot each year in early summer, the fleshy roots of most rot off each late winter and plants might just as well be started into new growth in new mixture.

HAEMANTHUS
(AMARYLLIDACEAE)

 WT

Haemanthus, bulbous plants from the savanna and warm temperate forests of South Africa, have showy flowers. Some lose their leaves in winter, others retain them. They are easy to grow provided they are given sun and are left undisturbed; repotting often upsets the flowering cycle for a year or two.

H. albiflos from South Africa keeps its leaves, which are fleshy, strap-like and arch over like the two sides of a saddle (saddle plant is its common name). A pair of new leaves appears each spring from the centre of the bulb and a pair of older ones from the bottom yellows and can be gently pulled away. In early autumn a stout, 22cm (9in) long flowerstalk appears,

carrying a shaving-brush flowerhead made up of masses of white stamens, tipped yellow.

H. katherinae and *H. multiflorus*: The former, from Natal, loses its lance-shaped leaves for a short period of the year; it produces a globular head of salmon red, tubular flowers, with a mass of stamens. The latter loses its oval-pointed leaves and sends up a red ball of tube-shaped flowers tipped with prominent stamens in late spring.

Watering: Water moderately at all times those that keep their leaves. Act the same for the deciduous kinds while they have leaves and stop watering when leaves yellow.

Potting mixture: Use soil-based mixture.

Propagation: *H. albiflos* makes many offsets; use in propagation. Other kinds can be split up or grown from seed.

Special points: Once potted, leave as long as possible (even when obviously potbound); feed rather than repot. Do this every two weeks with a high-potash fertilizer in the active growth period only.

HAWORTHIA
(LILIACEAE)

Haworthias are succulent plants from South and southwest Africa. They live in hot, dry areas but usually among rocks, stones and scrub grass that shade their roots and give some protection during some part of the day from the fierce sun.

Their leaves are arranged in a rosette shape but this can be low and tight or elongated up to 30cm (1ft) tall. Their whitish, narrow and tubular flowers are carried on very long, very thin stems.

There are two distinct kinds. Some, usually found almost totally buried in grit and sand, have soft leaves, patches of which are light sensitive (the patches taking in light like windows). Others either have hard leaves studded with tubercles (white bumps), or they are covered with bristles that catch evening dew and act as a sunscreen.

H. cuspidata, from the Cape of Good Hope, is low-growing and makes a tight, pale-green rosette around 7.5cm (3in) across. Its triangular leaves are thick flat-topped and slightly translucent near the tip.

H. margaritifera (from Cape Province to Karroo) makes a dumpy rosette to 15cm (6in) across. Its thick and rigid leaves point upwards and are a deep green, heavily spotted with white warts.

H. reinwardtii also has hard, up-pointing leaves but the rosette is elongated and may in time need the support of a thin cane. Its dark-green leaves are densely covered with tiny whitish warts – in full sun the leaves take on a purplish hue.

H. tessellata grows 5–7.5cm (2–3in) across and hugs the ground. Its

thick, tooth-edged leaves curve downwards with the upper surface rounded and marked with an attractive network of white lines.

Watering: During the growing season water moderately, allowing the mixture to dry out a little between waterings. In winter give only enough water to prevent leaves shrivelling.

Potting mixture: Use a mixture made up of $\frac{2}{3}$ soil-based potting mixture and $\frac{1}{3}$ coarse sand or perlite.

Propagation: Offsets develop freely around the base, often already have roots attached and quickly develop on their own once potted up.

Special points: Haworthias are shallow-rooting and half pans suit them best.

KLEINIA
(COMPOSITAE)

Officially the genus *Kleinia* is now included in *Senecio*, but these plants are well known under the earlier name.

Kleinias are small succulent shrubs from the Cape Province of South Africa, some are very easy to grow, others more difficult.

K. articulata (*Senecio articulatus*) is the popular and easy-to-raise candle plant with cylindrical grey-green segments joined together and topped by a tuft of small, fleshy, arrow-shaped, green leaves. These leaves appear in winter and may fall off in late spring.

K. tomentosa (*Senecio haworthia*) has branching stems packed with 25mm (1in), fleshy, cylindrical leaves, the whole plant covered with white hairs. Sensitive to change.

Watering: These plants rest from mid-spring to early autumn but need some very moderate watering during that period. Water moderately at all times.

Potting mixture: Use $\frac{1}{3}$ sand or perlite and $\frac{2}{3}$ soil-based mixture.

Propagation: 7.5cm (3in) stem cuttings of *K. articulata* root easily in a sandy mixture in late summer and early autumn; those of *K. tomentosa* need to be kept only *just* moist during the rooting period.

Special points: No feeding is normally required. Repot in early autumn, it is normally sufficient to take off some of the old mixture; replace it with fresh and use the same pot size.

LITHOPS
(*AIZOACEAE*)

Lithops are very small succulent plants from South and southwest Africa. Their stone-like bodies lie half buried in sand, gravel or stones that protect them from the drying effects of hot winds and fierce sun. Each plant consists of two fleshy, semi-circular leaves merged together for most of their length. Large, daisy-like flowers (one per plant body) appear in summer from the slit between the leaves. After flowering, the leaves slowly shrivel and are replaced in early spring

Many kinds are available: the most popular are forms of *L. fulleri* and *L. lesliei*.

Watering: Lithops rest in winter when they should be kept cool and completely dry. Start watering in late spring when new leaves are fully developed, making the mixture just moist, and keep this up through to mid-autumn. Ideally use rain water.

Potting mixture: Use an equal-parts mixture of coarse sand or perlite and soil-based mix.

Propagation: By division of overcrowded clumps at the time of full growth (but do this only when the pot is really filled with plant bodies).

Special points: No feeding

is necessary. Use small half pots or pans. Take away dead (shrivelled) plant bodies only when they come away easily.

PELARGONIUM
(GERANIACEAE)

Thousands of hybrid pelargoniums are available today, as well as many of the species. The parentage of the hybrids is involved (and sometimes obscure) but they have all been developed from South African species.

There are several distinct groups of pelargonium. The most familiar are the zonals – these are the standard bedding-out "geraniums" of parks, with flowers in a gamut of colours including the popular scarlet, from orange to pink, magenta and white. Flowers are usually single but some doubles are available. The leaves almost always have an attractive dark band or "zone". Some varieties have leaves variegated with yellow, orange, red or a mixture of these. Zonals usually flower all summer long.

Miniatures are similar to zonals except in size,

having small leaves and flowers and compact growth.

Regal pelargoniums have plain but frilly-edged leaves and large flattish flowers usually with a central contrasting blotch. Colours are often very vivid: carmine, shocking pink, magenta – though there are pale pinks and some of sombre purple and maroon. Blooms are mainly produced in spring and early summer.

Ivy-leaved pelargoniums have trailing habit and are therefore good in hanging baskets. The usual colours seen are pink and mauve but there are red and white varieties. Leaves are plain-coloured, and fleshy.

Finally there is a large group of scented-leaf kinds with leaves of greatly varying size, shape and odour. Most familiar are lemon, orange, peppermint and cinnamon, but there are many others. Most of these are undeveloped species and have rather small, usually pinkish flowers in tight clusters.

The standard kinds (regals and zonals) are best for sun-porches, conservatories and lean-tos. For indoor rooms the miniatures, trailing kinds (ivy-leaved) and scented-leaved sorts are more suitable. All need sun to produce tight growth, good scent and lots of flowers.

Watering: Water moderately, allowing the mixture to almost dry out before applying more. In the winter rest period give only enough water to prevent complete drying out.

Potting mixture: Use a soil-based mixture.

Propagation: All kinds root easily if tip cuttings 5–10cm (2–4in) long are taken in summer or autumn. Water very sparingly during the rooting process (otherwise, black-leg or black stem rot can set in).

Special points: Pinch out growing tips of young plants to encourage bushy growth. Feed the flowering kinds with a high-potash liquid fertilizer every two weeks from spring to end-summer; use standard liquid fertilizer for the scented-leaved kinds. Do not, however, be too generous or soft, sappy growth will develop. Pot on into larger pots only when plants clearly need more root room. Keep cool for the winter rest period.

PLUMBAGO AURICULATA
(PLUMBAGINACEAE)
(syn. Plumbago capensis)

P. auriculata is from the Cape area of South Africa, and commonly called Cape leadwort. It is a strong-growing shrub, up to 1.2m (4ft) tall with rather coarse, medium green leaves arranged in whorls around thin, arching stems. Flower clusters are on short side shoots and comprise up to

10 tube-shaped blooms flaring out at the tip into 5 pale-blue petals. Blooms start to open mid to late spring, and can continue until mid-autumn. Flowers appear only on the current years growth, therefore any amount of pruning can be undertaken early in the spring. They look good trained around hoops of cane or wire, in a large cool porch or conservatory.

Watering: Water plentifully during active growth and sparingly in the winter rest period.

Potting mixture: Use soil-based mixture.

Propagation: Use 7.5–10cm (3–4in) semi-ripe cuttings in spring.

Special points: Feed with a high potash fertilizer every two weeks during active growth period. Move on into larger pots each spring. Keep cool in winter.

ROCHEA COCCINEA
(CRASSULACEAE)

R. coccinea is a small South African succulent shrub with small leaves packed tight together in four ranks against virtually upright stems. In spring and summer, dense clusters of

small, bright red, tubular flowers appear at the tips of the stems. These are long-lasting and often scented. White, and red and white flowered forms exist.

Watering: Water moderately during the growing season and sparingly in winter.

Potting mixture: Use $\frac{2}{3}$ soil-based mixture and $\frac{1}{3}$ coarse sand or perlite.

Propagation: 5–7.5cm (2–3in) tip cuttings root easily in late spring and summer.

Special points: Feed every two weeks with a high-potash fertilizer once flower buds first appear until flowering ceases. Pot on into larger pots as necessary. Nip out growing points to encourage bushy growth. See that they get a cool winter rest.

SANSEVIERIA TRIFASCIATA
(AGAVACEAE)

Mother-in-law's tongue or bowstring hemp are two common names given to the tall, sword-shaped-leaved plant from the Transvaal, Natal, and E. Cape. The fleshy, marbled leaves rise from a thick rhizome that runs over and just under the surface of the potting mixture. They are arranged in small groups, in loose rosette shape, and can reach 60cm (2ft) in length. Sansevierias are tolerant of a wide range of growing conditions but cannot stand cold and wet conditions.

S.t. Laurentii is the most popular with marbled leaves boldly edged with a golden-yellow stripe. *S.t.* Craigii has an even wider yellow stripe, and a recent introduction, *S.t.* Moonshine, makes plain green (unmarbled) silvery grey leaves. Totally different is a squat-growing form (looking like a small aloe), *S.t.* Hahnii. Often incorrectly listed as a separate species, there are silver and golden forms.

Watering: Water moderately during the active growth season, but very sparingly during the winter rest period. No water for up to three months will not kill this plant; too much water for one month in winter will.

Potting mixture: Use a soil-based potting mixture.

Propagation: Offsets are the easiest way of increasing plants. Detach in spring with some root attached and pot up individually. Alternatively, leaves may be cut up crosswise into 5–7.5cm (2–3in) pieces and potted shallowly in very sandy rooting mixture, but none of the variegated leaves will produce like offspring in that way.

The late-spring flowering Haemanthus multiflorus

Special points: Leaf growth is from the tip. Any damage to the awl-shaped tip means that no further growth will be made by that leaf. Feed actively growing plants with a half strength liquid fertilizer every two weeks. Pot on into larger pots only when the loose rosettes of leaves totally occupy the surface of the growing mixture.

SELAGINELLA KRAUSSIANA
(SELAGINELLACEAE)

Selaginellas form tight moss-like hummocks or loose fern-like fronds. Although not ferns they often resemble them and do produce spores rather than seeds. All thrive on high humidity and are best suited to the bottle garden or Wardian case. The genus is very large and covers large tracts of the world's surface.

S. kraussiana (South Africa) is fast-growing, creeps over the surface, rooting down at intervals but reaching up to one foot tall.

A form, *S.k.* Aurea is yellow-green.

Watering: Water plentifully throughout the year – never allowing the mixture to dry.

Potting mixture: Use a mixture of $\frac{2}{3}$ peat and $\frac{1}{3}$ coarse sand or perlite.

Propagation: Take short tip cuttings 25–50mm (1–2in) long in spring, keep warm and humid until rooted.

Special points: Do not feed at other than $\frac{1}{8}$-strength standard liquid fertilizer every two weeks during the growing period. "Normal" feeding will result in coarse, untypical growth. Use shallow pans or half-pots. Move on into larger pans as plants grow over the edge of the older ones. Make the air more humid by standing on trays filled with moist pebbles, or grow in a terrarium.

SENECIO
(COMPOSITAE)

The senecios grown as house plants are trailing or

climbing plants from South or South West Africa. Two look very much like ivy (*Hedera*), the other looks like its common name, string of beads. All have soft and fleshy leaves and typical daisy (or groundsel) flowers.

S. macroglossus (waxvine) is grown in its variegated-leaved form, *S.m.* Variegatus, and comes from E. Cape Province. Stems are purple, leaves medium green, very heavily marked with creamy-yellow.

S. mikanioides (German ivy) has green stems and rather coarse green leaves with sunken vein areas. Has naturalized in England and California.

S. rowleyanus (string of beads) has creeping stems, round, fleshy leaves with pointed tips, stems can grow to 60 or 90cm (2 or 3ft).

Watering: Water moderately during the growth period but sparingly in winter.

Potting mixture: Use a mixture of ⅔ soil-based and ⅓ coarse sand or perlite.

Propagation: Take tip cuttings of all kinds in spring or early summer.

The shoots of *S.m.* Variegatus that are all yellow (lacking chlorophyll) will *not* root.

Special points: All can be allowed.to trail from hanging baskets. The two "ivy" types can be guided up thin canes or other supports. Feed actively growing plants once a month with half strength fertilizer. Watch out for aphids that tend to collect on the young shoots.

SPARMANNIA AFRICANA
(TILIACEAE)

In South Africa sparmannias grow as small trees; in the confines of a pot they are fast-growing large shrubs. Two years growth will produce a plant 1.2–1.8m (4–6ft) tall. It is usually best to start afresh with young plants every other year.

Leaves are roughly heart-shaped, light-green and slightly hairy. They are held on 15–23cm (6–9in) long leafstalks, well away from the woody stems, giving a pleasant open look to the shrub. White flowers, up to 25mm (1in) across, appear

in large clusters (up to 100) towards the end of winter, and open in succession until mid-spring. Four papery petals surround a mass of yellow and red stamens.

Although rarely seen, there is a double-flowered form, Flore Pleno, and a dwarf kind, Nana.

Watering: Thoroughly moisten the mixture but then allow it to begin to dry out again before applying more.

Potting mixture: Use a soil-based potting mixture.

Propagation: Tip cuttings root very easily in late spring, even when stood in water.

Special points: Move on into larger pots as necessary (perhaps twice a year) but topdress with fresh mixture when maximum pot size is reached. Feed every two weeks throughout most of the year. Stakes are not required, stems are stout enough. Pinch out growing points during the summer months if stems don't branch naturally.

STAPELIA VARIEGATA
(ASCLEPIADACEAE)

S. variegata is a succulent and has the common name

starfish plant, from the shape of the yellow, purple spotted flower. The flowers are very unpleasant smelling and can appear at any time from spring to early autumn. Stems are four-sided, with soft teeth at the edges, they branch freely from the base and quickly form dense clumps, rarely above 15cm (6in) tall.

Watering: Water very sparingly at all times. Because of the clustering stems they are best planted in shallow pans and left to stand in water for 20 minutes to allow the mixture to take up as much as the plants need. Allow the mixture to dry out completely before repeating the exercise.

Potting mixture: Use ½ soil-based mix and ½ coarse sand or fine grit.

Propagation: By seed or stem cuttings (the latter should be allowed to dry for 2 or 3 days before planting) in spring.

Special points: Feed once a month (adding the liquid fertilizer to the dish of water) from spring to early autumn only. Move on into larger pans or half pots in spring, when the stems have covered the surface area of the mix. Avoid wetting any cut or damaged sections of stem until properly healed, otherwise rot can set in.

STRELITZIA REGINAE
(STRELITZIACEAE)

Best suited to a conservatory or large porch, the bird of paradise flower, *S. reginae,* comes from the Transkei-Bantu

95

area of South Africa and needs space. Its spear-shaped leaves are carried on 60–90cm (2–3ft) stalks. It has a remarkable flowerhead at the top of a 90cm (3ft) flowerstalk. A green bract houses the orange and deep blue flowers. This plant enjoys warmth during the summer but prefers a cool winter rest (around 50°F (10°C)).

Watering: Water moderately during the growth period and only enough during the rest period to prevent the mixture from drying out.

Potting mixture: Use a soil-based mixture.

Propagation: Divide old, overcrowded, clumps (perhaps with a sharp knife) in the spring. Also seed.

Special points: Flowers are only produced on mature plants. Pot on each spring until 20 or 25cm (8 or 10in) pots are reached, thereafter top dress. Plants flower best when potbound and when left undisturbed. Feed every two weeks from spring to end of summer with standard liquid fertilizer. Sun is essential for flowering.

STREPTOCARPUS
(GESNERIACEAE)

The genus *Streptocarpus* is mainly concentrated in Africa and Madagascar, ranging from southern Ethiopia almost to the Cape and across the continent to Angola. A few (rarely grown as house plants), come from Southeast Asia. The wooded ravines and valleys of the Drakensburg mountains are a typical habitat.
Growth habit varies enormously: some make just one huge leaf, others are small bushy shrubs, but those grown as house plants are more often of rosette shape.

Quite the best kinds are recent hybrids – Constant Nymph, variants of that hybrid and the John Innes Hybrids, the latter developed at the John Innes Institute and all bearing girls' names. All have manageable-sized leaves, strap-shaped, and resembling those of the primrose in texture – a common name is Cape primrose. All are extremely free-flowering and virtually non-stop. Flowerstalks, 15–23cm (6–9in) long, carry funnel-shaped flowers that flare out at the tip into 5 rounded segments. Blooms, around 5cm (2in) across, are nearly always arranged in pairs and can be followed by long, twisted seedpods. Young plants flower early in life.

A selection giving wide colour range could include: Constant Nymph – Deep violet blue with deeper veining from the yellowish

white throat;
Maassen's White – Pure white with a yellow eye;
Snow White – Compact plant, small, freesia-like, white flowers with yellow eye;
Diana – Deep cerise, white throat;
Fiona – Pink with wavy edged petals;
Karen – Magenta-pink, lower petals veined darker colour;
Marie – Dusky purple, veined white at throat;
Paula – Reddish purple, darker lower petals, veins into yellow throat;
Tina – Pale pink, deeper in the centre.

S. polyanthus (Natal), *S. rexii* (S. Africa) and *S. saxorum* (Tanzania) are species rarely met with although the last makes a decorative plant with branching habit, soft, velvety, grey-green leaves and pale lilac flowers.

Watering: Thoroughly moisten and then allow the mixture to dry out before applying more.

Potting mixture: Use a soil-based potting mixture to which has been added a ¼ part coarse peat or perlite.

Propagation: Mature plants normally make clumps of growth, and sections can be taken off and potted up on their own. New plants may also be made by cutting leaves across into 5–7.5cm (2–3in) sections and rooting them in peat and sand, or perlite. Leaves may also be filleted of their prominent midrib, placing the cut edges into contact with the rooting mixture, when a whole row of small plants will grow from the "raw" edges.

Special points: Stand plants on trays of moist pebbles to increase humidity. Streptocarpus will tolerate a very wide range of temperatures, with a minimum of around 50°F (10°C). Watch out for aphids which tend to collect on the flowerstalks and buds – they rarely attack leaves. Do not overpot as too large a pot encourages rampant leaf growth at the expense of flowers. Feed every two weeks with a high-potash fertilizer from spring to mid-autumn. Take off embryo seedpods (the flowers fall off) and cut off flowerstalks at the base when all blooms have fallen. Encourage plants to have a short winter rest by reducing watering.

VALLOTA SPECIOSA
(syn. *V. purpurea*)
(AMARYLLIDACEAE)

Vallota speciosa is a bulbous plant which produces striking, trumpet-shaped, bright scarlet flowers in late summer and autumn. Each bloom may be 7.5–10cm (3–4in) in diameter, in a cluster of

The lithops' succulent leaves aid survival in fierce heat.

three to eight, at the top of a 45–60cm (18–24in) flowerstalk. Leaves are dark green, tinged purple at the base, 20mm ($\frac{3}{4}$in) wide and 30–38cm (12–15in) long; they are retained through the winter. The brown-skinned bulbs are the size of a shallot and should be planted so that they are only half buried. They reproduce rapidly, developing small bulbs at the base and quickly form dense clumps of mature and small bulbs. There is a white-flowered form *V.s.* Alba, and one with pale salmon-pink blooms, *V.s.* Delicata. Plants flower best when they are left undisturbed; repotting often results in a loss of flowers for a year or two, but is in time inevitable. Vallotas are tolerant of a wide range of temperatures but do best if given a cool (50°F (10°C)) winter rest.

Watering: Water generously during the active growth period but allow the mixture to dry out a little between applications. Water very sparingly during the winter rest period.

Potting mixture: Use a soil-based potting mixture.

Propagation: Increase plants by taking off well-grown bulbs in spring, potting several bulbs up together.

Special points: Feed

plants with a high-potash liquid fertilizer every two weeks from spring to mid-autumn. In spring repot, or pot on, only when the bulbs completely crowd the growing area. Topdress plants with fresh compost in spring in other years. Some sunlight is essential for the production of a good crop of bloom.

VELTHEIMIA
(LILIACEAE)

Veltheimias are bulbous plants with fleshy leaves and a tall flowerspike hung with many narrow, tube-shaped flowers clustered together at the top. The bulb has a dormant period (in the wild the hot, dry summer). In cultivation growth normally starts in late summer or early autumn, first with the production of the leaves arranged in rosette shape from the tip of the bulb, followed by the flowerspike pushing up from the centre in mid-winter and developing slowly over two or more months.

Veltheimias lie dormant to survive the summer.

V. capensis has blue-green leaves with wavy edges, a purple-spotted flowerstalk and pale pink blooms.

V. viridifolia's leaves are a glossy viridian green and flowers pinky-purple.

Watering: Be very sparing with water as bulbs start into growth, but increase the amount given as top growth develops; never more than moderate. In late summer start to reduce watering, and eventually stop.

Potting mixture: Use $\frac{3}{4}$ soil-based mixture and $\frac{1}{4}$ really coarse sand or grit (or perlite).

Propagation: Mature bulbs make offsets most years and these should be detached as bulbs start into growth in late summer and grown on.

Special points: Use a high-potash liquid fertilizer once a month when leaves are 15–20cm (6–8in) tall until flowers fade. Bright light, including some sun, is needed to bring these winter-flowering plants into bloom, but once the light gets stronger they will tolerate poorer light. Watch out for aphids, which tend to cluster around the developing flowerspike. Repot into fresh mix, just as new growth starts.

Madagascar

With more than 4,000 species of flora growing in widely varying habitats, Madagascar is an important source of plants in cultivation. The polka-dot plant (*Hypoestes phyllostachya*) is at home on the shady rain-forest floor where it spreads (and roots down) in its search for light (in unnatural confinement it needs bright light to make an attractively compact plant). Here too are the Madagascar periwinkle, the colourfully leaved *Dracaena marginata*, the best staghorn fern – *Platycerium bifurcatum*, and from sclerophyllous regions, the kalanchoes and crown of thorns.

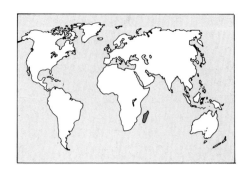

Madagascar is a large island that covers about 230,000 sq miles and is about 940 miles long. Its climate is entirely tropical; the northernmost point of the island is about 12° south of the equator and it reaches down to about 25½° south. The variety of climatic and local conditions means that there are many varied ecological environments. In fact, the only type that is missing is very high mountain; the highest mountain mass reaches to 2,900m (9,500ft) above sea level.

The relief of the land and prevailing winds determine the main plant formations. The narrow coastal plains in the east, the steep rise of the mountains and the high plateaux (constantly exposed to the trade winds) all receive much rainfall, at least 1,500mm (60in). In these areas dense rain forest still covers large areas. On the other side of the island, from about 800m (2,600ft) altitude, the land gradually slopes towards the coastal plains. Here the trade winds bring little or no rain, and the area is hot, dry and arid. These areas, however, come under monsoon influences during the summer, but this monsoon effect rapidly dwindles towards the south.

In other words, rainfall declines from east to west on one hand, and from north to south on the other; the very south of the island receives only a small amount of irregular rainfall (about 300mm (12in)) and the dry season lasts about ten months.

These rainfall gradients result in a gradation of vegetation from tropical rain forest to dense dry forest to deciduous or even sclerophyllous forest and finally to open bushland in the south. In both the south and west, the drought is often intensified by the sandy and limestone soils which hold little water. There, some plants show extreme adaptations to conserve moisture.

Throughout the country, most of the rain that falls does so during the hottest time of the year. Average temperatures are about 80°F (27°C) at their highest and 73°F (23°C) at their lowest, though the greatest variations are in the south. Altitude affects temperature by reducing them by about 2°F (0.5°C) for each 100m (325ft) increase in altitude; in some areas of the high plateaux, at about 1,000m (3,300ft) altitude, it actually freezes for a few days each year.

Madagascar is divided into two major phytogeographical regions that are distinct in both their vegetation and climate; these are the Eastern Malagasy Region and the Western Malagasy Region. Each of these regions is subdivided into domains.

Eastern Malagasy Region

East domain
This reaches from the eastern coast up to an altitude of 800m (2,600ft). The rainfall is high, up to 4,000mm (158in), with well over half falling during the hot season. The humidity and temperature are always high and there is no dry season. The climax vegetation is dense rain forest.

Sambirano domain
In the north of the island this continues westwards towards the coast on the western side of the plateau. It covers only a relatively small area and is essentially similar to the east domain.

Centre domain
This includes the central plateaux area, the mountains and both the east and west slopes above 800m (2,600ft). The rainfall is fairly high, above 1,500mm (60in), but it nearly all falls during the hot season and, consequently, the dry season may last for several months. The aridity is moderated by the effects of fog and condensation, however, and towards the east, the climax vegetation is a tropical rain forest. This is not as tall as that of the east domain but it is much richer in epiphytes. Towards the east, on the other hand, where the trade winds are hotter and drier, the climax vegetation is only a low sclerophyllous type of forest.

High mountain domain
This is the land above 2,000m (6,500ft).

Western Malagasy Region

West domain
This is below 800m (2,600ft) and the rainfall decreases from 1,500mm (60in) in the north to 500mm (20in) in the south; the dry season, when the air is very dry, lasts from six to eight months. The climax vegetation is of various types of forest, usually dense, dry and deciduous. The northernmost tip of the island is included in this domain.

South domain
This is most notable for its increased aridity and its low and irregular rainfall of no more than 500mm (20in); there are often long periods of drought. The climax vegetation is either deciduous forest or wooded country or dense bush with many highly adapted leafless succulent plants.

Vegetation
The great variety of conditions and

the richness of the flora account for the very varied and often original types of vegetation found on the island. The wetter tropical rain forest areas, at least superficially, resemble tropical rain forest elsewhere. On the other hand, the dry areas have certain plants morphologically well-adapted to survive drought, and they give these areas a very characteristic appearance: rocky areas with aloes, kalanchoes and succulent composites and the southern areas with didierias and euphorbias; all form very unusual landscapes.

Between the dry and wet extremes, all types of intermediate vegetation can be found. Many of these plant formations have now, unfortunately, either completely disappeared or can only be found in small patches. This is particularly so in the central and western regions where, on the whole, the natural climax vegetation has been destroyed.

Wooded areas
The eastern domain stretches nearly the whole length of the island but it is rarely more than 50km (30 miles) wide. The vegetation, where it has been destroyed by clearing, consists of low altitude dense rain forest. This is conventional tall tropical rain forest with three well defined layers. The upper stratum is of trees about 25–30m (80–100ft) tall and is mixed with masses of lianas; the whole layer appears very uniform despite the wide variety of species that are its constituent parts. The trees of the middle stratum are totally different, much shorter and more substantial and, of course, fairly shade-tolerant.

The lowest stratum, the ground layer, is not at all continuous, with large areas of bare ground covered with dead leaves and branches. Here and there, either separated or in small groups, grow ferns, dwarf palms, herbs and shrubs. Epiphytes, mainly consisting of ferns and orchids, grow commonly in all layers of the forest.

In the Sambirano domain, where the structure of the tropical rain forest is very similar to that found in the eastern domain, the species do differ.

Tree ferns in a dense rain forest

In the eastern part of the central domain grows a medium altitude dense rain forest. This still has a high annual rainfall but a somewhat more marked dry season and a lower minimum temperature. This is a dense forest, more or less all evergreen, and containing a very wide variety of species. The trees are in one layer 20–25m (65–80ft) tall, beneath which is an underground of plentiful shrubs and herbs. The undergrowth contains tree ferns as well as many shade-loving plants, closely related to temperate region plants. Once again epiphytes are abundant, not only orchids, ferns, cacti *(Rhipsalis)* and crassulas, but also mosses and lichens that often completely cover the tree branches. With an increase in altitude the degree of mossiness increases, and, at higher levels, the forest is often called 'mossy and herbaceous undergrowth forest'.

Between 1,300 and 2,000m (4,250 and 6,500ft) lichen forest replaces mossy forest. This is a sclerophyllous type of forest with small leaves and twisted trees reaching only to a height of about 12m (40ft). Again, epiphytes abound, and on trees coated with moss masses of them grow, especially ferns and orchids. Many of the epiphytic species also grow on the ground in the thick covering of moss and lichen that seems to smother the forest floor. This forest has now mainly been destroyed and only small pockets now remain. It is often replaced by bushland with heather-like plants.

On the bare rocky outcrops, which are virtually soil free, grows a very low type of vegetation adapted to extremely arid conditions as well as a high intensity of sunlight. Although found in rocky places throughout the island, this vegetation type is best developed in the high mountain regions. The plants may have succulent stems like euphorbias, or succulent leaves like kalanchoes, or they may be so-called reviviscent species. These plants apparently dry up and shrivel when water is not available, but when wetted by rain they swell and grow; they are often called resurrection plants.

On the western slopes of the central domain the natural vegetation is a sclerophyllous forest, but it is only found in very small patches and often poorly degraded, appearing like a densely wooded savanna as the undergrowth has been replaced by light loving grasses. The forest is very susceptible to fire, and is replaced by woody savanna or grassland. In the valleys a rich forest still grows with many palms and species that are common in the eastern domain.

The vegetation of the western domain is, once again, mainly forests, but very different to those so far described. The main difference is that most of the trees are deciduous and lose their leaves during the dry season. Understandably, as the dry season grows longer (mainly by moving south), more plants highly adapted to survive drought are found, such as leafless euphorbias and plants with swollen trunks for water storage.

There are also true savannas, the grasses forming a dense carpet over much of the western domain.

In this area the factor limiting growth is available water and, consequently, the soil type has a large influence on the vegetation that does grow. In fact, several types of forest can be distinguished depending upon the nature of the soil. On lateritic clays the soil is humus-rich as organic matter decomposes only slowly due to the lack of water. The forest is

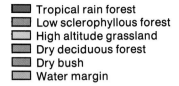

- ▨ Tropical rain forest
- ▨ Low sclerophyllous forest
- ▢ High altitude grassland
- ▨ Dry deciduous forest
- ▨ Dry bush
- ▨ Water margin

1. *Bryophyllum daigremontianum*
2. *B. tubiflora*
3. *Catharanthus roseus*
4. *Cyperus alternifolius*
5. *Dracaena marginata*
6. *Euphorbia milii*
7. *Hypoestes phyllostachya*
8. *Kalanchoe beharensis*
9. *K. blossfeldiana*
10. *K. pumila*
11. *K. tomentosa*
12. *Platycerium bifurcatum*

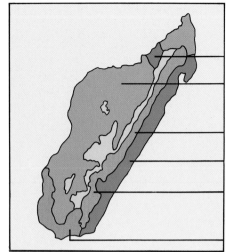

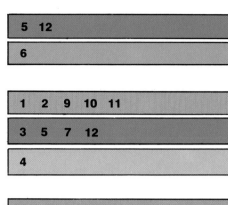

5	12
6	
1	2	9	10	11
3	5	7	12
4	
8	

sparse, about 15m (50ft) or so tall with a wide variety of species; lianas are abundant and there is a shrubby undergrowth. Epiphytes are rare, in fact only a few orchids with highly drought resistant leaves grow. This type of forest is found in the north and north west of the island.

On soils that are sandy, forests are widespread. In the most humid areas the vegetation is similar to that found on clay; tamarind trees are very common. Further south, where it is more arid, the forest takes on a peculiar appearence with bulbous trunked baobab trees and large leafless euphorbias.

On the limestone soils the vegetation is again different with the shrubby undergrowth thickly entwined with lianas. On the rocky escarpments the flame tree, *Poinciania regia*, grows. Where the soil is very thin and water is in very short supply, the vegetation resembles that found in the south of the island. Plants are often rooted deep into cracks in the rock and have small leaves or even spines; stems are often swollen into peculiar shapes. These dense and dry forests cover large areas on the limestone slopes, though elsewhere they have mainly disappeared due to fire and land clearing. In some areas odd palm trees remain, indicating the vegetation that used to grow there.

The main feature of the south domain is the small amount and irregularity of rainfall. Apart from water courses, the vegetation is all highly adapted to conserve water. On the whole, the vegetation is a type of thicket with leafless bushy euphorbias and didierias. The didierias very closely resemble cacti and the euphorbias have fleshy and spiny branches.

Other species of trees are rare; the bush species, however, are of quite a wide variety, but all have very small or no leaves and they all tend to be spiny. Little grows on the ground, though there is the occasional resurrection plant or fleshy aloe or kalanchoe.

The only other woody vegetation is the mangrove area along the western coast where conditions are most favourable to its development.

Dracaenas grow best in good to bright light and high humidity.

BRYOPHYLLUM
(syn. **Kalanchoe**)
(CRASSULACEAE)

Two are commonly grown, both native of Madagascar (E. region, C. domain), both succulent sub-shrubs to 90cm (3ft) tall and both carrying numerous young plants with aerial roots on their fleshy leaves.

B. daigremontianum rarely branches, bears deep-green leaves with brownish markings in opposite pairs. These are arrow or shovel-shaped and can be up to 25cm (10in) long, notched at the edges where the small plantlets develop. Flowers pink and yellow, on long stalks in winter.

B. tubiflora makes tubular, green and brown striped leaves set in three ranks around the stems. Young plantlets grow on the leaf tips. Flowers orange-red in autumn.

Watering: Water moderately during the active growth period and very sparingly in the winter.

Potting mixture: Use soil-based potting mixture.

Euphorbia milii – *the crown of thorns*

Keep Cyperus alternifolius, *a river bank plant, permanently moist.*

Propagation: Just plant the plantlets, or look around the base of the parent plants where plantlets have rooted.

Special points: Feed every two weeks with a standard liquid fertilizer during growth

CATHARANTHUS ROSEUS
(APOCYNACEAE)
Known as the Madagascar periwinkle and sometimes

called *Vinca rosea, C. rosea* is a small shrub found in both Madagascar (E. region, E. domain) and India. Its five-petalled, usually very pale pink flowers appear throughout the summer above glossy oval leaves. Height and spread are about 30cm(1ft).

Young plants appear on the market in late spring and prove valuable as house plants flowering until early autumn, when they should be discarded. White flowering forms and one with a carmine "eye" are available.

Culture: Grow in bright light, ideally a window that gets some sun each day, pot on as necessary during the summer using a soil-based mixture. Water plentifully and feed fortnightly with a high potash liquid fertilizer.

Plants are normally raised from seed sown very early in the year.

CYPERUS ALTERNIFOLIUS
(CYPERACEAE)

Cyperus are found along the river banks of north, tropical and southern Africa and in the adjacent islands. They are sedges and closely related to rushes and grasses with upright

101

stems (leaves are actually at the base and hardly noticeable) topped with bracts that look like leaves and brownish grasslike flowerheads. As house plants they should be stood in deep saucers filled with water to emulate the riverside home.

C. alternifolius, (Madagascar, Reunion and Mauritius) commonly called umbrella plant, reaches 1.2m (4ft) tall with slightly drooping bracts. There is a dwarf form *C. a.* Gracilis, and a white-striped (or virtually totally white) kind, *C. a.* Variegatus, that is very difficult to keep in good condition due to a lack of chlorophyll.

Watering: Keep permanently moist.

Potting mixture: Use a soil-based potting mixture.

Propagation: The easiest way is to divide overcrowded clumps in early spring. The umbrella shape of bracts at the top of the stalk can be induced to make roots by either standing it with 12mm ($\frac{1}{4}$in) of stem attached in water or damp sand. Pot up when some roots have formed and a little new growth appears.

Special points: Feed actively growing plants at monthly intervals with a standard liquid fertilizer. Pot on into pots two sizes larger each spring, or as required.

DRACAENA MARGINATA
(AGAVACEAE)

Often confused with a near relation, cordyline, dracaenas tolerate a wide range of temperatures.

D. marginata is popular and relatively easy, and comes from Madagascar. Each narrow deep green leaf has a fine red or purple margin. There is a variegated leaved form *D. m.* Tricolor with cream stripes in the green and a new form with red suffusing the whole leaf.

Watering: Water plentifully when in active growth, more sparingly in the winter.

Potting mixture: Use a soil-based potting mixture.

Propagation: Stem, tip and basal cuttings can be used in spring. Tips should be rooted in a propagator, basal shoots will normally have some roots attached and will grow if enclosed in a plastic bag. Set 7.5–10cm (3–4in) stem cuttings upright in a peat and sand mixture. With warmth they will send down roots and develop growing points.

Special points: Give extra humidity by standing pots on trays of moist pebbles. Feed every two weeks with a standard liquid fertilizer from spring to early autumn. Repot only when really necessary. Watch out for mealy bugs that may inhabit the leaf axils. The loss of older leaves is quite normal, leaving behind the quite attractive bare stem.

EUPHORBIA MILII
(EUPHORBIACEAE)

E. milii (syn. *E. splendens*) is the crown of thorns from

Madagascar, (W. domain, W. region), a succulent with viciously spined stems, elliptic green leaves and flowers with a pair of small bright red or yellow bracts. There is a dwarf form, *E. m.* Imperatae, rarely growing above 25cm (10in) tall, spined but surprisingly no more than prickly.

Watering: Water moderately in the growing period and sparingly in winter.

Potting mixture: Use a mixture of $\frac{2}{3}$ soil-based mixture and $\frac{1}{3}$ coarse sand or perlite.

Propagation: Stem cuttings 7.5–10cm (3–4in) long (dip cut end in water and spray the wound of the plant to stop sap flow); leave for 24 hours before planting in a very sandy rooting mixture.

Special points: Feed actively growing plants with the standard liquid fertilizer every two weeks. Move plants into slightly larger pots every other year; firm new mixture around the roots very thoroughly. Should lower leaves fall in winter this is quite natural; they will not be replaced.

HYPOESTES PHYLLOSTACHYA
(syn. *H. sanguinolenta*)
(ACANTHACEAE)

With a common name polka-dot plant, *H. phyllostachya* is a low-growing plant from Madagascar (E. region, E. domain) with oval-pointed olive-green leaves heavily marked with pink patches. Improved forms in recent years have given plants with at least half of the leaf surface coloured pink. Small lavender flowers appear in summer but are of little consequence. Really good light encourages the best leaf coloration.

Watering: Water moderately during the growing period; if kept too wet they will make elongated, untypical growth; for best, close, highly-coloured leaves a certain dryness between waterings is essential.

Potting mixture: Use a soil-based potting mixture.

Propagation: Best raised from seed, of which there are several new and improved forms.

Special points: Feed every two weeks with the standard liquid fertilizer during the active growth period. These are greedy plants and should be moved on into larger pots whenever they have filled their pots with roots. Pinch out growing tips to encourage bushy growth.

KALANCHOE
(CRASSULACEAE)

Kalanchoes are small succulent plants or shrubs occurring over a very wide area. Most of the more popular ones are from

Madagascar where they grow in full sun or in the partial shade of taller shrubs and small trees. Most are grown for their decorative fleshy leaves, but *K. blossfeldiana* is grown for its striking flowers.

K. beharensis from the Western region: South domain of Madagascar is the tallest kind grown indoors. It reaches 90cm–1.2m (3–4ft) but older plants tend to lose their lower leaves and some of their appeal. Leaves are arrow-shaped covered on the underside with white hairs and on the upper side with gingery-red hair – quite a distinctive colour. Flowers are rarely produced. Replace frequently.

K. blossfeldiana (E. region, C. domain) hybrids are now extremely popular (the wild species is rarely seen). Grows to 30cm (12in) tall with juicy-looking, deep green, red-edged leaves. Flowerheads are a dense cluster of small four-petalled flowers whose colour ranges from bright red to yellow or orange. In recent years specialist growers have produced flowering plants at all seasons by restricting the day-length – they are short-day (winter) flowering plants. (Often discarded when past their best). Good strains of seed are available.

K. pumila grows to 15cm (6in) tall and then sprawls. They came from the same area of Madagascar as *K. blossfeldiana*. Leaves are scallop-edged and they, and the stems and flower buds, are heavily encrusted with flaky-white meal. Flowers are pink and

appear in spring. Good in baskets.

K. tomentosa (Also E. region, C. domain) grows in a loose rosette shape with semi-erect, sage-green leaves, edges with rusty brown, the whole covered with short bristly white hairs.

Watering: Water sparingly through the growing season and very sparingly after flowers have faded. Leaves become gross and untypical if overwatered.

Potting mixture: Use ¾ parts soil-based mixture and ¼ part coarse sand or perlite.

Propagation: Tip cuttings and offsets root very easily in spring. Seed of *K. blossfeldiana* is difficult to grow and hardly worth the trouble.

Special points: Feed actively growing plants once a month with a half-strength liquid fertilizer. Pot on each spring into larger pots those plants that are long-term, discard *K. blossfeldiana* when all flowers have faded. Watch out for mealy bugs that are apt to collect in the leaf axils.

PLATYCERIUM BIFURCATUM
(POLYPODIACEAE)

Most of the platycerium species hail from S.E. Asia and Australia. They are

all epiphytes, growing high in the rain forests, clutching the rough bark of the trees for support with one kind of frond and reaching out for light with the decorative antler-shaped fronds. They are ferns – usually called staghorn ferns – and produce spores on the antler-like fronds. The basal or infertile, disc-shaped frond is fleshy and pale green at first but later turns brown and papery. New basal fronds develop over the old ones, the old in time decaying and catching forest debris on which the plant partly feeds. In the home they can be grown in pots, slatted wooden baskets or fixed to slabs of bark.

P. bifurcatum (syn. *P. alcicorne*) from Madagascar, Comores and Mauritius makes the best house plant. Fertile fronds broaden out from a narrow base and may reach 60cm (2ft) in length, split into typical antler shapes. They are a deep-green covered with a fine, silvery fuzz of hair.

Watering: Water generously and then allow the mixture to dry out a little (to the point where the fronds droop slightly, rather than too frequently). Plants grown in slatted baskets and on slabs of bark must be soaked in a bowl or bucket of water as required. Give brief soakings in winter under cooler conditions.

Potting mixture: Use a special orchid potting mixture, usually obtainable in small quantities and comprising equal parts very coarse peat and sphagnum moss. This mixture is suitable for small plants and for filling slatted, wooden,

hanging baskets. See special points for plants grown on bark.

Propagation: This is not normally practicable in the home.

Special points: Hand spray clay pots, cork or bark slabs and wooden baskets, regularly to increase atmospheric moisture immediately around the plants. The support of plants bought ready growing on pieces of cork or bark should be nailed (or glued) to larger supports when the basal fronds have almost completely covered their initial base. Any damaged fronds should be cut away completely at the base. Plactyceriums need little feeding: 2 or 3 feeds a year, during the summer, are usually sufficient.

STREPTOCARPUS
(GESNERIACEAE)

The genus streptocarpus is mainly concentrated in Africa and Madagascar, ranging from southern Ethiopia almost to the Cape and across the continent to Angola. A few (rarely grown as house plants), come from Southeast Asia. Growth habit varies enormously, some make just one huge leaf, others are small bushy shrubs, but those grown as house plants are more often of roughly rosette shape. For full information, see South Africa.

India

Hot, dry India (where most plants live only where moisture is available) is of course the home of *Ficus elastica*, the omnipresent rubber plant, less frequently seen in nature. Here too are the song of India (*Pleomele* syn. *Dracaena reflexa*), the parents of the beautifully marked *Begonia rex-cultorum* hybrids, the fishtail palms, and the brake or ribbon ferns from the Himalayas where in 1848 Joseph Hooker commented that "it is difficult to conceive a grander mass of vegetation . . . trees clothed for yards with a continuous garment of epiphytes."

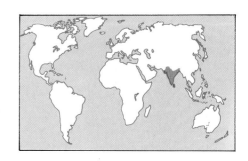

☐ Desert and ice desert
■ Sparse forest/woodland/grass
☐ Tropical rain forest
☐ Oasis
☐ Deciduous forest
☐ Savanna grassland
■ Montane forest
■ Temperate mountain forest

1. *Aeschynanthus marmoratus*
2. *Asparagus falcatus*
3. *Begonia alleryi*
4. *Begonia rex-cultorum*
5. *Caryota mitis*
6. *C. urens*
7. *Catharanthus roseus*
8. *Cordyline terminalis*
9. *Crossandra infundibuliformis*
10. *Ficus benghalensis*
11. *F. elastica*
12. *F. sagittata*
13. *Hoya bella*
14. *Plectranthus coleoides*
15. *Pleomele reflexa*
16. *Primula kewensis*
17. *Pteris cretica*
18. *P. ensiformis*
19. *Strobilanthes dyeranus*

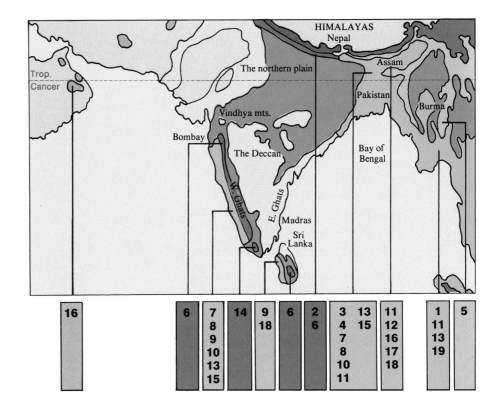

India and Pakistan cover an area of about 1.5 million sq miles from 33°N to 8°N, much of the land lying within the tropics. In the north, forming a barrier, are the Himalaya Mountains, with the highest Indian peak reaching 7,815m (25,500ft). Below, and further to the south of the Himalayas, is a vast lowland area (the northern plain), formed by the river basins of the Ganges, Indus and Brahmaputra. Below this lowland area is a large plateau area called the Deccan. Separating the northern plain and the Deccan plateau are the Vindhya Mountains. The plateau is at its highest in the west where it rises to about 1,200m (4,000ft) in the mountains called the Western Ghats. Towards the east the land slopes downwards towards the Eastern Ghats which rise to only 600m (2,000ft). Between the Western Ghats and the coast is a very narrow coastal plain, but between the Eastern Ghats and the Bay of Bengal is a wide plain crossed by many rivers. On Sri Lanka, the mountains rise to over 2,500m (8,000ft), and in Pakistan to over 3,000m (10,000ft).

Climate

India's climate has four distinct seasons: a cool season from December to February, a dry, hot season from March to May, the monsoon from June to October, and the 'retreating monsoon' season during November.

The cool season is dry and sunny, though there is heavy rain in the south around Madras; temperatures range from 57°F (14°C) in the north, to 75°F (24°C) in the south. *The hot season* is dry and sunny with temperatures averaging about 90°F (32°C). *The monsoon* season, from the south west, brings the country about 90% of its rain. Part of the monsoon blows in over the west coast and about 5,000mm (200in) of rain falls on the Western Ghats; the other part of the monsoon blows up the eastern side of the country, bringing up to 20,000mm (nearly 800in) of rain to a few places in the north and east. At the other extreme, the desert area on the Pakistan border receives an annual rainfall of only 120mm (5in). The southwest of Sri Lanka is the wettest and receives over 5,000mm (200in) of rain, whereas the rest of the island averages about 1200mm (47in).

Vegetation

With the exception of the higher levels in the Himalayas and the desert area in the north west, the vegetation is nominally classified as arboreal. Today, however, over 90% of the land has been cleared of trees. The remaining areas (where cultivation has been abandoned) include both natural forest and secondary forest.

Tropical forests

The wet tropical evergreen and semi-evergreen forests are typical tropical rain forest, and best developed in the areas with over 3,000mm (120in) of rain, where there is only a short dry period. True evergreen tropical rain forests grow in a band between 450 and 1,350m (1,300 and 4,500ft) along the Western Ghats to the south of Bombay, and also on some of the Assam hills. On the drier side this forest gives way to semi-evergreen forest and then to moist deciduous forest. Much of Bengal and Orissa was originally covered with semi-evergreen forest.

On the whole, the tropical rain forest is very dense with emergent tree crowns towering up to 60m (200ft) and the main forest canopy below them at 35–40m (110–130ft). Due to the extreme density of the canopy, the forest floor tends to be very bare, though where there are breaks there is a dense undergrowth of palms and bamboos. Epiphytes are very common. The forests are very rich in species. In the Assam area, large areas of bamboos form a transition zone between semi-evergreen and moist deciduous types of forest.

Spruce forest in the Western Himalayan foothills

Upland subtropical forest in the Sri Lankan mountains

The tropical moist deciduous or monsoon forest is the natural vegetation that would cover most of India, were it not for the interference of Man. Today, there is still a long strip of this vegetation along the eastern side of the Western Ghats as well as in the north-east of the peninsula and in the Siwalik Hills to the south of Kashmir. Most of the trees lose their leaves for about 6–8 weeks during the hot period, but different species lose theirs at different times; as a result the area is rarely leafless. During the dry period the forest has a generally dried up appearance; however, in the moister areas, the undergrowth is evergreen and often quite dense, and climbers and bamboos are both fairly common.

In areas with less than 750mm (30in) of rain, thorn forest grows; this is found to the northwest of, and in areas sheltered by, the Western Ghats. The vegetation is made up of stunted trees no more than 6m (20ft) tall and fairly widely scattered; many of the trees are euphorbias and acacias. This vegetation grades into the widespread bushland and into the desert in the north-west. Most of this area is now badly deteriorated due to overgrazing and fodder cutting.

The tropical dry evergreen forest only grows in coastal areas from Madras southwards where the humidity is high. The forest is low, only 1–13m (3–40ft) with a shrubby and spiny undergrowth.

Moist deciduous forest waterhole: hot and humid

105

Montane sub-tropical and temperate forests

These forests grow on some of the hills of the Western Ghats, the outer Himalayas and the Assam Hills. In the south, the sub-tropical forest grows above the tropical rain forest and one gradually blends into the other; above this a temperate type forest grows which blends into the sub-tropical forest.

The sub-tropical forest here is a slightly stunted form of tropical rain forest and is not as luxuriant. There are many local variants, but on the whole the trees are 15–18m (50–60ft) high and beneath them is a dense undergrowth; epiphytes, mosses, magnolias, rhododendrons, ferns and laurels are all very common. In the northern areas the trees tend to be taller, reaching 20–30m (65–100ft), and both epiphytes and climbers are common. Some northern areas have a sub-tropical dry evergreen forest; this is a low and scrubby vegetation that resembles the Mediterranean maquis; *Olea* and acacias are common with the ground often smothered by dwarf creeping palms.

The northern wet temperate forest is the most widespread of the Himalayan foothill forests; it occurs in areas where the rainfall is 1,000–2,500mm (40–100in). In the wetter east, broad-leaved evergreens are mixed with the conifers, but in the west they are rare. The forest is found between 1,500 and 3,000m (3,300 and 10,000ft) on the whole consists of a high but open forest with an underlying shrubby layer of oaks, rhododendrons, laurels and bamboos. At higher altitudes a dry temperate forest grows. It is an open forest with the trees showing water conserving characteristics. Precipitation is about 1,000mm (40in), but most of this falls as snow. In the main the trees are conifers, but there are also a few oaks and ashes.

Alpine forest

From about 2,900 to 3,500m (9,500 to 12,000ft) in the outer Himalayas, alpine forest and scrub form the main vegetation. Most of the plants are shrubs, often gnarled and twisted.

They grow to 7m (23ft) tall and include juniper, pine, birch and rhododendron.

Much of the northern hills and mountain areas have only been poorly explored, and it is probable that many new species of plant have yet to be discovered.

Assam

Tropical vegetation grows up to 900m (3,000ft) and includes tropical rain forest, semi-evergreen forest, dry and moist deciduous forest, grassland and swamps. The forests, on the whole, are dark, and the low light inhibits the formation of lower layers of vegetation. Lianas, climbers and epiphytes (especially orchids and ferns) are common, as are large specimens of bamboo. Many species of *Hoya* with beautiful bunches of star-like flowers grow here.

Above about 1,300m (4,250ft), the vegetation becomes more temperate. Unfortunately, much of this area has been cut and burned to clear for agriculture. Small areas of woodland (the sacred forests) have been left scattered here and there. Their rich flora gives an indication of what the whole area might have been. Most of the trees are heavily loaded with epiphytes, mainly orchids, ferns and aroids.

From 3,000 to 4,500m (10,000 to 14,750ft) a sub-alpine vegetation grows; pines and rhododendrons are common and the shrub layer is often very dense; a profusion of herbs grow on the ground. The alpine vegetation grows between 4,500 and 5,500m (14,750 and 18,000ft), above which plants become very scarce. There is no sharp distinction between the alpine and sub-alpine vegetation, but at the higher levels there are no trees, and the land resembles meadow or moorland. Rhododendrons are frequent, and sedums, saxifrages and gentians add a bright splash of colour.

Burma

The vegetation of Burma is very similar, but in general richer in species than that of Assam.

Plant hunting in India

Many of the ficus, which are still grown as house plants, have a long history in cultivation. The banyan, *F. benghalensis*, had been grown by the Earl of Portland as long ago as 1690, while by 1731 Philip Miller had obtained the peepul, *F. religiosa*. By 1759 he had also obtained *F. pumila* and *F. benjamina*. In 1786 William Roxburgh, the director of the Calcutta Botanic Garden, sent back *F. nitida* and in 1805 he followed this up by *F. repens*. There seems some doubt as to whether the plant grown under this name is correctly named or whether it might be *F. stipulata*. This was in cultivation about 1771, but no details as to who was growing it is obtainable.

A few of the most popular house plants were still to be introduced when the 18th century ended. The omnipresent Indiarubber plant, *Ficus elastica*, was not received until 1815. This presumably came from the Calcutta Botanic Garden. In 1815 Nathaniel Wallich was appointed temporary director of the garden in succession to William Roxburgh. Wallich was instrumental in the distribution of large numbers of plants, not only from India, but also from Eastern Asia, Mauritius and Madagascar, and there is a tendency to assume that any plants from those regions in the period between 1815 and 1840 are to be ascribed to him unless there is proof to the contrary. So it is fitting that the house plant grower should remember him when he looks at his Indiarubber tree.

Wallich's position at the garden was confirmed in 1817, and though poor health caused frequent absences, he was to remain director for thirty years.

Wallich was born a Dane and called Nathan Wolff. He became a surgeon and entered the Danish East India Company's service in 1807. In the same year, during the Napoleonic wars, hostilities broke out between Britain and Denmark and in 1808 their settlement at Serampore was captured and Wallich was taken prisoner. He was released to assist

Roxburgh and in 1812, owing to ill health, he went on leave to Mauritius, where he became friendly with Telfair, the director of the Botanic garden there, which also amassed many unusual plants, which he would send to Wallich.

Wallich was also instrumental in the expedition of John Gibson, who collected for the Duke of Devonshire and Paxton in the Khasia hills during the latter half of 1836. This expedition was the first large scale transportation of plants in which the Wardian case was used and the success of the expedition made its use regular practice for the future. The only plant among his sendings that is occasionally grown as a house plant was *Aeschynanthus grandiflorus*: the bulk of his collections was orchids, although he also sent back *Rhododendron formosum*, which would probably be as good a house plant as the so-called Indian azaleas, which in point of fact come from China. The Khasia hills are one of the wettest places in the world and Gibson, moreover, was there during the monsoon. One can imagine the problems of trying to dry out seeds and botanical specimens under such conditions. Since coal outcrops occurred in the neighbourhood, Gibson used to light roaring fires to dry out his seeds and specimens, which cannot have been too agreeable in the hot tropics.

300ft in diameter, the Ficus benghalensis *at Sibpur, Bengal*

AESCHYNANTHUS MARMORATUS
(GESNERIACEAE)

A. marmoratus is an epiphytic trailing plant which thrives in the high humidity of the warm rain forests of Malaysia, Burma and Thailand, and has very attractive foliage. Individual leaves are up to 10cm (4in) long, light green above marbled with darker markings, the underside flushed with rich red. Flowers are greenish yellow, marked with brown at the throat.

Full cultural details are given in discussion of the whole genus on page 129. Most of the species came from S.E. Asia.

ASPARAGUS FALCATUS
(LILIACEAE)

A. falcatus, from the temperate montane forests of Sri Lanka, is a climber with hooked spines and thin, sickle-shaped, 5-cm (2-in) long branchlets. It is, along with many fellow species discussed in the section on South Africa, a member of the lily family.

Watering: Water thoroughly, allowing the mixture to dry out a little before applying more during the growing season, but more sparingly in winter. Foliage falls if the mixture gets too dry.

Potting mixture: Use a soil-based potting mixture.

Propagation: Increase plants in spring by dividing overcrowded clumps. A sharp knife may be needed to cut through the mass of fleshy roots but retain as many as possible.

Special points: Old plants lose some of their vigour due to overcrowding: break up and repot the healthy younger pieces. Feed every two weeks with a general liquid fertilizer from spring to early autumn. When potting, leave the level of the potting mixture well below the pot rim level; as the fat, tuberous root sections grow they force the mixture upwards. Provide thin cane or string for support.

BEGONIA
(BEGONIACEAE)

Two begonias, described under the main entry for begonias in the section on S. American house plants, have their roots in India.

B. alleryi (a hybrid between *B. gigantea* (Sikkim) and *B. metallica* (Brazil) is one of the hairy-leaved – or hirsute – begonias, growing to 90–120cm (3–4ft) tall.

107

Tooth-edged, hairy leaves are browny-green with reddish veins on the underside. Flowers are pale pink and covered with fine, silky, silver hair.

B. rex-cultorum hybrids are prized for their beautifully marked leaves.

The original species from Assam is probably no longer in cultivation. Its descendants offer a very wide range of leaf colour and texture, including metallic markings, dense coating of fine hair in a sharply contrasting colour to the basic leaf colour and puckered or corrugated surface. Ancestry is highly complicated, resulting in some offspring that are easier to grow than others. Those with thin, soft and velvety leaves are usually difficult, those with thicker and rougher-textured leaves are usually easy. There are miniature or dwarf kinds and some with leaf edges that spiral.

CARYOTA
(PALMAE)

The fishtail palms are from montane forests of the Asiatic tropics and distinguished from all other palms in that the fronds of larger plants are twice

Caryota urens *in the bright light of its montane habitat*

pinnate. Fronds are made up of roughly triangular segments, each ragged at the edge, like a fish's tail. With age fronds arch over and develop the distinctive double division. Two forms are popular.

C. mitis, the Burmese, crested, or tufted fishtail palm can be found in the humid teak forests of Burma, Malaysia, Java and the Philippines. Unlikely to grow more than 1.8m (6ft) tall with six to ten fronds up to 90cm (3ft) long. Can cluster at the base.

C. urens is from India, Sri Lanka and Malaysia and is

called the sago, jaggery or wine palm. Segments are broader than *C. mitis*, darker green, and urens is unlikely to make offsets.

Watering: Water thoroughly and then allow a little drying out. There is unlikely to be more than a very short rest period, but reduce frequency of watering if temperature falls below 55ºF (12ºC).

Potting mixture: Use soil-based compost.

Propagation: Only *C. mitis* can be propagated by offsets; both by sowing seed, in heat.

Special points: See that the air is made extra humid, stand on moist trays and mist-spray regularly. Feed with a standard liquid fertilizer every two weeks while growth continues robustly. Repot only every other year. Watch out for scale insects.

CATHARANTHUS ROSEUS
(APOCYNACEAE)

Known as the Madagascar periwinkle and sometimes called *Vinca rosea, C. rosea* is a small shrub found in both Madagascar and India. Its five-petalled, usually very pale pink flowers appear throughout

Cordyline terminalis *Tricolor*

the summer above glossy oval leaves. Height and spread are about 30cm (1ft). Young plants appear on the market in late spring and prove valuable house plants flowering until early autumn, when they should be discarded. White flowering forms, and one with a carmine "eye", are available.

Culture: Grow in bright light, ideally a window that gets some sun each day; pot on as necessary during the summer using a soil-based mixture. Water plentifully and feed fortnightly with a high potash liquid fertilizer.

Plants are normally raised from seed sown very early in the year.

CORDYLINE TERMINALIS
(AGAVACEAE)

Cordyline are closely related to and often confused with dracaena. *C. terminalis* comes from the tropical rain forest of India, Malaysia and Polynesia and like it warm and humid.

C. terminalis (syn. *Dracaena terminalis*) has lance-shaped leaves, up to 60cm (2ft) long and 10cm (4in) wide that are arranged around an upright stem, most standing semi-upright, the older ones arching outwards. Leaf colour is coppery with bold red markings. There are a number of named forms, including the following:
Amabilis – bronze, tinged pink, cream-edged.
Baptistii – rich green, splashed red and creamy-yellow.
Firebrand – purple-red.
Redege – small scale, bright green and red.
Tricolor – creamy-white, pink and red.
All the forms of *C. terminalis* must have good light to develop best leaf coloration, but avoid hot, direct, summer sun. Good for an east- or west-facing window.

Watering: Water thoroughly during the active growth period, moderately during the winter rest.

Potting mixture: Use a soil-based potting mixture.

Propagation: Tip cuttings will root in a warm room or propagator in spring. Stem

Crossandra greenstockei, *a close relation to* C. infundibuliformis

cuttings (each with a growth bud) will send out a new shoot if planted in peat and sand in warmth.

Special points: Stand *C. terminalis* and forms on trays of moist pebbles, keep warm and out of draughts. Pot on into slightly larger pots each spring. Top dress older plants in spring. Feed actively growing plants with the standard liquid fertilizer every two weeks.

CROSSANDRA INFUNDIBULIFORMIS
(syn. *C. undulifolia*)
(ACANTHACEAE)

This crossandra is a shrub from the rain forests of southern India and Sri Lanka that prefers filtered or diffused light. Its shiny, dark green leaves which undulate at the edges are held in opposite pairs. Flowers appear in spring and summer from an upright tuft of green bracts. They have a tube-shaped base but flare out into a lobed disc, salmon-pink in colour and up to 38mm (1¼in) across.

Watering; From spring to early autumn water thoroughly and then allow the mixture to dry out considerably before giving more; water sparingly during the winter rest period.

Potting mixture: Use a

soil-based potting mixture and add up to one third extra peat or leaf mould.

Propagation: Take tip cuttings 5–7.5cm (2–3in) long in spring, and root in a heated propagator.

Special points: Stand on trays of moist pebbles for extra humidity. Feed every two weeks with a high potash liquid fertilizer during the growing season. Watch out for red spider mites; fine misting with a hand spray will discourage their getting a firm hold. Avoid hot sunny windows in summer; but if starved of light, flowering will suffer.

FICUS
(MORACEAE)

In cultivation, *F. benghalensis* is quite different from its parent in the wild. The Banyan tree grows to a great height and sends down wreaths of stilt-like roots. The famous banyan at Sibpur, Bengal, has a diameter of 90m (300ft) and the story is told that Alexander the Great and 7,000 men camped under one such specimen. Maximum height you can expect indoors is 1.8m (6ft). Its dark green leaves are oval and up to 30cm (1ft) long (when young they are covered with a fine, reddish-brown hair).

F. elastica is the ubiquitous rubber plant, from the mountainous regions of Nepal, Burma and north-eastern India. The species is rarely seen; improved forms with large, fleshy, oval leaves, 30–38cm (12–15in) long with a prominent midrib, being

preferred.
F. e. Decora – plain, dark-green leaves held at a perky angle;
F. e. Robusta – larger, more rounded leaves;
F. e. Black Prince – deep-green, almost black;
F. e. Tricolor – pink and cream markings on dark-green;
F. e. Doescheri – grey and cream markings and a deep pink midrib;
F. e. Variegata – narrower leaves slightly drooping, splashed yellow.

F. sagittata (syn. *F. radicans*) is a trailing plant from the E. Himalayas to the Philippines, but it is the variegated-leaved form *F. s.* Variegata, with grey and cream streaked, lance-shaped leaves (5–7.5cm) (2–3in) long that is grown indoors. Trailing stems can go to 60cm (2ft) long.

Watering: Water moderately during the growing period and sparingly during the winter rest period. Overwatering will cause the lower leaves to fall off.

Potting mixture: Use a soil-based mixture.

Propagation: Tip cuttings of the trailing kind, *F. sagittata*, can be taken and they may also be layered. Large-leaved sorts are normally air layered, but tip cuttings will root if a propagator is available.

Special points: The variegated-leaved kinds need slightly warmer positions and better light than the all green sorts. Give standard liquid fertilizer every two weeks from spring to early autumn. Move into larger pots only when this is

absolutely necessary – ficus do best when roots are a little restricted and can be grown in what may appear quite inadequate pots. Pot in spring. Top dress large specimens, in the spring. Keep the leaves clean by gently wiping with a damp sponge, or better still, stand out in gentle rain during the warmer months.

HOYA BELLA
(ASCLEPIADACEIAE)

Hoyas are epiphytic and terrestrial climbing and trailing plants from the forest that skirts the Himalayas in the north of India. Many start life in the soil and grow upwards, winding round tree trunks and branches, putting down aerial roots from tbe nodes whenever a favourable opportunity occurs.

H. bella. Leaves are matt surfaced, dull green, a pointed heart-shape and about 25mm (1in) long. Habit is trailing, with stems to 45cm (18in) long. Flowers are white with a purple centre and in groups of 8 or 10.

Watering: Water moderately during the active growth period allowing the mixture to dry out a little between applications. Be more sparing in winter.

Potting mixture: Use a soil-based potting mixture.

Propagation: Tip cuttings of *H. bella* (5–7.5cm) (2–3in) long root easily in the spring in a warm room. It is necessary to take more woody cuttings of the other kinds but these too will root

in a propagator or warm room.

PLECTRANTHUS COLEOIDES
(LABIATAE)

Most plectranthus have fleshy, four-sided stems which root at each node that comes into contact with a suitable moist rooting medium, making dense carpets in the open and under sparse-leaved shrubs and trees. Flowers are in a thin spike, white to light purplish and most are insignificant. Stems may reach 60cm (2ft) in length in one full growing season – excellent in hanging baskets.

P. coleoides Marginatus. The type comes from the Nilgiri Hills in South West India; Marginatus is a variegated form. It starts upright but later trails. Leaves are hairy, apple-green, and edged with creamy-white.

Watering: Water plentifully during the period of fast growth from spring to early autumn but sparingly during the short winter rest period.

Potting mixture: Use a soil-based potting mixture.

Propagation: Tip cuttings root very easily in the

spring and early summer, even in winter. Young plants are best, start afresh each year.

Special points: Plant 4–6 plants in one hanging basket to get the best, bushy effect. Nip out growing points regularly to encourage side branches to develop. Feed every two weeks with the standard liquid fertilizer during the active growing season. Encourage to rest in winter.

PLEOMELE REFLEXA VARIEGATA
(AGAVACEAE)

Popularly called Song of India and sold as *P. reflexa* this plant is now classified as *D. reflexa*. Its home is not only India but also Madagascar and Mauritius. Only the variegated-leaved form is popular. The lance-shaped green leaves with yellow margins are arranged close together around the thin stems. Stems are upright but the tip is held at a slight angle, straightening later. Stems need the support of thin canes after a foot or more of growth has been made. It is

usual and best to grow several plants in one pot.

Watering: Water moderately at all times.

Potting mixture: Use soil-based mixture, with ⅓ extra peat or leaf mould.

Propagation: Use 10cm (4in) long tip or side shoots in spring.

Special points: Feed every two weeks with the standard liquid fertilizer from spring to autumn. Move on into larger pots only when really needed – in spring. Stand on trays of moist pebbles.

PRIMULA KEWENSIS
(PRIMULACEAE)

Of the four kinds of primula popularly grown as house plants, three *(P.malacoides, P. obconica* and *P. sinensis)* originate in China and are described in the section about plants from C. & E. Asia. *P. kewensis* is a hybrid with *P. floribunda (Himalayas)* and *P. verticillata* (South Arabia) as parents. It is yellow flowered, fragrant, and displays fine white powder over its leaves and stem.

Culture: Give bright light, a cool position, thorough waterings (soakings if necessary), and fortnightly feeding with a high potash liquid fertilizer. All flower in late winter and spring; move to the greenhouse or garden frame when flowering is complete.

PTERIS CRETICA
(POLYPODIACEAE)
Commonly called brake or ribbon fern, these plants

have a very wide distribution. Many kinds are in cultivation.

P. cretica (Himalayas, India, Italy, Japan, Middle East, Florida) is the most popular of the genus. Fronds reach 30.5cm (12in) in length and are made up of several pointed pinnae or segments fanning out from a common point.

P.c. Albo-lineata has creamy white central lines on the pinnae, and *P. c.* Wimsettii, crested pinnae.

Watering: Keep well watered during the warmer months when growth is active, more sparingly if temperatures or light levels are low.

Potting mixture: Use a peat-based mixture.

Propagation: Divide overcrowded clumps in spring, seeing that some rhizome is attached to each piece.

Special points: Use half-strength general fertilizer every 2 or 3 weeks while growth is active. Make the air more humid by standing

pots on moist pebble trays and plunging in moist peat. Move into the next size larger pot each spring.

STROBILANTHES DYERANUS
(ACANTHACEAE)

S. dyeranus from Burma is grown for its decorative, purple-shot, metallic leaves. It has pointed, heavily-veined, dark-green leaves splashed with purplish-red, and with a deep purple underside. Pale blue flowers rise from a spike in the leaf axils of mature plants.

Watering: Water actively growing plants moderately and resting ones sparingly.

Potting mixture: Use equal-parts soil-based mix and leafmould.

Propagation: Tip and side shoots root easily in spring and early summer.

Special points: Apply standard liquid fertilizer every two weeks during the growing season. Pot on as necessary, but 12-15cm (5 or 6in) pots should be the maximum. If grown in warm rooms give added humidity by standing on trays of moist pebbles.

111

Central and East Asia

In China and Japan it is the warm wet temperate forests that are the natural home of most indigenous pot plants. The aspidistra, prized for its resistance to poorly lit rooms, grows in the cool, dense shade of mountain forests. But there are few true house plants here; more common are the flowering temporaries, such as *Primula sinensis* (brought back by John Potts in 1821) and the parents of our all-year-round chrysanthemum hybrids – their light and temperature symbols relating only to their flowering periods, which in nature occurs in winter (see page 158).

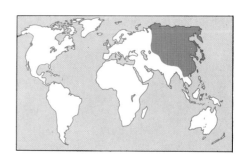

Steppe
High plateau & ice desert
Grassland
Tropical rain forest
High temperate forest
Temperate coniferous into deciduous forest
Temperate/sub-tropical/sclerophyllous forest
Monsoon forest and open jungle
Desert
Water margin

1. Acorus gramineus
2. Aspidistra elatior
3. Begonia grandis
4. Carex morrowii
5. Chrysanthemum morifolium
6. Citrus sinensis
7. Cyrtomium falcatum
8. Fatshedera lizei
9. Fatsia japonica
10. Ficus pumila
11. Hoya carnosa
12. Hydrangea macrophylla
13. Jasminum polyanthum
14. Pittosporum tobira
15. Podocarpus macrophyllus
16. Polystichum tsus-simense
17. Primula malacoides
18. P. obconica
19. P. sinensis
20. Rhapis excelsa
21. R. humilis
22. Rhododendron
23. Rohdea japonica
24. Rosa chinensis
25. Saxifraga stolonifera
26. Sedum lineare
27. S. sieboldii
28. Trachycarpus fortunei

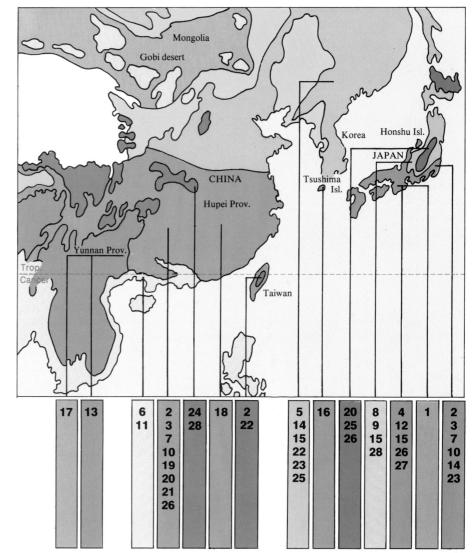

This massive area includes China, Mongolia, eastern USSR (Siberia), Japan and Korea. Western Siberia is a large lowland area about 2,000 miles wide; central Siberia is a raised plateau averaging 600m (2,000ft) and is rimmed by mountains in the south. Eastern Siberia is very mountainous. Mongolia consists of a large plateau 1,500–1,800m (5,000–6,000ft) high, with mountains in the north and west and dropping down to the Gobi desert in the south. Over half of

China is made up of plateau areas and mountains which are at their highest in the west and then descend gradually to the eastern plain. Both Japan and Korea are mountainous.

Climate
In the very north of the area the land is within the Arctic Circle and therefore has a very harsh climate. The area to the south of this, as far south as the north of Mongolia and eastern China, has a continental

climate with very cold winters and warm summers averaging 50°F (10°C) in the north and 77°F (25°C) in the south. The middle and south of China have mild winters and hot summers, with the southernmost areas actually tropical. Korea has cold winters and hot summers, as does the northern part of Japan; southern Japan is somewhat warmer.

Rainfall in the north of the area falls mainly during the spring and summer, and much of the area receives less than 600mm (24in), though some areas have appreciably more or less. Mongolia, on average, receives only between 50 and 300mm (2 and 12in) of rain, but further to the south, in the monsoon areas of China, as much as 2,500mm (100in) falls. Rainfall in Korea increases further to the south; in the north it is 600mm (24in), whereas on the south coast 1,400mm (55in) falls (however, typhoons are quite frequent in the south). Japan has a winter monsoon that brings heavy rain and snow to the western parts of the islands and dry but windy weather to the east. The summer monsoon from the south brings wet weather to the whole of Japan, which averages over 1,000mm (40in) of rain a year.

Vegetation
In the extreme north of continental Asia is a large area of tundra vegetation: a vast treeless waterlogged area.

To the south of this is the coniferous forest or taiga zone; this belt grows across most of Asia and Europe and is about 700 miles deep. These forests are made up of a variety of conifers including spruce, pine, fir and larch. They reach as far south as far as northern Mongolia and north-east China. To the south of this in Mongolia, the vegetation of the plateau is mainly steppe with the vegetation becoming sparse in the south-east, and eventually becoming more or less absent in the Gobi desert. Although at one time much of China was forested, most has now been cut and less than 10% is tree covered. Over half of the remaining forest is in the north-east, where there are extensive areas of conifers and deciduous trees. The other forested areas are in the tropical south-west of the country. Korea has been severely deforested, but still has temperate mixed conifer and deciduous forests. About two thirds of Japan is tree covered, and in the main, the forest is mixed conifer and deciduous trees, very much like those of Korea.

The vegetation of China is quite diverse and a brief rundown of the area follows.

Coniferous forest
This, the taiga, grows in the north, and at high altitudes throughout the country. It is essentially a single-stratum forest of mixed conifers and it has a very scanty ground cover and undergrowth, though epiphytic mosses and lichens are common. The ground is covered by snow for several months of the year, even at the higher altitudes in the south. There are, in fact two main areas of this vegetation; below 500m (1,600ft) in the north-eastern provinces, and above 3,000m (10,000ft) on the south-western plateau region.

Deciduous broadleaved forest

Forest at 5,000ft where subtropical plants give way to temperate

The deciduous broadleaved forest is the most extensive forest area in China, stretching from the Yangtze valley to south-eastern Siberia. There are four main types of vegetation distinguished by the main tree species; from north to south these are: birch, mixed northern hardwood, temperate broad deciduous and mixed. These are more complex than the coniferous forests, often having two different layers of tree, a shrub layer and a ground cover of herbs. Away from the coast and towards the desert areas, the forest is gradually replaced by wooded steppe and grassland; in the more arid areas, the forest is only found in the most wet or elevated places.

Evergreen broadleaved forest
There are three main types of this forest, and all are very distinct; they are sclerophyll, tropical rain, mangrove and seashore forest.

The sclerophyll is dominated by laurels and species with laurel-like leaves, oaks, and the chestnut-like *Castanopsis;* this covers large parts of southern China to the montane borders of Vietnam, Thailand and Burma. A well-developed area may have trees up to 30m (100ft) tall with rounded crowns. The underlayer of trees, the shrubs and the ground cover are not usually dense, though the ground is sometimes grassy. Lianas and epiphytes are common, but not as frequent as in most tropical rain forest. In areas where there is much mist and the humidity is high (the so-called cloud forest belt), the trees are smothered with mosses and liverworts, and epiphytic orchids, ferns and aroids are nearly always present. Like the rain forest, there is a wide variety of tree species, with over 150 different species of oak as well as many other types.

Tropical rain forest in China occurs throughout the tropics and as far north as 26°N along the coast and 28°N further inland. Much of this lowland forest has been cleared, but there are still well-preserved areas remaining and these continue southwards into Thailand, Vietnam, Laos and Burma. At higher levels, above 1,200m (4,000ft) the forest is composed of evergreen oaks. The rain forest has an uneven canopy with several tall emergent trees protruding. Most of the trees are evergreen, but there are a few semi-deciduous ones that lose their leaves in spring and then almost immediately grow a fresh replacement set which, at first, are light pink. Epiphytes and lianas are abundant, and many of the trees have buttress roots. Except in the areas where the canopy is somewhat open, the undergrowth is fairly scanty, though in areas where the sun does penetrate, masses of lianas, climbing rattan palms, epiphytes and shrubs can make the forest difficult to traverse.

The canopy, which is very dense, rises to 40–50m (130–165ft); it is so densely stacked with lianas and climbing plants that they can support a tree weighing several tons after it has been cut through at the base. The shrub layer is mainly small trees, shrubs, palms, bamboos and a few tree ferns; tree ferns are much more common at somewhat higher levels. Although the ground cover herbs are made up of many species, they are, on the whole, shade-loving flowering plants and ferns. Epiphytes occur everywhere, from the tops of the tall trees to the bases of the trunks. Many succulent climbers also grow as epiphytes, and parasitic mistletoes are common near clearings and on the upper branches of the trees. The lower level epiphytes tend to be deeply rooted in the bark, whereas those high in the canopy are more loosely attached and have more aerial roots.

Seashore vegetation, both strand and mangrove, is found on the islands and along the coast; as far north as 25–26°N on the mainland and up to 30°N on the Liukiu Islands. The vegetation is similar to that found throughout the tropics, and details are given in the S.E. Asia section.

Grassland and desert
There are vast areas of grassland and desert covering the arid heartland of the great Eurasian landmass. In China, this type of vegetation covers well over half of the land area in an unbroken expanse from the central steppe of the north-east, to the mountains of the Pamirs. The grassland is a wide semi-circular belt around the Gobi desert, with grasses naturally becoming more abundant further from the desert centre.

In areas where the grassland meets woodland, there is usually a savanna-like intermediate zone, often with quite luxuriant meadows containing many species of grass and flowering plant.

The deserts are mainly sand with some gravelly areas and, in general, the vegetation is very scanty; usually the occasional coarse grass or small shrub. Large areas of the desert are devoid of any vegetation.

Plant hunting in Central and Eastern Asia
A form of *Cordyline terminalis,* with purple leaves, long known as *Dracaena ferrea,* was introduced, apparently from China, by Benjamin Torin in 1771. Three years earlier Philip Miller of the Chelsea Physic Garden was growing *Dracaena fragrans,* although not with the variegated leaves that we cultivate nowadays.

The aspidistra was brought back by one of the gardeners sent out by the London (later Royal) Horticultural Society, John Parks. Since he was sent to Canton on the *Lowther Castle* both for the voyage out and that back, his stay at Canton must have been short. His most valuable introduction from this trip was a yellow tea rose, but the aspidistra also made an appearance through him.

There is no certain record as to who introduced the popular Wandering Jews, *Tradescantia albiflora* and *T. fluminensis,* from Central America; we do not even know when they were brought into cultivation. But a relative, *Commelina benghalensis,* with attractive blue flowers, that was tried for a short time as a house plant, had been obtained from tropical Asia by Sir Joseph Banks in 1794. (The other popular relative of the tradescantia, *Zebrina pendula,* was introduced before 1850 from Mexico, but we do not know by whom.)

China is not the home of any house plants, but has given us some notable flowering pot plants. Of these the first to arrive and the one most eagerly sought was the so-called *Azalea indica,* forms of *Rhododendron sinisii.* Before the introduction of the Wardian case this proved easily the most difficult of all plants to transport from China, although the plants were always for sale at Canton. Here is a description of what was regarded as a particularly successful importation in 1833. "The Chinese azaleas, lately purchased by Mr Knight from Mr M'Gillivray of the East India Company's *Orwell,* are as follows: of

the variegated azaleas nine plants were shipped at Canton, two of which are now alive, of the double red azalea six plants were shipped and one is now alive in England, of the red azalea, lighter colour, four were shipped and two survived the voyage ... of the large flowered azalea six plants were shipped and two are now in health."

In fact out of twenty-five plants, seven survived. This was outstandingly good. Reeves, who had greatly increased the successful shipment of Chinese plants, is reported to have said that he had dispatched five hundred of the variegated azaleas to England and not one had ever arrived safely. Even with this successful shipment we learn that Captain M'Gillivray and his officers had purchased some plants on their own account as a speculation, but not one had arrived in a saleable condition. Although after 1840 azaleas could have been imported fairly easily, it would seem that from the few kinds that had been received in Europe between 1804 and 1832 breeding was successfully undertaken.

A large number of different varieties must have been raised from really a very small number of cultivars. After about 1860 the raising of these azaleas became practically a Belgian monopoly and we do not hear of further Chinese sorts being imported, although it is not impossible that some were, to be released under European names.

The other popular Chinese pot plants are all primulas. *Primula sinensis* had for long been developed in China as a pot plant; indeed, its wild ancestor is still a matter of controversy.

In 1821 the London Horticultural Society sent out one of their gardeners, John Potts, to Canton and he returned the following year with a large quantity of *P. sinensis* seed and from this nucleus such different European cultivars as were raised derive, but, in truth, there seems little alteration between modern *P. sinensis* and those depicted in early 19th century Chinese paintings.

Primula obconica was brought back in 1879 by yet another Veitch collector, Charles Maries. The bulk of his collecting was done in Japan and consisted for the most part of plants that will thrive outdoors in Britain, but he did visit China on two occasions. During his last trip he collected *P. obconica,* not all that exciting in the wild, but when seeds of the original importation were sown, it began to show considerable variation. It has been the subject of controlled breeding ever since. Unfortunately many people find that the foliage sets off an allergic reaction resulting in dermatitis, so its popularity has been limited. Apart from this, it makes an excellent pot plant with a long flowering season and surprising tolerance of poor light (so often a concomitant of dwelling rooms).

The last of the pot plant primulas to arrive has been altered even more radically from the wild plant. This is *P. malacoides,* sometimes known as the fairy primula. This species was introduced by George Forrest, who spent many years collecting plants in Yunnan. The plant had actually been discovered by the great French missionary and botanist Jean Delavay, and seed was sent back by Forrest in 1908. The plant seems to have been subject to considerable cultivation almost immediately. Double-flowered forms were first reported in 1911, and tetraploid forms with larger flowers and considerable colour variation were first recorded two years later. Nowadays the colour range goes from carmine through various purples to the lavender colour of the original wild plant and to white. It is a far cry from the rather dwarf, small-flowered plant that germinated from Forrest's original sending.

ACORUS GRAMINEUS VARIEGATUS
(ARACEAE)

The variegated-leaved form of the grass-like acorus, a water margin plant from China and Japan (tolerant of a wide range of temperature) is the one popularly grown as a house plant. Its fine, 30mm (12in) long, arching, white-striped leaves provide excellent contrast to fleshy leaved plants. Leaves grow from a thin rhizome running just below the surface of the mixture.

Watering: Water generously at all times, they should never be allowed to dry out completely – often grown in aquariums. If grown alone stand in a saucer of water.

Potting mixture: Use a soil-based potting mixture.

Propagation: Propagate by dividing overcrowded clumps in spring, making sure that a piece of rhizome is attached.

Special points: Feed with a standard liquid fertilizer every two weeks from spring to early autumn. In warm rooms increase humidity by standing pots on trays of moist pebbles.

ASPIDISTRA ELATIOR
(syn. *A. lurida*)
(LILIACEAE)

Native of large areas of China, Japan, Taiwan and the East Himalayas, the aspidistra comes from the cool and often dense shade of mountain forests and is commonly called the cast-iron plant. Prized by Victorians for its ability to stand up well to poor conditions, it is stemless, sending up its 30–45cm (12–18in) oblong, elliptic leaves from a fleshy, creeping rootstock. There is a much more decorative, variegated-leaved form, Variegata, with wide patches of yellow or white streaking, though the variegation may seem to disappear. The dull-purple, star-shaped flowers are produced at soil level. In nature they are pollinated by snails.

Watering: Water very moderately at all times, allowing the mixture to almost completely dry out between applications. Feed every two weeks during the growing period.

Potting mixture: Use a soil-based mixture.

Propagation: Divide overcrowded clumps in spring.

Special points: Ideal for a poorly lit position, but don't expect too much new growth.

Use relatively small pots and only pot on when absolutely essential. Wipe leaves free of dust periodically.

BEGONIA
(BEGONIACEAE)

B. grandis (syn. *B. evansiana*) from Malaysia, China and Japan is the hardiest of all begonias. Green but red-spotted stem to 60cm (2ft) tall, fleshy mid-green leaves, burgundy-red on the underside and showing through the leaves at the vein areas on the upperside. Flowers large and a clear pink; also produces bulbils at leaf axils.

Full cultural details are given in Section 2 (South America) where the genus is dealt with in detail.

CAREX MORROWII VARIEGATA
(CYPERACEAE)

The variegated Japanese sedge grass, *C. m.* Variegata, which grows in open, wet areas is an extremely useful house plant providing rare leaf contrast to fleshy-leaved plants. Its arching leaves, 6mm (¼in) wide and up to 30cm (12in) long are white

115

in the middle with green margins and appear in tufts from a creeping rhizomatous rootstock. Like many sedges, leaf edges are armed with minute teeth – if you draw a hand along the leaf towards the tip it is smooth, but reverse the action, working towards the base of the leaf and it is met by thousands of rasping teeth. Flowers are small, light brown tufts and could go unnoticed.

Watering: Water generously but then allow a little drying out before applying more. There is virtually no stop to growth and water needs in winter are similar to other seasons.

Potting mixture: Use a soil-based potting mixture.

Propagation: Plants develop into dense clumps, divide each plant into several sections each carrying a good root system in the spring.

Special points: Carex will grow well in a wide range of temperatures but perfer cool, moist and humid conditions. Feed every two weeks with the standard

liquid fertilizer during the main growth period, late winter to mid-autumn. Move young plants on into larger pots when they have occupied completely the surface of the mixture.

CHRYSANTHEMUM MORIFOLIUM HYBRIDS (COMPOSITAE)

All-year-round chrysanthemum hybrids can now be bought cheaply because they are grown on a large scale by specialist growers that understand their needs – the original species (probably from China) were strictly autumn and winter flowering. Purchased plants have been treated with a dwarfing compound and "blacked out" for part of each day. They are mainly double-flowered but some have the typical dense ring of petals around a yellow disc; flower colour is white, pink, yellow and bronze shades.

Culture: Give good light, keep cool, water generously and plant in the garden when past their best.

CITRUS SINENSIS (RUTACEAE)

The exact region of origin or members of the citrus family is not known but *C. sinensis* is thought to have come from China. Known as the sweet orange, it grows to 1.5m (5ft) in a 30cm (12in) pot and displays its heavy fruit singly.

Watering: Water moderately throughout the growing season and sparingly during the winter rest period.

Potting mixture: Use a soil-based potting mixture.

Propagation: Seeds of bought citrus fruits will germinate readily: they make attractive foliage plants but cannot be relied upon to fruit. Fruiting plants are usually grafted or raised from cuttings – a slow process.

Special points: Move outdoors to a position getting full sun for the summer months. Feed with a high-potash liquid fertilizer every two weeks from spring to autumn. Watch out for scale insects that can collect on the

underside of the leaves and the stem. Mist-spray foliage regularly and stand on trays filled with moist pebbles. Pot on as necessary in spring.

CYRTOMIUM FALCATUM (POLYPODIACEAE)

The holly fern, *C. falcatum*, from the temperate forests of Asia (including China and Japan), is one of the most tolerant ferns. Its leathery fronds to 60cm (2ft) in length are divided into 7.5–10cm (3–4in), shiny, holly-leaf-shaped pinnae of a dark green. They spread, in time, to 60cm (2ft).

Watering: Water plentifully during the growing period, more sparingly if temperatures fall below 55ºF (12ºC).

Potting mixture: Use a mixture of equal parts peat and soil-based compost.

Propagation: By division of overcrowded clumps in spring, pull apart into

Fatsia japonica in a Japanese garden

Hoya carnosa *from southern China*

sections each having a piece of rhizome and 3–4 fronds.

Special points: Use half strength liquid fertilizer every two weeks during the growing period. Pot on into the next size pot only when the fronds fill the old pot. In warm rooms, increase humidity by standing plants on pebble-filled trays. Periods of poor light will be tolerated but growth will be slow.

FATSHEDERA LIZEI
(ARALIACEAE)

This bigeneric hybrid (a cross between two plants of different genera but the

same family) had the *Fatsia japonica* Moseri (the species hies from the temperate forests of Japan as one parent and the European *Hedera helix hibernica* (Irish ivy) as the other. The cross was made in France just before the First World War and was one of the first of its kind.

The hybrid's leaves share the characteristics of both parents – the leathery-textured, shiny surface and a tough constitution. The broad spread of the fatsia has been curbed, the stem of the ivy strengthened (a support may still be necessary) and the ivy-shaped leaf enlarged. Leaves may be up to 12.5cm (5in) across and ultimate height around 1.2m (4ft). Plants usually look best when 3 or 4 cuttings are planted around the edge of one pot, though flowers are not produced indoors. There is an excellent variegated-leaved form, Variegata, with white leaf edging.

Watering: Water moderately during the growing season and sparingly during the winter rest period.

Potting mixture: Use a soil-based potting mixture.

Propagation: Take tip cuttings 7.5–10cm (3–4in) long in spring or early summer.

Special points: Feed actively growing plants every two weeks with standard liquid fertilizer. Older plants quite naturally lose some of their lower leaves, if this is not acceptable, start fresh plants. Watch out for aphids at the growing tips.

FATSIA JAPONICA
(ARALIACEAE)

Regularly grown as a garden plant in temperate climates, *F. japonica* (Japan) makes a large shrub or small tree. Indoors it is very suitable for cool rooms, porches or conservatories. In high temperatures leaves and stems become "soft" and sappy, very prone to attack by pests and easily damaged. More typical plants with leathery, light green, hand-shaped leaves develop under cooler conditions. There are two variegated-leaved forms, *F. j.* Albo-marginata, with white leaf tips, and *F. j.* Variegata, but there is little to choose between them.

Watering: Water plentifully in the growing season (which can be most of the year),more sparingly in the depth of winter.

Potting mixture: Use soil-based potting mixture.

Propagation: Use basal or side shoots as cuttings in spring. Keep warm and humid – inside a plastic bag or propagator.

Special points: In warm weather stand on moist

pebble-filled trays. Pot on into larger pots (usually two sizes up) every spring, topdress older plants that have reached maximum pot size. Fatsias can be pruned quite drastically if they need to be kept to size.

FICUS PUMILA
(MORACEAE)

F. pumila (syn. *F. repens*), called the creeping or Chinese fig: it actually comes from Japan, north Vietnam, Australia and the warmer parts of China. It is used to high temperatures in summer and cool (around 50°F (10°C) in winter. Its leaves are thin, roughly heart-shaped and about an inch across. Useful for trailing – it will root down into suitably moist material, can also be trained up damp, moss-covered poles. This plant must *never* be allowed to become dry at the root, or leaves will shrivel. Stems may reach 60cm (2ft) in length.

Watering: Water moderately during the growing period and sparingly during the winter rest period. Overwatering will cause the lower leaves to fall off.

Potting mixture: Use a peat-based mixture.

Propagation: Tip cuttings can be taken and they may also be layered (see propagation).

Special points: Give standard liquid fertilizer every two weeks from spring to early autumn. Move on into larger pots only when this is absolutely 117

Ficus pumila, *known as the Chinese fig*

necessary – ficus do best when roots are a little restricted and can be grown in what may appear quite inadequate pots. Top dress large specimens, in the spring. Keep the leaves clean by gently wiping with a damp sponge, or better still, stand out in gentle rain during the warmer months.

HOYA CARNOSA
(ASCLEPIADACEAE)
H. carnosa from south China and Australia is the most commonly seen of this genus of epiphytic and terrestrial climbing and trailing plants. Its fleshy, elliptic leaves are shiny and have a slight twist to them (7.5cm (3in) long and around 25mm (1in) wide). White to very pale pink flowers with a red eye appear in clusters of up to 25.

There are two variegated forms freely available: *H. c.*

Exotica with a broad yellow line down the centre of each leaf and *H. c.* Variegata with leaves bordered with cream, in bright light pink tinges may appear in the latter.

Both *H. australis* and *H. carnosa* (the former coming solely from

Queensland in Australia) are fast growing and often produce long bare stems; the leaves appear later. All make short spurs; these same spurs make flowers in future years and should not be removed. The flowers of all are sweetly scented.

Watering: Water moderately during the active growth period allowing the mixture to dry out a little between applications. Be more sparing in winter.

Potting mixture: Use a soil-based potting mixture.

Propagation: Take woody cuttings and root in a propagator or warm room.

Special points; Feed plants every two weeks during the growing season with a general liquid fertilizer. Increase humidity by standing on trays of moist pebbles. Flower trusses are produced most freely on the climbers when the stems are trained horizontally; use a circular hoop of wire or cane and train stems around this.

HYDRANGEA MACROPHYLLA
(SAXIFRAGACEAE)

The popular, virtually hardy hydrangea, from the

temperate forests of the south coast of Honshu Island, Japan, can only be used temporarily in the home: its real place is the conservatory, porch, greenhouse or garden. The type commonly grown is *H. m.* Hortensia, a low-growing shrub with mop-heads of white, pink or blue flowers. Flower colour is affected by the acidity or alkalinity of the growing mixture. Plants are sometimes grown for sale displaying just one very large head of bloom, or with several heads.

Culture: Grow cool, in light but out of direct sun; keep the mixture thoroughly moist at all times (soak if necessary). Plant in garden after the show is over.

JASMINUM
(OLEACEAE)

Only one jasmine is a popular house plant, *J. polyanthum*, from Yünnan Province, western China. It is a very vigorous climber with dark-green leaves divided into 5–7 slim, pointed leaflets and large clusters of narrow, tubular, sweetly-scented flowers.

Flower buds are very pale pink but open up pure white and may appear from the latter part of winter to mid-spring. Young plants flower when only 4–6 months old. Best trained around cane or wire hoops pushed into the potting mixture.

Watering: Water plentifully while growth is active, sparingly in the winter.

Potting mixture: Use a soil-based mixture.

Propagation: Short tip cuttings or side shoots root readily in summer or early autumn.

Special points: Feed with standard liquid fertilizer every two weeks while growth is active. Stand on moist pebble-filled trays and mist-spray, particularly in warmer spells. Move young plants on into pots two sizes larger in late summer. Severely prune stems that have flowered – within a few millimetres of the base if necessary.

PITTOSPORUM TOBIRA
(PITTOSPORACEAE)

Pittosporum tobira and its variegated-leaved form, P. t. Variegata, are prized for their shiny, leathery leaves and sweetly scented, creamy-white flowers. They grow in temperate forests of China and Japan. Elliptic leaves are arranged in whorls around the woody, much-branching stems, flowering is in summer and in large clusters at the tips of the shoots. Good for a large, cool porch or conservatory.

Watering: Water plentifully while in active growth, moderately during the rest period.

Potting mixture: Use a soil-based mixture.

Propagation: Take tip-cuttings 5–7.5cm (2–3in) long, of half-ripe wood in late spring.

Special points: Feed every two weeks with the standard fertilizer during the growing period only. Pot on each spring into a larger pot. Pinch out growing tips during the early stages of the plant's growth to encourage bushiness and prune in spring by cutting out any straggly growths.

PODOCARPUS MACROPHYLLUS
(PODOCARPACEAE)

Native of central and southwest Japan, P. macrophyllus are conifers with needle-like leathery leaves and a dense habit of growth. They are very tolerant of a wide range of temperatures and are suitable for a cool conservatory or porch. They may be trained into various shapes by clipping, and being slow growing they remain much the same shape with little attention.

P. m. Maki is a variety from China.

Watering: Water moderately during growth and sparingly when resting.

Potting mixture: Use a soil-based mixture.

Propagation: Take tip cuttings in spring. May be slow to root.

Special points: Prune in late winter just before new growth is starting. Feed every two weeks while in active growth. Repot only when really necessary. Can be stood outside in summer.

POLYSTICHUM TSUS-SIMENSE
(POLYPODIACEAE)

This semi-tropical fern is native of eastern Asian

temperate forests (it gets its name from the Isle of Tsus in the straits of Korea). The base is a branching rhizome, making clumps of neat fronds made up of many fine pinnae, some prickly. Good for an east or west-facing window.

Watering: Water plentifully during the active growth period (most of the year) more moderately at other times.

Potting mixture: Use an equal-parts mixture of soil- and peat-based mixes.

Propagation: Divide overcrowded clumps in spring, cutting through the rhizome – each piece having several fronds attached.

Special points: Stand on trays of moist pebbles in warm rooms. Feed every two weeks during the growth period with a half-strength fertilizer. Move on into larger pots each spring.

PRIMULA
(PRIMULACEAE)

Four kinds of primula are popular house plants, usually best treated as temporary. Three are from China:

P. malacoides – bright pink, red or white flowers, carried in tiers.

P. obconica – large flowers, pink, red, salmon, mauve or white – all with a green "eye" – flower over a long period.

P. sinensis – pink or purple flowers in tiers, frilly-edged leaves and petals.

Culture: Give bright light, a cool position, thorough waterings (soaking if necessary), and fortnightly feeding with a high potash liquid fertilizer. All flower in late winter and spring; move to the greenhouse or garden frame when flowering is complete.

RHAPIS
(PALMAE)

Plants in the genus rhapis have the common name, lady palm. Originally from China (high altitude forests), but probably introduced into cultivation by the Japanese, two kinds are popular, both slow-growing fan palms with dark-green fronds.

R. excelsa has clustering stems, blunt-edged frond segments and may grow to 90cm (3ft) in the home.

R. humilis has very thin, reedlike stems and pointed tip segments. Can reach 1.8m (6ft) tall with a graceful, open appearance.

Watering: Water moderately during the growing season and sparingly in winter if temperature goes low.

Potting mixture: Use soil-based mixture.

Propagation: Take off basal suckers in spring. Also seed.

Special points: Feed actively growing plants once a month with the standard liquid fertilizer. As fronds age they first yellow and then dry up; simply cut out old fronds. Pot on into larger pots only when really needed, perhaps every two years. Top dress older plants.

RHODODENDRON
(ERICACEAE)

Two rhododendrons are popular temporary house plants, both commonly called azalea. They are sold as small autumn, winter or spring flowering shrubs with small, deep green, leathery leaves and bright, funnel-shaped flowers.

R. obtusum hybrids from

Japan have shiny leaves and small trumpet-shaped flowers, about 25mm (1in) across in twos or threes at the shoot tips. White, pink, red and magenta flowered kinds are available.

R. simsii hybrids from China and Taiwan and commonly, but incorrectly called Indian azaleas, have short bristly hairs at leaf margins and produce large "floppy" flowers in clusters.

These may be single or double, some with frilled or ruffled petal edging and in the same colour range.

Culture: Give light without sun, cool conditions, and stand on moist pebble trays to lift level of humidity.

Take off faded flowers, right to the base (including the embryo seed pod). *Never* allow the mixture to dry out completely, soak if necessary. If a greenhouse, or garden is available, pot on into an ericaceous (lime-free) potting mixture, keep well watered and fed (lime-free feed) when plants may bloom in later years.

ROHDEA
JAPONICA
(LILIACEAE)

Only one species of this genus is grown as a house plant, originally from China and Japan.

Leaves are leathery, arranged in two ranks with the leaf bases forming a thickened stem like a leek. Leaves however are up to 7.5cm (3in) wide 30cm (1ft) long. A rather arum-like flowerhead appears from the middle of the plant in early spring and can be followed by small red berries.

Watering: Water plentifully during growth and sparingly in winter.

Potting mixture: Use an equal-parts mixture of soil-based mix and leaf mould or coarse peat.

Propagation: By dividing up overcrowded clumps in spring. The base is a rhizome, ensure that a piece is attached to each division.

Special points: Feed fortnightly with the standard fertilizer while growth is being made. Keep cool for the winter rest.

ROSA CHINENSIS
HYBRIDS
(ROSACEAE)

Potted miniature roses are available in the shops through most of the spring and summer months. Each is a small-scale replica of the bushes we may grow in the garden. They have a dull, dormant period in the winter, they prefer a much higher level of humidity than we are normally able to give them indoors and are best treated as temporary room plants, to be enjoyed and then taken outdoors.

Culture: Give bright light, an east or west-facing window, generous watering (they are invariably in small pots), cool conditions and stand on trays of moist pebbles and handspray daily.

SAXIFRAGA STOLONIFERA
(SAXIFRAGACEAE)

S. stolonifera (still often sold as *S. sarmentosa*) and called mother-of-thousands, is a creeping plant from temperate forests of east Asia that produces rosettes of almost round, green and grey marbled leaves (wine-red on the underside). Red, hair-like stolons grow from the leaf axils and carry small plants. White, star-shaped flowers appear in clusters in early summer. Tolerant of cold, it is a useful plant for an unheated porch or conservatory. Good in small

hanging baskets when their stolons trail down. There is a bright-leaved form, *S. s.* Tricolor, with cream edging which turns bright pink in bright light.

Watering: Water plentifully while actively growing (most of the year) but sparingly in any short rest period.

Potting mixture: Use soil-based mixture.

Propagation: Snip off the plantlets that develop on the thin stolons and root them, or layer into a pot.

Special points: Feed actively growing plants every two weeks. Plant 3 or 4 young plants together in a hanging basket for best effect. Replace with young plants regularly. Watch out for aphids that collect on the new, young, stolons.

SEDUM
(CRASSULACEAE)

Sedums grow wild over large tracts of the globe. The kinds grown as house plants are mainly Mexican, succulent, mostly with fleshy, stalkless leaves, but they can be tiny-leaved creepers or small shrubs. Some produce flowers (usually white and small) at an early stage, others take a year or two.

S. lineare Variegatum is the preferred form of a species from China and Japan. Habit is trailing, stems clothed with many narrow, cream and light-green striped leaves.

S. sieboldii (Japan) is a trailer with pear-shaped, or nearly circular leaves that

Frost-hardy Trachycarpus fortunei

grow in whorls around the thin stems. The variegated form *S. s.* Medio-variegatum has leaves with white or cream centres and the whole leaf "shot" with pink.

Watering: Water moderately in active growth period and sparingly at other times.

Potting mixture: Use $\frac{2}{3}$ soil-based mix and $\frac{1}{3}$ coarse sand or perlite.

Propagation: By tip cuttings.

Special points: No feeding is needed. Use shallow pans, half pots or hanging baskets. Pot on, if necessary, into large pots in spring.

TRACHYCARPUS FORTUNEI
(PALMAE)

The windmill, Chinese fan or Chusan palm is from high evergreen forests in North Burma, central and east China and southern Japan. It is frost hardy and ideal for a large unheated

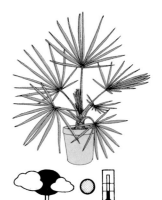

porch or conservatory or for standing outdoors for the summer. Growth is slow (two, or at most three new leaves a year) growing from a short, brown, husk-covered trunk.

Watering: Water moderately throughout the year.

Potting mixture: Use a soil-based potting mixture.

Propagation: Grown from seed, rarely produces offsets.

Special points: Feed every two weeks while in active growth only. Pot on into larger pots every other year in spring.

121

South East Asia

"No country in the world produces such ravishing perfumes as the Malayan islands . . . the woods abound in shrubs and flowers which delight the eye and attract the curiosity by their rich and gaudy colours or their delicate and beautiful forms." So said Hugh Low who brought back the orange-red flowering aeschynanthus in 1847. The region has provided us with many other treasured house plants, including the iron-cross begonia, the umbrella tree, the decoratively leaved coleus, the creeping pellionias, and many ferns.

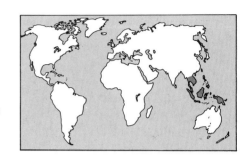

This area includes New Guinea, Indonesia, the Philippines, Malaysia, Laos, Thailand, Cambodia and Vietnam, and has a land area of over 1.6 million sq. miles. In all, there are thousands of islands (Indonesia alone has over 13,000) as well as the mainland. In some areas the mountains reach over 5,000m (16,000 ft.)

Climate
The whole of this area is within the tropics and therefore all of the area is hot and fairly wet. In the east it is hot and wet from November to April, but drier and less humid from May to October; rainfall on the higher land may be as much as 7,500 mm (300 in). Throughout most of Indonesia and Malaysia, it rains continuously throughout the year and it is always hot and humid; it is wetter from November to March, but only in the extreme south-east of the area is it actually dry from June to October. The average temperature at sea level is 79°F (26°C), though there are areas with appreciably higher and lower levels. Part of the Philippines and the mainland area to the north of the Malaysian peninsular have a monsoon climate similar to that of the east of India, but without the extremes of rainfall.

Vegetation
The vegetation is varied, but except for the high mountains, typically tropical. Forest, mainly tropical rain forest, covers much of the land, though large areas have been cleared for rice growing, maize, tobacco and other crops. As an average, about 60–70% of the area is still forested; Cambodia has 50% forest cover whereas Malaysia has 75%. As the area is so diverse and made up of so many very small facets, it is virtually impossible to give detailed

Plants adapted to salt-laden winds

geographical distributions of vegetation (indeed, much of the area is 'unexplored' and the details are not known).

Seashore
Sandy beach: At the top of sandy beaches are the seashore or strand plants which also form the zone of vegetation behind the mangroves (see right). This vegetation is made up of four main types; trees (some of which may be quite large), shrubs, woody climbers, and herbs. All of them are able to thrive in the vicinity of distinctly salty water. Seashore forests of similar composition are found in eastern Africa, Madagascar, Southern Asia, Micronesia, Polynesia, the Marquesas Islands and Hawaii, as well as throughout south-eastern Asia.

In general, this forest is not particularly dense. Coconut palms are widespread, and often associated with tropical island beaches. In nearly every case, however, they have been deliberately planted as a crop; they rarely grow here naturally.

Mangrove forest is found throughout the tropics but is most highly developed in the Malaysian region. The trees of the forest actually grow in salt or brackish water below the high tide line and have a peculiar appearence due to the mass of prop roots that extend downwards from the trunk, as well as aerial roots that grow down from the main branches.

This forest is usually best developed on estuarine mud flats that are protected from wave action and high winds. Mangroves may only be a narrow coastal strip a few metres wide, or, where there are wide mud flats, they may be a mile or more deep, but they never reach further inland than the limits of brackish water.

The characteristic plants are species of *Rhizophora,* and often large areas are covered by just one species. These are gloomy places with monotonous scenery and trees of a uniform height; the thick, glossy evergreen leaves shade out much of the light.

Slightly further inland the vegetation becomes more diverse and includes many of the plants that grow on sandy shores. Epiphytes are not very common; on the whole they tend to be ferns of which the best known is the bird's nest fern *(Asplenium nidus).* Two other epiphytic ferns that commonly grow here have swollen, creeping rhizomes which are hollow; these spaces are occupied by masses of small ants. It is thought that the ants provide some nutrients for the fern, and the fern gives the ants protection.

Secondary forest and grassland

Secondary vegetation: Throughout much of the area, man has long exploited the soil for agriculture, and, consequently, many once cultivated areas have now been abandoned and reverted to a wild but secondary vegetation. Often this is a dense forest, though coarse grassland may develop. Secondary vegetation, even if left alone, never reverts to primary tropical rain forest; it is always much poorer in species variety.

Secondary forests are composed of many well-branched small shrubs and trees; this makes travelling through the area very difficult. As the area ages, the variety of shrubs, climbers and trees increases until mature secondary forest has had time to develop. Eventually, the tallest trees grow up and form a dense canopy, and the resulting lack of light shades out and kills many of the shorter trees. In parts of southern New Guinea, where there is a distinct

Grassland midst secondary forest

dry season, more open types of forest are formed. This secondary forest resembles savanna, and frequent fires ensure that small woody plants do not become established.

Areas of grassland can be found throughout the area and they are always dominated by only a few species of coarse grass. In areas where there are also a few scattered trees, the grasses are more varied but still very coarse. Natural grasslands in this tropical area only occur in mountainous areas above 3,000m (10,000ft), and often much higher; most of these high level grasses are closely related to those that grow in temperate regions.

In parts of the Philippines and Malaysia, areas of open grassland with secondary forest are found; they are called 'parang'. These areas occur near centres of population and are usually an alternation of small areas of grassland and forest. Under natural conditions the whole area would eventually become forested. but the action of man ensures that this does not happen.

Nature's forests

Primary forest: This is the forest that has been undisturbed by man. The species make-up is very rich, and usually dependent on local soil and climatic conditions, favourable conditions result in a complex forest dominated by very large trees. Areas with dense populations, like Java, have intense pressures on their forest, and most of the forest below 1,200m (4,000ft) has long ago been cut. It is in places where there is less pressure, such as Sulawesi and parts of the Philippines, that large areas of primary forest remain.

Tropical rain forest

Most of the lowland primary forest is tropical rain forest with emergent trees up to 50m (160ft) tall and with two other distinct tree layers below these; there is a very wide variety of species that make up the canopy-forming trees. At the lower levels there are shrubs and saplings of the taller trees and often many types of palm, including the climbing and scrambling rattans. Large lianas are common, and along the edges of the forest, dense.

123

In areas with a longish dry season there is little ground cover, but in the perpetually wet regions, many plants adapted to low light conditions grow. Epiphytic and terrestrial ferns and orchids are common in wet areas, but rare where there is a dry season.

Two features that strike visitors to the forest are the large number of trees with buttress roots reaching way up the trunk, and the lack of large bright flowers. Many of the trees have their flowers high in the canopy, and they are often small and dull; a few have flowers that develop directly from their woody trunks and branches. Flowering branches of trees are often found on the forest floor, but due to the great variety and density of trees, it is often impossible to be sure from which tree the branch has fallen.

Lowland primary forest, Malaya

- ▣ Tropical rain forest
- ▣ Monsoon forest and open jungle
- ▣ Montane forest
- ▢ Savanna
- ▣ Sub-tropical/Warm temperate forest
- ▣ Water margin habitat

1. *Acorus gramineus* Variegatus
2. *Aeschynanthus lobbianus*
3. *A. marmoratus*
4. *A. speciosus*
5. *Aglaonema commutatum*
6. *A. costatum*
7. *A. crispum*
8. *A. modestum*
9. *A. nitidum*
10. *A. pictum*
11. *Asplenium bulbiferum*
12. *Begonia masoniana*
13. *Brassaia actinophylla*
14. *Caryota mitis*
15. *C. urens*
16. *Citrus limon*
17. *Codiaeum variegatum pictum*
18. *Coleus blumei*
19. *Cordyline terminalis*
20. *Davallia trichomanoides*
21. *Ficus benjamina*
22. *F. deltoidea*
23. *F. sagittata*
24. *Gynura sarmentosa*
25. *G. aurantiaca*
26. *Hemigraphis alternata*
27. *Heptapleurum arboricola*
28. *Hibiscus rosa-sinensis*
29. *Impatiens* New Guinea hybrids
30. *Pellionia deveauana*
31. *P. pulchra*
32. *Phoenix roebelenii*
33. *Pilea cadierei*
34. *Pteris ensiformis*
35. *Scindapsus pictus* Argyraeus
36. *Tetrastigma voinieranum*

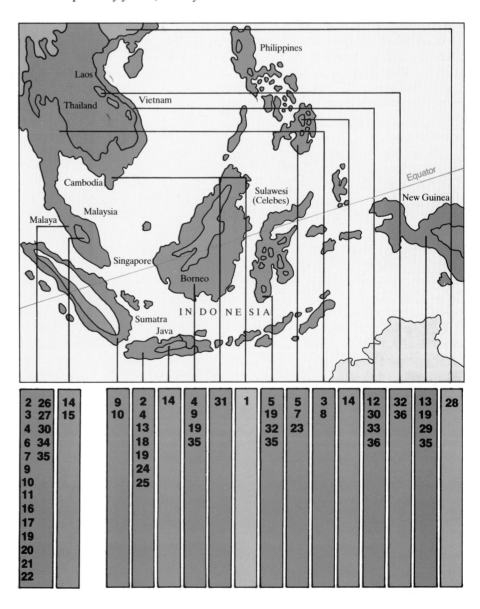

2 26 3 27 4 30 6 34 7 35 9 10 11 16 17 19 20 21 22	14 15	9 10	2 4 13 18 19 24 25	14	4 9 19 35	31	1	5 19 32 35	5 7 23	3 8	14	12 30 33 36	32 36	13 19 29 35	28

(Map labels: Philippines, Laos, Vietnam, Thailand, Cambodia, Malaysia, Malaya, Singapore, Sulawesi (Celebes), New Guinea, Equator, Borneo, Sumatra, Java, INDONESIA)

Tropical deciduous

In areas with a dry season, the forest gradually changes with the trees tending to become deciduous. The tropical rain forest trees are, of course, evergreen, their leaves constantly being shed and replaced. In the deciduous tropical forest, most of the trees lose their leaves during the dry season; some trees can be evergreen in tropical rain forest areas and deciduous in dry areas.

Above the lowland tropical rain forest, at levels above 600–900m (say 2,500 ft), the character of the forest changes. The large trees are replaced by smaller species without buttress roots, and tree ferns which are often very common. Probably the most noticeable characteristics of this forest are the two distinct tree layers and a sparse undergrowth of ferns, slender shrubs and treelets; epiphytes, mosses and climbing plants are fairly scarce. Towards the upper levels at which this forest grows, there is a noticeable increase in terrestrial ferns and herbs; and epiphytes are certainly more widespread.

Cloud forest

High altitude, moss-covered forest

At higher altitudes, some areas of forest are shrouded in cloud for much of the time. This ensures a very high

Cloud shrouds the forest near Mt. Piora, New Guinea.

humidity and a very wet forest, the ideal conditions for the growth of mosses. Everywhere, on the ground, on ledges, boulders, trunks and branches of trees, all the available space is covered by mosses, in which grow ferns, orchids and small flowering plants. Quite often there are masses of individuals of some of these small plants.

Above this mossy forest the trees are replaced by dense thickets of small shrubs with wiry stems; this forest is so dense that it is virtually impenetrable. Climbers scramble everywhere. On the tops of the tall mountains, above the tree line, open heath and grassland is found. Probably the most noticeable feature of these very high areas is that many of the plants are related to temperate plants and include cinquefoils, buttercups and gentians.

On the whole forests throughout the area are tropical rain forest, but on the mainland areas, especially towards the north of Thailand, the forests are predominantly deciduous.

Plant hunting in S.E. Asia

The Veitch collectors

Thomas Lobb, whose first contract was with the Veitch Nursery in 1843, was originally instructed to go to Singapore and then proceed to China, should that country be suitable for botanical collecting; but if not, Lobb was to use his own discretion as to where he went. His contract says that "next to China the island of Java appearing to offer the greatest advantages to a botanical collector (if facilities offer for exploring the same with safety) he is directed to proceed thither, but it is left to his own discretion." Lobb did not go to China, but it is not clear where he did go; we know little of his movements before 1845. These seem to have been as follows: 1845 he first explored the Malay peninsula. At the end of that year and in 1846 he was in western Java and may also have visited Bali. He returned in 1846 and signed a fresh contract with Veitch in 1848. This was the year he went to India and Burma. In 1849 he was in Borneo, Labuan and Sarawak and

125

may have visited the Philippines. He was back in India in 1850. There is now a gap until 1852 when he revisited Java and the Philippines. We owe the following to him: a number of Aeschynanthus species, *Hoya bella, Medinilla magnifica, Scindapsus pictus*, and *Sonerila margaritacea*, as well as numerous ferns and selaginellas.

We look in vain for any descriptions of the countryside from Lobb, but we do have some from Hugh Low, who was in Borneo from 1845 to 1847, collecting for his father's nursery.

Hugh Low in Borneo

"The flowers of Borneo and the archipelago generally are not less grateful and beautiful than the forests are grand and majestic. It has been said, perhaps too hastily, that no country in the world produces such ravishing vegetable perfumes as the Malayan Islands; and the well-known and widely distributed scents of the Kananga (Uvaria), the Champaka (Michelia), Melum (Jasminum) and many others would seem in a great measure to sustain them in this enviable pre-eminence; but though grateful perfumes are in such profusion, the woods also abound in shrubs and flowers which delight the eye and attract the curiosity by their rich and gaudy colours or their delicate and beautiful forms. As in all tropical countries the tribe of Orchidaceae is in profusion and beauty; and on the open banks of the rivers, where the sun can shed its vivifying influence upon them, these delightful epiphytes decorate with their fragile but showy forms the otherwise naked and unsightly stumps of decaying forest trees.

"On the banks of the rivers and growing as underwood in the dense jungles are found many beautiful species of the genera Ixora and Pavetta; the former with large bunches of flower of every shade from orange to crimson, the latter with tufts of pure and delicate white blossoms; other genera of the order Rubiaceae abound, and are amongst the most beautiful wild plants; many of them are fragrant.

"Perhaps the most gorgeous of the native plants are the various species of the genus Rhododendron, which here assumes a peculiar form, being found epiphytal upon the trunks of trees as in the . . . Orchidaceae. This habit, induced probably by the excessive moisture of the climate, is not, however, confined to the Ericaceous plants, but also prevails . . . with many others usually terrestrial. The roots of the Rhododendrons instead of being, as with the species inhabitants of cold climates, small and fibrous, become large and fleshy, winding round the trunks of the forest trees."

Apart from *R. formosum,* these members of the section Vireya were the first epiphytal rhododendrons to be discovered, although Thomas Lobb was also introducing the so-called Javanicum rhododendrons at the same time. It was six years before Hooker was to find the epiphytal *maddeniis* in the Himalaya. During the course of the 19th century, numerous hybrids, mainly from the Veitch nursery, were bred. Most of them are now lost, but they seem to be excellent house plants and it might be worth while for some breeder to recreate them.

Low goes on to describe various other plants, including a splendid Clerodendrum, *C. bethuneanum,* with crimson flowers followed by crimson calyces and blue berries. The only true house plant that came from this journey is thought to have been *Aeschynanthus speciosus.*

Although not particularly productive from the point of view of house plants, the expedition found many worthy plants and in his journal Low describes the discovery of one of the most spectacular, the orchid now known as *Arachnis lowii.*

November 22nd 1845. "I found myself indebted to my men for three plants of the yellow rhododendron, which they had insisted it was impossible to obtain, but which the offer of a dollar for each had caused them to exert themselves to procure. In coming here up the river, many shrubs were

in flower, particularly the sweet-scented kinds of Anthoscephalus, which attracted many beautiful butterflies. We had passed several of the gigantic Tapang trees, and two large shrubs of the magnificent *Clerodendrum bethuneanum,* which were in full flower. At night we slept in our boat and were free from the attacks of mosquitoes. Though sand flies had been troublesome during the day they did not disturb us at night. . . .

November 23rd. "Left Lubong Angin at 8 a.m., intending to call again on our return to look for more rhododendrons and anoectochilus: those we have already, having been planted in a box, are placed under the shade of a large Malvaceous plant. . . . In three quarters of an hour . . . we passed the village of Incotong . . . on a fine bamboo hanging bridge were standing some of the Dyaks, who wished us to stop at their houses; but this I did not do, as I wished to get on to Gumbang, while the fine weather lasted. Opposite a little gravelly islet, just above the village, I observed on a high tree a large mass of a new species of Vanda in full flower. The spikes of the flowers numbered upwards of a hundred, each being from 9 to 10 feet long. The foliage of the plant is very fine, being 18 to 24 inches in length and of a dark green colour; the chains of flowers rise out from amongst the leaves. . . . Each flower was three inches in diameter, of a light sulphur colour, transversely barred with bands of rich cinnamon brown; the small labellum is purple in the centre and spotted with brown towards the edges. . . . The peduncle of the flower is protected by a sheath over its upper surface; and this, with the footstalk and the flower stem are all densely covered with a beautiful mossy substance. . . . Having been delayed half an hour to secure this prize we pushed on."

Since Veitch and Low had done so well out of Malaysia, the nursery of Rollisson at Tooting secured around 1850 the services of John Henshall, of whom very little is known. In 1852 the *Gardener's Chronicle* published

A giant ficus embraces the Neak Pean temple, Cambodia

two "Memoranda from Java" from his pen, but they are not of much significance here, nor, so far as we know did he send back any plants that have since been cultivated in the home.

John Gould Veitch

The very opposite is true of John Gould Veitch a member of the nursery firm from the outset. In 1860 he was one of the first western collectors to be admitted into Japan, while on his voyage back he visited the Philippines, where he collected, among other plants, *Aglaonema commutatum*.

Scindapsus aureus seems to be a plant that John Gould Veitch failed to find on the Solomon islands and it is not known how or when it got into cultivation. The most likely source would seem to be the botanic garden at Buitenzorg in Java, under the direction of Treub and Röbelin, whose names keep cropping up as epithets in plants from Java and its environs. There are, for example, both an *Aglaonema treubii* and an *A. roebelinii*. It is to be expected that they not only made expeditions themselves, but also arranged for collections to be made on islands in the vicinity, and plants so collected would not take long before being introduced to Holland with its great tradition of glasshouse growing, and so into general cultivation. There is a great temptation, if plants from Malaysia were not introduced through a Veitch collector, to assume that Buitenzorg was its most probable source. However, there may have been many other collectors around of whom we know nothing.

Curtis and the Rex begonias

The last of the Veitch collectors in Malaysia was Charles Curtis. Although by 1878, when he set out, the Suez Canal was in full working order, he elected to go by way of Madagascar and Mauritius and from Madagascar he may have sent back the polka dot plant, *Hypoestes sanguinolenta* (syn. *phyllostachya).* Perhaps Curtis's most important sending from our point of view was a plant that is probably never seen today. This was *Begonia decora,* which came from Penang, where Curtis was director of the Botanic Garden. It is this begonia, which crossed with *B. rex* and to a certain extent *B. diadema,* gave the modern race of Rex begonias. Like petunias and verbenas the hybrids have survived and the parent species are probably no longer in cultivation.

The latest plant to come from this region is the popular Iron Cross begonia, brought back from the Singapore Botanic garden by Mr Maurice Mason, one of the few people who are collecting greenhouse plants nowadays. This plant, named in his honour *B. masoniana,* has yet to be found in the wild. At Singapore they thought that Vietnam was the most likely habitat, but no one knows for certain. The same would seem to apply to the aluminium plant, *Pilea cadierei,* which was brought back from Vietnam to France in 1938.

Botanical monkeys

One fascinating and quite recent method that must be credited to the inventiveness of botanical collectors in the area concerns the employment of berok monkeys as "assistants" by Professor E. H. Corner in the 1930s.

The berok is the Coconut or Pig-Tailed Monkey which, as is well known, is widely used in the East by Malays for gathering coconuts. The wild monkeys are caught as young as possible – so small even that they will sit in the hand; and they are trained   127 gradually to twist young fruits off the coconut inflorescences so that when they have grown strong enough they can climb the tallest trunks and drop the full-sized nuts from the crown. But it may not be so well known that a few of these monkeys are taught also such other jobs as plucking mangoes or pulling bunches of rambutans from the orchard trees. It seemed possible, therefore, that a monkey so trained would solve even the botanist's problem of obtaining specimens from tall trees, palms and climbers the height of which rendered them inaccessible.

Aeschynanthus speciosus

When Mr Corner was in Kelantan he was fortunate in finding a young berok which had been educated just as a botanist might wish. This monkey, called Merah, was brought to Singapore and after several weeks' training it complied with every expectation. On one occasion in Johore, for instance, it worked in the crown of a wild Chempedak at the height of 170 feet: on another day it collected specimens from 24 trees, all of which were over 100 feet in height. At Fraser's Hill it obtained good specimens from five of the giant palms, *Caryota equatorialis*, which seem to have been collected only once before in Malaya, many years ago, and of which there were no specimens in the Singapore Her-

barium: it revelled, too, in throwing down the fruits from so many plants of a big climbing fig that it was discovered for the first time that the gall-figs of this species (*F. calli-carpa* var.) were twice as big as the seed-figs and differently marked. Unfortunately this monkey developed an

obscure illness at Fraser's Hill, and though it became a patient at the College of Medicine in Singapore, it had to be put down shortly afterwards. In its somewhat brief career, it had collected specimens from more than 300 different kinds of tree at negligible expense.

ACORUS GRAMINEUS VARIEGATUS
(ARACEAE)

The variegated-leaved form of the grass-like acorus – a water margin plant from the rain forests of China, Southeast Asia and Japan – is the one popularly grown as a house plant. Its fine 5mm ($\frac{1}{4}$in) wide and 30cm (12in) long, arching, white-striped leaves provide excellent contrast to the fleshy leaves of other plants and it is often grown in bowls in which several plants are included. Leaves grow from a thin rhizome running just below the surface of the mixture.

Watering: Water generously at all times; they should never be allowed to dry out completely – often grown in aquariums. If grown alone stand in a saucer of water.

Potting mixture: Use a soil-based potting mixture.

Propagation: Propagate by dividing overcrowded clumps in spring, making sure that a piece of rhizome is attached.

Special points: Feed with a standard liquid fertilizer every two weeks from spring to early autumn. In warm rooms see that the air is made more humid by standing pots on trays of moist pebbles.

AESCHYNANTHUS
(GESNERIACEAE)

Aeschynanthus are a genus of trailing plants closely related to and resembling columneas which originate in the broad range from the Himalayas to Borneo and New Guinea. All thrive in the high humidity of the warm rain forest and all are epiphytic. In the wild their woody stems follow the line of the often moss-covered tree limbs, with their fleshy, elliptic leaves, arranged in opposite pairs facing the light. Roots go down into any suitable material available, when stems may branch. Flowers are large, mainly orange-red with a golden base, and appear in clusters of 3–10 on or very near the tips of the stems. Some have a prominent cup-like calyx from which the flowers grow. As house plants they tend to sprawl

and are best displayed in large hanging baskets.

A. lobbianus (syn. *A. radicans*) is commonly called Lipstick plant. From Malaysia and Java, this aeschynanthus has dark-green leaves, around 4cm (1$\frac{1}{2}$in) long. Its bright-red, 5cm (2-in) long flowers are backed by deep purple calyxes.

A. marmoratus from Malaya, Burma and Thailand, has very attractive foliage. Individual leaves are up to 10cm (4in) long; light green above marbled with darker markings; the underside flushed with rich red. Flowers are greenish yellow, marked with brown at the throat. A recent hybrid with *A. marmoratus* as one parent, Black Pagoda, is an improvement being easier to grow and with a longer flowering season.

A. speciosus (Borneo, Java, Malaya) also has large but plain green leaves and clusters of yellow-orange flowers marked with red.

Aglaonema commutatum

AGLAONEMA
(ARACEAE)

Aglaonemas are grown indoors for their spear-shaped, subtly-patterned leaves. Mature plants also produce typical arum flowers (a spathe) followed by red berries. They come from the moist rain forests of Malaysia, the Philippines, Thailand, Borneo and Sumatra, where they enjoy high humidity and warm to high temperatures. They thrive as house plants provided humidity is high and temperatures do not fall below 60ºF (16ºC) – they will tolerate relatively poor light. Plants rarely grow taller than 90cm (3ft), but may develop a short trunk.

A. commutatum (Chinese evergreen), Philippines and Celebes, has glossy dark-green leaves with silvery grey markings. Two forms:

Watering: Water moderately during the growing season, allow the mixture to dry out a little before giving more, but very sparingly during the winter.

Potting mixture: A light mixture is essential, use equal parts coarse peat, perlite and leaf mould.

Propagation: Tip cuttings, 10–15cm (4–6in) long, root easily in warm and humid conditions – best taken in early summer.

Special points: Best in hanging baskets. If stems are pinned into contact with the growing mixture they very often branch and make side-shoots, the more growing tips the more flowers. Feed every two weeks with a high-potash liquid fertilizer from late winter to early autumn.

A. c. Pseudobracteatum, (with creamy-white markings) and *A. c.* Treubii (similar, but smaller) are popular.

A. costatum, from Perale in Malaya, has dark-green leaves spotted with small white dots and a white midrib.

A. crispum (syn. *A. roebelinii*), from the Philippines and Malaya, has leathery, 30cm (12in) leaves, longer than most other aglaonemas. They are grey-green except for the midrib and leaf borders, which are olive green. *A.c.* Silver Queen is boldly streaked with silver.

A. modestum, found from Kwangtung in China to Thailand, is the easiest with plain, deep-green leaves.

A. nitidum (syn. *A. oblongifolium*), from Malaya, Sumatra and Borneo, makes a large plant with 45cm (18in) long medium green leaves, the form *A.n.* Curtisii has silver markings following the vein areas.

A. pictum, from Sumatra and Malaya, has deep blue-green leaves with irregular patches of paler green and silvery grey.

Watering: Water generously during the

active growing season but sparingly during the winter.

Potting mixture: Use a soil-based potting mixture.

Propagation: Take cuttings from the base of the plants, some may already have roots attached.

Special points: High humidity is an essential element for success; stand on trays covered with moist pebbles. Feed every two weeks during the active growth period only with a general liquid fertilizer. Avoid hot summer sun as this can cause scorch marks. A north-facing window suits them best.

ASPLENIUM
BULBIFERUM
(POLYPODIACEAE)

The parsley or mother fern comes from Australia, New Zealand, India and Malaysia and produces much divided, mid-green fronds (like carrot leaves) on black stalks, arranged in a rosette shape. Small, brown bulbils are carried near the tips of the fronds, each with a tiny frond attached and a capability of developing into a new fern. Full cultural information is given on pages 141–142.

BEGONIA
MASONIANA
(BEGONIACEAE)

B. masoniana (syn. *B.* Iron Cross) has bronze-green leaves puckered into hundreds of raised bumps, each topped by a short hair and a very distinctive

129

German iron-cross-like central marking. Most of this genus came from Brazil, and the culture for all begonias is discussed in detail in the section on South America. The Iron Cross begonia makes a spectacular house plant.

BRASSAIA ACTINOPHYLLA (ARALIACEAE)

The umbrella tree widely listed as *Schefflera actinophylla*, comes from Queensland (Australia), New Guinea and Java. Tall growing (and with scarlet flowers) in the wild, it reaches 1.8m (6ft) in a pot in the home – no flowers. Oval-pointed leaflets are shiny and leathery, up to 30cm (12in) long and 7.5cm (3in) wide on a sizeable plant.
See page 142.

CARYOTA (PALMAE)

The fishtail palms are distinguished from all other palms in that the bipinnate fronds are made up of roughly triangular segments, each ragged at the edge, like a fish's tail. With age, the fronds arch over and develop their distinctive double division.

C. mitis can be found in the humid teak forests of Burma, Malaya, Java and the Philippines. Unlikely to grow more than 1.8m (6ft) tall – a quarter of its natural size – with six to 10 fronds.

C. urens is from the Himalayas, India, Sri Lanka and Malaya and is commonly called the sago, jaggery or wine palm. In nature it can reach 30m (100ft) and makes a fine, majestic palm. Segments are broader than *C. mitis* and darker green.

Watering: Water thoroughly and then allow a little drying out. There is unlikely to be more than a very short rest period, but reduce frequency of watering if temperature falls below 55°F (12°C).

Potting mixture: Use soil-based compost.

Propagation: Only *C. mitis* can be propagated by offsets; both by sowing seed, in heat.

Special points: See that the air is made extra humid, stand on moist trays and handspray regularly. Feed with a standard liquid fertilizer every two weeks while growth continues robustly. Repot only every other year. Watch out for scale insects.

CITRUS LIMON (RUTACEAE)

The two forms of lemon, *C. limon*, are the two best

grown in pots and in the home. These are Meyer and Ponderosa, the former with pale-yellow, thin-skinned fruit and the latter coarser skinned, orange-yellow fruit.

Watering: Water moderately throughout the growing season and sparingly during the winter rest period.

Potting mixture: Use a soil-based potting mixture.

Propagation: Seeds of bought citrus fruits will germinate readily; they make attractive foliage plants but cannot be relied upon to fruit. Fruiting plants are usually grafted or raised from cuttings – a slow process.

Special points: Move outdoors to a position getting full sun for the summer months. Feed with a high-potash liquid fertilizer every two weeks from spring to early autumn. Watch out for scale insects that can collect on the underside of the leaves and the stem. Mist-spray foliage regularly and stand on trays filled with moist pebbles. Pot on as necessary in spring.

CODIAEUM VARIEGATUM PICTUM (EUPHORBIACEAE)

Originating in the hot and humid forests of Malaysia and the Pacific islands, all are commonly called croton. Growth is upright but bushy, eventually reaching tree-like proportions but when grown in pots, shrub size.

Leaf size, shape and colouration may vary enormously, some are large and pointed oval, some thin and finger-like, a few twist or curl in a spiral. They may be any combination of green, red, orange, yellow or bronze. Flowers are insignificant. Good in an east- or west-facing window. Full cultural details are given on page 143.

COLEUS (LABIATAE)

The first *C. blumei* to be introduced into Europe (in 1851) was not a wild species but one collected from a garden in Java, where the plants had been cultivated for some considerable time. Its exact area of origin can now only be guessed at. Plant breeders in Victorian Europe quickly started to hybridize the then available species and hybrids and produced the kind of plants we know today. Leaves can be virtually any colour, and range from rounded, heart-shaped to thin, twisted strips. Plants are bushy and multi-branched 30-38cm (12-15in) tall, and produce simple, light purple flower spikes which most growers pinch out to encourage the development of bushy sideshoots. Named varieties were produced but are now rarely available.

Cordyline terminalis

Today they are mostly raised from seed and quickly develop into useful and highly decorative plants.

Watering: Water generously to keep the mixture thoroughly moist. If the mixture dries out plants will collapse, and although they will recover, leaf loss will occur, leaving bare branches.

Potting mixture: Use a soil-based potting mixture.

Propagation: If facilities are available raise new plants from seed each year. Tip cuttings will root, however, and can be overwintered in a bright window.

Special points: Beware of red spider mites which tend to infest coleus in warm rooms. Nip out growing tips regularly to encourage bushy growth. Feed with the standard liquid fertilizer every two weeks during the active growth period. Can make good hanging basket plants when several plants are used together.

CORDYLINE TERMINALIS
(AGAVACEAE)

C. terminalis (syn. *Dracaena terminalis*) comes from the warm, humid rainforests of Eastern Asia – from India to Malaysia and Polynesia. Its lance-shaped leaves (up to 60cm (2ft), long and 10cm (4in) wide) are arranged around an upright stem, most standing semi-upright, the older ones arching outwards. Leaf colour is coppery with bold red markings. There are a number of named forms, including:

Amabilis – bronze, tinged pink, cream-edged.
Baptistii – rich green, splashed red and creamy-yellow.
Firebrand – purple-red.
Rededge – small scale, bright green and red.
Tricolor – creamy-white, pink and red.
All of the forms of *C. terminalis* must have bright light to develop best leaf colouration, but avoid hot, direct, summer sun. Good for an east or west-facing window.

Watering: Water thoroughly during the active growth period, moderately during the winter rest.

Potting mixture: Use a soil-based potting mixture.

Propagation: Tip cuttings of *C. terminalis* will root in a warm room or propagator in spring. Stem cuttings (each with a growth bud) will send out a new shoot if planted in peat and sand in warmth.

Special points: Stand *C. terminalis* and forms on trays of moist pebbles, keep warm and out of draughts. Pot on into slightly larger pots each spring. Top dress older plants in spring. Feed actively growing plants with the standard liquid fertilizer every two weeks.

DAVALLIA TRICHOMANOIDES
(POLYPODIACEAE)

D. trichomanoides (syn. *D. bullata*) from the tropical rain forests of Malaysia is the squirrel's foot fern with short brown fur and long silvery threads. It is tolerant of relatively dry air and makes a good basket plant.

Watering: Water moderately, allowing the mixture to dry out a little between waterings. Davallias grown in baskets should be soaked.

Potting mixture: Use a equal-parts mixture of peat-based and soil-based mixture.

Propagation: Use 5–7.5cm (2–3in) long sections of rhizome, each with 2 or 3 leaves attached. Pin down into contact with the mixture and enclose in a plastic bag or put in a propagator.

Special points: Feed actively growing plants every two weeks with a standard liquid fertilizer. Use half pots or pans as root system is shallow. Plant several small rooted sections in a hanging basket. Stand pots in trays of moist pebbles and mist fronds, rhizomes and baskets with a handsprayer (perhaps daily).

FICUS
(MORACEAE)

Ficus are native of the warmer parts of the Eastern hemisphere. Those grown as house plants are prized for their decorative leaves, which can vary in scale from less than 25mm to 60cm (2ft) or more in length. Habit varies from trailing to sturdy and rigid.

F. benjamina from south and south-east Asia and tropical parts of north Australia, aptly carries the common name weeping fig as its 5–10cm (2–4in) shiny, medium-green leaves "hang" on short stalks, and

131

its upright stems send out branches that weep like those of a willow. There are a number of forms available including an excellent variegated-leaved form, called Hawaii. To 1.5m (5ft) tall indoors.

F. deltoidea, the mistletoe fig (syn. *F. diversifolia*), from West Malaysia, has triangular, fleshy leaves (named after the Greek capital letter, Delta). Small, inedible, light-yellow fig-shaped fruits appear from the leaf axils for most of the year.

F. sagittata (syn. *F. radicans*) is a trailing plant from the Philippines, but it is the variegated-leaved form, *F. s.* Variegata, with grey and cream streaked, lance-shaped leaves that is grown indoors. Trailing stems can grow 60cm (2ft) long.

Watering: Water moderately during the growing period and sparingly during the winter rest period. Overwatering will cause the lower leaves to fall off.

Potting mixture: Use a soil-base mixture.

Propagation: Tip cuttings of the trailing kinds can be taken and they may also be layered (see propagation). Large-leaved sorts are normally air layered, but tip cuttings will root if a propagator is available.

Special points: Give standard liquid fertilizer every two weeks from spring to early autumn. Move on into larger pots only when this is absolutely necessary – ficus do best when roots are a little restricted and can be grown

in what may appear quite inadequate pots. Top dress large specimens, in the spring. Keep the leaves clean by gently wiping with a damp sponge, or better still, stand out in gentle rain during the warmer months.

GYNURA (COMPOSITAE)

Gynuras are grown for their distinctive, velvety, purple leaves. In their native Java they enjoy high humidity and warmth. Two kinds are popularly sold but it is probable that the one sold as *G. sarmentosa* is but a juvenile form of *G. aurantiaca*.

G. sarmentosa has creeping stems and coarsely-toothed deep-green leaves overlaid on both sides with soft, dense, purple hair.

G. aurantiaca stands erect with stout stems and large heart-shaped or pointed oval leaves. Flowers are orange, groundsel-like and unpleasant-smelling.

Watering: Water moderately during the growing season and sparingly at other times.

Potting mixture: Use a soil-based potting mixture.

Propagation: Both kinds root easily if tip cuttings are taken in spring. Pot several of the trailing kind together for best effect.

Special points: The trailing form looks good in a small hanging basket, particularly when viewed against the light. In warm rooms, stand on trays of moist pebbles. Watch out for aphids around the growing tip. Can be trained up canes and trelliswork.

HEMIGRAPHIS ALTERNATA (syn. *H. colorata*) (ACANTHACEAE)

H. alternata, from Malaysia, loves warmth and high humidity. Its red stems start upright but later sprawl and make them suitable for hanging baskets. Leaves are oval or heart-shaped, a metallic green with a deep reddish-purple underside.

Watering: Water plentifully during the active growth period and moderately in winter.

Potting mixture: Use equal-parts peat and leaf mould.

Propagation: Tip cuttings root easily in warmth in spring.

Special points: It is essential to make the air more humid by standing pots on trays of moist pebbles. Feed standard liquid fertilizer every two weeks during the growing period. Move these fast-growing plants on into the next size pot two or three times during the growth period. New, young plants are much better than old.

HEPTAPLEURUM ARBORICOLA (ARALIACEAE)

H. arboricola is a native of south-east Asia and related to *Brassaia*. Often called green rays from the way the 7 or more, glossy, elliptic leaflets radiate from the end of a leafstalk, 15–23cm(6–9in) long.

Plants reach 1.5–1.8m (5–6ft) in 4–5 years. Two forms are freely available, one with pointed leaflet tips – Hayata, and one with rounded leaflets – Geisha girl.

Watering: Water moderately at all times.

Potting mixture: Use a soil-based mixture.

Propagation: Tip or stem cuttings, 7.5–10cm (3–4in) long, root easily under warm conditions in the spring.

Special points: Stand on trays of moist pebbles, especially if grown in warm rooms, look out for scale insects and red spider mites. Feed every two weeks while in active growth with the standard liquid fertilizer. Pot on into the next size pot as required, perhaps once in spring, but if growth is very vigorous twice in the year.

Three young cuttings in one pot make for a bushy-looking plant. Stake with thin canes as needed.

HIBISCUS ROSA-SINENSIS
(MALVACEAE)

Symbolic of Hawaii, but distributed throughout the whole of tropical Asia and widely grown in all warm countries of the world, *H. rosa-sinensis* makes a good house plant for a warm or medium, brightly-lit room. Without enough bright light they will not flower as profusely as they should – an east- or west-

Impatiens, New Guinea hybrid

facing window, with some sun is ideal. Leaves are rather coarse, tooth-edged and deep green. Flowers are normally of five petals, white, red, pink, yellow or orange, but some new forms have petals in several layers. The single-flowered kinds have a prominent tubular column of stamens. *H.r.-s.* Cooperi has pink flowers, and leaves boldly streaked with white.

Watering: Water moderately during the growing season and give enough during the winter to prevent the mixture from drying out.

Potting mixture: Use soil-based mix.

Propagation: Tip and side-shoot cuttings root easily in spring if kept warm and moist.

Special points: These are greedy plants and need feeding every week during the growing season. Alternate between a standard and high potash liquid fertilizer. Stand on moist pebble trays. Pot on into larger pots, once or even twice a year. Severe pruning should take place in early spring, cutting new growth down to within 15cm (6in) of the base.

IMPATIENS
(BALSAMINACEAE)

All the worthwhile impatiens (busy Lizzies) grown today as pot plants are highly developed hybrids – none of the wild species are now popular. The new arrivals are of two main types, those used for bedding and in greenhouses developed from *I. wallerana* (Tanzania – Mozambique) – Africa, and the New Guinea hybrids. The latter have been developed in America

from species collected in New Guinea in the early 1970s and have very decorative leaves.

Watering: Water generously while the plants are in active growth, more sparingly in winter.

Potting mixture: Use a soil-based potting mixture.

Propagation: Seed sown in early spring will quickly give flowering-sized plants. Tip cuttings will root quickly at almost any time of the year, in water or in rooting mixture – spring is best.

Special points: Plants will only make short, tight growth and flower profusely if light is bright (but not hot,

direct, summer sun). Feed actively growing plants with a high potash liquid fertilizer every two weeks. Beware of aphids and red spider mites. In warm rooms make the air more humid by standing pots on trays of moist pebbles.

PELLIONIA
(URTICACEAE)

Pellionias are creeping plants with highly decorative multi-coloured leaves from the tropical rain forests of Burma, Vietnam and Malaysia. As house plants they are excellent for hanging baskets, or for covering areas of potting mixture under large plants. They root whenever stems touch the mixture. Avoid hot summer sun, best for an east or west-facing window.

Pellionia daveauana

P. daveauana has pink stems and leaves of variable colour from light apple-green, through bronze shades to almost black.

P. pulchra has purple stems and leaf undersides, deep emerald green leaves with almost black veining. Both may develop 60cm (2ft) stems, but these are often bare at the base and it is best to renew plants frequently.

Watering: Water plentifully during the active growth period but sparingly for the winter rest period.

Potting mixture: Use a mixture of 2/3 soil-based mix and 1/3 coarse leaf mould or peat.

Propagation: Take tip cuttings 5–7.5cm (2–3in) long in spring or early summer.

Special points: Feed growing plants every two weeks with standard liquid fertilizer. Pot on into slightly larger pots in spring.

PHOENIX ROEBELENII
(PALMAE)

P. roebelenii from hot and humid Laos makes a low spreading shape when young with very narrow, deep-green segments on gracefully arching fronds. Segments have thin white scales on them that look like threads.

Watering: Water thoroughly during the growing season and very sparingly during the winter rest period.

Potting mixture: Use a soil-based potting mixture.

Propagation: Offsets occasionally occur, detach and pot up in spring.

Special points: Feed every two weeks with standard liquid fertilizer during the growth period. Pot on into larger pots only when a mass of fine roots can be seen on the mixture surface. Top dress those that have reached maximum pot size.

PILEA CADIEREI
(URTICACEAE)

Pileas are generally low-growing, creeping-stemmed herbs spread widely through the tropical Americas as well as south-east Asia. They are prized for their decorative, often beautifully textured leaves; flowers are insignificant – rarely more than dust-like pollen sacs. Some have been in cultivation for many years, others are newcomers that have quickly become popular. All the kinds grown as house plants look best when planted in shallow pans – they are surface-rooting.

P. cadierei (aluminum plant) has a loose upright habit (to about 30.5cm (12in) tall), but can get straggly. Leaves are a mid-green with four rows of raised silvery patches.

There is a dwarf form, *P.c.* Minima.

Watering: Water moderately during active growth, more sparingly in the winter rest period.

Potting mixture: Use a peat-based mixture, or an equal-parts mixture of peat and soil-based mixtures.

Propagation: Tip cuttings and side shoots root very easily from late spring, through the summer. Start new plants each year.

Special points: Stand on moist pebble trays. Feed fortnightly from late spring to late summer.

PTERIS ENSIFORMIS (POLYPODIACEAE)

Commonly called brake or ribbon fern, these plants have a very wide distribution. Many kinds are in cultivation.

P. ensiformis originates in the Malay Peninsula, Samoa, and in Australia. It has narrow pinnae on fronds reaching 50cm (20in) long, but with some shorter and broader sterile fronds at the base. Vein areas are silvery. *P. cretica*, the most popular species, grows in India, *P. tremula* in Australasia. See page 149 for full cultural information.

SCINDAPSUS PICTUS ARGYRAEUS (ARACEAE)

S. pictus Argyraeus (syn. *Pothos argyraeus*) has matt olive green leaves, irregularly spotted grey-green, and comes from Malaya and Borneo. In the wild it clambers up the trees of warm, humid forests using its aerial roots for support. Indoors it can be trained to grow 1.2–1.8m (4–6ft) tall, or be allowed to trail.

Watering: Water moderately during active growth but sparingly for the winter rest.

Potting mixture: Use a soil-based mixture.

Propagation: Use tip cuttings 7.5–10cm (3–4in) long in spring.

Special points: Stand on moist pebble trays. Move plants on into the next size pots each spring. Include several plants in one hanging basket for a full look. In spring cut out any weak growth that may have developed in winter, and prune to keep within required bounds. Feed active plants once every two weeks with the standard fertilizer.

TETRASTIGMA VOINIERANUM (VITACEAE)

A very large climbing vine from Laos, *T. voinieranum*, makes a good, fast-growing, large-leaved climber for a large space (it would swamp a small one). Leaves are divided into five leaflets (arranged like those of a horse chestnut), glossy, dark olive-green above but with soft, felty, brown hair below. Stems grow in fast bursts and in obvious sections. The plant has the disconcerting habit of dropping whole sections of

stem if conditions are not right for it – giving it its common name lizard vine (from the way that reptile sloughs its skin if frightened).

Watering: Water moderately during the active growth period and sparingly in winter.

Potting mixture: Use a soil-based mixture.

Propagation: Propagation by cuttings is difficult because it is not easy to find short lengths of stems without large leaf surface areas. Use 23cm (9-in) long pieces of stem with one (or preferably two) leaves attached; keep in a propagator or within a plastic bag in a warm room. Spring is best season.

Special points: Feed every two weeks during the growth period with a general fertilizer. Pot on into pots two sizes larger each spring. Provide really stout supports as stems are very bulky. Avoid draughts and sudden changes in temperatures – the commonest cause of stem drop. Good in a large conservatory or heated porch.

135

Australia, New Zealand & Pacific Islands

Tall-growing brassaias from tropical rain forests . . . humidity-loving ferns, including the popular maidenhair and bird's nest . . . graceful coconut palms that fringe the islands of the Pacific Ocean . . . stately howea palms . . . epiphytic and terrestrial climbing and trailing plants (Hoya and the kangeroo vine) . . . tree-like crotons . . . frost-hardy cordylines: these are just some of the rich flora of this vast area that we grow as indoor plants. The region covers the Southern Pacific from 115°E to 130°W. For convenience, it has been divided into three major sections.

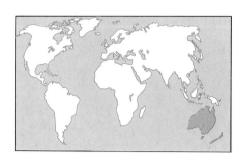

Arid areas
- Desert
- Dry semi-desert
- Grassland
- Scrubland
- Sclerophyllous grass-steppe

Semi-arid areas
- Grassland into savanna

Humid areas
- Tropical rain forest (monsoon type)
- Warm temperate forest
- Wet sclerophyll forest

Bonin Island
Hawaii — 20°N
Caroline Island
MICRONESIA
Equator
MELANESIA
Solomon Islands
POLYNESIA
Samoa
New Hebrides
Fiji
Tahiti
20°S
New Caledonia
Trop. Capricorn
Norfolk Island
Lord Howe Island
New Zealand
40°S
Tasmania

| 1 3 17 32 | 4 6 17 23 24 28 29 32 | 1 3 7 18 20 27 29 30 33 | 27 | 19 | 33 | 8 9 | 34 | 5 14 | 5 14 16 28 | 21 22 | 1 3 10 11 26 27 33 | 2 | 13 | 32 | 4 9 12 15 25 28 31 | 9 12 | 9 |

1. *Adiantum hispidulum*
2. *Araucaria heterophylla*
3. *Asplenium bulbiferum*
4. *A. nidus*
5. *Blechnum gibbum*
6. *Brassaia actinophylla*
7. *Cissus antarctica*
8. *Cocos nucifera*
9. *Codiaeum variegatum pictum*
10. *Cordyline australis*
11. *C. indivisa*
12. *Cyrtomium falcatum*
13. *Davallia fejeensis*
14. *Dizygotheca elegantissima*
15. *D. kerchoveana*
16. *D. veitchii*
17. *Ficus benjamina*

18. *F. rubiginosa*
19. *F. sagittata*
20. *Grevillea robusta*
21. *Howea belmoreana*
22. *H. forsterana*
23. *Hoya australis*
24. *H. carnosa*
25. *Pandanus veitchii*
26. *Pellaea rotundifolia*
27. *Pisonia umbellifera*
28. *Platycerium bifurcatum*
29. *P. grande*
30. *Plectranthus australis*
31. *Pseuderanthemum atropurpureum*
32. *Pteris ensiformis*
33. *P. tremula*
34. *Scindapsus aureus*

Australia

Climate

As Australia covers more than 30° of latitude, it understandably has a varied climate that is modified by oceanic influences and the absence of high mountains. The northern part of the land is within the tropics and has high temperatures, heavy rain and cyclones; annual temperatures are from 73°–86°F (23–30°C) and most of the rain falls in the January to March wet season, on average about 1,500mm (60in) a year.

Over half of the country is within the temperate zone and has warm summers and mild winters; average winter temperatures are about 60°F (16°C), while those in the summer are often 77–86°F (25–30°C). Snow falls and lays on the south-eastern alps during the winter. Rainfall is uneven; westerly winds bring light rain to the south, but much of the interior receives only 150mm (6in) a year.

Vegetation
The Australian climate is really an arid centre surrounded by concentric belts where the country is progressively wetter. After a central desert there is scrubland to the south and grassland to the north, followed by woodland and then forest. In the south, large areas are covered by scrub where woodland might be expected to grow. This is due entirely to the soils which are low in nutrients; the climate has very little effect.

Desert
The deserts are either sandy or stony. On the sandy desert, sclerophyllous grassland is found, where the grasses themselves have sclerophyllous leaves. The landscape is frequently made up of parallel ridges of sand, often over 150 km (90 miles) long and up to 2 km (1¼ miles) apart. Both the hollows and dunes have grassy vegetation. Apart from the grasses, a few shrubs grow, including species of *Grevillea*.

In the rocky areas the same grasses are found, but the vegetation differs by having different species of shrubs.

Arid areas
Around the deserts are arid areas where perennial grasses and scrubby plants grow. In the north, where it rains in summer, the grasses are prominent, whereas in the south, where it rains in winter, small shrubs replace the grass. In Western Australia a sclerophyllous grass-steppe type vegetation grows, this has dense tussocks of grass about 1m (3ft) apart; this vegetation merges into the scrub in the south and into savanna in the north. The scrub tends to be dominated by bushes of *Acacia*,

though in Queensland dwarf eucalyptus also grow. In the arid areas ephemeral (short-lived) species are very common and this part of the flora is often made up of a very wide range of species.

Semi-arid areas
Further out from the desert, as the rainfall increases, the plant communities become very grassy (except in the south where the scrubland persists): These are the grassland and savanna areas. The savanna often has areas where trees grow in clumps and form small patches of woodland.

Rainfall is usually in the region of 350–750mm (14–30in). The southern scrubland is dominated by species of *Eucalyptus*, the other woody plants being sclerophyllous. Much of this area has now been cleared of its natural vegetation and forms some of the best Australian wheat growing land.

The savanna (woodland) covers large areas in the east, and in the tropical areas, extends as far as regions receiving about 1,200mm (47in) of rain a year. The wooded areas, although superficially similar in both the north and south, differ by having different species of *Eucalyptus* tree.

In Western Australia, on sandy but poor soils, woodland is substituted by small sclerophyllous plants that resemble heathers.

Sub-humid areas

The savanna woodland of N.W. Queensland, not far from monsoon-type tropical rain forests.

With further increases in rainfall the vegetation changes and becomes forest and tall woodland. In the north, especially where the rainfall is higher, a form of monsoon vegetation grows in a dense community of trees and shrubs; palms and cycads are common. Apart from the eucalypts, most of the plants are species common in Southeast Asia.

In some areas merging into the savanna woodlands, or the wet sclerophyll forests, are the dry sclerophyll forests. These are *Eucalyptus* forests with a dense undergrowth of sclerophyllous shrubs.

Humid areas

The warm, temperate, wet evergreen forests of south east Australia. It resembles the tropical rain forests but the temperature is lower.

The wet sclerophyll forest is made up of tall *Eucalyptus* trees with a small tree or tall shrub stratum. Ferns are widespread, and in the gullies tree-ferns grow. Rain forest is either of the tropical or temperate type. In both cases the trees are densely covered with dark green leaves; plank buttresses supporting the trunks are common, especially in the tropical areas. In all of the rain forests there are masses of woody climbers and palms and, especially in the tropical areas, the undergrowth may be very thick. In fact, the major difference between the two types of rain forest is not the overall structure, which is very similar, but the actual species of *Eucalyptus* trees that grow.

New Zealand

New Zealand covers an area of just over 100,000 sq miles and is situated from 34°S to 47°S, well outside the tropics but in the southern temperate zone.

Climate

The climate ranges from sub-tropical in the north to almost continental in the centre of South Island. Conditions, however, are not extreme; the winters are mild and the summers warm. The lowest average temperature in the lowlands in the south is 37°F (3°C), and during the summers the temperature averages 66–73°F (19–23°C). The daily range of temperatures, like the annual range, is small. Ground frost is frequent everywhere except the north of North Island and crops often suffer, even late in spring.

Prevailing westerly winds bring rain to the west coast throughout the year, but in the east it is drier, especially in summer and autumn, when hot and arid north-westerlies blow. There is no dry season. In winter, the peaks are snow-covered, and in the lowlands in the south the snow occasionally settles.

Rainfall on South Island is mainly 500–1,000mm (20–40in), though a wide strip to the west of the mountain range has over 2,500mm (100in) and the mountains themselves have at least 5,000m (200in).

Most of North Island has over 1,000mm (40in) and the mountains over 2,500mm (100in).

Vegetation
Sub-tropical forest

In the North Island sup-tropical forests grow; these are made up of the conifer *Agathis australis* and assorted palms. Along the coast mangroves have developed, though they are not as complex or rich in plant species as those found in the tropics. It is surprising to find that the *Agathis* forests, typical of sub-tropical climates, are also found on South Island probably due to the absence of a cold winter in the low-lying regions. Southern hemisphere

Warm temperate forest showing tree ferns.

conifers are very common here, and species of *Nothofagus*, or Southern Beech, characteristic of colder areas closer to the Antarctic, are found throughout both Islands.

Steppe

On the eastern side of the South Island, where the rainfall is not too high (300mm – 12in) and there is a fairly dry period, a form of steppe vegetation grows. The main characteristic of this grassland, as with most steppe in the southern hemisphere, is the formation of masses of large tussocks about 1m (3ft) apart.

Pacific Islands

The island groups of the Pacific are traditionally divided into three major groups, Micronesia, Melanesia and Polynesia. Micronesia, the 'Tiny Islands', covers a land area of about only 1,100 sq miles and is made up of the Caroline, Mariana, Marshall and Gilbert archipelagos, Nauru and Ocean Islands. Polynesia, the 'Many Islands', covers a land area of about 3,750 sq miles and includes Samoa, Ellice, Line, Phoenix, Tokelau, Wallace, Futuna, Tonga, Cook, Nieu, Pitcairn and Easter Islands as well as French Polynesia. Melanesia, the 'Black Islands', is most westerly and covers about 35,000 sq miles. It includes the Solomon, New Hebrides, New Caledonia and Fiji islands.

Climate

The climate of Micronesia and Polynesia is influenced by both the latitude and the sea, but it is of course tropical. Humidity is always high, at least 80%, as are the the the temperatures which show little variation throughout the year, averaging 80°F (27°C); even on the remote Easter Island the temperatures are fairly high, though the nights can be cold.

Rainfall is, however, not so uniform. Across the eastern and central Pacific, the trade winds bring rain to the windward coasts, and western Micronesia suffers monsoons throughout the year as well as being subject to typhoons from July to November. The relief of the land greatly affects the amount of rainfall, with the high islands, like the Carolines, receiving as much as 10,000mm (400in) a year, while the nearby, but low, islands of the northern Marshalls receive only 500mm (20in).

In Melanesia there is a wet season from November to April followed by a slightly drier and less humid period from May to October. The rain, up to 3,000mm (118in), falls with no degree of regularity and often only during very violent storms.

Vegetation

The islands tend to be of two different and distinct types: Either low (atolls that are only a few metres above sea level), or high (the summits of ocean-floor volcanoes) and able to trap rain. It is the higher islands that are often very densely wooded. Normally, the flora of the low islands consists entirely of plants whose seeds and fruits are distributed by the ocean currents. This strand or seacoast vegetation consists of trees (some of which may be large), shrubs, woody climbing plants and herbs. Where forests grow they are not usually particularly dense.

Sea-shore

Mangroves are widespread, though it is on the larger islands of the western and south-western Pacific that they are most obvious. In places they may consist of a fringe of trees, whereas, where there are wide mudflats (covered by the sea at high tide), they may be a mile or more wide. Such mangrove forest is usually dark and gloomy as the trees are fairly close together; when mature, they are of a uniform height and the thick glossy evergreen leaves form a dense canopy. It is common in mangroves to find very large areas where only a single species grows. There is virtually no undergrowth except on the landward side where the ground rises above the high tide level. Prop roots are everywhere and make travelling through this forest very difficult and dangerous. There are no mosses, liverworts and lichens, but certain specialized orchids and ferns may be quite common, including the widespread bird's nest fern *Asplenium nidus*.

Secondary forest and grassland

On many of the larger islands, areas of rain forest have been cleared for agriculture, and then abandoned.

Tropical rain and temperate forest

The areas that have been unaffected by man cover large and often fairly inaccessible areas. These forests, the "typical" tropical rain forests, are rich, and vary according to local soil, degree of exposure, drainage, rainfall, etc. This is where many of the islands' indigenous house plants grow.

The upper layer of trees usually reaches about 30–35m (98–115ft) high with the second layer just beneath the crowns. A third layer consists of small trees, shrubs, seedlings and saplings of the taller trees, and various palms. The ground cover often has masses of climbing palms (rattans) and lianas, as well as plants adapted to low light conditions. Epiphytes, especially ferns and orchids, may be very common.

With an increase in altitude, the large trees are replaced by different and smaller species and tree ferns become common. The trees only form two layers with the tallest about 15m (50ft) high. As in the lowland forest, species of *Ficus* are very common. The undergrowth, however, is sparse, and consists mainly of ferns, shrubs and small trees; epiphytes and lianas are rarely present.

Somewhat over 1,000m (3,000ft), the mossy forest starts: here everything is covered by mosses, ferns, orchids and other small flowering plants; the moss blanket is always smothered with moisture. When there is no rain, the forest is kept very damp by shrouds of moisture-laden clouds. Epiphytes abound, and the climbing insectivorous pitcher plants, *Nepenthes*, are common. At the higher altitudes, very dense elfin woodland grows, made up of thickets of small shrubs with wiry stems and often interlaced with climbers. To penetrate this vegetation is difficult. Even higher, above the tree line, open grass and heath is found where many common temperate plants grow.

Plant hunting in Australasia

We can pinpoint the discovery of the Kangaroo Vine, *Cissus antarctica*, with confidence: George Caley sent it back in 1790. He also introduced another popular house plant, the Elkhorn fern, *Platycerium bifurcatum*, which did not arrive until 1808. Caley was an interesting figure, although not lovable. He was employed as a stable boy at the age of twelve and is said to have become interested in botany while searching for herbs to physic the horses under his care. In 1795, aged about 25, he wrote to Sir Joseph Banks asking for some botanical work. Banks, of the Royal Gardens at Kew, suggested that he start as a labourer in the Chelsea Physic garden and Caley accepted the post, only to complain shortly that his salary was not enough to live on. He refused to transfer to Kew, since the wages there were even lower, and wrote fairly abusive letters to Banks. To his credit Banks realized that beneath the prickly exterior there was genuine scientific interest, and eventually arranged a passage to Australia.

Further Australian house plants were collected by two other agents of Sir Joseph Banks. We know their names as George Austin and James Smith and that is the full extent of our knowledge. Through them Banks obtained *Ficus rubiginosa* in 1789 and *Araucaria excelsa* (syn. *heterophylla*), the Norfolk Island Pine, in 1793. This, incidentally, was the first araucaria to get into European cultivation, arriving three years before the Monkey Puzzle.

In 1864, John Gould Veitch (of the Veitch family nursery) visited Australia, whence many forms of popular plants emanated. Some came through the good offices of the director of the Sydney botanic garden, Charles Moore; others from the director of the Melbourne garden, William Guilfoyle. Indeed the Veitch nursery had many correspondents in Australia. Sir William MacArthur of Camden Park, Sydney, seems to have specialized in breeding crotons, while quite a few cultivars were named 'Baptistii' after John Baptist

& Sons of Sydney. Ships of the navy often made expeditions among the Polynesian and Melanesian islands and were not averse to taking botanists or plant collectors with them. The Sydney director Charles Moore had been on such a trip and on another John Baptist had sent a collector, a Mr Parcell, who returned with a variegated ficus, *F. parcellii,* which had a brief career as a house plant. It was however John Gould Veitch who was most significantly to enrich European greenhouses and later our homes. Far from being an exciting writer his prose style is rather dull, but it is interesting to have the collector's account in his own words:

"Sydney, June 4, 1865. On my return ... I was informed that Commodore Sir William Wiseman proposed visiting the various groups of the Polynesian and Melanesian islands. ... It was my intention to have finally quitted Australia about this time, but such an opportunity offered too many advantages to be thrown away and I could not resist the temptation of seeing so interesting a part of the world and one so likely to repay me.

He embarked with "8 Wardian cases filled with soil". At many of the places they did not stop for long and Veitch sometimes complains of insufficient time to make proper investigations. Among the islands visited were Tonga, Samoa, Fiji, the New Hebrides, the Solomons, and New Caledonia. Of all these it was the Solomons which most impressed Veitch and here are some of his notes on them.

"No islands can be more luxuriant. Tropical vegetation in all its beauty covers every yard of the ground from the water's edge to the tops of the highest peaks. ... All are mountainous. Guadalcanal rises to an elevation of 8,000 feet. Orchids, I have no doubt, are plentiful; I found several without being able to ascend any of the mountains. ... I noticed noble specimens of some Eugenias and Ficus, several species of palms and of Pandanus, *P. odoratissimus* being the most common; one species

of tree fern and *Cycas circinalis,* with stems 10 or 12 feet long. Amongst ornamental foliaged plants there are numerous Crotons, Coleus, Aroids, Anoectochilus, Amaranths, Acalyphas etc. Ipomoeas, Hoyas and other climbers overrun the forests to such an extent as to render it necessary to cut one's way in many places. Flowering shrubs did not appear to be plentiful; one or two Gardenias and Melastomas, two brilliant Heliconias, an Eranthemum and an Ixora are the principal. The average temperature during our stay was 82°.

"It was very vexing to see these places and not be able to explore them. Some day it is to be hoped that the natives will be more friendly; at present it is necessary to be very cautious in going amongst them, for at any moment one may, most unintentionally, offend a prejudice and excite their anger. Every one not belonging to their own district is a deadly enemy. The race is naturally becoming extinct." In spite of this

Veitch concluded: "The Solomon Islands are, I think, the most peculiar and interesting group we visited during our cruise."

The result of this cruise included 13 different crotons and 8 forms of *Cordyline terminalis, Dizygotheca elegantissima, D. osyana* and *D. veitchii, Oplismenus imbecillus* Variegatus, and the variegated *Pandanus veitchii*. He also brought back some very brilliant coleus, from which later Bause was to raise the most varied and brilliant crosses. It is not clear whether the coleus, cordylines and codiaeums were cultivated or wild plants; in the tropics the distinction is not always clear as plants from such regions seem to escape from gardens and naturalize themselves in a manner unlike those of temperate climes. Veitch was evidently a brilliant collector and his tragically early death at the age of 31 from tuberculosis was a calamity.

Asplenium nidus *in a Queensland forest.*

ADIANTUM HISPIDULUM
(POLYPODIACEAE)

Maidenhair ferns are among the most popular of all indoor ferns. The genus has a worldwide distribution but the most popular house plants are those from tropical America. In nature they may grow on moss-covered rocks or fallen trees on the floor of humid forests, but some are epiphytes. None will thrive unless the rooting mixture is moist yet free draining, as in nature they are subject to almost daily downpours of rain. Indoors too they must have very high humidity.

A. hispidulum (Australian maidenhair) from the Old World Tropics has hairy stalks and stiff fronds divided into pointed sections like the fingers of a hand. Young fronds have a bronze hue at first but turn to medium green.

Watering: Keep moderately moist at the roots but never sodden. Fronds will shrivel if the mixture dries out completely; dunk periodically in a bowl or bucket of water for ¼-hour in warmer months.

Potting mixture: Use ¼ peat, ¼ leaf mould, ¼ sharp sand or perlite and ¼ soil-based potting mixture.

Propagation: Divide up overcrowded clumps in spring.

Special points: Stand pots on trays of moist pebbles. When older fronds start to brown at the edges, cut them down right to the base; new ones will take their place. Avoid draughts. Very little feeding is necessary, do so only every two or three months during the growing season and with a fertilizer at half strength.

ARAUCARIA HETEROPHYLLA
(syn. *A. excelsa*)
(ARAUCARIACEAE)

This tall growing pine from Norfolk Island in the southern Pacific Ocean (900 miles north of Sydney, Australia) rarely exceeds 1.2–1.5m (4–5 feet) indoors and will not tolerate the

bright light that a mature plant may accept in nature. Dry heat is anathema to this plant. Its horizontally held branches appear in tiers and carry 12mm (½-in) needles. New growth, produced mainly in the spring, is mainly bright green, in time turning dark green. Slow growing.

Watering: Water plentifully during the active growth period and very sparingly in the winter.

Potting mixture: Use a soil-based potting mixture.

Propagation: New plants are grown from seed – a slow business.

Special points: Stand pots on a tray of moist pebbles. In warm rooms keep well away from radiators; dry air causes needles to brown and fall. Feed every two weeks from spring to early autumn. Move on into larger pots each spring; top dress older plants.

ASPLENIUM
(POLYPODIACEAE)
Only two species of asplenium ferns are popular house plants. They are very different in appearance.

A. bulbiferum (parsley or mother fern) comes from Australia, New Zealand, India and Malaysia and produces much divided, mid-green fronds (like carrot leaves) in a rosette shape on black stalks, Small, brown bulbils are carried near the tips of the fronds, each with a tiny frond attached and the capability of developing into

141

a new fern. It grows naturally in tropical rain forests (and requires high humidity in cultivation), but is also to be found in neighbouring temperate forests.

A. nidus (bird's nest fern) has shiny, undivided, apple green fronds with a pronounced central midrib arranged in a shuttlecock shape. Fronds may reach 60cm (2ft) in length. These ferns are from Queensland, as well as tropical Asia – including southern Japan and Polynesia. Can make large plants.

Watering: Water generously during the active growth period but sparingly through the winter rest period.

Potting mixture: Use a mixture with a high proportion of coarse organic material. An equal parts mix of coarse leaf mould, peat, sharp sand, and perlite or vermiculite will give free drainage yet be moisture retentive.

Propagation: In spring plant the small bulbils that develop on *A. bulbiferum* in small pots filled with a peat-based rooting mixture. *A. nidus* is propagated by spores that develop on the underside of its fronds.

Special points: Roots of aspleniums are fine and densely packed together, a pot-bound plant will develop a deep, spongy layer on the top of the potting mixture. Use half-pots for young plants as the root system is shallow. Pot on every other year. Feed with a high-nitrogen liquid fertilizer every month from spring to early autumn. Stand pots on trays filled with moist pebbles or sand.

BLECHNUM GIBBUM
(POLYPODIACEAE)

Blechnums are ferns that grow in the tropical islands of the south-west Pacific (New Caledonia, New Hebrides, Isle of Pines) and in the West Indies and tropical America.

B. gibbum (syn. *Lomaria gibbum*) is the most popular of the genus. Pinnae are shiny, medium green, and form fronds to 60cm (2ft) long by 30cm (1ft) wide. A short black trunk develops after many years.

All blechnums grow in forests, either tropical rain or temperate. They like good light but not the direct heat of the summer sun.

Watering: Water generously during the growth period and moderately in winter.

Potting mixture: Use equal-parts soil-based mixture and leaf mould or coarse peat. Provide good drainage.

Propagation: The tree-fern-type blechnums occasionally send up small offsets at the base. Use these for propagation.

Special points: Increase humidity with pebble-covered trays, and mist fronds in particularly warm weather. Move on into the next size pot only when pots are filled with roots.

BRASSAIA ACTINOPHYLLA
(ARALIACEAE)

Widely listed as *Schefflera actinophylla*, botanists tell us that this plant from Queensland, New Guinea and Java is a brassaia. Tall growing (up to 28m – 100ft), with scarlet flowers in the wild, it reaches 1.8m (6ft) in a pot in the home (sadly, no flowers). Oval-pointed leaflets are shiny and leathery, up to 30cm (12in) long and 7.6cm (3in) wide on a sizeable plant, each held on a short stalk radiating from a common point. The popular name, umbrella tree, is apt (stalks resemble framework of an umbrella).

Watering: Water moderately, allowing the mixture to dry out a little between applications from spring to early autumn; be more sparing in winter.

Potting mixture: Use a soil-based mixture.

Propagation: Normally grown from seed.

Special points: Move on into the next size pot each spring. Top dress older plants that have reached maximum pot size. Feed with a standard liquid fertilizer every two weeks while growth is active.

CISSUS ANTARCTICA
(VITACEAE)

Cissus are related to the grapevine, two are popular house plants. Both climb, or trail (though they rarely climb into the canopy) and are tolerant of a wide temperature range and light intensity. When given good light, growth is fast (with short gaps between the nodes).

C. antarctica (kangaroo vine), from the warm temperate forests of Queensland and New South Wales, has leathery, oval-pointed leaves tooth-edged and netted with slightly sunken vein areas. Leaves are a light green and carried singly on short red leafstalks.

A group of multi-coloured codiaeums.

Watering: Water moderately during the growing period, and sparingly during the winter.

Potting mixture: Use a soil-based mixture.

Propagation: Take tip cuttings in spring, keep warm and humid, either in a propagator or within a plastic bag.

Special points: Feed every two weeks during the growing season with the standard liquid fertilizer. Tendrils attach themselves to supports, but plants should be trained into place. Nip out growing tips periodically to encourage bushy growth. All are capable of making 1.8–2.4m (6–8ft) plants, pruning will keep them within bounds. Cut out any spindly growth after winter. Watch out for red spider mites, particularly if the air is dry.

COCOS NUCIFERA
(PALMAE)

You may have seen for sale a large coconut shell sitting half in and half out of potting mixture having sprouted one or several large, often virtually undivided frond(s). These are *Cocos nucifera* from Melanesia, now widely cultivated through the tropics. The coconut palm is a typical feature of tropical shores. Indoors they can be kept for a few years but eventually they need more root-run than afforded within a pot, and are best planted in a bed in a warm greenhouse.

Watering: Water copiously during the active growing season but very sparingly if warmth cannot be maintained consistently during winter.

Potting mixture: Use a soil-based mixture.

Propagation: Not possible indoors.

Special points: Make the air very humid, use pebble trays and a handsprayer regularly.

CODIAEUM VARIEGATUM PICTUM
(EUPHORBIACEAE)

All of the codiaeums grown as house plants are forms of one variety of a single species originating in the shrub layer of hot and humid forests in Malaysia and the Pacific islands. All are commonly called croton. Growth is upright but bushy, eventually reaching tree-like proportions but when grown in pots, shrub size. Leaf characteristics vary enormously; some are large and pointed oval, some thin and finger-like, a few twist or curl in a spiral. They may be any combination of green, red, orange, yellow or bronze. Flowers are insignificant. Good in an east- or west-facing window.

Watering: Water thoroughly in the active growth period and sparingly in winter.

143

Potting mixture: Use a soil-based potting mixture.

Propagation: Use small side shoots (staunch the flow of latex by putting the cut end into water) and root in a propagator, or within a plastic bag in a warm room.

Special points: Stand on damp pebble trays. Handspray periodically in warm rooms – this helps to discourage red spider mites. Pot on into the next size pot each spring and top dress older plants that have reached maximum pot size.

CORDYLINE
(AGAVACEAE)

Species require different positioning as to their different places of origin. Those from New Zealand (described below) grow naturally at a higher altitude and in the face of greater temperature fluctuation than their relatives in Eastern Asia. Consequently, the former are almost frost-hardy and suited to a large unheated porch or in summer a terrace or patio, whereas those from the tropical rain forests of India and Malaysia to Polynesia definitely prefer it warm and humid.

C. australis (often called *Dracaena indivisa* – cordyline in general are often confused with dracaena to which they are closely related) is popularly called the cabbage palm. It has sword-shaped, leathery, arching leaves arranged in a rosette at the top of a leafless trunk.

C. a. Atropurpurea is a reddish-hued form; *C. a.* Doucetii, is one with white striped leaves.

C. indivisa is similar to *C. australis*, and also comes from New Zealand, but it is larger all round.

Watering: Water thoroughly during the active growth period, moderately during the winter rest.

Potting mixture: Use a soil-based potting mixture.

Propagation: The New Zealand kinds can be grown from seed which is freely available.

CYRTOMIUM FALCATUM
(POLYPODIACEAE)

The holly fern, *C. falcatum*, from Asia, South Africa, Polynesia, Celebes, and Hawaii, grows in tropical rain forest zones, and is one of the most tolerant ferns available. Its leathery fronds to 60cm (2ft) in length are divided into 8–10cm (3–4in) shiny, dark green, holly-leaf-shaped pinnae. Spread, in time, to 60cm (2ft).

Watering: Water plentifully during the growing period, more sparingly if temperatures fall below 55°F, 12°C.

A hare's foot fern, davallia, with rhizomes spreading over the base of a palm tree.

Potting mixture: Use a mixture of equal parts peat- and soil-based compost.

Propagation: By division of overcrowded clumps in spring, pull apart into sections each having a piece of rhizome and 3–4 fronds.

Special points: Use half-strength liquid fertilizer every two weeks during the growing period. Pot on into the next size pot *only* when the fronds fill the old pot. In warm rooms it is necessary to increase humidity, stand on pebble-filled trays.

Periods of poor light will be tolerated but growth will be slow.

DAVALLIA FEJEENSIS
(POLYPODIACEAE)

Davallias are epiphytic, rhizomatous ferns with creeping, furry rhizomes that give rise to their common names.

D. fejeensis (the hare's foot fern) grows in the warm, wet and humid rain forests of Fiji. It displays tan-coloured fur on the rhizome, and fronds 45cm (1½ft) long.

Potting mixture: Use equal-parts mixture of peat-based and soil-based mixture.

Propagation: Use 5–7.5mm (2–3in) sections of rhizome, each with 2 or 3 leaves attached. Pin down into contact with the mixture and enclose in a plastic bag or put in a propagator.

Special points: Feed actively growing plants every two weeks with a standard liquid fertilizer. Use half pots or pans as root system is shallow. Plant several small rooted sections in a hanging basket. Stand pots on trays of moist pebbles and mist fronds, rhizomes and baskets with a handsprayer.

Watering: Water moderately, allowing the mixture to dry out a little between waterings. Davallias grown in baskets should be soaked.

DIZYGOTHECA
(ARALIACEAE)

Dizygothecas are from the tropical western Pacific and provide a rare leaf shape and coloration indoors. Growth is upright, with little branching (new growth may appear from the base). Leaves are coppery-red to almost black, with narrow leaflets radiating, like fingers, from a common point. Each leaflet is no more than 12mm ($\frac{1}{2}$in) wide and 8–10cm (3–4in) long, and is serrated, or notched at the edges. Maximum height around 1.8m (6ft) after many years and perhaps 60cm (2ft) through. Flowers are not produced indoors.

D. elegantissima enjoys warm, wet and humid conditions (temperature 68–86°F (20–30°C)) in its native New Caledonia.

The Polynesian *D. kerchoveana* has a prominent white midrib.

D. veitchii makes leaflets occasionally to 25mm (1in) wide with a red underside in its native New Caledonia.

Watering: Water sparingly at all times, allowing considerable drying out between applications.

Potting mixture: Use a soil-based potting mixture to which has been added up to $\frac{1}{4}$ part extra coarse sand or perlite.

Propagation: New plants are raised from seed – a propagator is needed.

Special points: Soil mixes should never be wet but they enjoy really high humidity. Stand on trays of moist pebbles and mist with a fine hand spray regularly. In dry air they are very prone to attack by red spider mites. Feed actively growing plants every two weeks with a general liquid fertilizer. Avoid draughts.

FICUS
(MORACEAE)

F. benjamina grows in tropical parts of north Australia and carries the common name, weeping fig – its 5–10cm (2–4in), shiny, medium-green leaves "hang" like willow leaves on short stalks and the upright stems send out branches that weep, also like the willow. There are a number of forms available including an excellent variegated-leaved form, called Hawaii. To 1.5m (5ft) tall indoors.

WT
F. rubiginosa (syn. *F. australis*) from New South Wales, enjoys temperate conditions throughout the year. The common name rusty fig comes from rusty-coloured powder on the undersides of the 7.5–15cm (3–6in) dark-green leaves. A variegated-leaved form, *F. r.* Variegata, has cream, grey and green marbled leaves. Normal height 90–122cm (3–4ft).

F. sagittata (syn. *F. radicans*) is a trailing plant from the Caroline Islands as well as the Philippines. The variegated-leaved form, *F. s.* Variegata, with grey and cream streaked, lance-shaped leaves 5–7.5cm (2–3in) long the plant is grown indoors. Trailing stems can go to 60cm (2ft) long.

Watering: Water moderately during the growing period and sparingly during the winter rest period. Overwatering will cause the lower leaves to fall off.

Potting mixture: Use a soil-base mixture.

Propagation: Tip cuttings of the trailing kinds can be taken and they may also be layered. Large-leaved sorts are normally air layered, but tip cuttings will root if a propagator is available or when pot and cutting can be placed in a large plastic bag in summer. The problems normally are loss of water through the large leaves for the relatively long period they need to make roots.

Special points: The variegated-leaved kinds need slightly warmer positions and better light than the all-green sorts. Give standard liquid fertiliser every two weeks from spring to early autumn inclusive. Move on into larger pots only when this is absolutely necessary – ficus do best when roots are a little restricted and can be grown in what may appear quite inadequate pots. Top dress large specimens in the spring. Keep the leaves clean by gently wiping with a damp sponge, or better still, stand out in gentle rain during the warmer months.

FUCHSIA
(ONAGRACEAE)

Though the genus is native to New Zealand, today's house plants are mainly derived from *F. fulgens* (Mexico) and *F. magallanica* (S. Chile and Argentina). See South America.

145

GREVILLEA ROBUSTA
(PROTEACEAE)

The silk-oak, *Grevillea robusta*, grows to a tall tree in the forest regions of Queensland and New South Wales, where it is hot during the day and cool at night with infrequent periods of heavy rain. Small plants just a few inches tall can be bought here (it is grown from seed) and quickly grow to 1.8m (6ft) in a 25cm (10in) pot. Leaves are finely divided, like the fronds of a fern, tinged coppery-red and with silky white hair when young. In the wild these trees grow in full sun but adapt well to medium light in the home. Tolerant of a wide temperature range.

Watering: Water throughly and then allow a little drying out before applying more. Be more sparing in winter rest period.

Potting mixture: Ideally use a lime-free, soil-based potting mixture, but fairly adaptable in this respect.

Propagation: Seed germinates easily in spring.

Special points: Move on into pots two sizes larger every spring, or as often as required – they can be very fast growing. Provide extra humidity by standing on moist pebble trays, this helps to discourage red spider mites.

HOWEA
(PALMAE)

Two howea palms are popularly grown as house plants. They are from the temperate forests of Lord Howe island in the south Pacific, and for years were called kentia after the capital of the island. Both are feathery (pinnate) palms with divided fronds held on long stalks, the stalk becoming the midrib of the blade, with leaflets arranged in ranks on either side of it. Both make tall plants in large pots or small tubs.

H. belmoreana (curly or sentry palm) has 20–25cm (8–10in) leaflets, growing close together and held nearly erect, like a V-shaped trough.

H. forsterana (thatch or flat palm) has a flat-topped appearance, a wider spread and the gaps between the leaflets are greater. The blade of the frond is held almost horizontal with the leaflets drooping a little.

These palms have dark green, leathery fronds which contribute to their tolerance of a wide range of light intensity, from a bright sunny east or west-facing window, to a certain amount of shade; they will not however grow much in really poor light. Warm or medium rooms suit them.

A climbing hoya

Watering: Water plentifully during the active growth period, allowing the mixture to dry out a little between applications. Water sparingly during the winter rest.

Potting mixture: Use a soil-based mixture.

Propagation: Offsets are occasionally produced and can be detached in spring. Otherwise they are grown from seed.

Special points: Feed every two weeks during the growing season with the standard liquid fertilizer. Move young plants on into the next size pot every other year, topdress older plants instead. See that the mixture is well firmed around the roots. Keep fronds clean by wiping with a moist sponge and stand out of doors in gentle rain in warmer spells.

HOYA
(ASCLEPIADACEAE)

Hoyas are epiphytic and terrestrial climbing and trailing plants from the tropical rain forests of Australia, India and south China. Many start life in the soil and grow upwards, winding round tree trunks and branches, putting down aerial roots from the nodes whenever a favourable opportunity occurs.

H. australis has waxy, almost round leaves (with just a tiny point), 63mm (2½in) long and around 50mm (2in) wide, arranged in opposite pairs, close to each other. Flowers are white with a red centre and in a cluster of around 15.

H. carnosa from south China and Australia is the most commonly seen. Its fleshy, elliptic leaves are shiny and have a slight twist to them, 75mm (3 in) long and around 25mm (1in) wide. White to very pale pink flowers with a red eye appear in clusters of up to 25.

There are two variegated forms freely available: *H. c.* Exotica with a broad yellow line down the centre of each leaf and *H. c.* Variegata with leaves bordered with cream, in bright light pink tinges may appear in the latter.

H. australis and *H. carnosa* are fast growing and often produce long bare stems, the leaves appear later. All make short spurs on which the flower trusses develop, thse same spurs make flowers in future years and should not be removed. The flowers of all are sweetly scented.

H. bella is from India.

Watering: Water moderately during the active growth period allowing the mixture to dry out a little between applications. Be more sparing in winter.

Potting mixture: Use a soil-based potting mixture.

Propagation: Take woody cuttings; these will root in a propagator or warm room.

Special points: Feed plants every two weeks during the growing season with a general liquid fertilizer. Increase humidity by standing on trays of moist pebbles. Flower trusses are produced most

freely on the climbers when the stems are trained horizontally, use a circular hoop of wire or cane and train stems around this. Move the climbers into pots one size larger each spring.

PANDANUS VEITCHII
(PANDANACEAE)

Commonly called screw pine from the way the bases of the leaves spiral around the stem, pandanus make large shrubs or small trees in their native Polynesia. As house plants they do not grow tall, but do spread considerably and need plenty of room. *P. veitchii* is the most popular kind with thin, pointed, sword-shaped leaves striped green, yellow and white. Leaf edges are barbed with very fine teeth.

Watering: Water plentifully while growth is active, sparingly at other times.

Potting mixture: Use a soil-based mixture.

Propagation: Small offsets (suckers) may appear around the base or from the stilt-like roots older plants make. Detach these for propagation in spring, but only when they have developed leaves 15–20cm (6–8in) long.

Special points: Make air moist by standing on pebble-filled trays. Spray foliage in warm weather. Move on into slightly larger pots each spring. Topdress when maximum convenient size is reached. Feed every two weeks from spring to mid-autumn.

PELLAEA ROTUNDIFOLIA
(POLYPODIACEAE)

WT

P. rotundifolia is from the mountainous regions of New Zealand and is able to survive in areas where rainfall is inconsistent, relying on an underground rhizome for moisture.

Fronds are up to 30.5cm (12in) long and carry round, shiny, dark-green pinnae up to 12.5mm ($\frac{1}{2}$in) across either side of the stalk. Shallow rooting. Commonly called button fern.

Watering: Water plentifully during active growth and moderately in winter.

Potting mixture: Use a peat-based mixture.

Propagation: Divide overcrowded clumps in spring, each piece with a section of rhizome and two or more fronds.

Special points: Feed actively growing plants every two weeks with the standard liquid fertilizer. In warm rooms stand on moist pebble tray and mist-spray foliage. Move on into the next size pot when growths become cramped.

PISONIA UMBELLIFERA
(NYCTAGINACEAE)

Only the variegated-leaved form of this tree from the temperate forests of Australia, New Zealand, Bonin Island and Mauritius, *P. u.* Variegata, is grown as a house plant. In a pot it will reach 1.2–1.5m (4–5ft) tall with large, soft, pointed-oval leaves green, pale green and cream, finely netted with dark veins.

Watering: Water moderately while in active growth and sparingly in the winter rest.

Potting mixture: Use a soil-based mix.

Propagation: Take tip cuttings 7.5–10cm (3–4in), and root in a heated propagator (or within a plastic bag in a warm room) in spring.

Special points: Feed every two weeks with the standard liquid fertilizer from spring to early autumn inclusive. Move plants on into larger pots each spring.

PLATYCERIUM
(POLYPODIACEAE)

Platycerium are all epiphytes, growing high in the rain forests, clutching the rough bark of the trees for support with one kind of frond and reaching out for light with the decorative antler-shaped fronds. They are ferns – usually called staghorn ferns – and produce spores on the antler-like fronds. The basal or infertile, disc-shaped frond is fleshy and pale green at first but later turns brown and papery. New basal fronds develop over the old ones, the old in time decaying and catching forest debris on which the plant partly feeds. In the home they can be grown in pots, slatted wooden baskets or fixed to slabs of bark.

Platycerium bifurcatum, *the staghorn fern*

P. bifurcatum (syn. *P. alcicorne)* from Polynesia and Australia makes the best house plant. Fertile fronds broaden out from a narrow base and may reach 60cm (2ft) in length, split into typical antler shapes. They are a deep-green covered with a fine silvery fuzz of hair.

WT
P. grande from Australia and the Philippines has larger fronds held like a fan

in a more upright angle with more splits in the edges.

Watering: Water generously and then allow the mixture to dry out a little (to the point where the fronds droop slightly). Plants grown in slatted baskets and on slabs of bark must be soaked in a bowl or bucket of water as required. Give brief soakings in winter under cooler conditions.

Potting mixture: Use a special orchid potting mixture, usually obtainable in small quantities and comprising equal parts very coarse peat and sphagnum moss. This mixture is suitable for small plants and for filling slatted, wooden, hanging baskets. See special points for plants grown on bark.

Propagation: This is not normally practicable in the home.

Special points: Hand-spray clay pots, cork or bark slabs and wooden baskets regularly to increase atmospheric moisture immediately around the plants. The support of plants bought ready growing on pieces of cork or bark should be nailed (or glued) to larger supports when the basal fronds have almost completely covered their initial base. Any damaged fronds should be cut away completely at the base. Platyceriums need little feeding, 2 or 3 feeds a year, during the summer, are usually sufficient.

PLECTRANTHUS AUSTRALIS
(LABIATAE)

The fast-growing, creeping and trailing forms of

plectranthus are those most popular as house plants.

The species are widely spread through both temperate and tropical rain forests in India, Africa and Australia. Most plectranthus have fleshy, four-sided stems which root at each node that comes into contact with a suitable rooting medium, making dense carpets in the open and under sparse-leaved shrubs and trees. Leaves are oval or nearly round, lightly toothed at the edges and often covered with soft, downy, hairs. Stems and leaves have a distinctive odour if brushed against. Flowers are in a thin spike, white to light purplish and most are insignificant. Stems may reach 60cm (2ft) in length in one full growing season – excellent in hanging baskets.

P. australis (S. E. Australia) starts by growing upright but later sprawls. Leaves are medium green and shiny.

Watering: Water plentifully during the period of fast growth from spring to early autumn, but water sparingly during the short winter rest period.

Potting mixture: Use a soil-based potting mixture.

Propagation: Tip cuttings root very easily in the spring and early summer, even in water. Young plants are best, start afresh each year.

Special points: Plant 4–6 plants in one hanging basket to get the best, bushy effect. Nip out growing points regularly to encourage side branches to develop. Feed every two weeks with the standard liquid fertilizer during the active growing season. Encourage to rest in winter.

PSEUDERANTHEMUM ATROPURPUREUM
(ACANTHACEAE)

Pseuderanthemums are capable of growing into small shrubs in the warm and humid forests of the Pacific islanda that are their home, but they have also "escaped" from cultivation and become naturalized in much of tropical America. As house plants they make small upright plants with highly decorative leaves, mainly purple in colouring but subtly and haphazardly marked white, pink and dark olive-green. White flowers may appear in spring in a central spike.

Watering: Water moderately throughout the year.

Potting mixture: Use a soil-based mixture.

Propagation: Take tip cuttings in spring, keep warm and humid (ideally in a propagator).

Special points: Feed every two weeks from spring to early autumn with the standard liquid fertilizer. Provide extra humidity by standing on moist pebble trays. Renew at least every other year.

PTERIS
(POLYPODIACEAE)

Commonly called brake or ribbon fern, these plants have a very wide distribution. Many kinds are in cultivation.

P. ensiformis (Australia, Samoa, Malay Peninsula) has narrow pinnae on fronds reaching 50cm (20in) long, but with some shorter and broader sterile fronds at the base. Vein areas are silvery.

WT
P. tremula (New Zealand, New South Wales/Australia and Tasmania) grows tall (to 91.5cm (3ft)) with finely-cut fronds.

Watering: Keep well watered during the warmer months when growth is active, more sparingly if temperatures or light levels are low.

Potting mixture: Use a peat-based mixture.

Propagation: Divide overcrowded clumps in spring, seeing that some rhizome is attached to each piece.

Special points: Use half-strength general fertilizer every 2 or 3 weeks while growth is active. Make the air more humid by standing pots on moist pebble trays or plunging in moist peat. Move into the next size larger pot each spring.

Scindapsus aureus

SCINDAPSUS AUREUS
(ARACEAE)

Scindapsus are epiphytic climbers from the Solomon Islands, Malaysia and Indonesia where they clamber by their aerial roots up the trees of the warm and humid forests. Indoors they grow 1.2–1.8m (4–6ft) tall, if trained, or can be allowed to trail in hanging baskets. Leaves are leathery and heart-shaped.

S. aureus – dark-green streaked yellow. Two forms are more brightly coloured; *S. a.* Golden Queen (golden yellow in large patches), *S. a.* Marble Queen (mainly white, marked green).

Watering: Water moderately during active growth but sparingly for the winter rest.

Potting mixture: Use a soil-based mixture.

Propagation: Use tip cuttings 8–10cm (3–4in) long in spring.

Special points: Stand on moist pebble trays. Move plants on into the next size pots each spring. Include several plants in one hanging basket for a full look. Cut out in spring any weak growth that may have developed in winter and prune as necessary to keep within required bounds. Feed active plants once every two weeks with the standard fertilizer.

149

Gardening indoors

Bringing plants into the home

When it all began

The habit of growing plants in dwellings is rather longer established than one might think. To most of us the cult of house plants is a post-war phenomenon which came to Britain from Scandinavia, but in point of fact the habit is much older. It is true that often the plants were only temporarily in the dwelling. As early as the 17th century the chimney campanula, *C. pyramidalis*, would be stood in fireplaces in summer. In 1706 Louis Liger recommended that the space in front of the grate should be centred with the campanula "with a pot of tuberose one each side of it and a pot of scarlet lychnis on each side of the tuberose and with small pots of Sweet Basil and Marum Syriacum neatly ranged in front." The last named plant was a form of marjoram.

In 1722 that great gardener Thomas Fairchild published *The City Garden*.

Fairchild is famous for being the first gardener to make a deliberate hybrid; in his case it was made between the carnation and the Sweet William. He had a nursery at Hoxton and anything he says merits serious consideration. He was all in favour of growing plants indoors. He noted that vines would do particularly well and he also recommended the true Virginian Creeper as suitable to grow indoors and train around the windows. Young orange and myrtles were, he said, suitable for balconies, but "those orange trees which are grafted and will blossom and bear fruit will do much better in chambers, tho' in the summer time, than stand out of doors." At this period in the early 18th century there was apparently a thriving trade in flowering bulbs, which Fairchild thought his readers were unwise to encourage. It was far better, he advised, to purchase the dry bulbs and bring them oneself to fruition.

There were, however, ornaments of a different nature for the chamber: "Many sorts of aloes, which will do very well in London and also some of those strange plants called torch thistles and also some sorts of the fig marigolds or ficoides . . . In Aldermanbury, Mr Smith an apothecary has a very good collection of these succulent or juicy plants, which he has kept for many years." This is more like our modern collection of house plants. Aloes were the same then as they are now, but the torch thistle was a globular cactus, possibly a mammillaria. The fig marigolds were mesembryanthemums and were grown satisfactorily by Mr Smith, although one doubts if they would have flowered particularly well. These could have been placed outdoors in the summer, but they must have been brought into the home for the winter. It would seem, therefore, that the earliest true house plants were succulents.

As more plants were introduced, many were tried in the home either temporarily or as a permanent fixture. In his famous *Gardener's Dictionary* Philip Miller writes of *Saxifraga cotyledon* "When these plants are strong they produce very large pyramids of flowers, which make a fine appearance, so are very ornamental for halls or to place in chimneys, where, being kept in the shade and screened from wind and

An early plant window provides light, humidity, and tranquil mood.

rain, they will continue in beauty much longer than if kept in the open air." One does not normally think of Georgian houses as being ornamented with rock garden plants, but since they have agreeable leaves as well as flowers it is easy to understand their attraction.

By the time we get to the early 19th century we find people with no greenhouse overwintering indoors such plants as scarlet geraniums. Mary Russell Mitford's *Our Village* is one authority for this practice and she also indicates that richer people would have pot plants as ornaments. She tells us that Hannah had a room "light and simple, and tasteful and elegant, with nothing fine except some beautiful greenhouse plants." It is fairly safe to assume that when literary men start to take note of a fashion, it has become fairly widespread. In *Dombey and Son*, (1848) Dickens does not seem to think there was anything unusual in Mrs Pipchin's room. "In the window of the front-parlour, which was never opened, Mrs Pipchin kept a collection of plants in pots, which imparted an earthy flavour of their own to the establishment. However choice examples of their kind, too, these plants were of a kind peculiarly adapted to the embowerment of Mrs Pipchin. There were half a dozen pecimens of the cactus, writhing round bits of lath like hairy serpents; another specimen shooting out broad claws like a green lobster; several creeping vegetables, possessed of sticky and adhesive leaves; and one uncomfortable flower pot hanging to the ceiling, which appeared to have boiled over, and tickling people underneath, with its long green ends, reminded them of spiders." No one has ever accused Dickens of being a botanist, but one would have little difficulty in re-creating Mrs Pipchin's bower. The pot that boiled over must be mother of thousands *(Saxifraga sarmentosa)* and the rat-tail cactus was wound round the laths. The creeping plants with sticky leaves present the only serious problem.

The impression given by Dickens's house plants is definitely sinister, but it is sweetness and light compared to those described by the late 19th century French writer, J K Huysmans. In his *A Rebours* his perverse aesthetic hero Des Esseintes goes in for exotics with a host of unpleasing analogies. He starts off with a collection of caladiums. "Some were extraordinary, some pinkish like 'La Virginale', which seemed made from lacquered cloth like English taffetas, some were quite white, such as 'L'Albane', which seemed to be fashioned from the transparent membrane surrounding an ox's lungs or the translucent bladder of a pig; some of them, especially 'Madame Mame', seemed made from zinc; they resembled pieces of engraved metal which had been dyed an imperial green and then splashed with oil paint in blotches of scarlet or cerise; others, such as 'Le Bosphore' gave the illusion of heavy calico begemmed with crimson and dark green; others, such as the 'Aurora Borealis' displayed a leaf of the colour of raw meat, striped with purple ribs and violet veins, a leaf swollen and sweating wine and blood.

"Next to 'L'Albane' the 'Aurora' illustrated the two extremes of anaemia and apoplexy.

"The gardeners brought in even more varieties. This time they presented an appearance of artificial skin, furrowed with veins and for the most part as though they were ravaged by syphilis or leprosy, showing livid flesh disfigured by pustules and pock marks and spots; some showed the bright pink of recent scars or the brown of scabs, others were bubbling with cauteries and puckered with burns; still others had hairy skins pitted with ulcers and cankers; others even appeared to be covered with bandages which had been dressed with black mercuric ointment and green belladonna and dusted with yellow mica and iodoform . . . .

"A fresh plant, not unlike the caladiums, was *Alocasia metallica*. This was coated with green bronze in which silver reflections could be seen. It was superbly artificial; one would have thought it was made from a

piece of stove pipe by the chimney sweep.

"The men then unloaded some tufts of lozenge shaped leaves from the midst of which there ascended a stem at whose summit there quivered a great Ace of Hearts, as shiny as a capsicum; as if to mock all the recognised qualities of plants there stuck out, from the centre of this brilliant scarlet ace, a fleshy tail, which was yellow and white; in some this was straight, but in others was like a corkscrew or a pig's tail. This was the anthurium which had only recently been brought from Colombia. . .

"Now came a further series of monsters. In the echinopsis flowers like bleeding stumps emerged from wads of cotton wool; the nidularium showed gaping raw fundaments in the midst of sabre blades and *Tillandsia lindeni* displayed chipped door scrapers of the colour of wine must."

Des Esseintes was slightly ahead of his time in his selection. Most people would only have had such tropical subjects as caladiums and anthuriums in their houses if they could be overwintered in the hothouse; the

Below: *an aquarium and fernery;* left: *a typical Victorian Wardian Case*

more permanent inhabitants of Victorian houses were somewhat different. Rather oddly the aspidistra does not figure very prominently in the lists of desirable subjects, but even so the emphasis was then, as it still is, on attractive foliage.

When foliage became the point of interest

The sudden interest in foliage that was either attractively coloured or very large and majestic is a rather odd phenomenon, which started in the 1850s. It would seem to have originated with a Parisian park director, M Barillet, who ornamented the Parc Monceau in a style that was described as sub-tropical bedding. Here greenhouse subjects with very large leaves were the main constituent, but also plants with coloured leaves were involved, particularly *Begonia rex* and its hybrids with other species. *Begonia rex* was discovered in Assam by a government apothecary called Simons, who, together with Captain Jenkins, made pocket money by sending back Indian plants and botanical specimens. Whether the begonia was actually introduced by Simons is not certain, but since we do not know who did introduce it he can at least have the credit for its discovery.

Presumably this interest in foliage came as a reaction from the rather garish bedding of such plants as scarlet geraniums and yellow calceolarias, which tended to disfigure the larger Victorian gardens. Victorian gardeners were always being convicted of "crazes". The bedding craze was to be followed by the fern craze and it must, indeed, have been agreeable to rest one's eyes on the delicate green tracery after the glare of the more strident beds. Ferns do not seem to have been so attractive to continental gardeners and they reacted with the foliage of the subtropical bedding, and the fashion for this spread to Britain.

Owners of smaller gardens could not provide either the space for subtropical bedding nor the battery of greenhouses necessary to preserve the plants in winter, and the foliage plant moved indoors. There were, not unnaturally, problems concerning their upkeep and these tended to become more pronounced as technology improved. Mr Pipchin's room was illuminated at night by oil lamps and warmed by an open coal fire. Provided they did not smoke excessively the fumes from the oil lamps would not have done the plants much harm. Smoke from the open fires might make the plants dirty, but would cause little damage.

Early terrariums and plant windows
As the century advanced, people began using gas both for illumination and heating and this did create problems. Many plants, begonias are a notable example, find the fumes from gas extremely toxic, so the choice of plants became restricted. This problem was solved somewhat ingeniously. In 1829 Nathaniel Ward had discovered that plants growing in a glass case that was more or less hermetically sealed would continue to thrive without being damaged either by noxious fumes or by inattention. Since the water in the soil could not evaporate it condensed on the glass and was eventually reabsorbed. This glass construction was known as the Wardian Case. Plants in these cases could be protected from noxious fumes and it was also possible to

A mid-19th century interior reflects a new interest in foliage.

maintain a higher temperature during frosty weather. This was done by suspending the case above a tray of water warmed by a spirit lamp. The cases were often embellished with ornamental wrought iron and might be mounted on a table with castors, so that they could easily be moved both towards and away from windows as circumstances dictated. Nowadays we call such glass constructions terrariums, but they are simply a reworking of the Wardian Case.

These cases were often quite sizeable. A popular dimension was 122cm x 60cm high and wide, (4ft x 2ft x 2ft) but even more elaborate structures were made. Shirley Hibberd, one of the greatest writers on plants and gardening in the second half of the 19th century, devised what he termed a *hortus fenestralis*, a window garden.

These were more or less miniature greenhouses which were made to fit the lower element of a sash window. He recommended that it be positioned outside "the window that commands an unpleasant look-out, or where inquisitive eyes impose a limit on privacy, or perhaps tongues that defy propriety make unseemly noises without." Hibberd lived before the days of airports, but maybe there is a case for reviving the exterior hortus fenestralis. It was however the one that projected into the living room which gave scope for the more exotic plants. In an example given by Hibberd the plants are framed by a wire arch around which the German ivy, *Senecio mikanioides*, is trained. The centrepiece of the garden is a Norfolk Island Pine while around this were caladiums, dracaenas, coleus and selaginellas. Selaginellas, indeed, which are rarely seen indoors nowadays, were put firmly over most other plants to disguise the outlines of

A hortus fenestralis

pots and give an agreeable mossy effect.

Not every hortus fenestralis was glazed in: sometimes a bow window was furnished with a specially constructed jardinière. Here is the specification for one. "In the first instance a series of zinc trays 18 inches wide and the same in length, the depth being one foot. These fit closely together and are completely hidden by an ornamental skirting of rosewood, which can be removed in one piece, as it is attached to a front of deal. The zinc trays are all freely pierced for drainage and they rest on thin slips of wood on a slab of slate, which in its turn rests on the sill and the central support. The furnishing consists of a combination of pot plants with plants that are naturally rooted in the zinc boxes." The sashes could be opened or closed by a system of cords and pulleys within the room. The plants in the boxes were selaginellas and lycopodiums, while the pot plants in this particular instance were often renewed from the author's garden.

Apart from the risk of damage from gas fumes and, in the cities, from sulphur-laden air, the main problems that faced the Victorian house plant grower were the same as face us today – poor light and a dry atmosphere. The window garden was one way of overcoming the light problem, but it was cumbersome and

since during frosty nights plants are best moved away from the window, it was deemed better to have smaller cases, which stood on tables and could be easily moved into the centre of the room during frosty spells. The moss and selaginellas around the base of the plants may have helped enhance local humidity and anyway those in the cases would have had a moist atmosphere.

Rooms in Britain tended to be heated by open coal fires, while on the continent enclosed stoves were much more frequently installed. This kept the house much cleaner. Moreover in cold countries, such as Scandinavia and Russia, the stove was never allowed to go out during the winter months, and the room temperature tended to remain constant. With the open grate, the sitting room would be nice and warm during the evening and early part of the night, but when the family retired the fire was allowed to go out. No heating during what might well be the coldest part of the night was clearly an unsatisfactory state of affairs from a plant's point of view. Even so a large number of plants were freely recommended for growing permanently indoors, many of which have now dropped out of cultivation. Of the most popular, we still grow the Indiarubber tree, the silk oak and the blue gum, while the variegated aspidistra has returned to some popularity. We grow many ficus besides *F. elastica* (the rubber plant), but not the two that were recommended in the 1880s; these were *F. chauvieri*, a form of the banyan, and *F. porteana*, which is apparently capable of producing leaves 60cm (2ft) long and 30cm (1ft) across and should be highly impressive. The Norfolk Island Pine, *Araucaria excelsa*, is still grown, but none of the other species which at the time were equally popular. Agaves are thought of as being too spiky for home decoration nowadays, but presumably their tough thick leaves were proof against the worst of fumes and there were also some finer-leaved relatives such as *Nolina recurvata* (then known as beaucarnea) and *Dasylirion acrotrichum*. These sound worth a reintroduction, although our

Araucaria excelsa

lighter rooms might cause them a problem. The Victorians loved palms and grew many more than we do today, and the number of ferns they cultivated was enormous.

The cult of house plants seems to have fallen off during the 1914–18 war in many countries, although it persisted in Scandinavia. It spread again to much of Europe between the wars, but not noticeably to the United Kingdom where the vogue only restarted after the second world war. One reason for this is the much wider use of central heating, which keeps rooms warm and at a fairly even temperature throughout the winter months, and enormously increases the range of suitable plants. Philodendrons have lost some of their popularity in recent years, but they would scarcely have been possible at all in houses without central heating. It does not seem to have occurred to the Victorians to attempt bromeliads and they might be surprised to see them in the house for long periods, but the 19th century gardener would be familiar with most of the modern house plants, although he would be surprised that they were kept permanently indoors. He would miss many of the aloes, the nolina, the dasylirion and a Japanese liliaceous plant known as rohdea; and the paucity of palms and ferns would probably shock him, but there would be relatively few surprises.

153

Climate in the home

The house as plant habitat
The first part of this book described how and where our house plants live in nature, and how their preferred living conditions are defined by a series of different factors. Among these climate is all-important, and this is closely interrelated with topography, with altitude as a vital component. We saw how in one particular kind of vegetation complex at a given altitude, like the low-level tropical rain forest where the majority of our house plants grow, there are innumerable niches which re-define their needs still more specifically. Plants may inhabit the crowns of tall trees or live on the jungle floor in vastly different light conditions; the epiphytes are starved of continual water while ground-dwellers may have bogs to tap; soils also vary in many ways.

There is, therefore, no simple summary available of the growth conditions enjoyed by a plant just because it comes from a particular locality. Some plants will only grow naturally in very specific conditions, like the saintpaulia on its cliffs or the lithops in the baking sands of southwest Africa. But fortunately many plants do, with appropriate care programmes, take to domestic cultivation in pots, and those plants which serve us best as house plants are these adaptable kinds. In many cases we can say that natural conditions have pre-adapted them to the hardships they will face in our houses, and we must never forget that to most plants living in rooms *is* a hardship, a very unnatural circumstance.

Certain limits control plants' survival wherever they grow − limits of temperature, air humidity and light intensity. Those that have the widest tolerances to these are the easiest house plants. Where a particular factor is more critical, we may be able to select spots within the artificial house environment which correspond reasonably well to plant needs, or modify that environment. A whole set of factors which affect a plant's life in its natural conditions are entirely within our control −

Ferns enjoy the humidity of a bathroom.

water and food supply, soil reaction and texture. But first, we must understand our houses as growing environments.

Climate in the home environment
Let us begin by observing our house in terms of climate. Some houses are cold overall and most popular house plants simply cannot survive in them in winter: their temperature tolerance does not stretch in that direction. Some houses *seem* warm enough, but their atmosphere turns out to be dry: the plants' temperature tolerance is matched but the humidity tolerance is not.

Within the overall limits each house will have a collection of different "local climates" or "mini-climates" in its individual rooms, and although it is dangerous to generalize, it is possible to lay down a few criteria that result from a look at typical room "habitats". Within each room we can locate various "ecological niches" (to borrow the plant geographer's idiom). There are hot spots and cool spots, well lit,

medium-lit and shady places. On the one hand plants known to grow naturally in certain conditions can be chosen for niches in various parts of the house; on the other hand, certain modifications can be made artificially to enhance the local climate. As we will see it is not difficult to improve local air humidity; insidious cold draughts should be controllable, and for special cases totally enclosed oases of warmth and high humidity can be created in glass or plastic containers or enclosures.

Measuring growing conditions
In the initial stages of introducing plants to a house, various instruments can help us assess the local climates − thermometer, hygrometer, light meter. As our knowledge of plant origins and experience of plant care increases we shall begin to *sense* what a plant needs, and how to improve matters if it shows distress. The more thought and consideration is given to siting each and every house plant we have, the more likely they will be to thrive.

Room habitats

Most rooms are set aside for specific purposes. Let us assume our house has a living room, a dining room, a kitchen, bedrooms and a bathroom, a hall, staircase and landings, possibly a porch and sunroom too; it may or may not have a basement. Flats and apartments follow the same principle though light levels are likely to vary according to elevation.

In the following sub-sections the potential climates of such rooms are described (assuming some central heating in winter and air conditioning in warmer areas). Temperatures mentioned are winter levels in colder climates when artificial heating is in use. In summer, temperatures overall are likely to be between 60° and 80°F (27°C), generally accompanied by adequate natural air humidity in temperate climates.

The living room

Temperature

Usually quite large and with at least one good window, the temperature of the living room will be around 65°–73°F (18°–23°C). If this is constant many house plants can be accommodated, but if heating is only supplied in the evenings the choice is reduced. Heating is often restricted at night but as long as it does not fall below 55°F (13°C) most warmth-loving plants should survive. Double-glazing will help in this respect, preventing windows from becoming freezing danger-spots on cold nights.

Air

The atmosphere is likely to be on the dry side and may be full of tobacco smoke. Frequent comings and goings may create draughts which need dealing with. Plants will, therefore, need local humidity aids and should be positioned away from drying agents such as radiators and night-storage heaters. They may also need frequent cleaning from stomata-clogging tobacco tar.

In one way this is the perfect place to show plants off, where visitors will admire them. Large specimens, including properly trained climbers, or bold groupings to provide set pieces, are more valuable than many small plants which will be disregarded and may get knocked about. But, *it is a room where people take precedence,* so the plants must not be in the way; kinds which will stand reasonable wear and tear are most valuable here.

Wherever people (and especially children) take precedence, plants with sharp-pointed or sharp-toothed leaves like yucca, ananas, and pandanus are best placed in the centre of groups; they may look best there too.

Light

Most "standard" house plants should grow in a living room. You could devote a south-facing window to succulents and temporary flowering plants; the other windows can be given over to foliage plants. Areas away from windows will be the choice position for warmth-loving plants that tolerate shade. Specialized and delicate plants are best avoided altogether, unless grown in a terrarium, bottle garden or plant window which of itself can be an interesting set piece.

The dining room

Temperature and humidity

In many homes the dining room sees little use. Economy may dictate that it is rarely fully heated. Temperatures of 65°–70°F (18°–21°C) may thus be reached in short spells, but more usually they will be around 60°F (16°C), less at night. Plants capable of standing long spells of fairly low temperatures are therefore appropriate. Air humidity will usually be relatively high. Within that limitation the room can be filled with vegetation according to the owners' desires: draughts and smokiness are less likely than in living rooms and overall the conditions may be more equable. Make use of windowsills, chimney-pieces (even in unused fireplaces where these exist) and dressers for smaller plants.

For the dining table a flowering pot plant or small foliage plant with good texture or markings can be effective.

The kitchen

Temperature and humidity

In use much of the time, the kitchen is usually comfortably warm, probably at least 65°F (18°C) most of the day and night, and may well be steamy. Given the right conditions of light or shade, quite tender plants, even some fairly difficult ones, often succeed admirably. Being the centre of operations, kitchen plants will be continually under someone's eye and be given extra attention accordingly.

Light

The kitchen windowsill is one obvious place for small gems; saint-paulias (African violets) often do well here. If it gets full sun it could display succulents (cacti and other prickly subjects being avoided, perhaps, because of the danger of brushing into them), or the window-sill could be used for growing the more compact herbs as an easy-reach alternative to the garden. Plants grown from pips and stones could also find a place here; children love to watch the "magical" development of orange and lemon trees, avocadoes, dates, pineapple tops, a coffee plant, not to mention carrot tops and the like.

There are often suitable positions at the back of a working surface, shelf units, or among crockery, pots and pans, and the like. Here supplementary lighting may be useful, and is described later.

Plants in a kitchen should never be in the way and that will mostly restrict your choice to small compact specimens. However, in large kitchens in old houses, or in modern houses with a dining recess, there may be scope for larger plants.

Bedrooms

Temperature and humidity

In bedrooms, as in dining rooms, the temperature is variable, rising for relatively short periods of time. The likely peaks are 65°–70°F (18°–21°C), with daytime levels of perhaps 55°F (13°C). Air humidity will be reasonably high.

A kitchen windowsill, a bedside table: ideal positions for a few choice plants

Display

Only the keenest enthusiasts fill bedrooms with plants, but a few select specimens can give great pleasure especially first thing in the morning. The bedroom tends to be a place for relatively small plants, including maybe one choice specimen or tiny group on bedside and dressing tables, but where space allows one or two large plants can be effective, with perhaps a climber trained alongside the window, and a hanging plant trailing down the side of a chest of drawers or wardrobe.

The bathroom

Temperature and humidity

Because of the moisture in the air the bathroom has similar potential to a kitchen, but in many houses it will not be so warm – an average of 60°–65°F (16°–18°C) is likely. Light varies from one to another, of course, but in many it is limited: windows are usually of opaque or frosted glass, while in urban areas bathrooms often face into the narrow gully between detached houses, and in apartments may have small windows in a central well. Such very dark conditions restrict your choice to ferns and other real shade-lovers, but otherwise rather cool-tolerant plants can be chosen for medium light conditions.

Display

Positions for plants are apt to be rather limited and can get in the way.

Plants which cascade, like asparagus ferns, or have drooping leaves like *Ficus benjamina,* echo the watery principle of the room. It is particularly important to have no prickly or spiky plants here!

Halls, stairs and landings

Growing conditions

These areas of communication in house or apartment are generally quite unsatisfactory for plants. To start with they are often rather dark and prone to draughts. There is nothing to keep the air particularly humid, though the temperature range will echo that of the living room if the house has central heating – probably around 65°F (18°C) by day, less by night.

Display

Nevertheless, these areas do often have windows around which a plant or two can be placed. A hall ought to be a pleasant welcoming place and a large specimen or plant group there can contribute greatly to this, while plants sited on stairs and landings effectively provide light relief to what are sometimes austere and uncared-for areas. In these positions smaller plants will probably be needed.

Apart from the usual need for shade-lovers, your selection should be dominated by tough plants which will stand draughts and occasional severe cold, especially if they are near the front door. Draught-proofing both doors and windows is sound economic sense, as well as increasing your own comfort and that of your plants.

Finally, it is often best to think of plants in these areas as only semi-permanent; if they show signs of distress take them elsewhere for a spell of recuperation – a spare bedroom is often a good place – and replace them with others held in reserve.

Basements

Light

Many houses have basements and sometimes these are self-contained as a flat or apartment. In some cases the windows may be level with the ground outside, when no special light problems arise. In others, however, the basement is sunk below ground level to a whole floor's depth. There may be a small sunken yard outside, but often just a narrow gully and the only outlook, a retaining wall.

The main problem created by these situations, in varying degrees, is obviously one of low or very low light. Painting the retaining wall (or the yard walls) white will undoubtedly help, as well as making the prospect more pleasant. In such basements the use of artificial light should be considered.

Humidity

Basements are often rather damp and though this produces problems it does make the overall air humidity greater and thus improves the growing potential for house plants.

Once again, if one chooses plants with the appropriate tolerances it is almost always possible to grow a reasonable range even in a dark basement.

The porch

Growing conditions

Many houses have glassed-in porches which provide shelter from wind and some frost but, even if carefully draught-proofed, not from winter cold. Even so, it is surprising what some plants will stand if kept almost dry in cold spells: citrus, acacia, fuchsia and eucalyptus, for example, and even pelargoniums, will overwinter in a weatherproof but unheated porch even with 15° of frost outside. It can be kept full of flower in spring and summer, and provide welcoming greenery in winter.

If you have no greenhouse, a porch is a natural spot for plants which are too tender for the open garden but otherwise need only protection from severe frost. These are frequently described as cold greenhouse plants.

One often unsuspected cause of trouble in porches is ornamental glass, especially the popular circular-effect, bottle-glass panes. These will focus the sun's rays like a magnifying glass and cause severe scorching on plant leaves.

The sunroom

Many people build a sunroom simply as an extra room which is heated like a living room. In these circumstances, depending of course on the temperature maintained, the sunroom can form a habitat for most of the "standard" house plants.

Ensure that they are not scorched by direct sunlight by installing blinds or thin white curtains to diffuse the rays. Good ventilation will also be needed

in hot weather, and the normal sunroom windows may need supplementing with greenhouse-style vents, preferably automatically controlled.

The more adventurous might use the sunroom as a conservatory (which is nothing more than a glasshouse fixed to a house wall with access from inside the house), deploying large specimen plants in big pots or tubs and small plants on wooden staging or in wire jardinières.

Splash water over stone-flagged or terraced floors on hot days to ensure good humidity. This means using suitable furnishings – metal, plastic-covered or outdoor-treated timber chairs and table, rather than orthodox furniture, and rush matting rather than carpets. In many ways this creates such a contrast with both the rest of the house and with the garden (to which it is a halfway house) that it is a more attractive option than having an extra orthodox room.

In these circumstances the sunroom can become a home to frost-tender greenhouse plants, most of which are grown for their flowers, rather than for the foliage house plants many of which need higher winter temperatures. Their choice comes rather outside the scope of this book. Success depends on the winter temperature maintained, which is most easily and efficiently done with electric fan heaters or banks of thermostatically controlled tubular heaters.

Some of the plants which will thrive with a winter minimum of 45°F (7°C) include azaleas, bougainvilleas, callistemons (bottle-brush), citrus, clivia, datura, eucalyptus, fuchsias, several jasmines, some passifloras, pelargoniums (regal, zonal and ivy-leaved "geraniums"), plumbago, greenhouse primulas, winter-blooming prostanthera and purple-flowering tibouchina. With a few degrees more heat it is easy to succeed with abutilon, hibiscus, brunfelsia, and many more. The conservatory-sunroom opens a whole new world of plant possibilities.

Where to site plants in your home
All genera of house plants described in this book are listed here and categorized as to their temperature and light preferences.

Temperature categories:

 Cool: 45–55°F (7–13°C).

 Medium: 55–65°F (13–18°C).

 Warm: 65–75°F (18–24°C).

Cool/bright light

Cineraria T
Crocus T
Cytisus T
Hyacinthus T
Narcissus T
Passiflora
Primula T
Senecio (wide temp. tolerance)
Strelitzia (wide temp. tolerance)
Tulipa T

Cool/good light

Asparagus
Calceolaria T
Citrus
Erica T
Fuchsia
Jasminum
Nerium
Pittosporum
Plumbago
Trachycarpus

Cool/light shade

Acorus
Araucaria
Carex
Chrysanthemum T
Fatsia
Rhododendron (Azalea) T

See pages 172–173 for advice about measuring temperature and humidity. Temperature schedules can never be divorced from advice about humidity.

Light categories:

 Sunlovers: 100% full sun requiring a cool winter rest.

 Bright light: 75–60% full sun

 Good light: 50–25% full sun

 Light shade: 10% full sun

● Shade: 5–3% full sun

Rohdea
Saxifraga
Solanum T
Tolmiea

Medium heat/bright light

Achimenes
Coleus (wide temp. tolerance)
Hibiscus
Oplismenus
Rosa T
Setcreasea
Stenotaphrum
Thunbergia T
Veltheimia

Medium heat/good light

Aechmea
Aloe
Aphelandra
Begonia (+light shade)
Beloperone
Billbergia
Brassaia
Browallia T
Callisia
Campanula
Catharanthus (+light shade)
Chamaedorea
Chlorophytum
Clivia
Cordyline (*C. australis* & *C. indivisa*: light shade)
Cyclamen T

See pages 178–179 for how to assess light conditions in your home. The majority of plants will thrive in a higher category of light than specified, though *bright light* subjects rarely tolerate full summer sun.

"T" denotes temporary pot plants; many of those in the *bright light* category can stand a few hours direct sun each day. The temperature/light categories accorded temporary plants are only for the period when they are in flower or fruit. Many need higher temperatures (and corresponding humidity) to reach that stage. This is partly because in nature temperatures are higher at seed germination time.

Dracaena
Euphorbia pulcherrima (Poinsettia)
Ficus
Gasteria
Grevillea
Gynura
Haemanthus
Haworthia
Hippeastrum
Howea
Hoya
Hypoestes
Impatiens
Lantana
Neoregelia
Nidularium
Pachystachys (v. tolerant)
Pellionia
Philodendron
Phoenix
Pisonia
Plectranthus
Podocarpus
Pseuderanthemum
Rhapis
Rhoeo
Sansevieria
Sparmannia
Streptocarpus
Strobilanthes
Tetrastigma
Tradescantia
Vallota
Yucca

Medium heat/light shade

Blechnum

Capsicum

Capsicum T
Cissus
Cryptanthus
Cyperus
Cyrtomium
Dizygotheca
Epiphyllum
Fatshedera (wide temp. tolerance)
Hedera (wide temp. tolerance)
Heptapleurum
Hydrangea T
Maranta
Monstera
Nephrolepis
Pedilanthus
Pellaea
Phyllitis
Pilea
Platycerium
Polypodium
Polystichum
Pteris
Rhipsalidopsis
Schlumbergera
Scindapsus
Stromanthe
Syngonium
Zebrina

Medium heat/shade

Aspidistra
Asplenium
Davallia

Warm/bright light

Caryota
Exacum T

Mimosa T
Sinningia

Warm/good light

Aeschynanthus
Ananas
Brunfelsia
Caladium
Cocos
Columnea
Crossandra
Guzmania
Microcoelum
Pandanus
Peperomia
Pleomele
Saintpaulia
Smithiantha
Tillandsia
Vriesea

Warm/light shade

Calathea
Codiaeum
Ctenanthe
Dieffenbachia
Episcia
Hemigraphis
Ruellia
Spathiphyllum

Warm/shade

Adiantum
Aglaonema

Aglaonema

Anthurium
Fittonia
Selaginella

Sun lovers

Aeonium
Astrophytum
Bryophyllum
Cephalocereus
Cereus
Ceropegia
Chamaecereus
Cleistocactus
Cotyledon
Crassula
Dolicothele
Echeveria
Echinocactus
Echinocereus
Echinopsis
Euphorbia milii
Faucaria

Dolicothele

Ferocactus
Graptopetalum
Gymnocalycium
Hamatocactus
Kalanchoe
Kleinia
Lithops
Lobivia
Mammillaria
Notocactus
Opuntia
Pachyphytum
Parodia
Pelargonium
Rebutia
Rochea
Sedum
Stapelia
Trichocereus

159

Natural characteristics in display

Growth habits and display

Having decided which "niches", or micro-climatic zones in the house, best suit your plants' natural needs, it is time to decide how best to display them as decorative groups or solo features.

Whereas a study of natural growing conditions can provide us with principles for plant care in the home, with display it is advisable to "muse on nature with a poet's eye"!

To begin with, the plants we use as house plants come to us from many different parts of the world; those you choose may never grow naturally alongside each other. Natural groupings *can* sometimes be striking, but they tend to be fortuitous. Most of the time plant growth in the wild reflects a battleground of survival quite at odds with the tranquil effects we are after in the home.

However, natural growth habits can be important starting points. See, for example, how the epiphytic nature of small ferns, bromeliads and tree cacti can be exploited in decorative plant groupings. But even with growth habits, there is room for personal preference – climbers may be used as trailers, the erect growth pattern of other species can be "encouraged" to be more bushy (p. 202). In the end, display is largely down to individual taste, while taste may be inspired by an appreciation of our plants' natural characteristics and dispositions.

A spider plant used as a feature, making the most of its natural form

Balance your needs and theirs when positioning plants.

People often begin with two or three plants bought on impulse for their own attractiveness, placing these on saucers or in pot-hiders on a table or shelf.

Five or six plants can be absorbed in this way by the average room, but more than that begin to create untidiness and a feeling of restlessness: the plants begin to dominate the room – distract attention rather than contribute to the overall effect.

There are certainly many situations where single specimens can be used very effectively.

Practical considerations

At all times it is a question of balancing the needs of plants and people. And in practice, the essential activities of the family are the first consideration. Children seldom have any respect for plants: they barge into big ones and knock over small ones. With growing families one must select tough plants for child-ridden areas, and place more delicate specimens out of the way. Plants suffer if brushed into frequently, and, in any room situation they need to be placed away from habitual traffic.

This point has been made with regard to arrangements in the living room, especially, where large, tough specimens or groups are not only more effective visually but less likely to annoy than a multitude of vulnerable small plants.

The problem of too many plants applies equally to bedrooms, bathrooms and kitchens, and to any kind of working surface whether a kitchen worktop, a sewing area, a place for paperwork or a bedside table with its usual paraphernalia. Conversely, plants put in little-used places like spare rooms may get forgotten and neglected.

Only by thinking these points through will house plants give the pleasure they should.

Grouping plants

House plants may be grouped together in many ways. The least demanding of these is to keep each plant's pot on an individual drip saucer or in a waterproof pot-hider of plastic or china; self-watering and hydroponic containers lend themselves to this treatment and are usually quite attractive visually. If separate pots or pot-hiders are clearly visible, they should not detract from the plants nor clash between themselves.

Plants thus treated can be made into informal groups or placed along shelves, windowsills and ledges, where a communal drip tray can be used to good purpose.

Such positions also recommend the use of troughs in which to conceal the pots, and the trough can be used under a window or along a wall wherever straight-line grouping is convenient and attractive. Some troughs are available on stands.

In general, watertight troughs should be used; those with drainage holes have to have a drip tray. Within the troughs, pots can be embedded in peat or fresh sphagnum moss, or placed on a layer of pebbles, gravel or granules to improve local air humidity.

Equally suitable for appropriately shaped sites are the many containers now available in variously coloured plastic. These include wide oblong boxes, large circular planters, and ingenious quarter-circle containers designed to fit inside corners or to be pushed together in a group of three around a projecting corner.

Many domestic containers can be useful, especially those now prized as antiques – old soup tureens, fish kettles, copper pots and troughs, for whatever purpose they were originally designed.

Other ways of grouping plants involve metal or plastic trays of various shapes. Ideally these should be quite deep so that they can accommodate a good layer of pebbles or granules to which water can be added to aid

Bringing the jungle indoors – huge plants dominate this room, placed at strategic points each in a pot-hider blending with the furniture.

humidity. Alternatively they may be filled with peat into which the pots are embedded. Where the flooring is suitable, and they will not give rise to cleaning problems, large stones or cobbles can be heaped over such low trays, or even surround pots in individual drip saucers.

Containers are valuable only for groups of relatively small pots. Where a jungly effect is to be created by a group of large plants – say in a corner or even along a whole wall – keep them in their own pots, packing them together as close as their size permits.

When placing plants together in containers it is most unwise to "plant" them without their pots. Roots tangle together, making it difficult to move or extract plants later, and some plants will grow faster than others

and swamp them. As it is, plants in pots will push out roots into peat or damp pebbles and a periodic examination should be made. Mostly these surplus roots will have to be cut off because if they grow to any length it will be impossible to re-pot later without damaging them.

Colour in groups

The actual arrangement of the plants in any group is very much a matter of personal taste and degree of artistry: in many ways it resembles flower arranging. Although many house plants are basically green, there are gradations of green from pale to dark, and beyond that a vast range of plants with coloured leaves – reds, pinks, purples, bluish shades and silver. And there are patterns combining two or more colours in stripes, bands, strange regular designs or mottling. Gold, yellow or white variegation on green is the commonest two-colour combination, and this can be overdone in an arrangement. There are many others with which to experiment.

161

Size, shape and texture of leaf

If the colour palette gives endless scope for colour contrast or association, so the variation in leaf size and shape provides infinite permutations. Some, like monsteras, are even perforated with holes. Texture is a feature which not only reflects plants' ability to survive in certain conditions. Many leaves are shiny, some are matt-surfaced, others furry or hairy; the variations can be put to good effect.

Growth habit

Another set of variations comes from the growth habit of each plant – the rosettes of bromeliads, upright leaves of sansevieria, feathery look of ferns, solidity of rubber plants, airy fronds of palms, are examples.

Climbers have a place, perhaps less in groups than as solo specimens or design features. Creeping plants are invaluable to fill gaps between upright stems, and trailers to tumble over container edges: some plants trail naturally, like the tradescantia tribe, while others which normally climb, like ivies, are quite at home trailing or cascading until their growths become too long for the position.

In general plants which look alike lose their identity and interest if grouped closely together. *Contrasts* of growth habit and leaf shape, assisted by those of colour and pattern, make for the most interesting and striking arrangements.

Flowers in display

As we have seen, relatively few permanent house plants flower in cultivation. If and when they do, it is a bonus and one may wish to reshuffle a group to give them more prominence while in bloom.

Plants that flower indoors are more likely to be temporary pot plants, such as dwarfed chrysanthemums, cinerarias and bulbs like hyacinths. These are usually bought in bud or actually in flower and often last a relatively short time (though with the right facilities it may be possible to bring them into flower another year).

A flowering azalea brings colour to well contrasted foliage plants.

Viewpoint

In building up a group one vital consideration is viewpoint. Will it be seen from all sides, will it be ensconced in a corner or placed against a wall? If from all sides, the taller plants are best near the centre; in one-sided groups they need to be at the back. At all times one needs to remember that most plants will in time turn their leaves towards the light. It is very difficult to keep an arrangement looking right if, to succeed, it has to face away from the main source of light.

Plants least affected in this way include bromeliads, sansevierias and yuccas. With *Ficus benjamina* and asparagus "ferns" the phenomenon is never a problem in that they remain attractive from all viewpoints.

The 'care' factor

In general plants grouped together should have similar watering needs. The odd plant needing little water or an unusual amount of water is likely to be overlooked among those with average needs. So, for example, group together "hobby plants", especially cacti and other succulents, and also African violets, rather than interspersing them in multifarious groups. There is also something in the *character* of these plant groups that usually makes them look better with their fellows than mixed up with more orthodox kinds. But again, it is a matter of taste if cultural problems can be overcome. Indeed there are certain plants of similar appearance, notably the bromeliads, that do not necessarily look attractive packed together.

Individual plants as features

There are many places where a group is impracticable, but a single plant can be used to good effect. Such *focal-point* or *accent plants* can be of any size. An African violet or a single small fern, say on a bedroom table, a mantlepiece or in the centre of a dining table, can attract attention and enhance the area as well as a big specimen plant. But mostly it is big plants that are used in this way, especially in modern decor where a bold "statement" is often preferable to the diversity of a group.

Further, there are some plants whose qualities are obscured in groups unless they are allowed to dominate the arrangement. We can think of these as living sculptures, ranging from the chunkiness of big-leaved ficus, the geometry of a large palm, the graceful weeping effect of *Ficus benjamina* or the delicacy of a cyperus or dizygotheca.

Individual plants, large or small, need to be in perfect condition. The odd blemish on a leaf in a group will be insignificant, but on a solo performer it will stand out. By the same token the containers for large plants will be specially noticeable; they need to be attractive in their own right, complement the plant and fit in with the room decor.

The huge yucca is sufficient decoration for the room and holds its own against the strongly patterned paper.

Designing with plants

Most people grow plants indoors – whether large or small, individuals or groups – in order to create interest and to enhance the appearance of their rooms. There is no room in which space for plants cannot be found, and it is amazing how they can become an integral part of decor in any style and age. There is no need to keep aspidistra and ferns in Victorian clutter, nor to confine the modernistic lines of yucca and sansevieria to avant-garde interiors.

The gleaming green bird's nest fern contrasts well with the shining brass pot in an otherwise bare corner.

Interestingly enough, the clinical decor, chrome and glass of stream-lined modernistic interior design, are more in need of the introduction of plants to give a lived-in, personal feeling than the average room in most homes, with its clutter and sometimes miscellaneous furnishing. Grand rooms with marble floors and panelled walls are equally humanized by the living plant.

Settings and backgrounds must be considered when selecting plants. Plain backgrounds are generally preferable: a patterned wallpaper with plants in front of it is likely to look fussy unless large, bold-leaved specimens are used. Certainly any small, delicate foliage will be wasted against most patterns. Colour of paint or paper must also be considered: a red-leaved plant will hardly make its mark against a red background.

Plants can be chosen to contrast with coloured backgrounds, say red or purple leaves against blue or green shades, or vice versa. White usually enhances most plants, except those with much white or yellow variegation. Dark walls or wooden panelling however call for colour harmony or very pale green leaves.

In general, house plants go well against wood, stone or marble, but not so happily against red brick nor over highly patterned tiling, vinyl or carpet. Large-leaved, plain green plants are best for these situations. Plants are usually successful alongside most furniture, even the starkest, hard-cornered furniture or modern fittings. But they go especially well with wood or cane. Bright-coloured plastic needs the same selection for contrast as wall colours, but strongly patterned furnishing materials rarely improve plant groups.

An unused fireplace transformed with plants: the mirror doubles the effect and cobbles enhance the trough.

There are many particular spots that can be enhanced with well-placed plants. Fireplaces are an example (if they have not been closed up) especially those with Victorian or art-nouveau decoration. These tend to look best painted glossy white, the plants framed within. **163**

Enhancing views with plants

Windows can be framed with climbing plants trained up cords or wire (see p. 168), both sides and top can be so treated. Small windows of no particular interest are brought into focus by a suitable small plant on the sill. Also, attractive outside views can be effectively "framed" in this way.

Ugly features can be disguised with well-placed plants, including projecting pipes, air vents, cracks or badly painted areas. One of the most valuable uses of house plants is to distract the eye from ugly exteriors – the neighbour's wall, a central shaft in a block of flats, or a dingy cramped outlook from a basement window. The whole exterior scene can be virtually blotted out with large plants along a windowsill, or one or more shelves higher up can be filled with an array or smaller plants.

In most such positions light is already restricted, so further reduction by obscuring plants is no great loss – provided that plants needing low-light conditions are selected.

Choice of suitably tolerant plants is equally vital in halls, passages, landings and on staircases, but given basic light requirements, climbing plants can be grown from one floor to another, or trailers allowed to hang down from a landing. Plants on or at the bottom of stairs enhance views from all sorts of unexpected angles.

Plants as screens

Another interesting use for house plants is as a living screen or room divider. One might wish to partly screen a kitchen from a dining alcove, or use plants in an open-plan layout to define different areas of use. Plants do this in a positive, but less definitive way than a solid dividing wall. For this purpose a suitable number of plants of the same kind are almost always better than a mixture. Plants should be tall, fairly erect and leafy: examples include *Fatshedera lizei*, *Ficus benjamina*, podocarpus and sansevieria. Alternatively climbers can be fixed onto poles, cord, wire or, if preferred, a length of netting between uprights.

For room division the plants can be set individually in large square containers placed in line, or their ordinary pots can be placed in fairly large troughs: the containers will themselves have a divisive effect.

Special effects with plants

Some plant containers are designed to be hung on walls: these are usually pots or basket shapes with a flat side, of earthenware or china, and provided with a hole for a nail. These do not always create as satisfactory an effect in rooms as in loggias.

Again it is not always easy to place hanging baskets in the average room, but when properly sited they can be very effective. A basket calls out for trailing plants with some of the growths trained up the supports.

Baskets designed for use outside, made of wire or plastic, are basically unsuitable indoors because of the likelihood of drip; even the plastic kind with a built-in drip tray is easily

Top: *Climbing plants form a leafy window frame.* Below: *In an open-plan setting the entrance area is separated by an ingeniously fixed plant shelf.*

overfilled. It is better to buy ornamental wicker or macramé baskets big enough to hold a deep drip saucer and an ordinary pot.

Other special containers with limited scope but great effect in the right spot are Victorian jardinières. These take two main forms. One is an erect stand of wood or china, supporting an ornamental pot. The other is an ornate wire trough or tiered stand, sometimes semi-circular. These do need decor of an appropriate kind, and few houses can accommodate more than one example.

Bottle gardens and terrariums are once again so eye-catching that one large example will dominate a room. However, several small examples can be formed into a group with amusing effect and combine plant interest with that of a collection of unusual glassware.

Where space is very limited a wheeled food trolley can be valuable. Plants are ensconced upon it on suitable trays or in containers; the trolley could be kept near a window for the good of the plants most of the time and be wheeled out to become a focal point when desirable.

The Victorian-style wire jardinière is a fine set-piece. Right, *a cheerful collection of bric-a-brac is complemented by plants.* Below, *a rather bleak top-floor room is vastly improved by climbers and trailers.*

Other props for plant display
Plants and their containers on their own provide quite sufficient interest as interior decoration features among furniture or work surfaces. But if you enjoy collections, whether of miscellaneous objects or of one kind of object, you might include plants in among *objets d'art* and *objets trouvés* – stones, shells, statuettes, antiques, ceramics and glass objects, oriental birdcages or whatever takes the fancy. In such deliberate arrays of smallish objects the plant takes its place in graceful contrast, bringing a touch of life to the inanimate.

Finally, a mirror can sometimes be used to good effect. It can double the impact of a few plants and, especially in small rooms, give a feeling of added space. Perhaps the most effective place for a mirror/plant combination is in a narrow hall or passageway, where there may be room only for one plant – the plant looks more luxuriant, the passage seems longer, and the reflected light may help the plant.

Controlling growth in display

In nature, our house plants indulge their natural growth habits in a constant search for nutriments and in response to their environments. At the highest level of the tropical evergreen forests, the tall, upward-thrusting trees play host to climbers, epiphytic bromeliads and ferns as they struggle for space and light in a crowded domain. Below, stragglers and creepers spread their leaves to make the most of what little light penetrates the dense leaf canopies of trees and tall shrubs. In other, more open regions where plants stand alone, growth is a more defensive response to nature's elements with which they may be in constant direct contact. In arid regions, for example, it is the below-ground root systems that tend to develop far and wide in search of the moisture that all plants need.

Pruning

In our homes, an artificial growing environment and our own preference for tidier growth patterns place constraints on plant growth. By judicious pruning and, particularly in the case of climbers, by satisfactory support, we seek to solve the "problems" of overcrowded groupings or individual plants becoming leggy, unsightly, or simply outgrowing their allotted space.

Pruning takes two main forms, depending on the habit of the plant: pinching or stopping, and more severe cutting back.

Pinching or stopping

This procedure involves removing the growing top either by literal pinching between finger and thumb, with small scissors, or on woody plants with secateurs. Pinching or cutting should remove the tiny growth – only 6-12mm ($\frac{1}{4}$-$\frac{1}{2}$in) long – immediately above a pair of leaves (a node), the nearest or the second nearest to the shoot end. This operation starts the dormant shoots growing in the axils (angles) between leaf and stem lower down. By regular pinching of all stems during the growing season a tight, compact mass of foliage is obtained.

In the jungle plant life is in constant competition in a crowded domain.

Such treatment applies especially to coleus and to other quick growers like beloperone, hypoestes, iresine and *Pilea cadierei*. At the end of the summer some of these may, even after regular pinching have a framework of over-long branches. These can be reduced to manageable size at that time and the following spring be cut back nearly to their base; new stems will sprout near this point. Often the tips of the pieces removed can be used as cuttings.

Woody bushes (shrubs) like citrus can be pinched or cut back in a similar but slightly less drastic way to ensure compact, much-branched growth.

Sprawling plants like gynura, plectranthus and the tradescantia tribe including callisia, setcreasea and zebrina will also react to pinching, but many of these are better controlled by periodically removing stem ends, and rooting a number of these together to create a new potful; the old plant can be discarded or be cut back to the base to stimulate regrowth.

With variegated plants it is essential to cut out altogether any green shoots. These are reverting to the all-green wild original and, since they are usually much more vigorous than the variegated growth, are likely to swamp the plant in time.

Cutting back

Tall plants can exceed their welcome, getting too big for their position, even reaching the ceiling, and may sometimes lose lower leaves so that they look leggy and unsightly. In such cases the stems can be cut back and will usually produce fresh growth at or below the point of cut.

Plants like fuchsia, hibiscus and strobilanthes can be cut back to within a few inches of the base to encourage new growth low down.

Many fast-growing plants can readily become leggy. Stems cut back above a node soon make side growths and a rounded, bushy plant results.

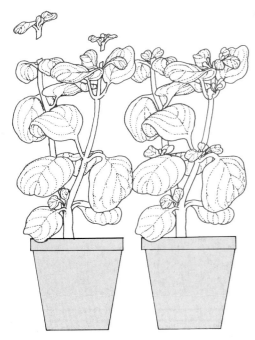

Supporting climbing plants

By their nature, climbers usually have thin flexible stems which will not stand erect on their own. Small specimens can be used as trailers if convenient, but in principle they need something on which to climb.

The easiest method of providing support is to insert two or three canes at the edges of the pot. The climbing stem can be tied directly up these or, if very long, spiralled around them, with fixings as required. With extensive climbers needing long canes the latter can be fixed together at the top; this looks better and also provides tension, keeping the bases of the canes firmly braced against the pot sides. Quick-growing climbers should be tied in regularly if they are not to become a congested tangle.

In many cases the upper part of the stem can be treated as a cutting and new short plants be produced as well. With some, for instance the familiar *Ficus elastica* with relatively large leaves, it is not practicable to root cuttings without special facilities. Then, air layering is the answer (see p. 202).

When stems are cut back, especially woody ones, the cut should be made with a really sharp blade just above a leaf or growth bud, either horizontally or sloping from a point above the bud to one opposite it. Cuts on plants which exude a lot of sap, or milky latex, as happens in the case of ficus, can be staunched by coating them with sulphur dust or charcoal powder.

Shrubs like citrus will benefit from the removal of crowded stems in the centre of the plant.

Pinching should generally be carried out only when plants are in active growth; severe cutting back is best confined to the beginning of the growth period, usually late spring and early summer; creating new growth by cutting in autumn may be hampered by lack of light.

Supporting growth in display

A number of non-climbing house plants are likely to need support if they are not to fall over or become lop-sided. This is true of tall, thin-stemmed plants like fatshedera and cane-stemmed begonias; and with flowering pot plants which often have large flower heads on soft or brittle stems. In such cases a single thin cane inserted fairly close to the stem and pushed through the roots down to the bottom of the pot will be sufficient. The stem is secured to the cane at intervals with soft wire rings, wire-centred "twist-its" of paper or plastic, or garden twine or cord. Never make a tie too tight or it may damage the stem; with twine or cord it is advisable to make a figure-8 loop around cane and stem which provides a "buffer".

When plants have several stems needing support, loops of twine can be passed round these and secured to a central cane, but it is usually more satisfactory to insert two, three or four canes round the edge of the pot at equal intervals, and secure the stems more closely to these. When re-potting, make sure the canes are pushed into the old, tightly-packed potting mixture.

The easiest way to support climbers is to push in canes at the pot edges and tie the growth to them.

Shaped wire frames can be bought or made at home; frames can be constructed from bamboo and flexible cane to create a variety of ornamental patterns. The main trouble with these is that though they look attractive at first they soon become swamped and ·outgrown by the climber. It is generally better to use a simpler method with a few unobtrusive canes.

Big thick-stemmed climbers like monstera and some of the larger philodendrons may need stout canes or poles pushed in by the stem near the centre of the pot; a good deal of support and careful tying may be needed for a ceiling-high monstera.

Such large plants are likely to become permanent fixtures because of the big containers needed, and in some cases it may be useful to fix a semi-permanent support. For instance, wire or cord can be arranged up a wall or around a window-frame. Secure this with screw eyes or long nails, and tie the plants to it. A stouter cord can be made taut between a large screw eye in a wooden floor and another inserted securely into a ceiling joist or fixed with an expanding toggle bolt.

To enable a large climber in a heavy container to be moved when required, place it on a small trolley made of a wide piece of wood standing on swivelling castors, and fix trellis behind the container.

The moss pole or surrogate trunk

In nature, some climbers, like ivies (hedera), philodendrons and scindapsus, make aerial roots to fix themselves to the moist bark of tree trunks. In room conditions, walls are too smooth and dry for aerial roots to attach themselves; even if they do manage to get a hold, they readily remove paint. However, it is possible to provide a porous support by the use of a natural or synthetic moss pole or cylinder.

Synthetic moss poles made of a porous, plastic foam material fixed around stiff plastic tubes are commercially available. They can be obtained in various lengths and thicknesses. However, natural moss poles can be produced at home in two ways, both requiring a quantity of fresh sphagnum moss, obtainable from florists. This can be bound to a thick wooden pole, or broom handle, with fine copper wire or nylon thread, criss-crossed to hold the moss firmly in place. Leave the base of the pole uncovered to push into the potting mixture.

Alternatively, form a piece of wire netting (chicken wire), of about 12mm ($\frac{1}{2}$in) mesh, into a tube about 50mm (2in) across. The piece will need to be 30cm (12in) wide for such a job, and its length will depend on the height required. Twist together loose ends from the mesh with pliers to ensure that the tube is firm and neat. Then push the moss into the tube, packing it as firmly as possible with a wooden rod. To simplify watering, a plant pot of appropriate size can be inserted into the top of the cylinder. When complete, the wire/moss cylinder should be "planted" in the pot to ensure stability, and the climbers planted around it.

The wire cylinder is easier to soak than the moss pole based on a rod, but wire cylinders more than 120cm (4ft) tall are likely to be unstable.

Plants can be tied to the poles with twine or, with the wire type, fixed with hairpin-shaped pieces of galvanized or copper wire.

The moss or plastic foam should be thoroughly moistened at the start and *must be kept moist at all times* if it is to ensure that the plants' aerial roots penetrate and do not shrivel.

After planting climbers round the wire-based moss pole they are fixed with wire "hairpins". Below, a well established monstera climbs its moss pole.

The wire tube is also sometimes called a fern column, reminding one that small ferns, bromeliads etc. can be pushed into the moss through the mesh where they will soon root themselves firmly and make an attractive display.

An epiphyte branch

A natural-looking support for epi-phytic bromeliads, ferns and tree cacti like rhipsalidopsis can be form-ed from a real tree branch to which moss is wired, the plants being fixed in position initially with wire or thread. Since the moss must be kept moist at all times, such entirely natural-looking supports can only be used where drips onto the floor do not matter. Stone paving or tiles are ideal, or the branch can be fixed into a large tray, attractively camouflaged with cobblestones or large pebbles. Epiphyte branches are most effective and easiest to manage in large plant windows.

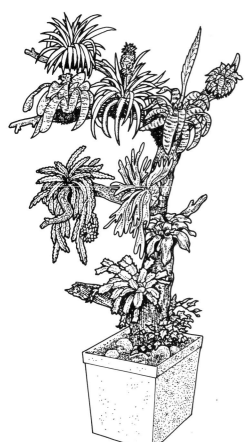

Epiphytic plants grow naturally on tree trunks and branches like these tillandsias in the Guatemala jungle (top right). A similar effect can be produced at home with a suitable cut branch fixed firmly into a large con-tainer (above); the effect is natural and striking (right). The plants grow in cushions of sphagnum moss wired to the branch so that the roots are held in place. But remember that they will drip when watered – the position must be right.

169

Acclimatizing plants to the home

Bringing house plants home

House plants for sale are grown in greenhouses where the conditions of temperature, air humidity and light are ideal for fast growth to saleable size. Such conditions are usually very different from those encountered in the home, and if the contrast between the two is very great the plants will receive a considerable check to growth, which can in some circumstances be fatal.

Similar problems apply when collectors bring tropical plants home from hot and humid natural habitats. Nowadays they will wrap them in plastic sheet to maintain humidity, trying to avoid long periods in low temperatures before they are flown back to greenhouses where they can be re-established.

Gardeners who raise half-hardy annuals, tomatoes, marrows, etc. under glass are accustomed to the procedure called "hardening off". Before setting them into summer quarters in the open, these plants are subjected to progressively cooler temperatures and increasing doses of fresh air.

A comparable procedure of acclimatization is recommended for house plants when first you bring them home. Unfortunately one has little control over the process unless plants are obtained directly from a supplier's own greenhouse. In winter, plants are generally transported from their warm cosy greenhouses in unheated vans to cold markets, before being displayed in draughty shops or even in the open. Christmas gift plants like azaleas, cyclamens and poinsettias most frequently suffer this process. The resulting shock is seldom apparent at that time; plants may take several weeks before leaves go yellow or black, or drop off.

The best way to minimize such checks is to obtain plants at a time when the difference between conditions in the growers' greenhouses and one's own home is smallest. Early summer is best because the plants will have the rest of the warm weather to acclimatize to their new

Many shops selling house plants display their wares outside. In summer this is fine, but on cold winter days the contrast between grower's greenhouse and pavement may cause a fatal check.

habitat, and gradually become accustomed to the poorer conditions of autumn and winter indoors.

If plants have to be bought in winter, avoid any which have clearly stood around in cold conditions, and get the supplier to wrap them well in several sheets of paper for transport home.

Coping with Nature's growth cycle

Earlier we saw how certain tropical and warm climates require plants to adopt resting periods. As equatorial climates give way to others with definite dry periods, a seasonal response is set up. It is a response due largely to rainfall patterns.

In temperate climates we are well

aware of this rhythm of plant growth. Most herbaceous species send up fresh growth from the root crown in spring, then flower, and their top growth dies down again during autumn in the same year. In winter the crown stays more or less dormant below the soil surface. Deciduous shrubs and trees put out leaves in spring, flowers during the spring or summer – the *active growth period* – and lose their leaves in autumn to start their *resting period*. This is a very easy growth cycle to follow and it is controlled largely by external temperature changes between seasons, and also by increasing light availability in spring.

The dormant or resting period of such temperate-zone plants must be maintained even when they are cultivated under glass. If they are forced to keep growing under artificial conditions (too much heat or food) they will probably die within a year or two.

There are, of course, evergreens in cold climates which do not lose their leaves. Among house plants, we can point to the ivies. Their essential growth processes continue in winter but at a greatly reduced rate, and they have various alternative biological devices which enable them to stand cold while carrying leaves. The leaf buds are in the same state of dormancy as those of deciduous trees; no new growth is made. If such evergreens are kept in higher-than-normal temperatures during the winter they too can rapidly run into trouble and may perish.

However, the majority of true house plants, though evergreens, come from tropical and sub-tropical countries, many of them from rain forests in equatorial climatic zones. In such climates and habitats there is little or no change in growing conditions throughout the year. There is therefore neither a specific season of active growth nor of dormancy, and the plants continue to grow without pause. Production of new leaves and flowers is often random even between individuals of the same species. Such forests display occasional bursts of colour from flowers and fresh leaves among an overall canopy of dull green.

Other plants originating from warm countries with seasonal rains and dry periods have distinct growing and

In the tropical rain forest plants grow all year round.

resting periods. Apart from the annuals and bulbs treated as temporary flowering plants the house plants which in nature display a seasonal rhythm of growth are cacti and most (but not all) other succulents. We find such plants in semi-deserts like those of New Mexico and Mexico, in the highlands of Argentina and other parts of South America, and in South and southwest Africa.

Succulent plants need a winter rest, cool and nearly dry.

These plants receive rain only occasionally, during which they replenish the water stored in their fleshy stems or leaves. Summer temperatures are very high and the intense sunlight by day is followed by considerable cold at night due to the virtual absence of cloud or insulation. Winter temperatures will be lower, some-

times markedly so as in the case of South American species. These lower temperatures also promote a seasonal response.

Resting periods in cultivation

Any plant whose natural growth cycle includes a resting period should have a similar cycle when grown at home. In temperate climates the easiest way is to follow the naturally occurring external seasons. In other words, rest these plants in your own winter. Resting is set up primarily by reducing watering and feeding; otherwise the plant may continue to grow which, in the reduced light and shorter days of winter, is likely to cause weak spindly growth which will not survive well.

It is clear why plants such as cacti need a rest period in cultivation. What of the evergreen rain-forest plants which do not rest in nature? In fact, these more than ever need similar care just because they are not suited to the reduction in hours and strength of daylight that is characteristic of temperate climates during winter.

Even if temperature is kept at the required level, rain-forest plants can suffer if, during our winter, they produce new growth as they do in the wild.

So if you live in a temperate climate and cannot re-create their natural growing conditions with artificial light (see p. 180), you must *impose* an artificial resting period on rain-forest plants so that they are in principle just "ticking over". With foliage plants resting is induced by a considerable reduction in watering (though pots should never dry out) and again cutting out feeding. With cacti a much lower temperature than in summer is essential; watering is greatly curtailed, and feeding entirely. Some plants sold as house plants are deciduous or partly so. Few are recommended here since they do not give a satisfactory year-round display; but if, for instance, you have bought a bougainvillea, which loses its leaves in winter, very little water is required in their natural rest period. 171

Temperature & humidity

Temperature

We have seen how each plant has a particular range of temperature tolerance. This is the first consideration to be given to a newly acquired plant. On pages 158 to 159, plants were accorded their preferred temperature ranges, so selection for this first vital factor is simplified. Plants which nature has conditioned to withstand higher or lower temperatures have also been mentioned. The lower temperature limit specified is in practical terms the crucial one to watch, as rooms are rarely as hot as the prescribed upper temperature limits.

In many homes heating is reduced or cut off at night. Fortunately most plants prefer a night temperature a few degrees below the daytime level. However, in the absence of continuous heating, cold winter nights can drag indoor temperatures down dramatically, often well below the tolerance of most house plants. Most plants react better to a steady temperature a little below their preferred level than to fluctuations greater than 15-20°F (8-11°C) between day and night levels.

Of course plants which prefer lower temperatures should be kept entirely out of well-heated rooms and in cool ones, porches or cool conservatories, and likewise those needing a winter rest in cool conditions must be taken out of heated rooms when the rest period begins.

In summer, indoor temperatures may sometimes rise to reflect outdoor levels of 80–90°F (27°–32°). This will not harm most indoor plants as long as the humidity is correspondingly high. But direct midday sun will scorch them.

Measuring temperature

The overall temperature of a room is easily measured with a thermometer. It is more valuable to use a maximum/minimum instrument which will show how high and low the temperature moves during a night, day or longer period. Move the instrument around the room over a period to reveal areas potentially problematic for more sensitive plants.

Problem points

Hot air rises, so spots above radiators, night-storage heaters, refrigerators and cooking stoves are particularly unhealthy positions. Not only does hot air scorch foliage, but it will also dry out the potting mixture.

The typical problem place, a shelf over a radiator, can be made reasonably beneficial for plants if the shelf is wide enough to deflect the rising air away from the foliage, and the plants are set on pebble trays or moisture troughs of some kind (see p. 174). Fit the shelf tightly against the wall to prevent hot air coming up behind the plant.

Cold is a more serious hazard. The typical danger spot is a windowsill. In cold weather, especially at night, a plant so sited can be chilled – plain glass is a poor insulator. If curtains cut the plant off from the overall warmth of the room the effect is still more severe. Chilling will not occur if the window is efficiently double-glazed. In winter, especially if frost is expected, move plants off windowsills at night, and *always* avoid shutting them between the window and a curtain.

Strong sun can scorch. This plant-filled penthouse room has blinds to draw at midday. Below, wide shelves deflect leaf-scorching, hot air.

Cold draughts are especially hazardous. These may be caused by ill-fitting windows or doors and will be worse in the direct path between windows, or windows and door. Another source of cold currents of air, more common in the U.S. than Britain, is the air-conditioning vent.

Apart from direct chilling and scorching from cold draughts or hot air rising, *any* air current will remove concentrations of water vapour which collect naturally around plants as they transpire, and increase the danger of wilting.

Air humidity

Many people find this factor difficult to understand, although even in temperate climates the occasional muggy or thundery summer day provides the sensation of a "close" atmosphere – the sign of high humidity. However, more and more people now visit the tropics or subtropics and experience high humidity first-hand. Again, anyone with a greenhouse will know the desirable humid "feel" of its atmosphere on a hot day. However, it is difficult to sense the humidity levels in which house plants will be reasonably comfortable and those they will suffer in.

In general, the levels of humidity preferred for human comfort are low. Unless an air humidifier is used to vapourize water continuously, many tropical house plants will suffer.

Air humidity is measured as "relative humidity" (RH) on a scale from 0 to 100. RH 0% is absolutely dry air; at RH 100% it is saturated and cannot absorb any more.

The relation between air humidity and temperature is the vital one to understand. Air expands when it

Symptoms of air dryness
Air humidity and temperature are inter-related. It is no good providing the correct temperature for a plant if the air around it remains dry. Local

Plants grown close together make their own microclimate of moist air.

becomes warm, so the amount of moisture that a given volume of air can hold increases with temperature.

The hotter we keep our rooms, the drier the air becomes, unless we take special steps to provide more moisture.

The greenhouse grower, especially if he is cultivating tropical plants or cucumbers, will do this simply by splashing water onto the floor and staging. This is known as damping down; if plant foliage is sprayed directly with water this is called overhead damping. The experienced grower will say of a properly damped

humidity is assured (left) *by placing the plant in a tray filled with pebbles and water. A plant may survive for a while in hot, dry air* (centre), *but soon the foliage will dry up* (right).

greenhouse that its atmosphere is "bouyant".

The purpose of providing additional moisture is to prevent plant leaves losing so much water by transpiration that they begin to wilt. Leaves, stem and roots are dehydrated and will literally perish. It is vital to realize that air humidity cannot be provided by keeping roots moist.

Measuring humidity

Humidity is measured on a hygrometer, and a simple dial hygrometer of reasonable accuracy can be bought cheaply. You may find dial instruments combining the functions of a thermometer and hygrometer. These are ideal.

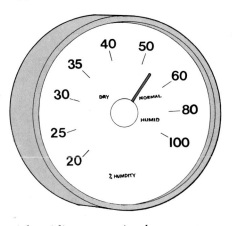

A humidity-measuring hygrometer.

Even succulent plants grown indoors need some air humidity; a level of RH35–40% is desirable for these.

The average, reasonably tolerant house plant needs at least 60%; delicate thin-leaved ones such as caladiums and calatheas more like 80%. Plants in warm spots, especially in rising hot air, must have special attention in this respect.

Sensitive house plants wilt entirely in dry air; at best, individual leaves will dry up. Typical symptoms are browning of leaf tips on plants with long narrow leaves (like chlorophytum and palms), or on leaf segments in plants like monstera. The stalked leaves of plants like some ficus and tetrastigma, may drop suddenly. Buds on flowering plants may drop or dry up, and flowers will wither more rapidly in dry air.

173

Providing air humidity

Obviously we cannot splash water on the floors or furniture of rooms like greenhouse growers. Instead, spray plant foliage finely with a mist-sprayer once or twice a day. This is always beneficial though its effect is relatively brief. If it can only be done once a day, do it during the morning or around midday. However, plants should never be sprayed if sun is or will soon be on them, since the droplets act like tiny magnifying glasses and scorch marks often result.

In summer, in temperate climates, the external air is likely to be moister than inside a house, so adequate fresh air will help.

Fortunately there are several quite simple ways of increasing local humidity around plants, which do not cause any extra work. The aim in each case is to produce a *microclimate* around the plants which resembles the overall humidity of their natural haunts. In still air, water vapour transpired by leaves will tend to remain close to the leaves, though in dry conditions it will quickly disappear into the atmosphere. Grouping several plants fairly closely will produce a concentration of water vapour among their foliage, creating an umbrella effect.

The peat or moss method

To enhance this effect the pots can be plunged into garden peat, or sphagnum moss, kept moist in a deep-sided container, which will give off water vapour around the foliage.

The pebble and water method

Alternatively place a layer of 12–20mm ($\frac{1}{2}$–$\frac{3}{4}$in) pebbles or gravel, or of moisture-absorbing clay granules (hydroleca) or of pulverised fuel ash granules (Hortag), at the bottom of the trough or tray on which the pots stand.

This layer should be at least 25mm (1in) deep and water poured into it should not rise above it. This is to avoid immersion of the base of the pot which may waterlog the roots, and give rise to further problems.

Three methods efficient in re-creating the humidity of a plant's natural home, relative to the temperature of its artificial environment:

Pebble and water, moist peat, and the capillary bolster.

These methods can be applied to groups of several plants or to single specimens. If the peat-plunging method is used the plant pot might stand in a larger ornamental china container or plastic pot-hider, with the peat packed between the two. Pebbles should be placed in a drip-saucer about 50mm (2in) wider than the base of the pot.

An alternative to pebbles is to stand the individual pot on a block of wood or even a half-brick in a water-filled drip-saucer or other container, but this is not so sightly.

Using capillary bolsters

One modern method is to use "capillary bolsters" in a container. These comprise an envelope of highly water-absorbent granules. Water is released gradually over a period to create local humidity around the plant: a 12.5cm – 15cm (5–6in) bolster can in fact absorb 250ml ($\frac{1}{2}$ pint) of water. These bolsters have cut down the frequency of watering as well as producing a humid micro-climate around the plants just like a wet pebble-layer. A similar effect can be obtained by using a double thickness of capillary felt matting.

All these methods are of benefit in any situation, but are essential in positions over radiators and other sources of heat (especially the peat-plunge which insulates the pot itself and thus prevents the soil mixture from drying out quickly. The only action needed is to keep the peat or pebble layer moist and this can be done when watering).

The only way to *ensure* high humidity in ordinary room conditions, and so to be able to grow particularly delicate plants which shrivel at average humidity levels, is to grow the plants in more or less sealed glass or plastic enclosures. The principle, discovered accidentally by Dr Nathaniel Ward in 1829, is that moisture absorbed by the plants is transpired through the leaves to make the atmosphere humid; surplus moisture condenses on the glass or plastic and returns as water to the soil. Any moisture introduced to the enclosure in excess of the needs of the plant roots remains in the atmosphere. The environment is virtually self-

A terrarium is the modern equivalent of the original Victorian Wardian case. Besides being an unusual and stylish container, it maintains ideally humid conditions for delicate plants.

supporting and little watering is needed.

Such containers do not provide the same decorative effect as plants in an open room, so retain them for special effects and to house particularly delicate plants.

The Wardian case and terrarium
Wardian cases, as the original glass containers become known, were very popular in Victorian times and have in recent years been revived (though not in such ornate designs). Modern, more or less portable glass or plastic containers are often called terrariums. In its simplest form the terrarium can be an aquarium or rectangular glass battery jar with a piece of glass as a lid; some are made like miniature greenhouses and in the U.S. some plastic forms are available.

Fill the terrarium with plants in individual pots and sink these into a deep layer of peat, this not only conceals the pots but helps to keep the potting mixture moist.

In the Wardian case – right, an antique example – water builds up in the air, condenses on the glass and returns to the soil – a self-supporting cycle.

The bottle garden

The bottle garden is a special form of terrarium created, as its name suggests, in a bottle or similar container. Small plants can be placed in brandy glasses, goldfish bowls and small glass bottles and jars, but real bottle gardens are mainly made in carboys or demi-johns of fair size. The bottle gardens which excite most admiration are those with openings too small to insert the hand! The effect is like that of a ship in a bottle.

The first stage in making a large bottle garden is to introduce a layer of small pot crocks plus some charcoal pieces through a short funnel of stout paper, or a cardboard tube. (This can be ignored for small bottles). Then pour slightly moistened peat-based potting mixture to a depth of at least 75mm (3in). This can be sloped across the bottle if desired. Spread out crocks and then mixture with a thin wood lath about 25mm (1in) wide, and make the mixture firm by pushing it down with a cotton-reel affixed to the end of a long cane.

Plan an attractive arrangement by first setting out the chosen plants on the floor or a table. You might try a relatively tall plant – a chamaedorea palm or a dracaena, perhaps – and surround it with others chosen for compactness or slow growth – such as cryptanthus, marantas and pileas, and low creepers like fittonias and selaginellas. Buy these as small as possible if you are planting a carboy, or their roots will not pass through its neck.

Once the arrangement is satisfactory start with a plant on the outer edge. Scoop away the potting mixture with the lath or a dessert spoon tied to a cane; remove the plant from its pot and push its roots through the neck, holding it by a topmost leaf if necessary. Tilt the bottle with the other hand till you can drop the plant into its hole. Then, using a cane to adjust the plant's position, push soil over the roots with the lath, and make firm with the cotton-reel.

Follow this procedure, plant by plant,

ending up with those in the centre so as to avoid mixture dropping on them from the roots of plants being introduced.

Condensation may develop in a stoppered bottle, obscuring the view of the plants. It is perfectly satisfactory to remove the stopper until excess moisture has dispersed.

When removing decaying leaves, cut the stem with half a safety razor blade pushed into the split end of a cane and bound with wire; lift the leaves by spearing with a sharpened cane. A small sponge at the end of a piece of stiffish wire is used to clean dirt or algal growth from the inside

surface of the bottle, adjusting the wire to the required position.

Eventually some plants may die or grow too large; then the bottle inhabitants may need pulling out (use a hook-ended wire to get at the roots) and a new planting made. But with well-chosen, well-spaced smallish plants to start with, a bottle garden can remain attractive for a year or more.

A bottle garden is much more a decorative object than an ordinary terrarium; but once planted, it can only be altered with difficulty, whereas the interior of a terrarium is much more accessible.

Glass containers of almost any size and shape make attractive miniature gardens, but a large demijohn, *carboy or apothecary's jar, with aperture too small for the hand, is best as a focal point.*

Natural and artificial light

Light intensity

The third important factor for house plants is the amount of light they receive. Earlier we have stressed the enormous differences between the natural light requirements of varying groups of house plants, ranging from full unmitigated day-long sunshine received (and hence expected) by cacti and many other succulents, to the tiny proportion of available light, perhaps 5%, received by plants on the floor of a tropical rain forest, like fittonias and calatheas. In each case the light level is adequate for the photosynthetic needs of the plant concerned; it is a result of gradual evolution in a particular natural "niche". The plant has a light-level preference quite as important as its temperature preference. A plant accustomed to full sun cannot thrive in deep shade, where it will become

Cacti enjoy all the sun they can get in a south-facing window.

etiolated – it will grow spindly and take on a yellowish tinge, both of which weaken it. By the same token, plants accustomed to the deep shade of the forest floor can react badly to strong light and will be scorched in full sunlight.

Fortunately, as with temperature, nature has conditioned plants to tolerate a range of light levels, but each has definite limits.

Most rooms have many more relatively shady places than bright ones, and it is no accident that most commercially successful house plants originate in shady habitats.

In a dense forest light intensity dwindles rapidly from the sun-drenched canopy to the floor where shade-lovers like Calathea ornata *grow.*

177

Measuring light

Just as with temperature and humidity, it is better to *measure* light in different parts of a room than to rely on one's senses. The human eye almost always overestimates light levels and as we shall see there are so many variable influences that measurements are desirable. The easiest way is to use a light meter – relatively cheap models, usually combined with moisture meters, are now available to the house plant owner.

A light and moisture meter

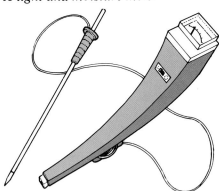

These work on exactly the same principle as a photographic light meter. One model at least has a chromatic filter which measures the kind of light specifically preferred by house plants.

Factors controlling light intensity

Aspect

The first factor influencing light intensity in a room is the direction its windows face. A window facing due south in the nothern hemisphere will receive full sun for a large part of the day; vice-versa in the southern hemisphere. Bear in mind that midday sun is almost always hotter than at other

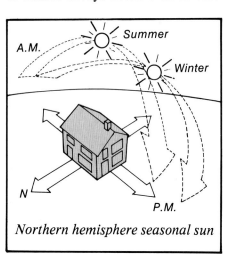

Northern hemisphere seasonal sun

times, and that it will be at least twice as hot in summer than in winter. The intensity of summer sun will, in the northern hemisphere, increase as one travels south. Plants which will stand full summer sun in Scotland, for example, will be in danger of scorching in southern England, and the difference between northern and southern United States is much greater. Many plants can tolerate winter sun but not full summer sun, and it is also necessary to realize that sun behind a closed window can have a more drastic effect than sun in the open. This is because indoors there is no air movement, while outside a light breeze can have a cooling effect.

Windows facing east or west will only receive sun for a few hours. Morning sun in an east-facing window is usually a little less strong than afternoon sun in a west-facing one. A window facing north will receive no direct sunlight at all in the northern hemisphere; but at least its light level will remain fairly constant.

Light reflection

Take into account that a white wall facing a window can reflect more light into the room; all-glass claddings will of course reflect light efficiently, and water is another reflector. Even within a room the colour of the walls will affect light levels, a white or pale-toned wall reflecting far more light than a dark one.

Light levels are affected by the colour tone of backdrops.

Screens

Various circumstances can reduce the effects of direct sunlight. Surrounding walls or buildings can curtail the number of hours of potential sunshine, and a leafy tree will filter it considerably. Similar diminution is created by curtains or blinds: direct scorching, the most serious effect of sunlight, can usually be prevented by a thin curtain of muslin or comparable material.

Some plants require screening if placed in the direct path of the sun

Light levels

Because the midday sun is high in the sky its direct rays can only illuminate the window itself and a relatively small proportion of the floor area. Once out of range of direct sun, the amount of light decreases rapidly the further one is from the window; the amount of light diminishes by 1–2% every 90cm (3ft) further from the window. Walls and room corners immediately beside a window will be relatively quite shady; they receive no direct light at all.

Light levels can vary quite dramatically, even within a few feet.

If we take direct, unobstructed sunlight as 100% light intensity we can qualify the amount of light in other circumstances as follows:

Sunlight passing through a thin curtain will range from 60–75%; a plastic venetian blind will reduce intensity to around 50%. But areas in a room beyond the direct sun-rays drop to a maximum of 20–25%, diminishing progressively the further away from a window they are.

A lace curtain can make the difference between "bright" and "good" light.

Light entering a north-facing window (in the northern hemisphere) will be about 10% of direct sunlight, near the window. Similar light intensity will be found in areas more than 30m (10ft) from a sunny window. Areas in corners of rooms which do not face windows, and even in windows facing nearby buildings or large trees, drop to 3–5% of full sunlight.

Needless to say the amount of light available in a given room depends on the size and number of its windows.

Light preferences
Earlier, we divided plants into three categories of light preference: plants needing maximum light and tolerating the effects of full midday sun – the *sunlovers*; this represents 100% light intensity. The next is for plants preferring *bright light* – anything between lightly filtered sunlight from a south-facing window and three hours sun a day from east- or west-facing windows; this represents 75–60% full sunlight. Outside the parts of a room reached directly by

Light categories
(see pages 158/9)

☀ *Sunlovers: 100% sun*

○ *Bright light: 75–60% sun*

◍ *Good light: 50–25% sun*

◐ *Light shade: 10% sun*

● *Shade: 5–3% sun*

the sun, there is a category of plants which will tolerate what we have called *good light* (50–25% full sun). *Light shade* describes sunless rooms with north-facing windows, or rooms with east- or west-facing windows where direct sun is obstructed (by a tree, for example); this represents 10% full sun. *Shade* – tolerant plants will accept about 5–3% full sun.

Few plants can tolerate the very deep shade found in rooms with no windows, very small windows, or windows which only face into deep narrow shafts between blocks of flats. In such places artificial lighting is valuable.

As with temperatures, all plants can tolerate a range of light levels. But do not subject them to widely *varying* light intensities. A plant that originated in South Africa (with attendant full sunlight) will be scorched if *suddenly* exposed to direct sunlight in the home after having been grown at a lower light level. Gradually accustom plants to stronger light.

Though all plants should be sited in suitable light conditions, most will retain their character and health if kept for decorative purposes, in too much or too little indirect light for periods of a few weeks at a time. But allow them recuperative periods of two or three weeks in light levels within their tolerance range.

The full summer sun
The one thing no house plant should be subjected to, other than those we have labelled as sunlovers, is full summer sun over the midday hours. This can cause irreparable scorching. The shock value to a plant reared in an artificial environment can be so great that even palms used to high intensity light when fully developed in nature, will suffer. Unlike the sun-loving cacti, etc., these palms do not develop their protective biological systems when reared away from their natural habitats.

One-way light
One last reaction to light has already been mentioned in the section called

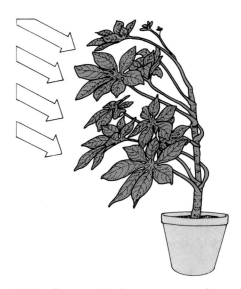

Light from a single source can draw a plant's beauty out of sight.

Display. If light reaches your plants from a single source, most will tend to turn their leaves to face it, just as they do in the wild. This does not apply to those with stiff erect leaves like sansevierias, nor to those spirally arranged as in dracaena. However, dracaena may bend their erect *stems* towards the source of light, and this stem-bending applies strongly to smaller much-branched plants. A white wall behind the plants will help diminish this effect.

In many positions in a room re-orientation of foliage to light source is not a problem. As in nature the resulting "leaf mosaic" ensures that each leaf receives the maximum light available, and if the plant or group of plants is sited at the sides or in the corners of a room the visual effect of the "mosaic" will usually be good. Exceptions occur where plants are positioned right up by the window, when their leaves will always be facing in the wrong direction from our point of view.

You can, of course, keep turning the plants around every two or three days. But, in the long term, it is not very good for them.

The problems of light-seeking by plants in one-way light conditions can be entirely resolved, however, by artificial lighting. Exposure to artificial light for even part of each day can improve the condition.

House plants
under artificial light

As we have seen there are many positions in rooms, and some rooms in any house, where the light level is generally low. In winter, this level decreases further and of course the number of daylight hours is reduced. Artificial light can be used to augment natural light, to supply good light in very shaded places, or even to replace natural light altogether.

There are two main kinds of artificial light available in houses – the incandescent filament bulb and the fluorescent tube.

Incandescent bulbs give out three-quarters of the electrical energy they consume as heat, only one quarter as light. In order to improve growth markedly, therefore, they will need to be placed so close to the plant as to scorch foliage and dry out its pot. A standard 150 watt bulb should be at least 75cm (30in) from a plant for safety, a 100 watt bulb 60cm (24in) and a 25 watt bulb 30cm (12in). Floodlights give off a little less heat in proportion to light and may be brought a little closer. In principle, then, incandescent lights are only of decorative value to highlight plants or plant groups, though if left on for several hours during winter evenings they will marginally improve growth and health.

Fluorescent tubes give out far more light than heat – they are often described as "cold light" – and can therefore be placed close enough to plants to supplant natural light altogether. Depending on type, their light production is at least twice as effective as incandescent lights.

A fluorescent tube gives out light of different colours which mingle to produce the basically white end product. There are various kinds of tubes, usually classed as "natural white", "cool white" and "warm white", though "daylight" and "colour matching" may be available. The different kinds of tube give out slightly varying amounts of colours, of which the orange/red and violet/blue parts are needed by plants.

Orchids, African violets, geraniums, begonias, bromeliads and foliage plants in a Flora Cart: ideal for a basement habitat.

Violet/blue is most important with shade-lovers which on the jungle floor receive little red light, since this is absorbed by the green foliage of the tree canopy far above.

All kinds of tube can be used to provide artificial lighting for plants, "natural" being probably the most effective for balanced growth, while "daylight" is deficient in orange/red. A pair of "natural" and "daylight" tubes provides the best overall combination.

There are also "plant-growth" tubes which are supposed to provide the closest approximation to natural conditions. They certainly enhance plant colours, but many growers believe that they do not in fact produce balanced growth, and they are far more expensive than ordinary tubes.

Outside the U.K. it is also possible to obtain very-high-output (VHO) tubes for plants such as cacti, pelargoniums and some bromeliads, which thrive in continuous hot sun. These VHO tubes give out nearly 30 watts per foot length while domestic and plant-growth tubes only provide 10 watts per foot. The VHO tubes are therefore three times more costly to run.

Placing tubes

A single tube will illuminate a row of small plants like saintpaulias adequately but for average-sized house plants two tubes 15cm (6in) apart is the minimum.

Plants vary in the intensity of light they need for healthy growth. Where tubes more or less replace natural light, they should be placed 30–60cm (12–14in) above foliage plants, 25–30cm (9–12in) above flowering ones, like saintpaulias.

The plants will soon let you know if the tubes have been poorly positioned. If they become etiolated – develop thin elongated stems, small widely spaced leaves, and fail to grow flowers when they should – the tubes are too far away. Scorched foliage, stunted growth and bleached colouring indicate tubes too close for comfort. Moving the tubes nearer or further from the plants in 75mm (3in) steps is the remedy.

The ideal set-up is, therefore, to have racks of tubes, 2 to 4 together (depending on the size and number of plants) which can be easily adjusted for height. Further fine tuning of light requirements can be effected by keeping the tubes alight for longer or shorter periods.

If tubes replace natural light entirely, they should normally be left on for 12 to 14 hours a day for foliage plants, and for most flowering plants 16 hours is the maximum time needed. When supplementing natural light, especially in winter, tubes can be put on in the evenings for 4 to 6 hours for foliage plants, 6 to 8 hours for flowering kinds. Electric timer switches are invaluable for such programmes.

A wall-fixture well suited to plants with trailing habit

Small plant lighting units, comprising a basal tray and a light tube held in place on legs above it, are available in Britain. In the United States many more such devices can be obtained, including wheeled "plant carts" with several shelves, each shelf having a pair of tubes fixed under it to illuminate the plants below.

More formal plant stands can be made with aluminium or stainless steel angle bars and wood shelves fitted with tubes underneath them; such stands can be designed for a particular position, such as a room divider, or as moveable plant display holders.

It is relatively easy to install fluorescent tubes in shelf and cupboard

A 22-watt 'lamp stand' light garden called Ripe-n-Grow

units, or above any flat surface suitable for a few plants, such as the back of a kitchen work-surface or a sideboard.

Small fluorescent tubes can be built into terrariums, and tubes will improve display and growth in large plant windows.

Square and circular fluorescent fitments are obtainable, and current developments promise more compact tubes giving good light but minimal heat in small units.

When constructing any fitment combining plants and lights do remember how lethal electricity is in the presence of water. All connections must be carefully water-proofed and earthed with sensitive fuses or trip switches in case of trouble; plants should *always* be housed on water-proof trays or troughs.

Plant care under lights
In principle there is little difference between growing plants in natural or under artificial light, except that under artificial light plants can be grown continuously and healthily without a rest period. In such circumstances, plants will need feeding without any winter break. Most tropical foliage plants which experience no alteration of seasons in nature will thrive in these conditions,

but plants with a natural resting period – cacti, for example (see page 171) – will not. Such plants should receive less light, heat, watering and food at a period to coincide with their natural rest.

Tube efficiency and life
If used for 12 hours daily, a fluorescent tube's normal effective life is about one year. During that time it slowly and indiscernibly loses its effectiveness, and after a year should be changed. An old tube still working can of course be used for plants needing lower light intensities. If two or more tubes are used in a unit they should not be changed at the same time: the extra light intensity that results can quite readily scorch plants.

A portable garden which includes a begonia, orchid and a geranium.

181

Potting mixtures and hydroculture

Roots are an essential part of the feeding mechanism of almost every cultivated plant, but some of our house plants are adapted to derive much of their water from the atmosphere, their roots being primarily for anchorage on other plants. For these, the potting mixture is just "somewhere for the roots to be".

We have also noted that many house plants come from tropical rain-forests in which the soils are lateritic. The litter of leaves, twigs etc. decays so rapidly in the high temperature and humidity that there is little organic humus of the sort that we aim for in our garden compost heaps; nor are there any earthworms to help in humus production. The forest soil is, consequently, low in plant foods and calcium, and does not retain water well; in some areas it may be composed almost entirely of sand.

Sand is also the major constituent of soils in those semi-desert areas inhabited by many cacti and other succulents. Such soils hardly hold moisture at all but they can be relatively rich in plant food since sand is rock, rich in minerals, in its final stages of breakdown.

Acid and Alkaline

Beside their needs for definite ranges of temperature, humidity, light and shade (created by evolutionary adaptation to specific habitats), plants display preferences for acid or alkaline conditions at their roots. This is known as the *reaction* of a soil or other rooting medium.

This reaction – the degree of acidity or alkalinity of a soil, fertilizer or of water – is measured on what is known as the pH scale. (pH stands for hydrogen ion concentration, but this is immaterial to the gardener.) It ranges from 0 (maximum acidity) to 14 (maximum alkalinity) with the neutral point at 7. However, plants only survive between pH4 and pH8.

The paper test and lime-testing kit

Damp soil, solutions of chemicals, and water can be roughly tested with litmus paper, which will turn red for

an acid reaction, blue for alkaline. Aquarium suppliers have more sensitive papers that give a range of colours to check against a scale. For soils and potting mixtures it is best to use an inexpensive lime-testing kit, which can be bought in garden shops. Simple to use, it produces a solution the colour of which can be read off against a scale.

Alternatively, it is now possible to obtain pH meters which give a direct reading when their probe is inserted into the potting mixture, though their results can be inconsistent particularly if you do not follow the manufacturer's instructions.

In outdoor gardens the best-known examples of acid-loving plants, sometimes called lime-haters (calcifuge), are rhododendrons, azaleas, almost all heathers and other members of the family *Ericaceae;* also the camellias, which are unrelated but often grown with them. In the presence of lime or an alkaline reaction these plants will

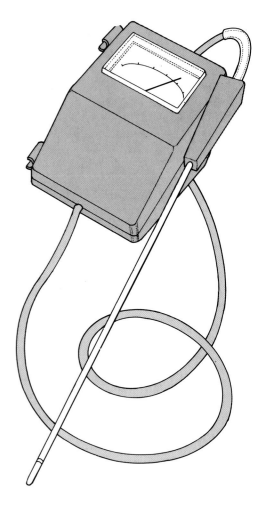

The Rapitest soil pH meter

sicken and die. At the other end of the scale many alpine plants, living as they do in limestone mountains, are lime-lovers (calcicole) and will become unhealthy in acid conditions.

Naturally alkaline reaction occurs in the proximity of chalk, limestone or limy soil water. Acid reactions occur in the presence of decayed organic matter or humus. Although humus accumulation is slight in the average tropical rain forest, it is a place of constant decay and there is usually enough to produce a slightly acid reaction, whether on the forest floor, in debris that collects in branches of trees, or among the aerial roots of tree-inhabiting epiphytes.

An unsuitable soil reaction works on plants in several ways. Apart from the direct effects of excess acidity or alkalinity, which can upset the plant's metabolism and health to a fatal degree, these conditions restrict the availability of plant foods. In alkaline

Plants display preferences for different levels of acidity or alkalinity: Heathers and azaleas insist upon an acid soil.

conditions the main food affected is iron which, though a minor element, is vital to healthy growth. In its absence plants tend to go yellow, and the essential operation of photosynthesis is disturbed. This yellowing is a condition known as chlorosis. The "locking up" of iron begins at levels about pH6.5, though it only starts to be serious about 7.5. Other trace elements such as manganese, copper and zinc are also affected.

Plants affected by chlorosis in over-alkaline conditions can be cured for a period by the use of compounds called sequestrols or chelates, which are watered onto the soil. Foliar feeding with a fertiliser known to contain iron and manganese will also help.

In acid conditions phosphorus becomes markedly less available below pH6.5. This is of course one of the all-important "big three" food elements, responsible in particular for root growth, and many plants which prefer acid conditions will be found to have limited root systems. This is generally true of plants from the tropical rain-forests, and thus the majority of house plants.

Choosing and preparing potting mixtures

Preparing a suitable potting mixture for a jungle house plant or succulent is a matter of compromise between what they are used to in nature and the growth factors that are available in the home. For jungle plants, air humidity is much lower in the home than in nature, and since there is no equivalent of heavy rainfall the mixture that you choose *must be* moisture-retaining. Also, because roots cannot roam freely in pots, potting mixtures must provide them with a reservoir of plant foods. The medium must also be porous because the roots of these particular plants need air to perform their functions and cannot survive in a waterlogged medium.

Succulents in cultivation need some moisture-retention in the food-rich mixture but, as in nature, free drainage is even more vital.

House plants from habitats outside low-lying equatorial or semi-arid regions will have a greater proportion of soil similar to what we are used to in our gardens. There, soil is made up of varying proportions of clay, sand, and organic matter created by the decomposition of vegetable and also animal matter.

During the centuries since man started to cultivate plants in containers an amazing variety of potting mixtures, sometimes containing the most bizarre ingredients, have been proposed. In the last fifty years or so these mixtures have largely been rationalized, mainly in response to mass-production of pot-grown plants of every kind, and it is possible to buy prepared potting mixtures (or composts as they are often called) in bags.

These fall into two overall categories; the soil-based and the soilless or peat-based.

Soil-based mixtures

The standard soil-based mixtures available in Britain are the John Innes Potting composts. These consist of 7 parts sterilized loam, 3 parts peat and 2 parts sharp sand, plus varying amounts of ground chalk and a specific base or balanced fertilizer. No. 1 compost has one part of fertilizer added, nos. 2 and 3, two and three parts respectively.

It is important to realize that the John Innes composts are not the sole property of any one particular manufacturer. They are based on formulas in which the quality of the loam is all-important. Since such high-standard loam is now very difficult to obtain, John Innes composts vary considerably and may contain soil with a high clay content, which packs down readily to become airless and waterlogged; beware of these. In all cases, however, the soil is sterilized so as to destroy weed seeds, harmful disease organisms and soil pests, without spoiling its other desirable qualities.

The John Innes composts are not known in the United States or Europe

though other soil-based mixtures are available there.

Other proprietary mixtures include sterilized soil, peat and perlite (a moisture-retaining substance).

John Innes composts are adjusted, by the addition of chalk, to be slightly acid at pH 6.0-6.3, which suits most house plants. It can be made more acid by adding extra crumbly peat, which will also retain more moisture.

Soilless mixtures

A number of potting mixtures made without soil are freely available. In principle these consist of finely milled peat, normally balanced by an alkaline compound (typically dolomite limestone powder, or calcium carbonate) to offset its natural acidity (because most house plants thrive between pH 5.5 and 6.5), plus a usually limited quantity of plant food. Some contain a proportion of rather fine sand, but perlite and vermiculite are also sometimes added to improve moisture retention and aeration.

These materials are undoubtedly an improvement on pure peat. A recently marketed synthetic product known as an acrylic copolymer is even more effective, holding over 100 times its own weight of water when added to a potting mixture. This material, which is as effective for moisture retention in soil-based as in peat-based mixes, greatly reduces the frequency of watering needed.

Acid-reaction, peat-based mixtures are available, specifically for azaleas and similar acid-loving plants.

In the United States such peat-based mixtures are sometimes known as Cornell mixes since much of the initial research was done at Cornell University. There are also U.C. mixes, developed at the University of California.

The standard soilless mixtures are adjusted to be slightly acid, but special formulations for acid-loving plants are also available and are slightly to be preferred for the majority of house plants. 183

Soil versus peat

The advantage of the peat-based mixtures is, primarily, convenience. They are relatively light – an important consideration if you have to carry bags upstairs to a flat – and clean: if you spill the material it is very easily swept up, and it will not become muddy if wet.

Lightness can, however, be a big *disadvantage* when you plant those large top-heavy plants. Other disadvantages are the low food levels (which need regular boosting), and the ease with which they dry out. They are also quite difficult to re-wet. For this reason peat-based mixtures are best in non-water-absorbent plastic pots, unless weight is a major consideration.

Soil-based mixtures are very much heavier, and relatively messy if spilt. Weight is an advantage for large plants which need a counterbalance. The great advantage of soil-based potting mixtures is their long-term food reserves. The loam has a "buffering" effect which allows the major plant food in fertilizers to be released steadily, and it usually also contains the minor minerals that are known as trace elements. Further, the organic matter in the loam contains bacteria which continue to produce food materials over long periods.

Soil-based mixtures retain water well and are less prone to drying out (and easier to re-wet) than peat-based ones. But sometimes you'll find they retain water too well. Excess clay in the loam can destroy porosity, and in time make them waterlogged, causing severe damage to the roots. This can be overcome by mixing 3 parts John Innes compost with 1 part extra crumbly peat. The end product should be easily workable and trickle readily through the fingers.

Note that peat-based mixtures need to be firmed rather less than soil-based ones when repotting.

Inevitably, chemical and biological changes occur in both kinds of mixture after they are made. Peat-based mixtures are usually sold dry and the changes are very slow. Soil-based mixtures may be moist and changes are likely to be faster; if possible such mixtures should be used reasonably soon after purchase – certainly within about six months. While these changes seldom affect plants being repotted, they can sometimes injure seeds and seedlings.

On the face of it soil-based mixtures score over peat-based ones. If peat-based mixtures are used it is absolutely vital to remember to feed at the intervals imposed by the fertilizers concerned (i.e. fairly often with standard liquid feeds, or according to instruction with tablets and long-term granules).

Home-made potting mixtures

Making one's own potting mixtures not only saves money but allows you flexibility in preparing the ingredients to suit different plants.

The cheapest and simplest method might seem to be to dig up soil from the garden, but this is seldom a sensible thing to do – especially in town gardens where soils are likely to be worn out and lacking in organic matter. Apart from varying immensely in quality and texture, any garden soil is likely to contain harmful organisms and weed seeds.

To be useful as a potting mixture soil should be fibrous, with neither too much clay content nor sand, and have the right level of acidity. But you must sterilize it to destroy harmful organisms and seeds. Small electric sterilizers can be obtained, or you can fill a baking tin with the soil, which should be averagely moist but not wet; cover it and place in an oven. Get the temperature up to 180°F (82°C) and maintain that level for one hour.

A *general-purpose soil-based mixture* can be made of:
1 part soil (fibrous and sterilized) +
2 parts horticultural peat +
1 part sharp sand, fine perlite or vermiculite (the latter two best where moisture-holding is important). $\frac{1}{2}$-part very coarse sand or grit aids stability in plastic pots.

To this should be added a balanced fertilizer or, preferably, slow-release fertilizer granules, according to instructions.

For a *general purpose peat-based mixture,* combine:
1 part horticultural peat (coarse rather than finely milled) +
1 part sharp sand or medium perlite +
1 part horticultural vermiculite or acrylic copolymer.

To this add a tablespoonful of dolomite limestone (calcium carbonate) powder to each quart of mixture, and fertilizer or granules as for the soil-based mixture. If desired, for reason of cost and to improve appearance (some people dislike the white granules of perlite in a mix), the proportion of peat can be greatly increased.

If one is making one's own potting mixtures, testing for acid reaction with a lime-test kit is essential. Soil-based mixtures clearly will derive their pH reaction mostly from the soil involved, and for house plants a slightly acid soil to start with is necessary. Too much acidity can be rectified by working in dolomite limestone powder to the mixture. Excess alkalinity can be overcome up to a point by adding more peat (though this may upset the overall balance of the mixture) and also by working in sulphur dust.

Special cases

Some plants prefer specific potting mixtures. Among house plants, most cacti and other succulents need extra sand, since of course they mostly grow in semi-deserts consisting of sand. Epiphytic orchids are the most extreme examples of plants which will not thrive in any orthodox potting mixture. Their roots, which attach themselves to trees and rocks, are specially developed to absorb moisture from the air. Placed in soil or peat-based potting mixture they will rot in the excess moisture.

Terrestrial orchids like cymbidiums on the other hand will grow in more ordinary mixtures which must always be extra porous.

Some cacti, like this Epiphyllum strictum, *are epiphytic and adapted to absorb moisture from the air.*

Mixture ingredients

Several materials besides soil have been mentioned in discussing both orthodox and special potting mixtures. These, and others which may have been mentioned in other references, are listed and described below.

Charcoal

Often recommended to keep mixtures "sweet", because of its capacity to absorb unwanted minerals and counteract decay of organic materials especially if too wet. Hence, pieces of charcoal are often added to mixtures which might get waterlogged, as in bottle gardens and undrained bulb bowls. Charcoal has a neutral reaction.

Dolomite limestone

A natural rock, chemically calcium carbonate, normally used in powder form to counteract the acidity of a peat-based potting mixture when required. Has a pH of 8.8; the more finely ground, the quicker it works. Also releases magnesium which is beneficial to plants.

Eggshells

Crushed eggshells are alkaline as they contain calcium carbonate. They can be used for the same purpose as dolomite limestone, to reduce acidity. They also help to "open up" a peaty mixture, to reduce water-logging and enable roots to "breathe". Their pH is 8.6.

Leaf mould

The result of leaves decaying for 2-3 years. Can be made at home by stacking leaves. Beech and oak leaves produce the best leaf mould; plane and holly are far too tough. Leaf mould is an organic material containing some nutrients; like peat, it is acid in reaction. Partly decayed coniferous leaf mould is occasionally recommended to provide a coarse, very porous, acid mixture.

Limestone chips

Sometimes recommended – and best in 20mm ($\frac{3}{4}$in) grade – to open up mixtures and to reduce their acidity, though their effect is slow.

Manure

Horse manure is not recommended as food for house plants even when thoroughly decayed. Cow manure, however, is a rich, organic plant food and when well rotted and dried can be crumbled into an inoffensive powder and stored; it has a slightly acid reaction.

Peat

This well-known material (called peat moss in the U.S.) is the result of plants which have decayed without oxygen, in waterlogged bogs etc. It contains virtually no nutrients and is effectively sterile, but holds water and plant foods, and offsets an excess of clay or sand in soil. Its reaction is very acid. According to its origin, peat may be labelled sedge peat or sphagnum peat, the latter generally to be preferred for house plants. Sedge peat is less acid and often dust-fine. For general guidance one can say that the coarser grades of peat, usually pale brown in colour, are far better for potting mixtures than finely milled grades, which are almost black and can pack down into an airless mass. Apart from being a basic constituent of most soilless mixtures, extra peat can be added with advantage to soil-based mixtures to improve texture and moisture-holding.

Perlite

A volcanic rock which has been heat-treated, and ground into grades varying from fine (almost powdery) to coarse, 3mm ($\frac{1}{8}$in) or larger. It holds water and nutrients and makes mixtures more porous, but its white grains may look peculiar in them. It has a neutral reaction.

Sand

Often used to open up potting mixtures, especially soil-based ones, to increase porosity; it is particularly invaluable to offset the effects of clay. It is essential to obtain sharp or coarse sand, which is rough to the touch; fine builder's sand is harmful. Coarse sand can be obtained in various grades up to about 3mm ($\frac{1}{8}$in). Sand from sea beaches contains salt and should not be used unless thoroughly washed. Sand has a neutral reaction (i.e. is neither acid nor alkaline).

Sphagnum moss

Live bog moss, sometimes used by specialists for very open, moisture-holding mixtures (as for orchids), or as a layer at the bottom of pots for specially moisture-loving plants. It has an acid reaction and little food content.

Tree bark

Ground, partly composted bark has similar uses to peat; like peat it is acid and contains very little plant food beyond a little nitrogen. The size variation of its particles gives an open texture, so it is valuable for plants demanding good drainage.

Vermiculite

Flakes formed from natural mica which has been heat-treated. Since they hold quantities of water and nutrients, they are valuable in seed-sowing mixtures, for rooting cuttings, and also to improve water-holding in potting mixtures. A horticultural grade with near-neutral reaction should be used; some grades used as building insulation are very alkaline.

Hydroculture

The idea of growing plants with roots in water, or in an inert aggregate standing in water, originated partly to succeed with plants in deserts, arctic wastes and other places where soil did not exist, partly to overcome soil-borne diseases, and partly to achieve tighter control over growth conditions.

There are various advantages over orthodox cultivation. It does away with annual repotting and the need for bulky potting mixtures.

But the greatest and obvious advantage concerns plant irrigation. Erratic watering is undoubtedly the major cause of failure with pot plants, over-watering being the most common problem. In hydroculture it is just a matter of topping up a reservoir at fairly long intervals; the element of human fallibility is virtually removed.

Another advantage is also the reason for its lack of popularity with some hobbyists; it so much reduces their need to attend to the plants! A good proportion of house plant owners talk to their plants as if they were pets, and hydroculture promotes far too clinical and scientific a relationship.

Roots develop a different structure, when growing in water, from those growing in soil. They become thicker, with expanded outer cells adapted to absorbing oxygen from water and storing it. This change explains why almost any plant – even succulents – can be grown by hydroculture in apparent defiance of all known natural principles. However it is difficult to transfer plants from one medium to the other, and far better to start with plants which have been grown since propagation as cuttings, in water-saturated aggregate.

Jar hydroculture

This involves rooting cuttings in water, a time-honoured method for many house plants, also used in the old-fashioned hyacinth jar. Use attractively shaped jars and bottles to enhance the pleasure of seeing the roots develop. Eventually, green algal growth inevitably forms inside a jar,

especially if plant food is added to the water, making any glass container unsightly. For this reason, this primitive method is at best a temporary one. Tall-growing plants are not suited to this method, as they will need support, so confine it to bushy or spreading kinds.

Hydroculture rids us of many of the orthodox cultivational problems, and suits more than the water margin plant, cyperus.

Use of aggregate

The more efficient methods depend on the use of an aggregate, partly or entirely immersed in water, which the roots permeate and which provides anchorage.

The aggregate can be made of 6mm–15mm ($\frac{1}{4}$in–$\frac{5}{8}$in) stone chippings, pebbles or gravel. Materials which absorb water, like perlite, vermiculite, and granules of expanded clay or pulverized fuel ash, are also used, but they can sometimes collect a harmful excess of fertilizer salts in normal hydroculture. (See also *Special methods* below).

Single-container method

The simplest method is to fill a single watertight container with aggregate. Add quarter-strength liquid feed to

Tradescantia in a single container

fill the lower quarter or third of the container. Insert the plants while the aggregate is being placed in the container; cuttings of rapid-rooting plants like tradescantias, zebrinas, ivies, impatiens, etc. can be pushed into it when full. Capillary action in the aggregate ensures that its upper levels contain enough moisture for rooting, though it is best to obtain a simple water-level indicator and push this down to the bottom of the container to make sure the correct water level is maintained.

The disadvantage of this method is that excess fertilizer is likely to build up in the solution. This means that every month or two the fertilizer solution should be poured off and replaced with fresh. At least once a year, the aggregate and plant roots should be washed clean of fertilizer under a running tap. Incidentally, unpainted metal containers should not be used as they will be corroded by reaction with fertilizer.

Double-container method

Most commercial hydroculture systems use an inner container which "nests" in a deeper and wider outer one. The inner container, which has holes in its base, holds the plant with its roots surrounded by aggregate. The outer container, which is water-tight and should be supplied with a built-in waterlevel gauge, contains the quarter-strength fertilizer solution to a level just above the base of the inner one. Capillary action brings the solution into the aggregate and

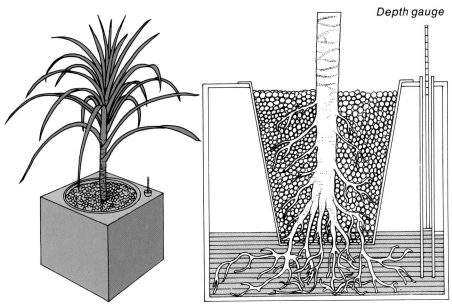

Dracaena in a double container

Depth gauge

into direct contact with the roots. Eventually the roots emerge through the basal holes and continue to develop in the solution.

As before, the solution should be replaced every month or two. Washing the aggregate and plant roots free of excess fertilizer is much simpler than in the single-container method, however. The inner container just needs lifting out and placing under a running tap for a couple of minutes.

It is possible to set up this method without expensive commercial double containers. A watertight outer container of china or plastic is selected.

The plant is put into a smaller "hydroculture pot", with slits round its base, and surrounded with aggregate. This pot and the plant are "planted" in the outer container and completely surrounded by aggregate, preferably a granular kind.

Special methods
One is a commercial double-container method originating in Germany, and also available in Britain (but used mainly in commercial situations where contractors deal with the plants).

It makes use of an absorbent aggregate made of heat-treated expanded clay granules (hydroleca),

plus a special fertilizer. This is supplied in a small "battery" which is fixed beneath the inner container, and then acts by ion exchange. In basic terms this means that the food materials are only released when the plant needs them, the remainder being taken up by the absorbent granules. The advantages are that there is no harmful excess of chemicals; further harmful chemicals in the water, like chlorine and fluoride, are largely absorbed. The fertilizer "battery" lasts for at least six months.

Moving plants on
Hydroculturally grown plants need moving into larger containers – the equivalent of repotting – much less often than when using orthodox potting mixtures. (Root systems in aggregate are compact and do not need to grow in all directions, as in soil, since water and food resources surround them). The main reason for moving on, indeed, is if the plant grows out of balance, aesthetically, with its container, or becomes dangerously top-heavy.

In single-container hydroculture a larger container must be found; in any double-container method a new set of inner plus outer containers is needed. A sink, bath or deep tray is desirable to contain excess liquid and aggregate during the moving-on

operation. The plant is removed from its container taking special care to avoid breaking too many roots (a particular problem with double containers).

Moving on is a good opportunity to wash the roots and aggregate. Remove any pieces of broken root, otherwise they will decay. Then, place a layer of aggregate at the bottom of the container, spread the roots out over this and, holding the plant at the desired level, fill the container up to its rim with more aggregate. The process is closely comparable with orthodox repotting.

Making a start
You may find it difficult to obtain young plants to grow on. If so, *start with cuttings*, which are rooted in an aggregate of small particles around 5mm ($\frac{1}{4}$in). A watertight tray or other container can be used, filled to half its depth or less with quarter-strength fertilizer solution; an alternative is to fill a number of 50mm (2in) plastic pots with aggregate; place these in a watertight tray, and partly fill this with solution.

Cuttings rooted in this way need similar treatment, as to heat, light and humidity, to those raised in soil or peat-based mixtures (see page 202).

It is possible to transfer plants grown in orthodox potting mixtures to hydroculture, but it tends to be rather traumatic for the plants. The first step is to wash all the potting mixture off the roots under a running tap. Then "pot up" in aggregate, as described. Because of the transition shock, plants should be kept warm and in a close, humid atmosphere as if they were regular cuttings, using a propagating case, or enclosing each plant in a larger plastic bag supported by canes.

In principle, plants will produce a new system of water-adapted roots after this treatment, and the old roots decay. For this reason, their root systems and the aggregate must be thoroughly washed after five or six months.

187

Watering, feeding and repotting

Watering

We have said that water is one of the essential components without which no plant can grow. It is required for the process of photosynthesis and is the means by which mineral food materials are transported via the roots from the soil to stems and leaves. Too little water means that the roots cannot supply the leaves with their vital and never-ending needs. Ironically, transpiration by the leaves adds to the urgent need of plants for water. Without it they will droop and eventually wither or drop off.

However too much water can result in drowning the roots, rotting the fine root hairs and eventually the main roots (roots need space to breathe in order to perform their function). Besides poorly aerated mixtures, permanently full drip-saucers can cause this.

How then do water plants, cuttings rooted in water, and indeed house plants grown by hydrocultural means, survive? The answer is that water holds a good deal of dissolved oxygen, and that roots immersed solely in water develop to take advantage of this oxygen. Roots used to soil will not survive.

The need for aeration of potting mixtures is greater for many of our house plants than for the average greenhouse plant, since so many of our house plants are epiphytic (like bromeliads and some ferns) and are conditioned to extract moisture continuously from the atmosphere, while others depend on very erratic water supplies in nature. Once again, this reminds us that *the more we know about how plants grow in nature the easier it is to keep them thriving in cultivation.*

In most natural situations an earth-rooting plant survives by steadily extending its roots in search of water and nutrients: experiments on rye plants (admittedly very vigorous compared with many house plants) showed an increase in total root length of 5 kilometres a day! In a pot, however, root growth is restricted

The banks of streams in Madagascar are home for Cyperus alternifolius.

and the plant is absolutely dependent on its owner to satisfy its water requirements. By forcing it into unnatural growing environment of a pot, the onus is on us to make amends.

How much water?

Many factors affect the water needs of any particular plant. The most important is, of course, its natural way of life and its natural expectations. A cactus from a semi-desert uses very little water compared with a rush growing in a bog, though its extensive root system will seek out a remarkable amount.

Growing conditions affect water uptake greatly. In hot weather, and equally in rooms heated well in winter, more water is lost by transpiration than in cool conditions. Water can also be lost by the soil – a pot in direct sunlight, or exposed to hot air from heating equipment, will dry out rapidly.

The state of activity of the plant is also important (see p. 170/1). When growing actively a plant needs much more water; to over-water when it is resting may be very harmful.

Drought-tolerant plants, or the xerophytes as they are known, often need virtually no water in their winter rest – they rely upon their natural water-storage mechanisms; by contrast a winter-flowering pot plant like a cineraria which is in active growth at that time will need watering every day or two.

Other factors relate to the water-holding capacity of the potting mixture and the pot itself. Water is evaporated more rapidly through an unglazed pot than through a glazed or plastic one. Potting mixture in a small pot usually dries out more quickly than a large one, and peat-based mixtures dry out more quickly than soil-based ones.

Finally, a large plant will need more water than a small one in the same-sized pot, because of the greater extent of the roots.

The need to maintain air around the roots so they can breathe, means that it is always better to water adequately at intervals controlled by the exterior factors outlined above, than to blindly water little and often. This tends to waterlog the potting mixture. Tiny air spaces among the roots and soil particles are vital for healthy growth.

When to water

It should now be clear that there can be no rule of thumb about when to water. The plant's own warning signs of wilting or drooping leaves, or

Echinocereus grows in the arid Mexican desert.

shrivelling stems in the case of cacti, are emergency signals which may be too late to rectify. To rely on them as regular watering guides is not at all good for the plant, since it will be weakened by repeated drying out, and leaves may go brown or yellow, or drop prematurely. Also, if a potting mixture dries out, it will soon shrink away from the sides of the pot, and require soaking in a container.

Remember that the surface of the potting mixture is an unsatisfactory guide: it may look dry when, overall, the potting mixture is quite moist enough. A finger pushed into the mixture will reveal whether it is damp an inch or so down. For deeper penetration one can use a pencil or small wooden rod; moist mix will stick to these and discolour the wood.

Until recently the classic way of determining soil moisture was to tap the pot with a little mallet: a dry pot would give a ringing tone, a wet pot a dull one. But this was with clay pots, and it is very rare to buy plants in other than plastic pots these days.

But another traditional method has its value — this is to lift the pot and gauge its weight in one hand, since dry potting mixture is much lighter than damp. Obviously this method requires experience, but this is true of all these methods.

As in measuring temperature and air humidity, it is possible to measure soil moisture with relatively cheap, foolproof electrical meters. Push the metal probe into the soil and read the moisture level on its scale. Most meters operate without batteries since the chemical reaction of moist soil causes a voltage differential between two distinct parts of the probe. Booklets supplied with the meters give the grower plant-by-plant advice on watering amounts.

With a large number of pots this procedure may become tedious, but it has special value with large containers, whose water needs may otherwise be difficult to assess, since it measures the water content well down in the pot among the roots. You may, of course, prefer to use small indicator sticks or probes that can be pushed permanently into pots and change colour when dry or moist. These are, however, apt to disintegrate in time, and only indicate moisture content in small pots or the upper levels of a large one.

The inexperienced will find that using a meter, and its accompanying booklet, helps them to gain an idea of the general water demands of their plants. The best moisture meters cannot supplant the need to be aware of each plant's needs and the environmental factors that influence these.

The amount to give at each watering again depends on the type of plant. In general terms, it is usual to give actively growing plants plenty at each watering, drenching the mixture enough for water to emerge from the base of the pot (if much ends up in a pot saucer it must be tipped out; roots will rot in standing water). This may be described as *generous* watering. More water is then given when the surface of the potting mixture begins to dry out, except in some cases, notably cacti, where most of the potting mixture should dry out before drenching it again.

Some plants needs less water than this: they need watering when the top half-inch or so of potting mixture is dry. Give only enough so that few, if any, drops of water emerge from the base of the pot. This so-called *medium* watering is also sufficient for most plants when resting.

Finally there are a few plants which need very little water: with these you can allow the upper two-thirds of the potting mixture to dry out between waterings.

When watering give only enough to make the mixture just moist. Such *sparing* watering applies for instance to cacti in the resting period.

The level of watering is specified earlier in the plant lists. Remember that these guidelines apply to plants in *active* growth, and that much less frequent watering is needed in a resting period. The golden rule is — when in doubt, don't. More plants die from overwatering than from drying out.

Finally, if you do not feel that you are sizing up a plant's water needs satisfactorily, knock it out of its pot as for repotting and examine the state of the potting mixture and roots. If the latter are soft and crumbly they are dead and have probably been overwatered; the same mistake will create an unmistakably soggy, airless potting mixture. A very dry mixture which falls away readily from the roots obviously means that watering has been insufficient.

How to water

The best watering can, for indoor use, is fairly small and light, with a long, thin horizontal spout, and holding not more than 2.5 litres ($\frac{1}{2}$ gallon). The spout is essential to direct water into a pot covered by the plants' leaves, and into individual pots grouped together.

Water can be applied onto the surface of the potting mixture or into a drip saucer below the pot. Drip saucer watering is valuable when irrigating large pots in which the lower levels of the potting mixture may often become dry if only watered from above. The method is also advised for plants with soft, hairy leaves set low down (especially rosette plants like saintpaulias) since it avoids the leaves becoming spotted or, in bad cases, leaves or crowns rotting. In nature these plants often live on vertical cliff faces so that water cannot lodge on leaves or in crowns. However, if the potting mixture is already rather moist, water can collect in the drip saucer and this must be emptied away. There is also the risk of mineral salts collecting near the top of the pot, though these can be removed by watering from above at intervals.

An alternative is to use self-watering pots which are provided with a reservoir and a water indicator, and need far less attention. However these tend to be expensive and more suitable for large plants or groups in offices or wherever plants may be neglected.

The narrow, porous, conical earthenware "irrigators", that are available for individual pots, tend to provide water continuously and thus may well destroy aeration in the potting mixture; the same applies to patent "drip-feed" systems which are in any case unsightly, though they have their use for holiday watering

Bromeliads are one unique clan of plants which in nature collect rain in urn-shaped leaf rosettes. Water for these can be directed into the rosettes with only an occasional moistening of the potting mixture.

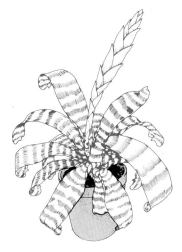

Vriesea: water can be directed into the rosette of leaves.

Water for house plants should never be much colder than the air surrounding them: this can cause a severe check to growth of delicate plants. The problem arises mainly in winter when the tap water can be very cold; then the easiest solution is to add some warm water to the can when filling it. You could, alternatively, leave the full can to stand in the room for some hours until it reaches room temperature.

Hard and soft water

The quality of the water may also need watching. Most house plants prefer rather acid conditions.

It follows therefore that "hard" (lime-containing) water is to be avoided. A level of over 120 parts per million of lime is unsatisfactory and over 150 ppm is likely to affect the general health of plants, retarding growth and making leaves go yellow. Hard water leaves unsightly deposits on leaf rosettes of bromeliads and on the surface of potting mixtures.

One can tell if there is a lot of lime in the tap water because kettles will "fur up" – develop an incrustation of lime. You can test for lime in water by using a pH indicator strip, obtainable from aquarium suppliers.

In country areas the problem of hard tap-water can be solved by collecting rain-water in a butt, and using this for your house plants. Unfortunately, in towns and near factories, rain-water is likely to be polluted by

sulphur dioxide and other chemicals, and should not be used.

Tap-water can be boiled to remove lime, but this is tedious. If mains water has to be used, the easiest solution is to instal a simple water filter. This is not the same as a water softener and in fact water which has passed through such a device is harmful to plants. A water filter will also remove high levels of chlorine if the mains water is chlorinated: this again can cause unsatisfactory growth. Fluoride in water is also harmful, and may cause leaf tips to go brown.

Holiday watering

If you are going away on holiday for more than three or four days, and cannot find a friend or neighbour to attend to your plants while you are away, you will certainly have to take precautions.

For a period of a week or so it may be sufficient to group the plants in a position which will receive no direct sun and, if possible, keeps cool. Place them on trays, preferably on a deep layer of pebbles or plunged into moistened peat-moss as deep as you can. Water liberally before leaving the plants.

In this situation self-watering pots come very much into their own. If you do not have these, you can improvise. Special wicks can be obtained which conduct water by capillary action from a container to the tops of pots arranged at a lower level; there are more sophisticated (though expensive) "drip-feed" systems with small capillary tubes.

Another very effective method is the capillary felt mat system. In this the pots are set on the felt in a tray; the free end of the felt being placed in a reservoir of water. A typical kitchen drainer surface is a good place to set this up, with the end of the felt dipping into the sink filled with water; but it works equally well in any waterproof tray of adequate size, on which the plants stand, in a position where the felt dips into a water container at a lower level.

Capillary matting

Another way of using the matting is to place it in a bath with the plants upon it, and leave the tap dripping very slowly. There is a danger here that the tap will stop dripping after a few days; experiment beforehand!

The capillary matting is, however, only really effective with plastic pots containing no drainage material, so that the potting mixture is virtually in contact with the mat. It does not work very well with plastic pots over 15–17cm (6 or 7in) in diameter. For large plastic pots and all clay pots, wicks must be inserted inside the base of the pot so that they emerge from the drainage holes and come into full contact with the felt matting.

Although proprietary plant-pot wicks are readily obtainable, you could use lampwicks or cut some capillary matting into strips about 25mm (1in) wide. To insert the wicks: either turn the plant out of its pot, insert the wick through a drainage hole and replace the root ball; or push a pencil into the root ball through a drainage hole to about 75mm (3in), and insert the wick into the hole that the pencil has made.

The plant-pot wick method

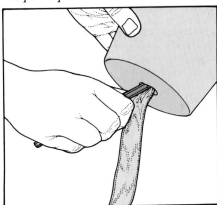

A quite different method is to water your plants thoroughly and the next day cover them with large plastic bags. These are supported on three or four thin stakes pushed in at the pot edge, which must be long enough to keep the plastic clear of the foliage.

Preserving moisture in a plastic bag

The plastic bag can be fastened around the pot rim with string: this is advisable for periods of 10–14 days. For shorter periods the bag can hang loosely over the pot. Place all the bagged pots in as cool a place as possible in summer, or between 60°–65°F (16°–18°C) in winter, and out of strong light.

There is a proprietary device called a plant dome which opens up to about 90cm (36in) high and 74cm (29in across) and works exactly like a polythene bag but has inbuilt rigidity. It will take a number of quite large

The plant dome method

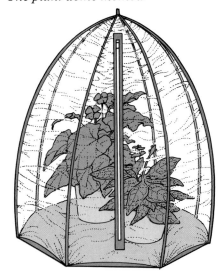

plants and, if they are well watered, should keep them thriving for at least two weeks.

Emergency watering
If for any reason the potting mix does dry out completely and the plant has wilted badly, immerse the pot entirely – over its rim – in a sink or bucket filled with water. Leave it there until bubbles stop rising from the potting mixture, then stand the pot where the surplus water can drain. Do this in a cool place, to give the foliage more chance to pick up satisfactorily.

It is, in fact, a good idea to give all house plants this treatment once or twice during the summer, so that any "pockets" of dryness (particularly common in large pots) are made wet.

A different kind of emergency occurs if water remains at the top of the pot for an abnormal time, refusing to be absorbed by the potting mixture. This may simply be due to caking of the surface layer, which can be broken up with a skewer or similar implement. If this does not cure the condition, the potting mixture is likely to be hopelessly compacted (probably due to using clay soil) and a repotting operation should be carried out in which as much of the mixture as possible is shaken off the roots (easier when it is becoming dry), before repotting the plant in a more satisfactory porous mixture.

Pointers for watering
Water more often if:
Plant container is unglazed clay.
Plant is large but pot relatively small.
Plant has filled pot with roots.
Plant is in active growth.
Temperature is high.
Air humidity is low.
Plant has large thin leaves.

Water less often if:
Plant container is plastic or clay.
Plant has not filled pot with roots.
Plant has recently been repotted.
Plant is small but in relatively large pot.
Plant is resting or dormant.
Temperature is low.
Air humidity is high.
Plant has succulent leaves or stems.

Besides light and water, continued healthy plant growth depends on a supply of mineral foods to supplement the sugar and organic materials derived from it after photosynthesis. These materials are almost always absorbed in the soil moisture by the roots, and in natural conditions this nutrition arises from two main sources. One is the slow breakdown and dissolving of particles of rock which releases minerals into the porous elements of the soil, or in the case of sand into the moisture which coats the particles in damp conditions (occasioned by dew or rain). The other is the decay of organic matter – fallen leaves, branches, dead animals (mainly the tiny ones which inhabit the soil). This decay is carried out by fungi and bacteria, and is greatly speeded up by the digestive processes of worms, termites and other soil-inhabiting animals.

In nature some plants develop huge buttress roots in search for food.

Most plants seek out additional food in the soil by expanding their root systems steadily. Some, however, obtain very little because of their natural habitat: examples are bromeliads, usually obtaining food only from the small amount of debris that collects around their roots, and cacti, with limited access to minerals because of the very slow leaching in the sand they live on.

In cultivation the process of solution and decay is at best slow. It does occur in soil-based potting mixtures, which contain mineral-based rock and sand particles, and bacteria which act on any organic matter

present. They do not, however, occur to a significant degree in peat-based mixtures, since peat decays so very slowly that it does not encourage normal soil bacteria.

It can be seen that artificial feeding of plants in pots is essential for health and continued growth. Plants in soil-based mixtures need less than those in peat-based mixtures, which *must* be fed regularly if they are to grow satisfactorily.

Plant foods
The three main plant foods are nitrogen, phosphorus and potassium. Each has an overall role in the plant's metabolism. Besides these major elements, a number of others, known as trace elements, are needed by plants in very small amounts to control their metabolism and ability to function (rather than building up tissue in the process of growth, which is the job of the major elements).

A balance of these plant foods is essential for healthy growth.

Nitrogen
Vital for active leaf and shoot growth and desirable for leafy plants in general. It is specially needed when plants start growing after a rest period, but less so towards the end of the active growth period when over-lush growth can be adversely affected by the poor growing conditions which winter can bring.

Phosphorus
Important for healthy root production and desirable when establishing young plants, and before and during flowering periods.

Potash
Helps to keep plants sturdy and well balanced, does much to improve disease resistance, and is specially valuable for encouraging future flowers and fruit. Thus after using high-nitrogen feeds to produce larger healthy plants, tomato growers switch to high-potash feeds to ensure good fruit production and ripening.

Such high-potash feeds are therefore very valuable with bulbs, and plants

and shrubs grown mainly for flower. There is no doubt that such feeds are good for all house plants especially if trace elements are guaranteed.

Since most house plants prefer acid rather than alkaline conditions, fertilizers labelled as "acid" or "acid-reaction" are preferable if available, but this is not of great importance in practice.

Fertilizer balance
The label of a plant food or fertilizer bottle or pack will indicate the proportionate presence of the "big three" elements, which are abbreviated as N (nitrogen), P (phosphorus), and K (potash). The label may spell out the proportions as in N=8%, P=6%, K=10%, or the percentage simply be expressed by the three numbers 8–6–10, the elements N, P and K always being shown in the same order. Most available fertilizers supply adequate trace elements, but to be sure of these choose a product which stipulates that trace elements are present: seaweed-based materials are usually rich in them.

The label will also give details of the required dilution. The proportions of N, P, and K in a feed that is coded 16–12–20, are the same as in one coded 8–6–10, but the first is twice as concentrated and needs double the dilution.

It will be clear that a fertilizer with the same numbers for each element, say 6–6–6, is exactly balanced; 12–6–6 is high in nitrogen, 6–12–6 is high in phosphorus, while 6–6–12 is high in potash.

Manufacturers produce many variations on these themes. Sometimes their fertilizers are recommended specifically for leafy or flowering plants, or for specific types of plant. Plants show much adaptability as long as they receive *some* additional food from time to time, but feeding is never a substitute for inadequacies in the other growth factors. If light or temperature levels are less than ideal, feeding may actually be harmful.

Most liquid fertilizers are made from

chemicals, often synthetically produced. Growers who prefer to use organic materials only should apply feeds made from seaweed. However, it must be said that the plant has no preferences: it can only absorb its necessary foodstuffs in their simplest possible forms, and there is no effective difference between a synthetically produced fertilizer and an "organic" one with the same mineral constituents.

Ways to apply plant foods

Fertilizers are supplied in various ways. The commonest forms are concentrated liquids to be diluted in water, and there are also powder and crystals to be dissolved in a specific quantity of water. Liquid foods are probably the most convenient, as feeding also supplies essential water.

The concentration recommended on the label should never be exceeded: overdoses can scorch and kill roots. Feeding at lower than recommended strength can never harm plants, and in many cases is to be preferred.

Powder and granular fertilizers intended for garden plants are not generally suitable for house plants, but there are certain granular materials specially made for the purpose. These can be scattered on the surface of the potting mixture (preferably worked lightly into it), or placed in a drip saucer if one is used; a measuring spoon or cap ensures the right quantity according to the size of the pot.

Other methods include tablets, "pins" or "spikes" of fertilizer chemicals in an inert "base", which are pushed into the potting mixture; some tablet products are supplied with a tapered plastic spike to make the necessary hole.

Most of the tablet, pin and granular house plant foods have relatively long-term action, in some cases over much of a growing season. These are variously labelled *slow release, timed release, controlled release* or simply *long-lasting,* and the instructions should be carefully followed. Because it is easy to forget when they have

been applied, it is helpful to keep records, either in a notebook or pencilled on a label inserted in the pot.

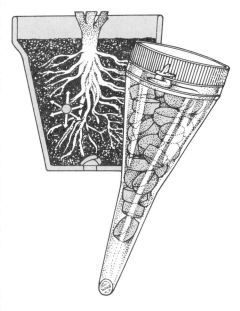

One other possible method of supplying plant food is *foliar feeding.* Surprisingly enough it has been found that plants can absorb suitably formulated foods in liquid form through their leaves; the method gives very quick results, so it is especially valuable for plants that look starved or in need of a tonic. Obviously foliar feeding is unsuitable for plants *in situ*: the spray would get onto furniture and carpets. Take them outdoors or put them in the bath for application via a sprayer. Plants with very hard or glossy leaves will not absorb foliar feeds as well as softer-leaved ones, and furry or hairy leaves may suffer.

As already stated, feeding should only commence when other growth conditions, notably light and warmth, have been properly seen to.

The other important factor is the potting mixture. The modern soilless mixtures, which are mainly peat-based, only contain enough plant food for about six weeks, and so newly bought or repotted plants in such mixtures should be fed after two months or so. Soil-based mixtures, however, can be left for three months or more, since their food reserves are much higher.

Feeding schedules

During the growing season most house plants will require regular feeding, at the manufacturer's recommended maximum strength, but not more frequently than every two weeks. Feeding every two weeks will make plants grow vigorously, and necessitate repotting perhaps once or twice in the season. If this is not desirable – space indoors is often at a premium – feed plants in soilless mixtures every 4–6 weeks; every 6–8 weeks for those in soil-based mixtures. Tablet, spike or granular feeds should be given according to the manufacturer's instructions on how long they will last.

In cold-temperate climates – say in Britain, northern Europe, Scandinavia, Canada and north-eastern U.S.A. – the growing season starts in early spring; a feed should be given then. This can be one high in nitrogen, and such a feed could continue into the first month of summer. After that, nitrogen should not be overdone, and in summer itself high-potash feeding will firm up the growth and make it better able to withstand winter. The last feed should be in early autumn at the latest. Feeding during a rest period in poor light is likely to result in thin, pallid leaves; growth may be frail and spindly, and liable to collapse.

Plants which need relatively little water, like cacti, can literally be "blown up" and start rotting if overfed; they need absolutely no nourishment in their almost-dry rest period.

In warmer climates, like the southern United States, the Mediterranean and Australia, most foliage house plants will usually grow continuously without a resting period, and feeding can continue all the year round. The same applies to plants cultivated in artificially light, hot and humid conditions.

It should, finally, be realized that feeding a plant in poor health is likely to harm it. First establish the cause of ill-health and rectify it if possible. Not until the plant is growing normally should it be fed routinely. 193

Plant containers

Most house plants are bought in hard plastic pots, but it is possible also to buy ornamental china ones, and styrofoam or polystyrene pots are sometimes seen. The traditional pot material, still obtainable, is of course unglazed clay.

Plastic pots

Less easily broken than clay, though the thinner kind are decidedly brittle and should not be picked up by the rim. Since they are impermeable no water is lost through the sides: this reduces the frequency of watering needed, but increases the possibility of water-logging. Plastic pots are easy to keep clean; they are light to handle, though they may not be heavy enough for large top-heavy plants; and they can be used with capillary felt watering mats. Not least of their merits is that they can be obtained in a range of decorative colours.

Glazed china pots

Comparable to plastic in many respects, though they can be broken and do not work with felt watering matting except with a wick.

Styrofoam or polystyrene pots

Made of an insulating material, these have the advantage of keeping the roots warm. This facilitates growth.

Pots of this material are soft and easily damaged.

Clay pots

Brittle, these pots need handling and storing with care. They are relatively heavy, but this makes them useful to house and counterbalance large top-heavy plants. They are permeable and lose water by evaporation through the sides. This action reduces the danger of waterlogging, but increases that of drying out in hot conditions. Clay pots cannot be used with capillary watering mats without a wick. Finally, they cannot be called decorative in most home situations, and are best concealed.

The main cultural difference between plastic and clay pots is in the frequency of watering they require. If both kinds of pot are used in a collection, problems can obviously arise.

Pot shapes and sizes

Clay and plastic pots are normally round and roughly as deep as they are wide. Clay pots usually have one quite large drainage hole in the centre, though very large ones may have three side holes as well. Plastic pots have many small holes at the bottom near the edge.

Square plastic pots are available in sizes from 5 to 15cm (2 to 6in). These hold more potting mixture than round ones of the same width and have the advantage that, placed together in a trough or on a ledge, no space is wasted; they are also visually effective.

Pans, dwarf pots or half-pots are shallow as their name suggests, less deep than broad. They are useful when growing seeds or taking cuttings, for shallow-rooted, spreading plants, and for massing quick-growing plants (such as tradescantias) from cuttings. Plastic half-pots are available from about 7.5 to 14cm (3 to 5½in) diameter. Larger sizes, often used by alpine plant specialists, are only available in clay and are very expensive.

A distinct kind of pot, much deeper than broad, known as a "long tom", is useful for plants with elongated roots or tubers.

Standard round pots are available in sizes from 25mm (1in) to 38cm (15in) diameter. The average increase between sizes is 12mm (½in) up to 20 or 23cm (8 or 9in) with a 50mm (2in) jump from 25 to 30cm (10 to 12in) and then a 7.5cm (3in) jump to 38cm (15in). Metrication has meant that pots no longer follow the traditional ½in or 1in increases and a wide range is offered by manufacturers.

Plant containers

There are sound practical reasons for choosing one type of plant pot in preference to another.

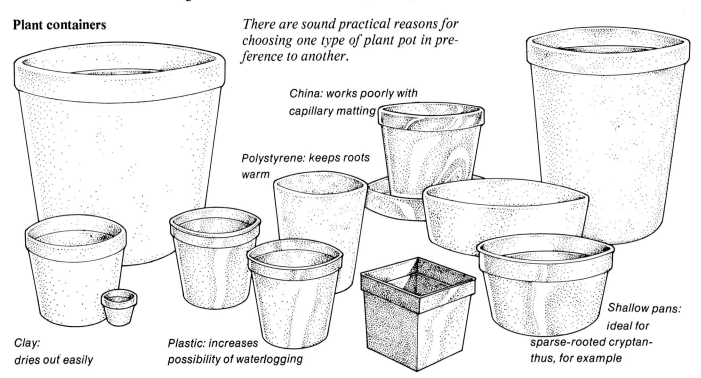

China: works poorly with capillary matting

Polystyrene: keeps roots warm

Clay: dries out easily

Plastic: increases possibility of waterlogging

Shallow pans: ideal for sparse-rooted cryptanthus, for example

Repotting

As already suggested, the greatest difference between house plants in the wild and in cultivation is that, in our houses, they have to live in pots or other containers. In nature their roots can roam as far as they need, but in cultivation they are confined.

It does not take long for most healthy plants to fill an average-sized pot with roots, and at a certain stage it is necessary to move the plant into a larger one, with some fresh potting mixture, if it is to continue to grow and thrive.

There is of course a kind of balancing act between repotting and feeding. A plant can be kept in reasonable health in the same pot for a remarkably long period if regularly fed, though after a time it may cease to show appreciable growth.

Some plants grow much faster than others; annual plants grown from seed, including several often brought indoors for a brief display; among these are cinerarias, coleus and primulas. In early stages, the young plants need repotting as soon as their pots are full of roots, or they will suffer a check to growth. (This does not of course apply to plants bought in flower.)

Some plants needing to be increased fairly often from cuttings are in the same category, like impatiens and tradescantias.

The standard repotting procedure

Fortunately the majority of house plants are satisfied to grow fairly slowly in the confines of a pot; usually one move a year into a larger pot will suffice. This process is known as potting on, moving on, or more often simply as repotting.

When is repotting needed?

Repotting should only be done when plants are in active growth. If they are resting, the roots will not grow into the new potting mixture, with the resulting danger that this may become waterlogged and "sour", which can in turn damage the roots.

The only sure way to know if a plant needs repotting is to turn it out of its pot and examine its roots. Certain signs may suggest the need: the most obvious is a quantity of fine roots coming out of the drainage holes, and if the plant is in a drip saucer one may find a positive mat of roots under the pot. A few roots peering out of drainage holes are not a reliable sign, however.

Some plants may produce roots at the top of the pot, especially thick-rooted ones like chlorophytum and clivia.

How to repot

Standard procedure is to place one hand, palm downward, across the top of the pot with the plant's main stem between your fingers: with low-growing plants – the rosette-forming saintpaulias for example – push the

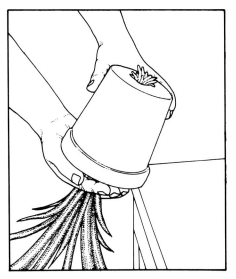

fingers below the leaves. Turn the pot upside-down and tap its rim gently on a hard surface like a table-corner; if this is not feasible tap the pot with a trowel handle or similar wooden object. It should then be possible to pull the pot off the root-ball (the mass of roots and potting mixture) with the other hand. Never try to pull a plant out of a pot by its stem.

Repotting a cactus

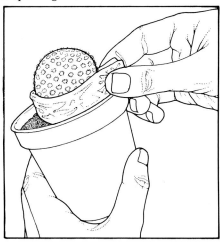

With a prickly plant it is best to make a protective band from folded newspaper; hold this around the plant before turning it out. Plants with brittle stems or leaves obviously need to be turned out with great care if damage is to be avoided.

Repotting large plants

Large plants in large pots cannot be dealt with in the same way. The plant must be laid on its side and the pot rim tapped, with a wooden mallet or block, to loosen it. If this fails to dislodge the plant, work the blade of a long thin knife around the inside edge of the pot. You may need help to pull the pot away while you hold the base of the plant. Sometimes pots grip so fast that they may have to be broken off (if clay) or, if plastic, cut away. This is usually only necessary if plants have been left for several years in the pot.

Once the plant is out of its pot, look at the state of its roots: if they are evenly and thickly spread over the whole surface of the root-ball, repotting is *desirable*. If there is a thick mat or spiral of roots at the bottom of the root-ball, repotting is *overdue*.

Plants that prefer being pot-bound

There are some exceptions to this rule. Some fleshy-rooted plants like clivias, and bulbs like hippeastrums, flower more readily if allowed to fill their pots with roots (this is known as being pot-bound or root-bound), and a few shrubs grown for flower are the same. Where this applies it is noted, earlier. The reason for this is that these plants naturally tend to flower in adverse conditions such as drought – one might say that the plant "feels" its life is threatened and its reaction is to produce flower and seed to disseminate the species. If the plants are regularly repotted they do not feel this urgency, make lush leaf growth and may not bloom. This does not mean that pot-bound plants should not be fed: they appreciate it even more, especially if given a feed high in potash, which encourages flower production.

There are other plants, notably bromeliads, which will need little repotting: for these, a pot is mainly for convenient anchorage, a receptacle for roots that would in nature be clinging epiphytically to a tree branch or rock. In a few cases, for instance tillandsias, pots are not normally used at all: the plants are grown fastened to pieces of cork bark, rough-barked branches, or artificial supports like moss poles.

Staghorn ferns require no pot at all.

Practical pointers for re-potting

★ Because of the amount of preparatory work, it is a good idea to repot a number of plants in one operation. Fresh pots, potting mixture, drainage materials etc., must all be gathered together, and if the work has to be done indoors provision must be made to avoid mess by spreading newspapers. Large trays are invaluable to contain plants and materials.

★ Preliminaries also include watering plants to be repotted an hour or two beforehand (this makes it easier to extract them from their pots with the root-ball intact), and to clean the replacement pots if they are not new. Clay pots may need to be scrubbed especially if discoloured with lime deposit; but plastic pots seldom need more than rinsing and rubbing round with a cloth. New clay pots should be soaked in water till air-bubbles no longer emerge, since fresh dry ones can suck moisture out of the potting mixture.

★ When repotting, only a small increase in pot size is needed. The reason for this, is that however porous and free-draining the potting mixture is to begin with, it is likely to become sodden quite quickly with ordinary watering. When plant roots permeate it, they introduce both air and water into the mix. Sodden, stagnant mixture will not be entered by roots, and can cause existing ones to decay.

★ For most house plants in pots the following size increases are adequate:

Pots up to 11.5cm (4½in) – 12mm (½in) increase.

Pots from 12.5 to 25cm (5 to 10in) – 2.5cm (1in) increase.

Pots larger than 25cm (10in) are normally only made in 30.5cm (12in) and 38cm (15in) sizes, and these increases are satisfactory.

★ With very fast-growing plants such as impatiens, plectranthus, and tradescantias and their relations, these increases in pot size can be at least doubled. Otherwise, pots quickly become choked with roots and, after a short time, their growth will cease. If annuals, such as cinerarias, are being raised from seed they need even larger increases, otherwise they can suffer severe checks which may stunt flower growth.

★ Clay pots normally have one large drainage hole in the centre. This should be covered with a crock (a broken piece of clay pot, slate, crockery or a pebble) large enough to cover the hole and prevent soil falling out; a few plants (as specified earlier) may need a deeper layer of crocks.

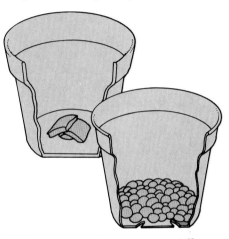

Different sorts of pot require different drainage methods.

Plastic pots have a number of small holes near the bottom edge and do not normally need special drainage material. However, if plants are usually kept standing on drip saucers, or in china or plastic pot-hiders, a shallow layer of small pebbles or clay granules placed in the base of the pot will protect them against accidental waterlogging should water collect in the saucer.

★ With the plant removed from its original pot, check the condition of its roots; remove any roots that are decayed or dried up, and if pests like root mealy bugs and weevil grubs are seen take remedial action.

Moss, liverwort or weeds on the top surface of the root-ball should be scraped off or pulled out. Remove any drainage material embedded among roots at the bottom.

★ To gauge how much new potting mixture can be placed in the bottom of the new pot, place the old pot inside it, adding sufficient mixture until the rim of the old pot, when so placed, sits at the same level as that of the new, or a little lower.

Remember also that it is necessary to leave an adequate space between pot rim and the surface of the root-ball for watering, roughly as follows:

Pot Diameter	Watering Space
Up to 12.5cm (5in)	12mm ($\frac{1}{2}$in)
14–19cm (5$\frac{1}{2}$–7$\frac{1}{2}$in)	20mm ($\frac{3}{4}$in)
20–23cm (8–9in)	25mm (1in)
25–30.5cm (10–12in)	38mm (1$\frac{1}{2}$in)
38cm (15in)	50mm (2in)

★ Put the old root-ball in the centre of the new pot and fill round its sides with potting mixture, pushing this down with the fingers or a wooden rod to make sure no air-pockets are left. Soil-based mixtures need to be packed down rather more firmly than peat-based ones, but never make either too solid or the roots will not penetrate them. To settle the mixture down, tap the filled pot a few times on a hard surface.

Settling the new mix correctly gives roots the best chance of survival.

★ If roots are exposed on the top of the root-ball, add enough potting mixture to cover them, while maintaining the watering space.

★ With some plants it is difficult to fill in around the root-ball – these include prickly kinds, wide bushes, and those with brittle or rosette-type leaves. The problem can be solved by using the old pot as a mould: after placing enough potting mixture in the base of the new pot, put the old pot in place and fill round this with mixture. When all is firm the old pot is removed and the root-ball can be placed carefully into its position. Again, tap the pot on a hard surface to settle the mixture.

A ctenanthe growing askew is corrected in the process of repotting.

★ If a plant has its central stem off-centre, it can be repositioned when repotting; similarly if the stem is slanting, place the root-ball at an angle to correct this, making sure that no air pockets are left anywhere below or around it, and build up mixture on top to make it level.

★ When repotting you may encounter a tiny pot in the centre. This is the plastic mesh pot in which the plant was originally rooted; roots grew through it before the initial potting and it cannot now be removed.

Top-dressing and root pruning
The largest pot that can usually be handled conveniently in rooms is 25–30.5cm (10–12in). Larger pots,

tubs etc. can be obtained but they are very heavy and unwieldy when filled. In any case, there comes a point where further potting on is impracticable. Still, roots continue to grow, and eventually fill the pot, the potting mixture having every particle of moisture and organic matter taken from it until it almost disappears.

The usual way of dealing with this situation is *top-dressing*. In this operation the top inch or two of potting mixture is removed, using a small trowel or perhaps an old spoon. Continue scraping away until the roots are exposed. Then, replace this layer with fresh potting mixture, high in nutrients, created by mixing a concentrated slow-release fertilizer into standard potting mixture or combining the latter with dried, fully decayed cow manure (an old-fashioned but excellent material for anyone who can lay hands on it).

Top-dressing can maintain large plants in reasonable health for many years, although growth will slow down by degrees.

An alternative method is to remove the plant from its pot every year or two and pick away soil from all round the root ball, taking care to damage the roots as little as possible, so that fresh potting mixture can be refilled around it as in normal potting on. Sometimes in this process it is found that the centre of the root-ball contains dead or dried-up roots; these can of course be removed, the space filled with potting mixture.

A drastic method sometimes used is actually to *root-prune* by removing slices of soil, roots and all, from the sides and base of the root-ball with a large sharp knife, after which the plant is repotted in the original container. Though some plants may be resilient enough to stand this treatment and produce new roots quickly, it can cause severe shock and is only a last resort.

In the end, it is best to propagate new specimens from old, and finally discard very large, root-bound specimens.

197

Nature is a battleground, and the first joust is between plants competing among themselves. Perhaps the most violent example is from the eastern tropics where rattans or climbing palms scramble up other trees, fixing themselves with hooked prickles and draping themselves all over their hosts. These suffer from lack of light to their leaves and may eventually collapse under the rattan's weight. Strangler figs germinating in the debris-filled crotch of a tree will send down roots all round it which, after many decades, literally strangle the host to death; the popular *Ficus benjamina* is one of these! On a much smaller scale almost microscopic plants and lichens grow upon leaf surfaces and obscure light intake – these are called epiphylls.

More orthodox predators attack plants by eating them. The rainforest has everything from scale insects and other tiny sucking species, to leaf-eating caterpillars and leaf-cutting ants, and finally larger creatures like monkeys. In some places elephants destroy whole trees and other vegetation, and herbivorous animals devour their leaves.

Attack, damage, collapse are commonplace for plants in the wild. In some parts of the jungle it is impossible to find a whole leaf, or to move without hacking through the debris of dead plants, while elsewhere some species, like the bromeliads, manage to make themselves so tough and unattractive to predators that they are seldom attacked.

But whereas the aim of a plant in nature is to survive and reproduce itself, its purpose in the house is to be decorative, and any blemish upon it is a misfortune.

Plant pests

Although plant pests are relatively uncommon indoors, they do manage to attack from time to time. Some arrive through windows in summer, others are brought in on new purchases – temporary flowering plants are often infested and should be carefully examined before placing among permanent plants. Indeed, all new house plant purchases should be examined not only for insects and mites but for tiny slugs and snails which can wreak havoc in a collection.

Certain pest infestations can sometimes be removed by hand, for instance scale insects and mealy bugs, but for most an application of suitable pesticide is needed. Mostly this involves spraying, and is best done in the garden or a garage outside (flat dwellers might take plants onto a balcony or use the bath). Unfortunately, most pest sprays have an unpleasant odour, and should in any case not be inhaled. Maximum ventilation is essential.

An alternative method is to use pesticidal granules or "plant pins" impregnated with pesticide. Granules are applied to the soil surface; pins are pushed into it. The chemicals within both these are released after watering, and absorbed by the roots. Insects that feed on upper parts of the plant are poisoned by chemicals rising in the sap. This action is known as *systemic*, and pesticide sprays that are absorbed by leaves work in a similar way. Such pesticides protect plants over a period, unlike contact or "knock-down" sprays whose effect is short-lived.

Spraying can be carried out with a small manual pump-action sprayer, a larger pressurised sprayer (very useful if many plants are involved) or an aerosol. If using aerosols, follow the instructions carefully; spraying too close can damage leaves.

When spraying it is essential to cover every part of a plant, particularly the leaf undersides. With smallish plants an alternative is to immerse the stems and leaves in a bath of diluted pesticide, wearing rubber gloves.

Pesticide materials

The active ingredient of a pesticide is always specified on the bottle or packet, usually in rather small print. Many manufacturers may offer the same chemical under different names. The label should also specify the pests controlled. Follow all instructions as to method of use and safety precautions to the letter. There are as many as 50 chemicals used for various pests. Here only a handful of those most widely used can be mentioned. Sometimes more than one chemical is used in a pesticide, for instance a knock-down pesticide with a systemic. It is always advisable to vary the material from time to time: some pests can develop resistance to one chemical.

Dimethoate is the most widely used systemic, but does not kill mites.

Butoxicarboxim is the systemic in plant pins and does kill mites.

Malathion is a pesticide which destroys virtually every pest.

Pirimiphos-methyl also has a wide range but does not destroy scale insects and mealy bugs; it is particularly effective against white fly and mites.

For those who prefer not to use materials intrinsically poisonous to humans and pets, *pyrethrum* is a safe pesticide made from a plant. *Resmethrin* and *bioresmethrin* are synthetic products, but similar to pyrethrum and equally safe. All these are specially valuable against white fly. *Derris* is another plant product effective against aphids and mites, but is harmful to fish.

Main house plant pests

Aphids. These insects, around 3 mm ($\frac{1}{8}$ in) long, are usually green – hence the name greenfly – but can be brown, pink, grey or black. They are sometimes aptly called plant lice. They favour new soft growth, and can attack almost any plant except bromeliads. Wash off small infestations with soapy water and follow with a clear water rinse, though chemical spraying or plant pins are usually needed.

Mealy bugs. These resemble miniature woodlice. The actual insect is oval, pinkish, 3 mm ($\frac{1}{8}$ in) long, but is usually concealed in a mass of white "wool", typically sited in the axils (angles) between leaf stalk and plant stems, although sometimes elsewhere. They specially favour succulents, notably cacti where there are many crevices in which to lodge.

Deal with small infestations by using a small, stiff artist's paintbrush dipped in insecticide solution or methylated spirits (alcohol in U.S.). Otherwise use systemic pesticide.

Root mealy bugs. These are similar to mealy bugs but infest root systems; succulents are again very prone to attack. If, when repotting, you see white patches on the root ball or wool on the roots, drench the potting mixture with pesticide, preferably systemic. Clean pots thoroughly before re-use.

Red spider mites. These pests are almost invisible to the naked eye. If leaves start to go pale yellow and if a fine web is seen coating leaves and stems, check with a magnifying glass on the leaf undersides to see if the tiny oval-oblong, 8-legged, red, pink or whitish mites are present. Badly infested leaves and stems are best cut off. Spray plants with malathion, resmethrin, derris, etc. Repeat spray after 3 days and again 10 days later. Hot dry air encourages "red spider"; regular mist-spraying is preventative.

Scale insects. These are sap suckers which after a mobile infancy settle down in one place under a hard shell, looking like a miniature limpet. Scale insects can vary greatly in size and colour, and some are specific to one host plant, but those likely to be seen on house plants are usually about 3 mm (⅛ in) long and brown.

Although scale insects can be killed by sprays – systemics are far the best – the actual scales remain in place, so for clean plants they must in any case be rubbed off manually with a soft cloth dipped in soapy water or pesticide solution, supporting the leaf underneath as you do so. Probe all crevices with a small paintbrush also. It is a tedious job, and prevention – by regular use of systemic pesticide – is much better than cure on susceptible plants such as asparagus, citrus

and oleander.

Weevils. Vine weevil insects are increasingly common pests of pot plants such as cyclamen, primulus, streptocarpus, and succulents. Their white grubs, about 1cm (⅜in) long and shaped like a letter "C", devour roots entirely, causing the plants to collapse. The adults are beetle-like, about 2.5cm (1in) long, with a distinct proboscis or "nose". An attacked plant is seldom to be saved, but adding HCH or other insecticidal dust to potting mixtures when repotting, or watering with insecticide solution, will prevent attack. Plants that have been so attacked and lost all of their roots can sometimes be rerooted.

Whitefly. Very small white, wedge-shaped, mothlike insects which flutter off in clouds when disturbed. These are more pests of conservatories, porches, etc. than rooms, but can come indoors, especially on flowering plants, and prove very hard to destroy. Repeated sprayings with different pesticides is essential, or use plant pins. The greenish or translucent larvae, produced in large numbers, are immune to pesticides, so infested plants need spraying every 3 days for at least a fortnight.

Plant diseases
Many fungal diseases and some bacterial ones attack plants, sometimes with fatal results. Fortunately very few are likely to affect house plants. Most relevant diseases tend to be triggered by faulty conditions, especially excess moisture, while sooty mould follows insect attack.

As with pests, chemical materials are available for disease control, but prevention of trouble is much more in the grower's hands.

Viral diseases are caused by sub-microscopic organisms that actually alter the composition of plant cells, and are spread by sap-sucking insects. They cause mottling, spotting and streaking of leaves, very often accompanied by distortion; they can stunt growth severely. In a few cases

ornamental variegation is the result of an otherwise harmless virus. Viruses hardly ever destroy house plants. There is in any case no cure for viral diseases, and affected plants should be destroyed.

Fungicide Materials. Again, many chemicals are marketed under brand names, but only a couple really need be named for indoor use. These are much less toxic to mammals than pesticides, but should not be inhaled. *Benomyl* and *thiophanate-methyl* are both systemic and useful against a wide range of fungus diseases.

Bacterial diseases are more difficult to control: in the U.S. antibiotics are used with success, including *cyclohexamide* and *streptomycin*.

Such materials can also be used on tissue which has started to rot and decay for any reason; this can happen especially to fleshy roots (bulbs, tubers etc.) when resting or stored. *Sulphur dust* is an old-fashioned remedy and still valuable against any kind of rot.

Main house plant diseases
Blackleg is a disease that typically attacks cuttings of fleshy plants such as pelargoniums, but it can attack mature plants. In either case it is due to overwatering or soggy soil. The remedy is to make cuttings of unaffected top growth.

Grey mould or botrytis is fluffy and grey, as opposed to mildew which is powdery and white. It can cover any upper part of a plant if air is too humid, especially in over-cool conditions. Over-assiduous mist-spraying and allowing moisture to lodge on foliage etc. encourages it. Saintpaulias are very prone to attack which can rapidly destroy their rosettes. Remove affected parts; apply a fungicide; water less frequently.

Leaf spot. Spots small and large, brown, yellow or white, and blister-like pustules may be caused by fungi or bacteria. They are almost always encouraged by letting water drops remain on foliage. Affected leaves

SYMPTOM CHART * denotes pests, diseases and control measures already described in the text.

	Symptom	Likely Causes	Action
LEAVES	Sticky	Excretions of sap-sucking insects	Check for pests*
	Covered with sooty growth	Sooty mould growing on insect excretion	Wash off mould*; destroy pests responsible*
	Bear small round spots	Water drops left on leaves; possibly fungal or bacterial leaf spot disease	If water drops not thought responsible use fungicide*. In bad cases discard plant.
	With brown, irregular, scorched-looking areas	Over-watering, hot dry air, sun scorch, over-feeding	Correct culture and/or conditions
	With black irregular areas	Overwatering especially if cold	Correct culture
	With yellow patches on edges	Probably over-feeding, possibly insect attack	Correct culture, check for pests*
	Go yellow overall and finally fall	Old leaves may do this naturally; premature yellowing due to over- or under-watering, over-feeding, worn-out potting mixture, excess heat or cold, gas or industrial fumes	Correct conditions
	Go yellow overall but remain on plant	Chlorosis due to limy potting mixture or lack of balanced plant food	Apply sequestrene; repot in acid mixture, give balanced feed if not resting
	Become mottled yellow	Suspect red spider mite attack; just possibly virus disease	Check for red spider mite*; if virus (all leaves affected, plant seeming generally unhealthy) destroy plant.
	Drop without other symptoms	Severe shock caused by chill, draughts, use of cold water, dryness at roots, gas fumes	Correct conditions; recuperate plant in best available conditions
	Wither at leaf tips	Dry air (difficult to avoid); people brushing into plant continually; sometimes, fluoride in water	Cut off unsightly tips; improve air humidity; mist-spray; reposition plant
	Go green when should be variegated	Either too little light, or if whole shoots affected reversion to type	Improve light; cut reverted shoots right out
	Tiny white insects on undersides	Whitefly attack*	Apply suitable pesticide every 3 days

should be removed in case it is an infection; fungicide spraying may prevent further attack.

Mildew makes white, powdery mould on leaves, stems and flowers. Soft-leaved plants are most likely to suffer; among house plants mainly begonias are affected, and it can be difficult to prevent the disease even by using fungicides, unless warmer conditions can be provided.

Sooty mould. Not a direct disease of plants, sooty mould grows on the sweet "honeydew" excreted by sap-sucking insects notably aphids and scale. Indeed the appearance of this unsightly black mould is a sure indication of pest attack. Sooty mould blocks leaf breathing pores and can totally obstruct photosynthesis, so it must be removed. Although it can be killed by fungicide spray, the black mould stays in place and it is better to remove it manually with a soft cloth dipped in soapy water or fungicide solution, supporting the leaf on its under-surface as you do so. It is time-consuming.

Tracking down trouble
Most house plant ailments are cultural, stemming from unsuitable growing conditions or faulty care, including failure to keep plants in a suitable "climate" of temperature, humidity and light level which has been stressed throughout this book.

The chart will help you tell what has gone wrong, though very often, as will be seen, one symptom might be attributable to a variety of causes. In addition, the actual shock to the plant's system, which shows up in leaf discolouration or whatever it may be, probably occurred several weeks before.

In the symptom chart an asterisk refers to the description of pests or diseases and necessary control measures already fully described.

Avoiding trouble
The best way of avoiding ill health in house plants is, as far as possible, to mimic the conditions of their natural haunts.

Routine examination of each plant should reveal symptoms of trouble at

SYMPTOM CHART

	Symptom	Likely Causes	Action
STEM & LEAVES	White "wool" at stem and leaf junctions	Mealy bug attack*	Apply suitable pesticide, if possible pick off with brush
	Enveloped in fine web	Red spider mite attack*	Apply suitable pesticide
	Covered in fluffy mould	Grey mould disease*	Apply suitable fungicide; reduce air humidity
	Covered in powdery mould	Powdery mildew disease*	Apply suitable fungicide; reduce air humidity
	Growth (especially young) distorted, probably yellowing	Check for aphids*	Apply suitable pesticide; may be necessary to cut out affected growth
	Encrusted with small brownish scales, sticky	Scale insect attack*	Apply suitable pesticide; clean off scales by hand
STEM	Rots at base	Basal rot*	Take top as cutting; ensure potting mixture does not get waterlogged
	Rots elsewhere	Rot: suspect physical damage, overwatering, severe chill	Take top as cutting; trim remaining growth to healthy tissue, dust with sulphur
ROSETTE	Rots in centre	Cold, overwatering, or water lodged in centre	Discard plant; avoid conditions next time
FLOWERS & BUDS	Drop	Usually fluctuating temperatures or sometimes just moving plant. Also over- or under-watering, over-feeding, chill, hot dry air, gas fumes	Correct conditions
ROOTS	Soft and rotten	Potting mixture too wet, or plant over-fed	Repot if possible; place plant in humid conditions while re-rooting
	Dried up	Inadequate watering	Soak pot thoroughly (allow to drain after)
	White woolly patches on roots and soil ball	Root mealy bug attack*	Drench root ball with suitable pesticide, preferably repot
WHOLE PLANT	Weak, spindly growth	Lack of adequate light, or growth induced by excess warmth, feeding etc. in dull winter rest period	Move to better-lit place; cut back to encourage new bushy growth; feed only in growing period
	Droops or wilts	Dryness at roots, severe over-watering, sun scorch, severe chill, gas or industrial fumes; also possibly attack by weevil grubs	Correct culture and/or conditions. If grubs seen in mixture dispose of this and try to re-root plant, or take cuttings
	Does not grow appreciably	If in winter, plant is probably resting – leave well alone; if in growing period, too small a pot, sometimes overwatering	Correct situation
	Dies altogether	Mixture allowed to dry out entirely or become sodden (water in drip saucer?); severe chill; sun scorch; draughts; very hot dry air; gas or industrial fumes; deep shade	Start again and try to do better!

an early stage; pest infestations especially should be nipped in the bud in this way. A weekly examination for pests is desirable, and can be carried out during watering. At this time also examine the surface of the potting mixture, a) to check watering needs (a hollow visible round the plant stem or the mixture shrinking away from the sides of the pot are sure signs of a dry soil ball); b) to confirm satisfactory drainage – green algal scum or the flat growths of liverworts suggest over-wet compost; c) to check feeding levels – white crust on the surface of mixture or on clay pots is a sign that too much plant food has been given.

House plant propagation

Multiplication of plants in nature
In nature house plants, like all wild plants, increase themselves mostly from seed or, in the case of ferns and selaginellas, spores. Every plant has this capacity though it is not always the *main* method of increase. Seed and spores are distributed in various ways which usually ensure that large numbers of young plants do not strive to grow in the same place.

Herbaceous plants – those other than trees and shrubs – have other ways of reproduction. Most increase steadily in size, the plant forming a bigger and bigger clump. In order to reproduce, the clump must be divided. Many perennials, like bromeliads and bulbs, produce offsets or sideshoots (young plants around the parent). These can again build up into large clumps but sometimes become detached on their own. Cacti also produce such detachable offsets.

Plants with runners, either above or below ground, produce their young at intervals on these stem growths which gradually spread outwards from the parent. The strawberry is a familiar example. Many creeping and also some climbing plants have stems which root at leaf joints when these touch moist earth. Among house plants, tradescantias are examples. In the course of time the old stem may perish but the stem tips, having rooted down, continue to grow.

There are a few plants that are viviparous – they carry tiny plantlets with ready-formed roots which may drop off, like bryophyllums, or root down when they touch soil, as with chlorophytum.

Many succulents including cacti, and a few other plants, have jointed stems which break quite easily and, when detached, can produce roots at the lower end even if not in direct contact with soil. Many leafy succulents have leaves which are very easily broken off and these too can put out roots and form new plants.

Propagation at home
This is the basis of the gardener's stem and leaf cuttings: one is taking advantage of the propensity of wounded plant material to produce roots under certain circumstances.

Growing from seed, cuttings, offsets, plantlets, rooted pieces of runner and so on are all methods open to the gardener who wishes to increase his plants. Apart from the pleasure of making new plants, and perhaps giving some to friends, it is a desirable practice when older ones become unmanageable or unattractive.

All methods except seed sowing involve the use of existing plant tissue, and are known as vegetative propagation. With very few exceptions plants propagated vegetatively produce offspring that are identical (variegated sansevierias grown from leaf cuttings are a notable exception). These methods are usually the most satisfactory and simple for rapidly increasing your collection of house plants or for regenerating old stock.

Seed sowing
Certain house plants, including most palms, are grown from seed because there is no other method of increase. With most, this process takes time to produce plants of worthwhile size, and sometimes a packet of seed results in an embarrassing number of seedlings. But there is much satisfaction to be gained by this method: if you can point to a huge dracaena or grevillea and say that you raised it from seed so many years back, it is an impressive achievement.

For seed sowing, a light porous mixture is essential: it should retain moisture, certainly, but never be waterlogged. Commercial mixes are obtainable; alternatively use a simple, equal-parts mix of peat and sand, or a combination of these with perlite or vermiculite. Sowing mixture for cacti and succulents should be fine, sandy and very well drained.

Very small seed (eg. begonias and most gesneriads) should be sown as thinly as possible without being covered. Water it in with a mist-sprayer or a fine-rosed can. Rather larger seeds should be just covered with finely sifted mixture; with succulents use fine sand. Sow thinly to avoid masses of tiny seedlings coming up very close together; they are difficult to separate and rapidly become "drawn" and spindly. Mix small seed with fine dry sand to ensure thin distribution. Some seeds, like those of palms, are pea-sized or bigger and should be buried in mixture to a depth of about twice their diameter.

Most seeds need warmth to germinate; packet instructions usually state the desirable temperature. If you do not have a heated propagator, place the seeds in a warm airing cupboard, but remember to look at them frequently because the seedlings must be brought into a good light as soon as they appear. In some cases germination takes a long time: make sure the mixture never dries out. This is much easier to ensure if the seed box is covered with plastic sheeting until germination occurs.

When the seedlings appear they will usually have a pair of leaves. Wait for the next pair of leaves – the first "true" leaves – before moving them on (or "pricking out" as the process is called). Palms and bulb plants are among those which do not produce these seed leaves; simply move them on when large enough to handle.

Plants from small seed can be pricked out and placed an inch or two apart into other seed trays of mixture, before a later move into small individual pots. Those from large seed usually make quite large seedlings and can be potted individually at once. After that the normal potting-on procedure (see page 189) should be followed.

Vegetative propagation
Division: Gently break up overcrowded clumps, pulling each section of growth free of the rest of the plant. Plants with very dense or matted roots may have to be separated by cutting through the clumps with a sharp knife, avoiding damage to large roots as much as possible. In most cases the new growths on the outside of the clumps are better than the

202

older ones situated in the middle of the clumps.

Gently separating a saintpaulia clump into rosettes for individual repotting

Using a knife to detach a sansevieria offset with roots of its own

Offsets: These are small new plants that appear around the base of such plants as bromeliads, most bulbs, cacti and succulents. Most produce some roots of their own while still attached to the parent. Detach when large enough to handle (not too soon for bromeliads), using a knife if essential. Pot up singly into small pots, carefully retaining what roots may already have been made, and keep warm and moist.

Plantlets: Some aspleniums, bryophyllums, chlorophytums, tolmiea and *Saxifraga stolonifera* produce small plantlets ready developed,

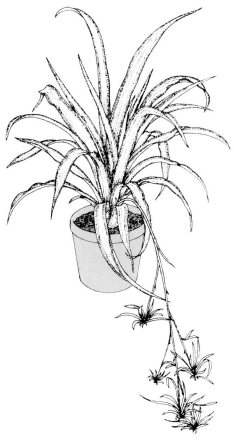

Chlorophytum plantlets, made on flowering stalks, root readily.

either on the leaf surface or at the end of a flowering stalk or stolon. They can be detached and treated as offsets. Alternatively, if on a long stem, peg the plantlet down (hairpins are very useful for this) into an adjoining pot filled with rooting mixture to encourage the young plant to make good roots while still attached to the parent plant. Cut free of the parent when strong, new growth appears.

Stem Cuttings: Taking stem cuttings involves using pieces of stem. These should be firm, not *very* young, soft and sappy. Use the main growing point of the shoot, namely the tip. The shoot you choose can be the main "leading" growth, alternatively a side branch. Some cuttings can be induced to make roots initially by placing them in a jar of plain water, but these should be transferred into growing mixture when only a very small amount of root has been made. It is more common to root in rooting mixture, which is exactly the same as for seed sowing.

With a sharp knife or razor blade cut 5–10cm (2–4in) of shoot (much longer shoots can be used on soft plants like tradescantias) from strong-growing stems. Make the cut immediately *above* a node (a slightly swollen point usually adjacent to a leaf axil). The parent plant will then make new growth from the growing point in the leaf axil. Then trim the cutting immediately *below* the node nearest to the cut and gently remove any lower leaves that would otherwise become buried in the rooting mixture, cutting them off if necessary. Push the prepared cutting into the rooting medium. You can assist the rooting process by dipping the cut end in a hormone rooting powder before planting, but this is not essential. The rooting mixture should be just pleasantly moist (not sodden) and should remain that way.

Trim tip cuttings of a cane-stemmed begonia just below a node.

An over-wet mixture will not encourage rooting: roots grow when in active search of water. Over-wet mixtures can also cause rotting.

A few woody house plants, notably cordylines and dracaenas, are increased from short leafless pieces of woody stem carrying at least one growth bud. These are sometimes pushed horizontally into rooting mixture but more generally vertically (make sure you remember to plant the bottom of the stem). In the tropics one can see hedges of these plants made simply by pushing short lengths of stem into the ground in a line. Stem cuttings of cacti and succulents should be allowed to dry 203 out for a day or two and be pushed very lightly into the rooting mixture, even better, prop them up with thin canes so that the cut surface is just resting on the mixture.

Leaf cuttings

The fleshy leaves of crassulas, echeverias and some other succulents will make roots and in time produce new plants, if they are set in, or just rested on, a moist, sandy material. Leaves of saintpaulias, peperomias and most kinds of rhizomatous begonias, with 25–50mm (1–2in) of leafstalk attached, will make new plants. Plant the leaves with their stalks 12–25mm ($\frac{1}{2}$–1in) deep, at a 45° angle; clusters of young plants will push through the rooting mixture in 5 to 8 weeks. When these can be safely handled they should be divided up into tiny individual plantlets, and potted up in small pots.

Multiplying a sansevieria from leaf cuttings

A few plants need some specialized treatment, for instance streptocarpus and sansevieria leaves are usually cut into sections. These details are made clear in the text describing individual genera and their culture.

In a few cases it is essential to use a leaf-bud cutting, meaning a short stem section bearing a leaf with a growth bud in its axil. House plants such as *Ficus elastica* are increased in this way commercially but the method is seldom feasible for the amateur because of the amount of heat required.

Propagating a Ficus elastica *by air layering: first, nick the stem $\frac{1}{3}$ way through and wrap with live sphagnum moss; finally sever from the parent and pot up.*

Air layering

This is a totally unnatural method of increase used with tall more or less woody plants, especially if they are getting too tall and have lost many lower leaves. Monstera and *Ficus elastica* are typical candidates. Their leaves are too large for cuttings to be successful in the conditions usually available to the amateur. The method involves nicking the stem, say 1/3 way through, or scraping off the bark in a ring, about 6–12mm ($\frac{1}{4}$–$\frac{1}{2}$in) deep, all round the stem at the point where new roots are required. The wounded part is then covered with a wad of moist, live sphagnum moss; this is wrapped around with a piece of plastic sheeting (a polythene bag cut open is fine) and fastened securely top and bottom to keep everything moist. New roots develop at the point of damage, perhaps only after a few weeks. These can usually be seen through the moss, or when sturdy new growth appears it is likely that the upper part has sent down roots into the moss. It can then be severed from the parent plant and potted up and treated as a new plant.

The basal section can be cut back to manageable height and will usually produce one or more new growths if the soil in the pot is kept moderately moist.

Equipment

A heated propagator is a considerable advantage, but is not essential.

Small, simple appliances are available consisting of a standard or half-sized seed tray covered with a clear, rigid plastic dome, but a plastic bag enveloping a pot in which seeds have been sown or a cutting planted is often just as effective. The purpose is to encourage humidity and prevent the mixture from drying out too quickly. Propagate in medium light, most certainly away from direct sun.

Sansevieras successfully propagated from leaf cuttings

Timing

The best time for practically all propagation in temperate climates is from spring to mid-summer. As the season progresses the need for artificial heat virtually disappears, though some seeds do require quite high temperatures. Certainly most cuttings will root successfully under a plastic dome, or a plastic bag, in summer room temperatures.

A dictionary of house plant terms

Annual A plant which is grown from seed to flower within one year, after which it dies. Examples are browallia and cineraria.

Biennial A plant is which grown from seed in one season and flowers, seeds and dies in the next. No house plants are of this type.

Bromeliad A member of the large family *Bromeliaceae*, almost all of which form rosettes and many of which are epiphytes. A rosette which has flowered typically dies afterwards. Examples are aechmea, tillandsia, vriesea.

Bulb A storage organ compound of fleshy scales which are modified leaf bases. Some are evergreens, eg *Haemanthus albiflos*, but most of those described in this book, like narcissus and tulipa, have a marked resting period when they are entirely leafless and rootless. Bulbs usually live underground but a few, including haemanthus, hippeastrum and vallota, remain above soil level. Individual bulbs live indefinitely, producing offsets (side growths) to increase themselves. The word is often loosely used to include corms, tubers and certain rhizomes.

Cactus A member of the family *Cactaceae*: succulent plants with very fleshy stems and almost invariably no leaves, though some like zygocactus have stem segments resembling leaves. Most are spherical or cylindrical and carry spines, as in echinopsis, mammillaria etc.

Climber A plant which grows upwards among more sturdy plants by various means, including scrambling through vegetation with the assistance of thorns (eg asparagus), attaching itself with aerial roots (eg philodendron), spiralling around other growths (eg *Cissus antarctica*), or with tendrils *(Cissus rhomboidea).*

Corm A subterranean storage organ formed from the thickened base of the stem, often enclosed in papery scales called the tunic. During each season a corm that produces leaves and flowers shrivels away and a new

Left: Nidularium innocentii, *a bromeliad;* right: Schlumbergera truncata, *an epiphytic cactus*

corm is produced above it. Tiny corms for increase are produced around the base. The crocus has a corm.

Creeper A plant with stems which spread on the ground or may produce roots to climb up trees etc; the distinction between climbers and creepers is often blurred. An example is *Ficus pumila.*

Deciduous Losing leaves in a resting period, in contrast to evergreens.

Epiphyte A plant which lives upon another but is in no way parasitic. In tropical regions many plants, notably bromeliads, ferns and orchids, live epiphytically on trees and also cliffs. Climbers which attach themselves to trees with aerial roots, like hederas and philodendrons, are also technically epiphytes.

Evergreen A plant which retains its foliage all year round, in contrast to deciduous kinds.

Herbaceous Soft-stemmed plants which have no woody tissue. Such plants can be annual or perennial.

Non-woody The same as herbaceous.

Perennial Plants with a long indefinite life, in contrast to annuals or biennials.

Rhizome A more or less underground stem which lasts at least one season. Many rhizomes are horizontal, as in aspidistra, but others are

upright. Some operate as storage organs as in smithiantha.

Shrub A woody plant with many branches and no main trunk as in a tree.

Succulent A plant with fleshy leaves and/or stems adapted to growing in arid conditions which act as water reserves.

Temporary Plant A "pot plant" usually bought in flower or fruit and discarded after its display is over. Such plants may include annuals, bulbs, corms, tubers and also shrubs like azaleas which can rarely be grown with success, to flower again indoors.

Tree A woody plant with a distinct main stem or trunk, in contrast to a shrub without a main stem. The distinction between trees and shrubs is sometimes blurred and trees grown as house plants are usually encouraged to develop a shrubby habit.

Tuber A storage organ, usually underground, which may be a thickened stem or root. Stem tubers, like cyclamen, produce leaves and flowers; root tubers, like those of chlorophytum and asparagus, do not carry growth buds and cannot produce stems or leaves.

Woody Plant tissue containing lignin, which ultimately forms the dense material called wood, and characteristic of trees and shrubs (including some climbers).

205

The illustrated plant index

Page numbers in **bold-face type** indicate major entries where the culture of a species is dealt with in detail. Common names of plants are cross-referred to the botanical names.

Page numbers in *italic-face type* indicate plant illustrations. Plant drawings appear above their botanical names. Synonyms are in brackets.

*Brunfelsia pauciflora
calycina* 41, **53**, *53*
Bryophyllum (Kalanchoe)
202, 203
*Bryophyllum
daigremontianum* 87, **100**

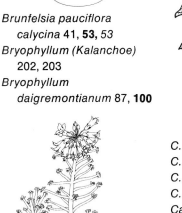

B. tubiflorum 82, 87, 100,
101, **101**
Bu'lrush, see *Cyperus*
Bunny's ears, see *Opuntia*
Busy Lizzie, see *Impatiens*

C

Caladium 7, 151, 152, 173

Caladium hortulanum 41,
53, *53*
Calathea 173
Calathea bachemiana 41,
56
C. lancifolia (insignis) 41,
56
C. lindeniana 41, **56**

C. makoyana 41, **56**, *56*
C. ornata 41, 45, **56**, *56*
C. picturata 41, **56**
C. zebrina 41, 45, **56**
Calceolaria 152

*Calceolaria
herbeohybrida* 41, **56**,
56
Callisia 166

Callisia elegans 20, **26**, *26*

Campanula isophylla 70,
71, *72*
Candle plant, see
*Plectranthus
oertendahlii*
Cape heather, see *Erica*
Cape leadwort, see
Plumbago auriculata
Cape primrose, see
Streptocarpus

Capsicum annuum 20, **26**,
26, 28, 41, **57**

Carex morrowii 112, **115**,
116

Caryota mitis 104, **108**,
124, *130*, **130**

Catharanthus roseus 100,
101, 104, **108**, *109*

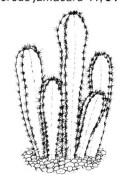

Cephalocereus senilis 20,
22, **24**, *24*
Cereus jamacaru 41, **54**

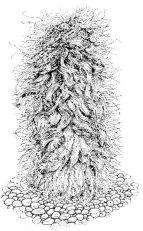

C. peruvianus 41, **54**, *54*
Ceropegia woodii 82, 87,
87

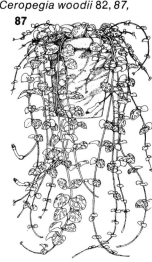

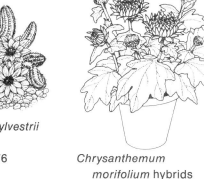
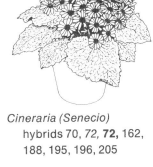
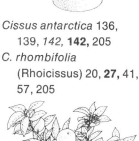

209

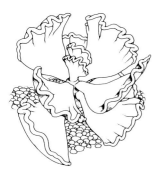
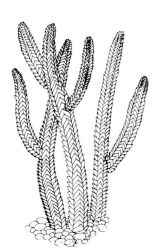

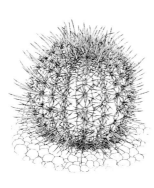

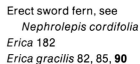

212

G

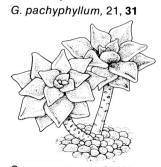

Gynura 166
Gynura aurantiaca 124,
132

G. sarmentosa 124, *132,*
132

Haemanthus albiflos 82,
91, **91,** 205
H. katherinae 82, **91**
H. multiflorus 82, **91**
Hamatocactus
hamatacanthus
(Ferocactus) 21, **26**

H. setispinus 21, **26,** *25*
Hammock fern, see
Blechnum occidentale
Hare's foot fern, see
Davallia fejeensis,
Polypodium aureum
Hart's tongue fern, see
Phyllitis scolopendrium
Haworthia cuspidata 82 **92**
H. margaritifera 82, 85, **92**
H. reinwardtii 82, 85, *91,* **92**

H. tessellata 82, 85, *92,* **92**
Heather, see *Erica*
Hedera 162, 168, 186, 205
Hedera canariensis 70, **73**
H. colchica **73**

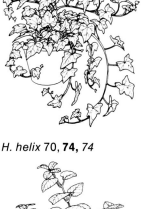

H. helix 70, **74,** *74*

Hemigraphis alternata
(colorata) 124, *132,* **132**

Heptapleurum arboricola
124, *132,* **132**

Hibiscus rosa-sinensis
124, *133,* **133,** 157, 166

Hippeastrum hybrids 46,
60, *60,* 196, 205
Holly fern, see *Cyrtomium*
falcatum

Howea belmoreana 136,
146, **146**
H. forsterana 136, **146**

Hoya 106, 140, *146*
Hoya australias 136, **146**
H. bella 104, **110,** 126

H. carnosa 112, *117, 118,*
118, 136, **147**

Hyacinthus orientalis 70,
74, **74,** 162

Hydrangea macrophylla
112, *118,* **118**

Hypoestes phyllostachya
100, *102,* **102,** 127, 166

213

Monstera deliciosa 21, **31,**
32, 162, *168,* 168, 173,
204
Moonstones, see
Pachyphytum oviferum
Moses-in-the-cradle, see
Rhoeo spathacea
Mother fern, see
Asplenium bulbiferum
Mother-in-law's tongue,
see *Sansevieria*
Mother-of-thousands, see
Saxifraga stolonifera

N

Narcissus hybrids 70, *74,*
74, 205
Neanthe bella, see
Chamaedorea elegans

Neoregelia carolinae 41,

62, *62,*
N. concentrica 41, **62**
N. marmorata 41, **62**
N. sarmentosa 41, **62**
N. spectabilis 41, **62**
Nephrolepis cordifolia 21,
32, *32,* 41

N. exaltata 21, *32,* **32,** 41

Nerium oleander 70, *74,*
74
Nidularium fulgens 41, **62**

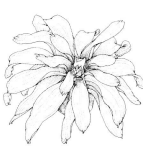

N. innocentii 41, **62,** *62*
N. purpureum 41, **62**
Norfolk Island pine
Araucaria heterophylla

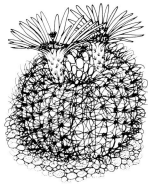

Notocactus apricus 41, **55,**
55
N. concinnus 41, **55**
N. leninghausii 41, **55**
N. ottonis 41, **55**
N. scopa 41, **55**

O

Old man cactus, see
Cephalocereus senilis
Oliveranthus elegans, see
Echeveria harmsii
Oplismenus 141

Oplismenus hirtellus 21,
33, *33*
Opuntia basilaris 21, **26**
O. cylindrica 26, 41, **55**
O. imbricata 21, **26**

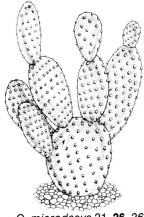

O. microdasys 21, **26,** *26*

O. rufida 21, **26**
O. salmiana 41, **55**
O. subulata **26,** 41, **55**
O. vestita **26,** 41
Ornamental monk's hood,
see *Astrophytum
ornatum*

P

*Pachyphtyum
amethystinum
(Graptopetalum)* 21, **33**

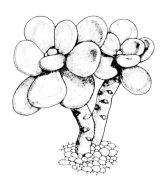

P. oviferum 21, **33,** *33*
P. pachyphytoides 21, **33**

Pachystachys lutea 41, **62,**
62
Painted fingernail plant,
see *Neoregelia
spectabilis*
Painter's palette, see
*Anthurium
andraeanum*
Pandanus 155

215

Pandanus veitchii 136,
141, *147,* **147**
Paper plant, see *Cyperus
papyrus*
Parodia aureispina 41, **55**

P. chrysacanthion 41, **55,**
55
P. sanguiniflora 41, **55**
Parsley fern, see
Asplenium bulbiferum
Partridge-breasted aloe,
see *Aloe variegata*
Passiflora 157

Passiflora caerulea 41, **63,**
63
Peacock plant, see
Calathea makoyana
Peanut cactus, see
*Chamaecereus
sylvestrii*

*Pedilanthus tithymaloides
smallii* 21, **33,** *33*

Pelargonium 82, 84, *93,*
93, 152, 157, 180, *180,*
181

Pellaea rotundifolia 136,
147, **147**
'P. viridis 78, **80**

Pellionia daveauana 124,
134, **134**

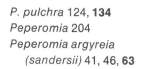

P. pulchra 124, **134**
Peperomia 204
*Peperomia argyreia
(sandersii)* 41, 46, **63**

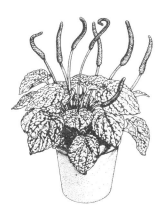

P. caperata 41, **63,** *63*
P. fraseri (*rotundifolia*) 41,
63
*P. griseoargentea
(hederifolia)* 41, **63**
P. magnoliifolia 21, 22, **34**
P. obtusifolia 21, 22, **34,**
41, **63**
P. orba **34**
P. scandens (serpens) 21,
34, 41, **63**
P. verticillata 21, **34**
Philodendron 7, *64,* 153,
168, 205
*Philodendron
angustisectum
(elegans)* 41, **64**
P. bipennifolium 41, **64**
P. bipinnatifidum 41, **64**
P. Burgundy 41, **65**
P. erubescens 41, **64**
P. imbe 41, **64**
P. pedatum (laciniatum)
41, **64**
P. scandens 21, **34,** 41, **64**

P. selloum 41, **64,** *64*
P. wendlandii 21, **34**

Phoenix canariensis 70,
75, *75*
P. dactylifera 70, *75,* **75**
P. roebelenii 124, **134**

Phyllitis scolopendrium
70, **75,** *75*
Pilea 176

Pilea cadierei 124, 127,
133, **134,** *166*
P. involucrata (see
spruceana) 21, **34**
P. mollis **34**
P. spruceana (see
involucrata) 41, **65**
P.s. Norfolk **65**
P.s. Silver Tree **65**

Pisonia umbellifera 136,
147, **147**

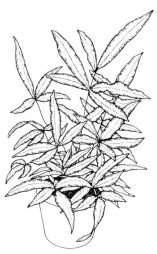

217

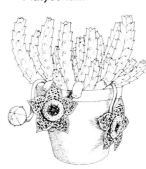

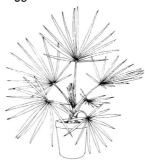

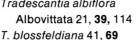

The general index

221

222

Acknowledgements

Pilot Productions and Anthony Huxley would like to thank all those who supplied information, assistance or photographs to the *World Guide to House Plants*.

Prof. E.A. Bell (Director, Royal Botanic Gardens, Kew)
Prof. J.P.M. Brenan
A.C. Burt (Glasshouse Crops Research Institute)
Fisons Ltd., Horticulture Division
Miss Gwen Goodship
Rex Grimes (Wilson Grimes Products Ltd.)
H.P. Hartley (BIF Ltd.)
Mrs Isobyl la Croix
Andrew Lauener (Royal Botanic Gardens, Edinburgh)
Peter Lihou (MDL Ltd.)
R.W. Manners (Phostrogen Ltd.)
David Philcox (Royal Botanic Gardens, Kew)
Thomas Rochford, Jock Davidson and P.F. Murison (Rochford Houseplants Ltd.)
Prof. H.B. Rycroft (National Botanic Gardens of South Africa)
Silvaperl Products Ltd.

For assistance with illustrations

Anthony Huxley
Charles Marden Fitch
G.R. Roberts
Royal Botanic Gardens, Kew (Dr. P. Brandham, F.N. Hepper, D. Philcox, Martin Sands) Crown copyright
Harry Smith Horticultural Photographic Collection
Alfred Byrd Graf
Dr. Giuseppe Mazza
Elizabeth Whiting and Associates
Pat Brindley
Leslie Johns
Robert Ornduff
John Criswick
John Bannochie
Ann Reaben Prospero
Takashi Sawano
Rod Shone/ONLP
Tim Shackleton
Jeff Grimes
Marijke Heuff, Amsterdam
Alan Toogood
W.L. Tjaden
B. Morley
Farnsworth
E. Molseed
G.R. Nichols
R. Saunders
David Hunt
Liz and Tony Bomford/Survival Anglia
Dieter and Mary Plage/Survival Anglia
Kenneth W. Fink/Ardea
Ardea
Museum der Stadt, Vienna
D. Hardy
Country Life Magazine
R. Brummitt
J. Vahmeyer
National Botanic Gardens of South Africa
Adelaide Botanic Gardens
Evans Bros

Pilot Productions would also like to thank

Jan Croot
Ruth Dodds
The staff of the Harry Smith Collection
Negs Photography
Safu-Maria Gilbert
Rob Hillier